DATE DUE

DEC 1 1 1999		
GAYLORD		PRINTED IN U.S.A

POOR RICHARD'S PRINCIPLE

POOR RICHARD'S PRINCIPLE

RECOVERING THE AMERICAN DREAM
THROUGH THE MORAL
DIMENSION OF WORK,
BUSINESS, AND MONEY

ROBERT WUTHNOW

PRINCETON UNIVERSITY PRESS
PRINCETON, NEW JERSEY

Copyright © 1996 by Princeton University Press
Published by Princeton University Press, 41 William Street,
Princeton, New Jersey 08540
In the United Kingdom: Princeton University Press,
Chichester, West Sussex

Library of Congress Cataloging-in-Publication Data

Wuthnow, Robert.
Poor Richard's principle : recovering the American dream through the
moral dimension of work, business, and money / Roberth Wuthnow.
p. cm.
Includes bibliographical references and index.
ISBN 0-691-02892-3
ISBN 0-691-05895-4 (pbk.)
1. United States—Moral conditions. 2. Work—Moral and ethical aspects—
United States. 3. Money—Moral and ethical aspects—United States.
4. Business ethics—United States. 5. Social values—United States.
6. Work and family—United States. I. Title.
HN90.M6W87 1996
306'.0973—dc20   96-6799

//

This book has been composed in Palatino

Princeton University Press books are printed on acid-free paper and meet the
guidelines for permanence and durability of the Committee on Production
Guidelines for Book Longevity of the Council on Library Resources

Third printing, and first paperback printing, 1998

http://pup.princeton.edu

Printed in the United States of America

10 9 8 7 6 5 4 3

And everywhere, through the immortal dark, something moving in the night, and something stirring in the hearts of men, and something crying in their wild unuttered blood, the wild unuttered tongues of its huge prophecies—so soon the morning, soon the morning: O America.

Thomas Wolfe, *The Web and the Rock*

CONTENTS

ACKNOWLEDGMENTS

A NUMBER of people contributed to the five years of research that went into writing this book, and I want to express my deep appreciation to them. Not least were the more than two thousand randomly selected people who patiently responded for more than an hour when an interviewer came to their home to ask questions about their work, their money, their families, and their values. Special appreciation goes to the additional two hundred people who answered semistructured, qualitative questions for more than two hours each. They spoke candidly about their struggles at work, how they manage their finances, what it has meant to be unemployed or to be discriminated against, what they learned from their parents and what they hope to teach their children about the American Dream, and in some cases what it has been like to be a new immigrant in the United States. As is customary, I have changed their names to protect their identities, but their stories appear throughout the book and greatly enrich our understanding of the moral discourses in which work and money are framed.

I was very ably assisted in conducting the survey and with the interviewing by Harry Cotugno, Roberta Fiske Rusciano, Natalie Searl, Elaine Friedman, Matthew Lawson, John Schmalzbauer, Tracy Scott, Timothy Clydesdale, Richard Flory, and Heather Behn. Natalie Searl oversaw the transcription process as well, and Timothy Clydesdale served as chief programming consultant for the quantitative analysis. Roberta Rusciano and Yvonne Veugelers helped with library work, and David Harrington Watt was a valuable consultant on the historical aspects of the study.

Correspondence and discussions with a number of people who know more than I do about many of the subjects dealt with in this book helped sharpen the research questions and kept me from falling victim to too many false hypotheses. I wish especially to thank Amitai Etzioni, Neil Smelser, Arlie Hochschild, Nathan Hatch, Martin Marty, Michéle Lamont, Mark Noll, Jeffrey Stout, Paul DiMaggio, Frank Dobbin, Robert Liebman, George Thomas, Virginia Hodgkinson, Wilfred McClay, Albert Bergesen, Viviana Zelizer, David Riesman, Miroslav Volf, Steven Tipton, Nicholas Wolterstorff, and Alan Wolfe.

During the course of the project, I was privileged to be given the opportunity to present working papers as lectures at the University of Michigan, the University of Pennsylvania, Rutgers University, the University of Florida, Indiana University, Biola University, Southern Methodist University, Princeton Theological Seminary, Southern Baptist Theological Seminary, Hope College, Eastern College, and Calvin College. Many of the comments that arose in these groups helped to refine my arguments. In addition, Robert Jackall and Kevin Christiano read the entire manuscript and saved me from some of my more egregious mistakes.

Funding for the research was generously made available by the Lilly Endowment. Fred Hofheinz and Craig Dykstra at the Endowment have been wonderful to work with because of their commitment to the issues dealt with in the book and their collegial support. The same has been true of my editor Peter Dougherty and the staff at Princeton University Press. As always, I am most indebted to my wife, Sara, and my children, Robyn, Brooke, and Joel, who, in this context, helped me especially to think hard about the balance between work and family that has always been delicately inscribed in the American Dream.

POOR RICHARD'S PRINCIPLE

Introduction

THE QUESTION OF MORAL RESTRAINT

WORK BECKONS. Money talks. Like a mysterious force, the economy waxes and wanes. It flourishes by following its own logic—seeking new markets, new opportunities for profits. So say the experts. Are beliefs and values relevant? Of course—but as ways to legitimate this incessant expansion. Advertising is thus a way to encourage consumers to buy more. Corporate subcultures ply bureaucrats with better reasons to put the company first. The Protestant ethic is relevant if it encourages workers to work harder. The American Dream promotes the endless pursuit of more prestigious careers and a more comfortable life.

The argument I wish to develop in this book is just the opposite. It suggests that economic commitments are embedded in moral frameworks, and that these frameworks significantly *restrain* our economic behavior. People may work hard, but they do not work all the time. And when they are asked to work longer hours, or to increase their level of productivity, or to take on dehumanizing or overly stressful responsibilities, they sense that something is wrong. People may want money and material possessions, but they are unwilling to do just anything to realize these wants. They may be driven by the needs of their families to make tough economic choices, but they have ways to distinguish these choices from the ends they were meant to serve. They create space in their thinking for family commitments that cannot be reduced to economic considerations. Their sense of community, and the importance they attach to having a respectable identity within their community, may lead them to pursue certain economic goals. But people limit these pursuits long enough to behave in neighborly and in charitable ways.

As an example, consider a man in his late thirties, an entrepreneur at the height of his career. He lives frugally but has accumulated considerable wealth. He budgets his time, recognizing its monetary value. And he focuses so much of his attention on his work that we might think being a successful businessman was the sole aim of his life. Yet, were we to pay closer attention to this man, we would see that his carefully orchestrated daily schedule also calls for an extended period of reading and meditation. He devotes his evenings to the arts. And he is intensely involved in community affairs. Thinking him interested in nothing but work and money, we would be surprised to learn that only a few years later he retires from his business to pursue a life of philanthropy, science, and politics.

Readers will perhaps recognize the identity of this man: Benjamin Franklin. Though he has been considered the epitome of the Protestant work ethic, Franklin illustrates how the pursuit of work and money are restrained by moral commitments deeply ingrained in his character. These commitments did not prevent him from working hard or from accumulating wealth. They did not keep him from contributing enormously to the economic progress of our nation. But they did, paradoxically, give work and money *added* meaning by making them *less* than the ultimate end of life itself.

The American Dream is a moral framework. It encourages people to work hard, giving them hope that their work will be rewarded. Simplistic understandings make it out to be little more than a materialistic value system, holding forth the prospect of a high-paying job, a comfortable home in the suburbs, and opportunities for one's children. But closer consideration of the American Dream, I shall argue, shows it to be much more than this. It supplies understandings about why one should work hard and about the value of having money, but it does so in a way that guards against money and work being taken as ends in themselves. It creates mental maps that allow distinctions to be drawn between economic behavior and other commitments. It draws deeply on implicit understandings about the family, community, and the sacred. It comes in many varieties, reflecting different ethnic, religious, regional, and occupational subcultures. But its core assumptions transcend these subcultures.

During most of our nation's history, this dominant paradigm served us well. It reconciled our economic pursuits with a commitment to basic human values. It provided an integrating set of assumptions about the nature of work and money. It gave us a reason to work hard and to expect this work to pay off. It anchored our sense of the value of money. It showed us how work and money contributed to the realization of personal, family, community, and spiritual values. It reinforced the incentive structure undergirding our nation's businesses and schools. And it defined major policy debates about economic growth, the nation's place in the world, and the role of government in economic affairs.

This consensus was clearly in evidence at the start of the nineteenth century when America was just beginning its long period of agricultural and industrial expansion. It found expression in the writings and speeches of popular theologians, literary figures, and moralists of the day. But for the most part it was simply taken for granted. It gave us an implicit definition of the American Dream, allowing us to focus on the business at hand without having to think very often or very deeply about what we were pursuing, or why.

By the end of the nineteenth century a significant alteration in the American Dream was taking place. New scientific conceptions of work and money were being advanced by political economists, making it more difficult to integrate moral considerations into formal discussions of economic life. Work and money became more intimately linked to each other, but farther removed from those conceptions of the human spirit that had once constrained them. Still, the American Dream lived on in the popular mind, drawing much of its strength from established communities of faith, from local neighborhoods and settlements of new immigrant groups, and from a growing sense of professionalism. It continued to legitimate hard work and to validate the place of work and money in relation to other human aims and aspirations.

Even today, much of the moral strength embedded in the American Dream remains intact. To think of it as a moral framework, however, has become less common. Much of the recent literature uses the term to mean little more than the desire to own a home or to frame arguments about the aspirations of minority groups for economic equality. Economistic thinking dominates discussions of work and money, while questions of moral commitment, character, and human values seem more difficult to relate to economic behavior.

Signs of erosion in the moral meanings once supplied by the American Dream are in fact everywhere. An overwhelming majority of Americans say their work is enormously meaningful and fulfilling, and yet they also feel pressured, dissatisfied, and uncertain about how their work fits in with the rest of their lives. Average family incomes for most Americans have edged up steadily during the past four decades, reaching record highs, but money still seems to be in short supply. People worry not only about having money, but also about the fact that they are worried in the first place. They don't know how to think about it or talk about it. Getting money sometimes seems more like playing the lottery than the outcome of rational effort. Consumerism still dominates our spending habits, but growing numbers of Americans worry about the blight of materialism and confuse marketing experts by giving mixed signals about quality, price, and value. Business leaders have started throwing organization charts and cost-benefit calculations out the window in favor of talk about "values management" and "corporate cultures." Ethicists argue that a radical shift in incentive structure must be made to head off repeat performances of the financial scandals that rocked the nation in the 1980s. Educators ponder the improbable task of gearing the schools for greater technological competitiveness, on the one hand, while trying to bring values more actively back into the curriculum, on the other hand. National policy debates seem increasingly to be caught up in a permanent stalemate over the promotion of economic growth versus the implementation of social programs.

But can all this really be taken as evidence that the old consensus is breaking down? Or is it merely a hodge-podge of unrelated, perhaps even insignificant, developments? Consider the following. A nationally prominent team of journalists (say, from CBS or *Newsweek*) venture out to Centerville, Iowa, to find out how the typical American is faring these days. They spend time with the Gormans and the Ishkowitzs. The Gormans are prospering like never before, both spouses working hard at professional careers. The Ishkowitzs aren't faring as well: they're employed but have to watch what they spend and defer major purchases. Much of the write-up sounds familiar. It deals with trends in disposable income, inflation, unemployment, and consumer credit. But the story also has an unexpected twist. The Gormans aren't trying to decide whether to buy stocks or real estate; they're considering cutting their jobs back to half time so they can plant a garden, play with the kids, and work with a local environmentalist group. The Ishkowitzs aren't just making it by shopping for bargains, working overtime, and squirreling away their nickels; they're holding their lives together by inviting the neighbors over and by attending church. Trivial? On the surface it would perhaps seem so. But decisions such as this, amplified nationwide and implemented amidst a much louder chorus of anguished questioning of personal values, add up to something profound.

The relationship between economic life and the quest for deeper human values, I shall argue, is becoming increasingly problematic. On the one hand, the work we do, the money we make, and the things we buy all remain very much at the heart of the American Dream. They are the fundamentals, the stuff of which life itself is composed. It is hard to imagine what life would be like if we did not have work, did not struggle to earn money, and did not have material things to purchase. Yet, on the other hand, these economic commitments seem increasingly to get in the way of other needs that cry out from the depth of our souls: the need to cultivate intimate relationships with our families, the desire to be part of a caring community, the quest for spirituality and truth, and, perhaps most of all, the longing to know ourselves better and to grow as persons. As a result, we experience an internal tension between the material side of our lives and what in an earlier time was called the human spirit. For some of us, it is little more than a tug pulling at our conscience when we get home from work too late to tuck the children into bed. For others of us, it becomes a raging war within ourselves. It seizes our attention, forcing us to question our basic commitments. How should we live? How much should we work? How much money do we really need? What goals are we trying to accomplish anyway?

In recent years this tension has been aggravated by pressures in the workplace, by the state of the economy, and by profound changes in the society at large. Slower economic growth means heightened competition for good jobs and promotions. Even the more fortunate feel compelled to work longer hours and complain of diminished free time. For the vast majority of women now in the labor force, career opportunities and disposable incomes have expanded, but workplace demands raise new questions about relationships with spouses and place heavy burdens on those who try to maintain parental responsibilities. In an economy dependent largely on consumer goods and services, advertising and commercialism also impose rising demands on family budgets, and these budgets are already strapped by high taxes, credit-card debt, mortgage payments, and numerous nondiscretionary expenditures.

At a time when income levels for many people have reached record highs, a growing number of people are thus feeling sufficiently pressured to question whether economic success is enough. Some bury their heads, denying that enough is enough, and insist that even more economic success is all that matters. Others magnify economic pressures to the point that no time is left to think of anything else. And yet, good jobs, meaningful careers, and adequate salaries notwithstanding, a persistent restlessness appears evident. Increasingly people are asking:

What else does life have to offer? How can I balance my job and my family? Is it possible to be successful and have a life too?

The reason these questions are being voiced with increasing urgency, though, is not simply that they have been forced upon us by economic conditions. To assume that it is, in fact, is still to take the old paradigm for granted, rather than realizing the full extent to which it has fallen into question. The old consensus would suggest, for example, that both the Gormans and the Ishkowitzs are still fundamentally pursuing the American Dream. Its defenders would argue that economic prosperity for the Gormans had reduced the marginal utility of additional income, causing them to shift their utility function in the direction of greater free time. The Ishkowitzs, in contrast, are probably victims of a recession or a temporary realignment in the labor force. Their decision to postpone major purchases constitutes "rational" behavior under the circumstances. Their interest in neighbors and church is probably a reversion to a kind of barter economy in which shared tasks can take the place of cash payments. Note, however, that these arguments fail to say anything about the struggle both families are having trying to decide how to live their lives. The issue is not simply economic, but moral, having to do with personal decisions about basic human values.

These questions carry enormous implications for public policy but lie largely outside the realm of policy deliberations themselves. Policymakers can try to stimulate economic growth, provide programs for the disadvantaged, and keep taxes at levels amenable to private investment and consumption. But what people do with their time and money is up to them. The role of public policy is only to guarantee the freedom to make individual choices in these areas. As long as these choices are lawful, policy does not attempt to make these choices for us.

The private sector of course flourishes on this freedom, incessantly turning it into new markets for goods and services. But it too offers little positive guidance in how to lead our lives. Especially when the choices are not between one product and another but concern how much of our lives to devote to economic pursuits at all, the guidance of the private sector is more likely to be a hindrance than a help. Workplace incentives are structured to make us work harder, not to make us take more time off. Financial advisers are in business to help us invest our money, not to decide against trying to make it in the first place. Indeed, the advice we receive on all sides encourages us to think in economic categories, rather than giving us ways to transcend these categories. It comes through the mass media, telling us to prefer one brand to another, but fundamentally to spend our money on something. It comes through educational programs that challenge us to prepare for better careers. And it comes through the workplace itself in encouragement to be more productive and competitive.

Where then do we find the encouragement to cut back, to keep our work commitments within bounds, to curb our wants, to abide by rigorous ethical standards, to take more time for ourselves? Where do we turn for support in trying to cultivate the deeper, historically cherished values of the human spirit? These choices lie in the nether world of obscurity—except when advertisers attempt to package them as economic goods, such as exercise equipment, health clubs, cruises, and movies. The pressure is still to spend our money on consumer goods, not to limit our involvement in the economic sphere entirely.

Few of us would nevertheless doubt the importance of being able to make choices governed by something other than economic considerations alone. No price can be put on beauty or truth or happiness. No career is worth sacrificing our integrity for, and no fortune can guarantee our self-esteem or our children's well-being. These are high values that transcend the economic life in any society. Some of them can perhaps be obtained more easily by those who work hard in their jobs and who earn handsome livings. But they are also values that at some point require us to limit our economic pursuits.

The stakes are very high, individually and collectively. On the one hand, economic realities are so intertwined that our very way of life seems to depend on ever-expanding markets, on creating new jobs, on promoting higher productivity in those jobs, on learning new skills, and on stimulating consumers to purchase the goods and services we produce. On the other hand, what have we gained if economic prosperity is bought at the price of our fundamental human needs?

The aim of this book is to demonstrate that Americans must recover a moral language in which to bring their deeper human values directly to bear on their economic decisions. For much of the past century we have bracketed most of our values out of these considerations, letting economistic thinking, consumerism, and narrow concerns about profitability, efficiency, "getting ahead," and "making it" dominate our collective thought processes. That bracketing served us very well. It contributed to a high standard of living. It promoted industrial and technological expansion. It simplified our lives, allowing us to proceed much more efficiently than if we had to think more deeply about what we were doing. But those days are over. We know they are when we hear the cold facts being presented again and again about the ill effects of our way of life on the physical environment. We realize it in a way that is perhaps even more difficult to deny when we see ourselves suffering health problems because of too many responsibilities at work, when we experience increasing stress on the never-ending ladder to material success, when our spouses and children receive less of our attention than they deserve, when ethical shortcuts come to be the best way to get ahead, and when we simply have trouble focusing our attention on anything but what we do at work and what we see on television.

There is mounting evidence that Americans *are* beginning to think seriously about how to bring values back into the center of their lives. All across the country, churches and synagogues are drawing people to workshops on how to apply their faith in the workplace. Self-help groups for workaholics and compulsive shoppers are trying to rein in materialistic addictions. Men's groups are voicing questions about the relationships between careers and families. Women's groups have been addressing the same issues for some time. In countless corporate boardrooms, seminars are being given about humanizing the workplace. Colleges and universities are sponsoring new programs in ethics and values. Teachers and parents are struggling to find ways to bring values back into the curriculum.

The question that must be asked, however, is whether the current quest for values will make any difference. Will it affect the ways in which Americans comport themselves economically? Or will it simply be a "side show," pursued in our leisure time or when we are young, but forgotten when the chips are down? Posed another way, can economic commitments be reintegrated into the wider social practices that have long been a source of collective values in our society? Or will these commitments continue to be dominated by cost-benefit calculations that fail to answer any of the fundamental questions about how our work and money contribute to the realization of our dreams?

Instead of adding to the long series of discussions of how we must reform our economic aspirations, then, the present argument requires us to pay close attention to the ways in which people *already* think about their work, their money, their consumer behavior, and the relationships between these commitments and other parts of their lives, such as their families, their ethical orientations, their communities, and their religious faith. The problem is not that people are simply over-worked and strapped for money. If that were the problem, some straightforward adjustments in the incentive structure of the workforce itself might be sufficient to get people to scale back their commitments and desires. These are *symptoms* rather than the underlying problem. It is important that we understand how serious they are, for much of the public rhetoric voiced by business leaders and politicians ignores them entirely. And yet they must not be framed strictly in economic terms.

Much of the problem our society faces today in trying to bring its economic commitments back into alignment, I shall try to show, is rooted in the way we *think*, that is, in the moral frameworks we use in ordering our priorities and deciding how to lead our lives. Work is not something devoid of values, separated from the rest of our lives. It could never be that. The fact is that most Americans are deeply com-mitted to their work. They find it meaningful and derive personal ful-fillment from it. The same is true of money. Even our material goods are fraught with meaning. What does this suggest? Are values already an integral part of our economic commitments? Yes and no. They are in that these commitments are seldom ends in themselves or means sim-ply to attain other economic ends. Work, money, and the goods we buy have meaning because they are connected to a substratum of thinking about individual freedom, personal growth, devotion to family, the re-alization of variety, and a whole variety of other seldom-stated aims and aspirations. But values are still seldom fully integrated into our thinking about these commitments. We live out our work lives with a kind of "work self" that provides temporary meaning, but we com-partmentalize our work from many of the other values we hold dear. The same is true of money. It is the means to attain our values, we tell ourselves, but how we think about it is often so poorly formulated that we consider it a deep mystery.

It is for this reason that I insist on the importance of moral language. The quest for values has too often been framed in meaningless general-ities. Parents and schoolteachers talk about bringing values back into the classroom. College administrators discuss the collapse of a "value-free" approach to the sciences and social sciences. Marketing experts champion a new approach to their trade called "value marketing." What do these words mean? Usually little more than the fact that people have preferences (biases, when conceived negatively). The current crisis of values hinges on the simple fact that we have no basis on which to make these choices. Calling for more attention to values is merely to identify the problem. To move positively toward its resolution requires paying closer attention to the way in which choices are actually made.

How we choose lies basically in the realm of morality. This is an old-fashioned word, relegated mostly to questions of such dubious gravity as whether to cheat on exams or have sexual intercourse before marriage (or both). But the need to restrict our economic appetites is as important as the need to curb permissive sexuality. Everywhere we see the ill effects of material promiscuity—in the greed that plagued brokerage houses and that cost taxpayers billions in bailing out gutted savings and loan companies, in the career stress that results in alcoholism and broken families, in the incessant consumerism that has itself become the consumer of our nation's youth, and in the daily stress and strain that stems from overwork. The costs to ourselves, our children, and our society are enormous.

And yet little attention has been devoted to the moral arguments we must make in order to restrain our economic passions. The culture tells us to be responsible, to work hard, to earn as much money as we can, and not to bend the rules (unless we can get away with it). It provides us with few legitimate reasons for restricting our material pursuits. Short of having a heart attack, the commonest excuses for not devoting all our energies to the grindstone and the counting house are that we lack the necessary talent or admit to being lazy. In the land of opportunity, not trying to be as successful as we can be is often a source only of shame.

Thinking morally about our commitments to material pursuits, on the one hand, and to higher values, on the other hand, is not something we know very well how to do. As public discourse has shifted increasingly toward politics, consumerism, and narrow contentious definitions of personal morality, we have lost touch with an important segment of our cultural heritage. For we do have a strong, but neglected, tradition of argumentation about the moral limits of the economic life. It is a heritage embedded deeply in our religious institutions, but one that is also profoundly a part of our literary and artistic traditions. It is a heritage that in the eyes of many contemporary observers needs desperately to be rediscovered.

To do this, some would perhaps argue that all we need do is reconsider the classic arguments of the nineteenth-century moralists, reminding ourselves of what they had to say about the limits of economic life, and applying these arguments to our own situation. But normative appeals of this kind are not likely to be compelling unless they coincide with our basic assumptions about how the world actually works. If life is fundamentally governed by economic laws and the principles of self-interest, as we are so commonly taught to believe, then arguments about moral restraint in the name of high values are likely to be regarded as idealistic at best and whimsical at worst.

For this reason, we need to begin not by appealing to the moralistic arguments of the past but by reconsidering our present assumptions about work, money, and material goods from the ground up. We need, moreover, to do this not by engaging in recondite debates with armchair economists about the premises of their models but by listening to people to find out how they actually live their lives. Only by listening to the ways in which people make sense of their lives can we discover the integral relationship—the relationship we all sense intuitively from our personal experience—between the material realm and our commitments to the human spirit.

PART ONE
THE UNREALIZED AMERICAN DREAM

Chapter One

HAVING IT ALL—AND WANTING MORE:

THE SOCIAL SYMPTOMS

OF CULTURAL DISTRESS

WHEN MARK LATHAM graduated from college, he had no idea what he wanted to do next. Like many other young people with talent and good credentials, he decided to maximize his options by getting into something where he could make a lot of money. That meant Wall Street. Within two years, Mark was a successful analyst negotiating leveraged buyouts for a major corporate finance firm. Now, at age 26, he works for another firm arranging financing for huge real estate deals. Handling sales in the $400 million range has become routine. He knows he could become enormously successful if he really tried. He says, "It'd be great to be famous, having everybody wanting to talk to you, going to interesting parties, not having to worry about money, traveling, living in a nice home."

But Mark Latham is not so sure this is the life he wants. "Someday, our planet's going to be a speck of dust," he muses, "so what's the point of making a lot of money?" He fears he will spend his whole life trying to fill it up with possessions, only to have someone ask, "Did you really make a difference? Did you give a little more than you took? Or did you just take a lot?" He is no visionary, but he wants to be remembered as a decent person who left the world a little better than he found it.

John and Mary Phelps, both age 30, have achieved a comfortable standard of living compared with most Americans. After finishing his MBA, John moved up the corporate ladder in various finance and marketing positions in Minneapolis. Mary runs her own graphic design business. They own their home and have enough money to buy most of the things they want. Both find their work intellectually stimulating and see a rosy economic future ahead.

They do not aspire to the fast track, but even in the driving lane they have discovered more pressure and frustration than they ever imagined. Recently John gave up his marketing position because of sixty-plus-hour weeks, back stabbing, and office politics, only to find himself in a job with grueling deadlines and endless paperwork. He says he comes home and just screams to relieve the tension. Mary feels the pressure, too, especially when clients insist she work evenings and weekends. She wants to have children but fears she will not have time to be a good mother. Both would like to play a more positive role in their community—developing environmental projects and helping the disadvantaged. They are uncertain whether they will ever realize these dreams.

RETHINKING THE AMERICAN DREAM

Throughout much of our nation's history people pursued the American Dream by trying to attain high-paying jobs, working hard to become materially successful, and striving for an economically comfortable life. But to a growing number of Americans, the life envisioned in this dream is no longer enough. Having moved securely into the professional-managerial class, they want more than simply an above-average standard of living. Working harder just to climb the corporate ladder and acquire more economic resources no longer seems as appealing as it once did. Instead, concerns are being expressed with increasing frequency about the ill effects of working too hard, of subjecting oneself to relentless job pressures, and of becoming focused so single-mindedly on material pursuits that other human values are neglected. People are now reconsidering the benefits of family life, community service, spiritual pursuits, and self-realization, in opposition to the search for material success alone.

"The New American Dream," writes family sociologist Arlene Skolnick, "mixes the new cultural freedoms with many of the old wishes—marital and family happiness, economic security, home ownership, education of children."[1] But, she cautions, there are more twists and turns to be faced. In part, this is because economic conditions themselves may provide fewer opportunities than they did in the past. But it is even more a result of uncertainty about what the American Dream should include.

Observers assess the current mood with differing emphases but agree that serious rethinking of the American Dream is taking place. Increasingly, writes Graham Hueber of the Gallup Poll, "Americans

[are] seeking more personal satisfaction through recreation, family life, friends, religion, and a search for meaning in life—not through work."[2] There is "a great craving," notes a leading business magazine, for a slower pace and the time just to relax and do other things besides work.[3] Finding how to do this might even make our work more productive, counsel the editors of another magazine, because "the human spirit, strangely and wondrously made, always turns out to be a surprise."[4]

As the lives of people like Mark Latham, John and Mary Phelps, and millions of others demonstrate, however, economic aspirations and the demands that go with them are seldom easy to escape. In all periods the great sages and social visionaries hoped for a better way. Aristotle predicted a time when people could expend a minimum of energy working, saving most of their time for reflection and pleasure. Centuries later, the explorers who came to American shores envisioned a land of plenty in which the toil and drudgery of the past could be forgone.[5] But, for all the industrial and technological advancement that has happened since then, these dreams have failed to be realized.

Even the more prosperous members of our society find themselves beleaguered to the point of exhaustion with economic commitments. In one sense, they have everything—talent, connections, opportunity, prosperity, freedom from back-breaking labor, the ability to live securely and comfortably—but they clearly want more. Economic well-being is only a means to realizing the other aspirations they hold more dearly. Indeed, it is a means that sometimes gets in the way of these other aspirations. The economic portion of their lives seems to be ever on the move, expansive, demanding, threatening to encroach on every other realm of their lives. And so they struggle to find legitimate ways in which to restrain their economic commitments, still feeling the need to work hard, but also experiencing high levels of stress, periodic burnout, and the constant desire to achieve greater fulfillment.

The ambivalence toward economic commitments that seems to characterize a growing number of middle-class Americans has been expressed well in a recent book by psychologist Sam Keen. Reflecting on his own ambivalence, Keen writes, "I don't know who I would be without the satisfaction of providing for my family, the occasional intoxication of creativity, the warm companionship of colleagues, the pride in a job well done, and the knowledge that my work has been useful to others." Keen's devotion to his work, however, is plagued by unease about the price of this devotion. He adds, "But there is still something unsaid, something that forces me to ask questions about my life that are, perhaps, tragic: In working so much have I done violence to my being? How often, doing work that is good, have I betrayed what is better in myself and abandoned what is best for those I love? How many hours would have been better spent walking in silence in the woods or wrestling with my children?"[6]

Such questions of course are not popular in many circles. If there is anything wrong with the American Dream, say the politicians and corporate analysts, it is that most people are not pursuing it hard enough. Sagging productivity, inflated salaries, long lunch breaks, padded expense accounts, lax supervision, too little interest in doing the job well, an education system that provides inadequate training in technical skills—these are the problems. Not a rapacious economic system that extracts too much from its workers. Even to suggest that economic commitments may need to be reined in is to fly in the face of most conventional wisdom. Yet a growing body of evidence demonstrates clearly that the vast majority of Americans who have achieved a comfortable level of economic well-being are experiencing the pressures of work and monetary commitments so acutely that they wonder how to make room for the more basic human values these commitments were once intended to achieve.

WORKING HARDER

Long hours on the job signal the first line across which material pursuits embark in their relentless quest for a greater share of our lives. Compared with the Japanese, the American worker has often been made to feel like an outright shirker. Faltering national competitiveness in world markets has been blamed on the U.S. worker taking too many holidays and vacations, watching too much television, cutting hours, and idling the time away while on the job. The Japanese, critics point out, work longer hours each week and take fewer vacations. Americans also fall behind their German counterparts, apparently valuing free time at the expense of the national economy. These accusations square well with other impressions of American society: that it is devoted increasingly to leisure and relaxation, that the decline of agriculture and heavy industry has led to a more humane life for the average worker, and that the proverbial work ethic nurtured by Puritan strictness has long been on the decline. But portraying the American worker in this manner is to engage in a massive deception.

Statistics on the average workweek did register substantial declines (about 10 percent each decade) between 1900 and 1940. Since then, however, the workweek has remained remarkably stable. It does so, moreover, when estimates of holidays, paid vacations, and sick leaves are taken into account. Comparative figures from other countries also show that workers in countries such as Japan and Germany put in about the same number of hours as American workers when actual time in similar-sized companies is considered, and that working hours in many other advanced industrialized countries have been declining in contrast with those in the United States.[7]

Labor statistics show that the typical hourly worker in the United States still receives wages for a workweek of approximately forty hours. What these figures mask, however, is the fact that an increasing number of people—who are not paid by the hour—generally work longer. At present, approximately 40 percent of all men in the U.S. labor force put in more than forty hours a week at their jobs—and a quarter put in more than fifty hours. Among women, the figures are still somewhat lower, but at least one woman in five works outside the home more than the standard forty hours. These figures are even higher in professional and managerial occupations and reach the highest levels among married men and women—precisely those whose time is likely to be fullest with other responsibilities, such as child-rearing.[8] The fact that many Americans take their work home with them, mulling it over while they watch television or mow the grass, also means that official estimates give a distorted picture. One national study found that one American in three thinks about his or her work a lot outside of the workplace itself.[9] Some evidence also indicates that an increasing share of the American workforce is now *required* to work evenings and weekends, rather than being able to restrict their jobs to the conventional "nine-to-five" working day.[10]

The most substantial increase in the typical workweek has come from more and more women participating in the labor force. When the workweek for individual workers is counted, this fact is missed. But for most people, the relevant fact of life is that they and their spouse *both* work now, whereas a generation ago only one spouse was likely to be employed outside the home. In 1950, for instance, only 37 percent of all women between ages 25 and 54 were gainfully employed, meaning that the typical household contributed about forty hours a week to the labor market, or if this 37 percent were averaged in, no more than about fifty-five hours. By comparison, 81 percent of all women in this age-group are now employed, meaning that the typical household involves dual careers, or at least eighty hours a week on the job.[11] When work from all these various sources is taken into consideration, some estimates suggest that per capita involvement in the labor force may on average be as much as an extra month per year, compared with only two decades ago.[12]

As a result, large numbers of the American public complain of having too little time to do anything but work. According to one recent survey, 48 percent of the U.S. labor force say they have too little time to spend with their spouse, and 39 percent say they have too little time for their children. Thirty-two percent of those polled felt they had to spend too much time working.[13] In my survey, 66 percent of the labor force said the statement "I'm working harder than I did five years ago" described themselves very well or fairly well. One person in two (52 percent) said the same about the statement "I wish I could work fewer hours than I do."[14]

In another national survey 41 percent complained of having too little time to spend with their families, and three-quarters said they sleep fewer than eight hours a night; indeed, four people in ten sleep only six hours a night or less.[15] And, while many adults may feel this is the only way to get everything done, research is beginning to document its serious negative consequences. As one writer observes, "Evidence is mounting that sleep deprivation has become one of the most pervasive health problems facing the U.S."[16] Many people, it appears, might agree. In my survey, 48 percent said the statement "I should get more sleep than I do" described them very well or fairly well.[17]

Despite the fact that leisure time is probably more abundant than it was a century ago, many people are thus pressured to find enough time to relax or pursue any of their other interests. With both spouses working, less time is left over to care for children or engage in community activities. Even with labor-saving devices such as household appliances, and the growing availability of professional services, people find that much of their free time must be spent maintaining these labor-saving devices, traveling to and from work, and doing routine household and personal chores.

"The hours are a real pain in the ass," says Jena Forsythe, 29, a New York securities trader who specializes in Japanese equities and bonds. At work every morning by seven-thirty, she spends at least five evenings a week at the office in order to be in contact with her counterparts in Tokyo. In eight years, she has found little time to pursue personal relationships, let alone get married or think about having children. Yet, even without these commitments, she finds it virtually impossible to do the things she needs to do for herself. "Like, this morning I'm thinking, oh my God, I do not have an ironed blouse in my apartment and somehow I've got to figure out how to get my blouses ironed so that I have some clothes!"

In the same way that labor statistics have sometimes given a misleading impression of the American workforce, studies of leisure time have also been deceptive, leading many observers to assume that people actually have more free time than ever before, despite their protests to the contrary. But when viewed more closely, these studies indicate how small the segment of American society is that has actually gained greater free time in recent years. Since 1975, for example, leisure time appears to have edged up by as much as two hours a week for the American population as a whole. Yet, when subgroups are examined, this increase turns out to be limited almost entirely to men and women in their fifties and sixties. Among married people with children, there has actually been a decrease in leisure time.[18]

With a wife and two daughters, Stuart Cummings, 33, a corporate lawyer in Chicago, is beginning to resent the long hours his job requires. "On a good day," he says, "I'm away from seven to seven, and many nights I don't make it home before my kids go to bed at nine." He says he has trouble accepting this as the way it will be for the next thirty years. But, like many other Americans in high-level professional positions, he sees no immediate way of escaping these requirements.

On objective grounds alone, then, it appears that many middle-class people are putting in long hours on the job, despite the fact that prosperity is already relatively widespread among this segment of the population, and that automation and other labor-saving devices seem not to have done much in recent decades to reduce the overall workweek. Some would argue that these conditions have been created by economic laws operating in the marketplace itself. These objective conditions, however, do not fully explain why their subjective correlates take the form they do. Previous generations might well have complained about being physically exhausted from too much work, but the current sense that one has a moral obligation to choose between working and other commitments hinges on much more recent definitions of the self and the social context in which it must function. Without yet trying to make sense of these definitions, we can at least begin to see that understanding the nature of work and the ways in which it might be reconciled more fully with other human aspirations will require us to consider it in relation to broader cultural assumptions involving moral meanings and conceptions of the good.

THE GOLDEN HANDCUFFS

One of the reasons why so many Americans find it difficult to cut back on the work they do, according to their own accounts, is that they are caught up in a cycle of lifestyle expectations that leaves them financially dependent on every marginal gain they can possibly earn. Henry David Thoreau once wrote critically of this financial dependence as "golden or silver fetters."[19] But in current management parlance "the golden handcuffs" have evolved into a strategy for cultivating corporate loyalty. Pay people enough, build in fringe benefits, encourage them to lead a lifestyle in keeping with rising economic expectations, and they will have trouble quitting or slowing the pace.

Corporate executives seldom have to bend employees' arms to apply these handcuffs, for economic obligations tend to rise during the life course of most individuals. Married couples typically spend more on housing than do singles, and as children enter the picture, housing, food, clothing, and education costs all escalate, usually at a rate equal to or above annual salary increases. Only as they reach their late fifties, do most people begin to feel they can afford to consider such options as working shorter hours in order to have more free time.[20] In my survey, people between the ages of 35 and 49 were particularly subject to financial concerns: 44 percent in this age bracket were trying to save money for children to attend college, 43 percent were paying off credit card debts, 57 percent were saving for retirement, 40 percent were either saving to buy a house or meeting high mortgage payments, and 31 percent were paying for medical bills.[21]

American culture is also geared to encourage rising material expectations across the life cycle. Rising costs associated with a growing family may induce greater economic pressures, but so do rising expectations about consumer goods, luxury items, and other material comforts. In one national survey, 56 percent of the respondents age 18 to 34 admitted that their desire to have "nice things" had risen within the past five years, as did 42 percent of those age 35 to 49.[22]

The result is that fewer and fewer Americans are able to escape the cycle of working harder to buy more things and to pay the bills for what they have already purchased. Some evidence of this pattern is evident in public opinion polls. In my survey, for example, 69 percent of the U.S. labor force admitted they had more money now than they did five years ago; yet 53 percent said they worry a lot about meeting their financial obligations, and 84 percent wished they had more money than they do.[23]

Better evidence comes from economic data themselves. In the last two decades alone, consumer borrowing on charge accounts has risen from $8.7 billion to $20.4 billion—a figure that now comprises approximately 21 percent of U.S. disposable income.[24] Over the same period, bank-card delinquencies have grown steadily.[25] Personal savings have experienced a corresponding decline, putting an increasing number of families at the mercy of short-term swings in the economy; for example, in one survey, half the respondents said they had managed to save less than $3,000, and 40 percent said it would be a "big problem" for them to receive an unexpected bill for $1,000.[26]

On balance, the most serious indication of how the golden handcuffs have increased their hold on the American public is probably the fact that household debt, which only a decade ago was 20 percent below the average level of household income, is now 10 percent higher than household income.[27] Much truth, it seems, is borne by the bumper sticker "I owe, I owe, so off to work I go."[28]

John Phelps, the Minneapolis businessman, had recently become acutely aware of the golden handcuffs he was wearing. Climbing the corporate ladder, he began to feel he was no longer being true to the values his parents had tried to instill in him; instinctively, he knew he wanted to pursue something else. "I definitely wanted to drop out," he recalls, but he postponed doing it. "They talk about the golden handcuffs in the corporate world where you get the nice benefits and the high pay, and you build a lifestyle around that." He knew he was tied to the corporation by financial necessity. "It's hard to leave," he admits, "no matter what you're thinking."

Stuart Cummings, the Chicago lawyer, also knows he is a victim of the golden handcuffs. "I get troubled," he muses, "but I am attracted by the lifestyle that I have built up in just 8½ years of practicing law. It's easy to talk about chucking that lifestyle when you're by yourself. But when you've got a wife and two girls, then you begin thinking—you almost get altruistic about it—about having a nice home and that kind of thing because you did it for your kids. So you get sucked into it. You face a whole set of conundrums at that point."

He is at least candid about it. Others have succumbed to the lure of a comfortable lifestyle to a point where they no longer experience the tension evident in his remarks. For them, the magic of the American economic system has become complete. As literary critic Leslie Fiedler once wrote, it no longer produces things, but "dreams disguised as things."[29]

The wisdom in Fiedler's remark is perhaps evident in the fact that most Americans disavow wanting to be rich or even having a lot of money for its own sake—indeed, there is much concern in our society that too much emphasis is being placed on money—and yet the desire to realize a comfortable lifestyle is nearly universal. In one poll, 98 percent of the American public said "living a comfortable life" was at least fairly important to them, and 77 percent said this was very important. In the same poll, only 37 percent valued "making a lot of money" this highly.[30] Evidently it is the lifestyle we want most, including the dreams and the security that go with it, but it is needing the wherewithal to buy these dreams that keeps our shoulders to the wheel.

ETHICAL EROSION

For a disturbingly large number of people, the desire for material advancement has also led them beyond the boundary of conventional moral restraint. "Greed is all right," declared arbitrageur Ivan F. Boesky to the graduating class of the School of Business Administration at the University of California, Berkeley, at the height of his climb to financial success. "You can be greedy and still feel good about yourself."[31] But within a year Boesky had been charged by the Securities and Exchange Commission with obtaining insider information from Drexel Burnham investment banker Dennis Levine, and soon after, plea bargaining by Boesky's lawyers resulted in a felony settlement and $100 million in fines and restitution. Five years later, with numerous lawsuits and investigations still pending, Drexel Burnham and several of its top managers, including Michael Milken and Bruce Newberg, had been indicted on nearly 100 counts of fraud and racketeering and forced to pay more than $600 million in penalties.

"I can talk about it now because they're out of business," says Teri Silver, 29, a systems analyst who worked at the Beverly Hills office of Drexel Burnham where Milken and others developed their lucrative junk bond industry. A sardonic smile crossed her face as she recalled, "One time we were told we couldn't use the door going to our computer room, and we couldn't use it for like three days. They said, 'Whatever you do, don't go through that door, you have to go through the other door.'" Teri soon found out why. "Overnight they had built a wall around our computer room, so that anybody who just came in wouldn't know there's a computer in there. And the reason was, we had auditors there. They didn't want them to know that we ran our own computer system in Beverly Hills. They wanted them to think that everything came from New York, because Beverly Hills was very secretive with their high-yield bond stuff. It was just bizarre. And they told us if somebody were to ask us if we had a computer—basically we were lying for them—just to play real dumb."

Teri Silver's experience is undoubtedly an extreme case of corporate disregard for public ethics, but such violations are by no means unique, either in the world of business or in politics. Personal stories reveal, often more profoundly even than the scandals publicized in newspapers, that ethical erosion is also an endemic problem in the world of politics.

Karen Kelsey grew up in a mansion on Rodeo Drive in Beverly Hills. After graduating in business and economics from one of the nation's most prestigious (and expensive) private universities, she landed a posh job in the nation's capital. She planned to spend several years gaining experience, then attend law school, and eventually embark on a career shuttling back and forth between Wall Street and the federal triangle. Soon, however, she was feeling profoundly dissatisfied with the high life of politics, and within a few years she dropped out. Today she earns a modest living as a therapist. She had the talent and training to make as much money as she wanted, but she opted for less because she wanted more. Why?

The triggering event that led Karen Kelsey to abandon Capitol Hill for a career in counseling was discovering that the senator she worked for was breaking federal laws. "He was basically committing felonies," she recalls. When she documented them and confronted him, he retaliated. "I was trying to get a top secret clearance from the Department of Defense because I did his defense work. And he told me that if I didn't just forget about everything I knew, he would go to the Department of Defense and say that since I'd been in psychoanalysis he didn't think I was mentally stable enough to have a clearance, and then I wouldn't be able to work in defense, which I loved at the time. So I had to go to the assistant secretary of defense myself in person and say this guy's blackmailing me, can you help me? And the assistant secretary of defense gave me my clearance personally."

Just how widespread these ethical problems may be is of course difficult to gauge, but some studies suggest that the potential for misconduct may be very widespread indeed. For example, a study conducted by the National Association of Accountants revealed that 87 percent of American business managers were willing to commit fraud in one or more of the cases presented to them. Another study, including more than 400 industrial salespeople, suggested that the likelihood of getting caught, not a commitment to moral principles themselves, was the only thing preventing people from breaking the rules.[32] In my survey, 48 percent said it was okay to bend the rules sometimes at work, and 32 percent said they had actually seen people at work doing something unethical within the past month.[33]

Whether the potential for misconduct is generally realized or only considered, there is also a deep sense in the public at large that morals and ethics in the workplace are found wanting. While a majority of Americans rate the honesty and ethical standards of clergy, physicians, and college professors "very high" or "high," for example, only 30 percent give the same rating to bankers, and even fewer express confidence in the ethics of business executives (21 percent), members of Congress (19 percent), real estate agents (17 percent), and stockbrokers (14 percent).[34] Over the past decade the ethics ratings of bankers, reporters, journalists, lawyers, and stockbrokers have all dropped substantially.[35] In another national survey, respondents were asked simply whether most corporate executives are honest: fewer than one person in three said yes.[36]

Corporations have begun responding to these negative perceptions by instituting ethical codes, but prevailing cynicism can also be a self-fulfilling prophecy when executives believe slippery morals are simply the norm. According to one study, this belief is indeed widespread:

four-fifths of 1,000 upper-level executives surveyed said people are "often" or "occasionally" unethical in their business dealings, and slightly more than half indicated that "bending the rules" was common among their own acquaintances. Junior executives and middle-level managers were thought to be particularly prone to engage in unethical practices in order to achieve success. Compounding the problem was a widespread perception that ethical dilemmas are not an appropriate subject for discussion among colleagues. Most executives said they would resolve such a dilemma by themselves or discuss it with their spouse; only one in ten said he or she would discuss it with someone at work.[37]

Wanting to Contribute

But it is not just the unscrupulous and the greedy who raise concern about finding appropriate limits for our material pursuits. It is also the virtuous among us, those who want to do more with their lives than simply make a handsome living. A long-standing American tradition says contribute something to the world, pay back your debts to society, make humankind better. Mark Latham was clearly echoing this tradition in saying he wanted to give back more than he took.

The desire to contribute something positive to the world is deeply embedded in American religious history, in the humanitarian ethos of liberal arts education, and in the service ethic of our nation's voluntary organizations. The same concern is evident in the service ethic of the professions themselves and is even part of the language of the for-profit world. Business leaders want their activities to be viewed as beneficial to society as well as financially profitable. Not surprisingly, making a contribution is also a widely shared value in the American public at large. One survey showed that 96 percent of the public said "making the world a better place" was at least fairly important to them, and 78 percent said it was very important or absolutely essential in their lives.[38]

Wanting to contribute fits happily with many jobs, and where there may be no obvious social benefit, people can still feel worthwhile by treating their customers with extra kindness or by giving some of their money to charities. But there is often an inherent tension between making larger contributions to the world and keeping up with the daily pressures of the job, especially when specialization requires people to engage in ever narrower kinds of work. As a result, people may be earning a good living but feeling they want more, including the opportunity to serve others and to do something even more meaningful with their lives.

Real-estate appraiser Norm Lundström brings in a six-digit income, finds his work personally fulfilling, and figures he basically has a pretty good deal in life. But after eighteen years in this line of work, he is seriously considering dropping out. He complains that everything in his present job revolves around money. "I would dearly love to contribute something significant to humanity," he says. Yet he sees no way to do that as a real-estate appraiser. "I will never do that in the job. I will not save somebody's life who's contemplating suicide. I will not cure a major disease. I will not make a significant scientific accomplishment. I would love to become an astronomer—discover something in astronomy or solve Fermat's last theorem or something. I would like to get into something where I could contribute. Write some poetry. Or maybe write a novel that would exist far beyond my own life and contribute to people's happiness or thought patterns sometime. I won't be doing that in the job I'm in right now, and I think that's sad. I would like something more than that."

For people at Norm Lundström's age, the urgency to contribute before it is too late becomes all the more acute. But younger people often feel the same frustrations. Still sensing the idealism that led him into a law career, Stuart Cummings worries that more and more of his time is spent helping the rich protect their assets than helping to realize his own values. "Isn't there some way I could make a bigger difference?" he asks. It troubles him to think he is spending the best years of his life helping wealthy people make more money. He still dreams that someday his talents will be used "in a way that's more directly and obviously beneficial to this world and the people in it."

TIRED TO THE DEATH?

Yet despite these yearnings for something more, work itself has retained considerable appeal. A generation ago, writers and pundits proclaimed that the human cost of American capitalism was to be counted chiefly in boredom, drudgery, faceless similarity—in short, a meaningless existence. Willy Loman, "tired to the death," symbolized the fate of the American breadwinner.[39] But that image seems not to have stood the test of history. The problem with middle-class work today is often that it is *too meaningful*. Increasingly, the Willy Lomans who see themselves as hard-working drummers, destined for the ash can because their work has no intrinsic meaning, appear to be a distinct minority.[40]

Virtually everyone claims their work is a major source of personal fulfillment. In one national survey, 83 percent of the American public said work was an important source of their basic sense of worth as a person.[41] In another study, the same proportion (83 percent) said they were satisfied with their job, while only 11 percent said they were dissatisfied.[42] In my survey, 84 percent of those working full time said their work was absolutely essential or very important to their sense of personal worth, and 82 percent of the entire workforce said the statement "my work is very meaningful to me" describes them very well or fairly well.[43] For many, the reason may be that so-called postindustrial society does provide more interesting and varied careers to pursue than was ever possible in preindustrial or industrial settings. For others, work may provide a sense of security at a time when the familiar moorings of the past seem to be unsettled. "How is purpose, seriousness, or meaning found in life when it is not given by earthly necessity?" asks historian Benjamin Hunnicutt. His research has convinced him that Americans are trying desperately to answer these questions by turning work into an end in itself, creating a new work ethic that is distinctively modern and secular.[44]

John Phelps, having shed the golden handcuffs to become an economic development specialist, does not let his work substitute for other values he holds dear, but his work is indeed a source of deep personal satisfaction. He says it is especially fulfilling when he is able to help disadvantaged people realize their dreams of starting their own business. "It's exciting to me," he says, "because that's a symbol of hope for people in that income group."

Lou Candela, 50, a Boston schoolteacher, finds his work enormously fulfilling, too. Sometimes he fears he will never do anything really significant in life, such as finding a cure for a major disease or making a scientific discovery, but he revels in the excitement of seeing the students in his woodworking class create something they can truly call their own. "When we make some projects, like these carousels that have to spin without wobbling and everything, I help the kids do the final steps, and they're so excited that it works!" He fairly glows as he describes how happy that makes him feel. "It just really feels great!"

What makes meaningful, fulfilling work problematic is that people find it so engaging they have trouble setting boundaries around it. They want to save time and energy for other things, but they become absorbed in their work and eventually their lives just slip away. Philadelphia lawyer Stanton Haynes, 43, expressed the sentiment of many when he remarked, "I feel I should take more time off to do things I would enjoy more than my work, but unfortunately I always seem to take things too seriously to do that."

At one time the tension between work and time for other activities might have been more easily resolved. Work was perhaps the curse of Adam and therefore unlikely to be intrinsically fulfilling, but at least it was necessary for survival. Now work is less a physical necessity, but it is supposed to contribute to our sense of dignity and personal worth. When it does not, the Willy Loman complaint about meaninglessness sets in. But when it does provide meaning, it is still only one of the components of ordinary life that is supposed to do so. Family life, leisure activities that expand our sense of being, and free time just to reflect on ourselves also have intrinsic merit. Furthermore, the burden is on the individual to allocate time and energy among these various realms of ordinary life in a way that is most fulfilling.

BUCKLING UNDER AND BURNING OUT

Even the most interesting work can also be the bearer of mind-numbing stress. "From the corner office to the factory floor," declares *Business Week*, stress is "epidemic in U.S. business."[45] According to the National Center for Health Statistics, a majority of the U.S. labor force complains of experiencing stress on a regular basis, and nearly as many believe this stress has had a negative impact on their health. The highest rates of stress, moreover, are experienced in upper-income categories and by men and women at the peak of their careers.[46] With growing evidence of demoralization among physicians, career dissatisfaction among teachers, and mental health woes among lawyers, studies conducted in specific professional occupations point to the same conclusion.[47] In the labor force as a whole, a majority of people complain that they have too little time to spend relaxing, three-quarters

wish they were better able to limit the job-related stress they experience, and one person in five says his or her health has been seriously
affected by the demands and pressures of work.[48] My survey showed
that 46 percent of the workforce sometimes feels burned out in their job,
44 percent feel they seldom get enough time for themselves, and 39
percent believe they are under a lot of pressure in their jobs. Among
full-time workers, 59 percent said they were bothered by stress in their
job situation at least once a week, and one person in six was bothered by
stress almost every day. The survey also showed that stress is consistently related to the number of hours a person works each week, rising
to one person in four who experiences stress on a daily basis among
those who work fifty hours or more each week. Moreover, those who
say they are bothered this often by job-related stress are significantly
less likely than other workers to say they are satisfied with their jobs
and less likely to say they are happy with their lives in general.[49]

Other evidence also suggests that stress is playing an increasingly
costly and devastating role in the U.S. labor force. For example, the National Institute on Drug Abuse estimates that 25 percent of the American labor force is affected by chronic alcoholism, drug addiction, or substance abuse—either their own (10 percent) or that of a member of their
immediate family (15 percent) who, in many cases, may be acting out
problems endemic to the whole family.[50] Much of the problem, say experts, is that people turn to these various addictions as a way of coping
with the mental and emotional turmoil they experience in their daily
lives.

In addition to the long hours that many people work and the accom-
panying lack of exercise and loss of sleep, the conditions that put many
Americans into the pressure cooker include heightened responsibility
and competition in professional and managerial jobs, fear of job loss,
lack of control over one's work, nonsupportive supervisors or co-workers, ethical conflicts, and uncertainties about job performance and promotions. Add to these the periodic stress of losing an important contract, experiencing a string of bad fortune, or having to struggle harder
to keep the business from going under, and many people simply buckle
under the pressure.

Whatever the specific reasons, a growing number of workers are becoming dissatisfied enough with job-related stress to sue their employers for damages. What began as a trickle of stress suits in the late 1970s
grew to 5 percent of all workers' compensation cases in 1980 and then

reached 15 percent of all cases in 1990. Among the plaintiffs, women and younger workers in white-collar jobs are particularly prominent. But suits are also aggravated by plant closings, relocations, mergers and acquisitions, and the rapid growth of highly stressful service industries.[51]

Another indication of the pressures that characterize the American workforce is the fact that approximately ten million people—one person in ten—change occupations every year. Given an average work life of nearly forty years, this means that the typical individual changes occupations between three and four times during his or her career. These changes, moreover, are not limited to the young or to persons undergoing a proverbial "midlife" crisis but are scattered evenly across all age categories. Nor are they limited to persons in less desirable jobs where higher turnover rates might be expected. They are actually highest among white-collar workers with college educations.[52] As this segment of the labor force grows, it is also expected that occupational switching will increase. In one national survey, 29 percent of the men and 36 percent of the women polled said they planned to change their overall career or type of work in the next five years.[53] In my survey, a striking 76 percent of the respondents said they had been in more than one *line of work*, not counting jobs held while they were growing up. One person in two had been in at least three different lines of work. And one person in ten had been in five or more different lines of work.[54]

Average turnover rates also mask considerable variation across different occupations. In lower echelons of the white-collar labor force, particularly in sales and clerical work, turnover rates account for as many as one worker in four each year. But other white-collar jobs involve extensive occupational switching as well. Banking and finance, for example, have experienced higher than average rates of turnover in recent years. And among workers in the helping professions, such as nurses and occupational therapists, levels of switching have been exceptionally high.[55]

Available evidence does not support the view that occupational mobility occurs mainly because of burnout or serious career dissatisfaction. Most is voluntary and seems to be motivated by a desire to find more interesting work or improved working conditions.[56] Even when burnout is part of the problem, people often say in retrospect that the change provided a healthy transition in their lives. "It was good for me to burn out, because then I could relight my fire," Mary Phelps observed about leaving a job she had held for five years. But the process itself is terribly costly. For employers, it means hiring and training a replacement. For the person herself, it often means enormous emotional turmoil, insecurity, and self-doubt. Mary Phelps became extremely nervous and found it one of the hardest things she had done when she decided to quit. She hadn't realized before how dependent she was on the security of her job.

There is, however, clear evidence that frequent occupational switching is associated with some level of dissatisfaction with work. In my survey, 29 percent of those who had been in five or more lines of work said the statement "I'm working myself to death" described themselves very well or fairly well, compared with only 15 percent of those who had stayed in the same line of work. In contrast, only 11 percent of the former expressed high levels of satisfaction with their current job, compared with 26 percent of the latter.[57] Career change itself is allegedly one of the leading sources of emotional difficulty in the American population, ranking nearly as high as such trauma-producing events as divorce or the death of a loved one.[58] In comparison with these events, it generally does not result in far-reaching soul searching or questioning of one's values and priorities. And yet for a minority it does become a deeply unsettling experience. In one national survey a quarter of those who had voluntarily changed jobs, for example, said the experience had affected their thoughts about the meaning and purpose of life a great deal.[59]

"I was just dying inside," admits Amy Oldenburg, 39, a hospital chaplain in Los Angeles. She was a successful registered nurse, engaged in meaningful work caring for other people, but there seemed to be no sense of herself in this career. "I just put myself on a shelf. I was out there trying to be this little goody-two-shoes. And it was disgusting. It made me sick." From the time she was little, Amy had been taught to be responsible, so she became a nurse to please her parents and to make sure she could earn her own living. Deciding to quit nursing and enter training to become a chaplain was the hardest thing she had ever done. In addition to the usual stress of having to learn a new job, she had to evaluate who she was and fundamentally reassess what she wanted in life. "I was completely exhausted and grossly depressed," she recalls. "It was like I was fleeing for my life. Making the change was the biggest risk I'd ever taken."

In their book *The Good Society*, sociologist Robert N. Bellah and his coauthors have described the pain and uncertainty expressed by people like Amy Oldenburg in more general terms. Having drunk deeply for so many generations at the well dug for us by John Locke, Adam Smith, Benjamin Franklin, and other inventors of the American Dream, they argue, we are now beginning to realize the unanticipated costs of pursuing that dream. "In our great desire to free the individual for happiness," they write, "we Americans have tried to make a social world that would serve the self. But things have not gone quite according to plan. We have made instead a world that dwarfs the self it was meant to serve. Especially in the economic realm Americans find themselves under the pressure of market forces to which the only response seems submission."[60]

There is, then, considerable evidence that work and the pursuit of material possessions is taking its toll on the American population. More time spent at the grindstone, even when work itself is meaningful and enjoyable, leaves us exhausted, feeling pressured, and wanting more from life than material success alone. Growing numbers of people are registering concern that the good life is filled more with labor than with the nourishing fruits of this labor. Most Americans still work hard and feel it is meaningful and important to do so, but a majority (77 percent in one study) also worry that they have become workaholics—addicted to something that may be preventing them from realizing the full measure of life.[61] Despite their interest in material possessions, a large majority (72 percent) readily admit that they "want more from life than just a good job and a comfortable lifestyle." Most (78 percent) say they do think a lot about their values and priorities in life, but a sizable minority (35 percent) also claim they "need more time to think about the really basic issues in life."[62] Economic progress, it appears, has produced material abundance but not enough time to think about how to translate this abundance into qualitative improvements of life itself. How to rein in our economic commitments—or at least steer them in more desirable directions—is the question we seem increasingly to be asking.

Chapter Two

MAKING CHOICES: FROM SHORT-TERM
ADJUSTMENTS TO PRINCIPLED LIVES

W
ITH INCREASING levels of burnout, career dissatisfaction, substance abuse, alcoholism, and costly job-stress suits, a growing number of American corporations have started paying attention to the possibility that people are simply working too hard, taking on responsibilities that do not nurture themselves as human beings, and putting themselves under too much pressure. General Motors has more than 100 staff psychologists dealing with problems of drugs, alcohol, burnout, and depression on the assembly line. Motorola, Xerox, Levi Strauss, and a few other large firms have initiated task forces in recent years to study the relationship between work and family problems among their employees.[1] But thus far the response from business has been mainly to invoke stricter policing in hopes of curtailing substance abuse and to encourage workers to live healthier lives through fitness programs and health evaluation clinics. Stimulating productivity while protecting their firms from undue costs has been management's top priority.

Quick-Fix Solutions

Typifying this priority is the kind of advice found routinely in managerial columns for employers faced with stress and burnout among their employees. One such column advises readers to screen employees better for preexisting "mental maladies" and to solicit information from other workers that might be useful in warding off lawsuits. Presuming that it is the worker's own responsibility to limit stress, the column makes no mention of firms themselves trying to reduce job pressures.[2] Other columns suggest that managers deal with work-related stress by making corporate myths more visible to middle-level employees.

More generally, analyses of the work and money pressures facing the American population usually take a sadly limited view, attributing them to bothersome but endemic features of corporate life, the managerial personality, and the business cycle. Most of the trouble, say the analysts, springs from crisis situations such as being laid off, landing under the thumb of a dictatorial boss, or simply having a sudden string of bad luck.[3] Others emphasize economic and demographic factors, both of which have simply made it more difficult for the present generation to realize the American Dream.

What to do? Find ways to cope. Here, for example, is the advice given by a leading news magazine:

Maintain a sense of humor.
Meditate.
Get a massage.
Exercise regularly.
Eat more sensibly.
Limit intake of alcohol and caffeine.
Take refuge in family and friends.
Delegate responsibility.
Stand up to the boss.
Quit.[4]

These tips are not dissimilar from ones found in countless advice columns, employee newsletters, and self-help books. They encourage people to take more minivacations, play softball, go fishing, collect stamps, see the doctor regularly, and take themselves less seriously. Meditation and physical exercise are increasingly among the most frequently cited recommendations. Other hints include visualizing a pastoral scene while sitting at one's desk, making lists of fun things to do after work, and cultivating friends who stroke one's ego. A few corporations have even begun trying to help their employees relieve stress in these ways. Ben & Jerry's Ice Cream Company, for example, has initiated a Joy Committee to help employees lighten up. The Fun Committee at Odetics, a robotics firm in California, has been sponsoring Hula-Hoop contests and bubble-gum-blowing competitions for the same reason.[5]

Such activities and advice may be helpful for getting through a particularly stressful day, but they will not do anything to solve the underlying problem. "Stress cannot be dealt with by psychological tricks," Sam Keen has written, "because for the most part it is a philosophical rather than a physiological problem, a matter of the wrong worldview."[6] Coming from a writer who himself has long been associated with the pop-psychology industry, this is a sobering warning indeed.

The reason quick-fix solutions can be of little enduring value is that stress and overwork are built into the American way of life. They are not just the nettlesome by-products of having an ill-tempered boss or seeing a prospective contract turn sour. They are rooted in endemic characteristics of the modern workplace and the international markets in which most corporations now compete. Certainly these economic realities play a significant role in the work and money pressures so many middle-class Americans are experiencing. But there is an even deeper source of many of these pressures. They are part of the values we have inherited and the way we think. They reflect both long-standing and changing conceptions of ourselves as individuals, of our responsibilities and what we most cherish in our lives.

Research evidence points clearly to the inadequacy of quick-fix solutions. If these ideas were really that useful, we would expect to find people faced with stress on a frequent basis using them more. If they actually worked, we might also observe that people who used them were less likely to register feelings of stress than people who didn't. But neither of these is the case. When faced with stress, large numbers of the American workforce resort to such tactics: 71 percent talk to close friends, 60 percent engage in physical exercise, 56 percent work on a hobby, 40 percent go shopping, and 30 percent take a few days off. But those faced with frequent stress are neither more nor less likely to engage in these activities than other people. Nor are those who engage in these activities any more satisfied with their work or any less likely to be worried than other people.[7]

The evidence also points clearly to one of the reasons why quick-fix solutions do not work. Job-related stress stems from factors other than just those associated with unpleasant situations at work, and it raises questions about a much broader and deeper range of issues. Of people in my survey who said they experienced job-related stress almost every day, for example, only a quarter complained of conflict with co-workers (26 percent), an unsupportive boss (25 percent), or an unpleasant work environment (22 percent). In comparison, nearly half complained of not having enough time for their family (49 percent), feeling burned out (49 percent), needing more time for themselves (48 percent), and wanting other things in life (42 percent).

To be sure, unpleasant situations at work can contribute significantly to job-related stress. For instance, among those who said they experience stress on a daily basis, 26 percent said they had had an argument with the boss in the past year, 21 percent felt they had experienced discrimination, 16 percent had been reprimanded, and 8 percent claimed to have been sexually harassed—all higher percentages than among those who registered little or no stress. And yet the percentages for whom stress had raised broader issues were much higher. Among the frequent-stress group, 53 percent had been wondering if they were in the right line of work, and 55 percent had been feeling seriously burned out within the past year.

The one thing that stress relates to more powerfully than anything else, in fact, is thinking about basic values in life and trying to juggle commitments to a wide range of values. In the labor force as a whole, for example, 29 percent said they think a lot about their values and priorities in life; but this proportion rose to 40 percent among persons experiencing stress almost every day in their jobs and was 56 percent among those who felt they were working themselves to death. Moreover, the more frequently respondents experienced stress, the more likely they were to say they attached value to other commitments such as family, morality, taking care of themselves, and relating to God.

Fun committees and advice columnists seldom pay any attention to these underlying values. They simply assume that people are going to work too hard, try to buy too many things, and eventually burn out. So the only thing to be done is provide a little humor along the way. They are part of the current mentality that tells us we must also work hard at keeping fit and keeping our stress down, our self-esteem up, and our outlook bright. It is little wonder that we find everything from getting a massage to quitting our jobs on the same list. The advice columnists can think up easy solutions to our problems, but they help little in thinking through the hard issues of what we really want in life.

Brad Diggins illustrates well how tough these issues can be. Owner of a travel agency in southern California, he finds he has to work twelve hours a day, six days a week, to keep the business afloat. For years he's been searching for a way to stop putting his work first. But every time he thinks he's figured out how to change things, he laments, "it doesn't change; it just gets to be more." Nearing his mid-forties, he knows he has to change things before it's too late. "Somehow I've got to create a life," he ponders. But much of the time he isn't even sure anymore what kind of life he wants.

THE DISEASE MODEL

If quick-fix solutions are too shallow, the disease model that has been advanced in recent years to understand problems with work, money, and other economic commitments goes to an extreme in the other direction. Rather than linking stress and burnout to specific situations at work, it associates them with an underlying malady in the worker's personality. The problem, say proponents of this view, is "workaholism"—a malady taken to be exactly parallel with alcoholism. Suffering from some fundamental insecurity, the workaholic tries to discover true happiness by working too hard. Compulsiveness is often present, causing the individual to "binge" on day-and-night working sprees and then to feel utterly dissatisfied and unmotivated. Money problems may stem from the same problem: an insatiable longing for happiness that is wrongly pursued by trying to accumulate riches or by spending money wildly on unneeded purchases.

The disease model is valid up to a point. It does recognize the importance of questions about personal identity, commitments, values, and the need to settle on priorities. The compulsive behavior it describes does characterize a segment of the population. But, like so many other contemporary applications of the literature on addictions, it carries the argument too far. Workaholism may be similar to alcoholism in some respects, but its chemical basis is fundamentally different. Just how widely applicable it may be is also debatable. That it may have limited applications is suggested by the fact that only one person in six actually feels like he or she is working to death, and only one in seven claims to experience stress on a daily basis. Moreover, of this frequent-stress group, only 4 percent say they are seeing a therapist to help them with stress, and only 6 percent try to find help in a support group.

Proponents of the disease model, of course, argue that the fact people are not seeking help is all the more reason to be concerned. But the model ultimately suffers thereby from being impossible to confirm or disconfirm empirically. Many of its assertions focus so broadly on such "problems" as rushing, busyness, making lists, and caring about one's work that virtually everyone falls into the category of the diseased. Other assertions make valuable connections and yet lead away from a valid understanding of these connections. For example, one widely publicized book on the subject asserts that "work addicts are dishonest, controlling, self-centered, perfectionistic, and abusive to themselves and others." It is little wonder, the author expostulates, that "their morality" is askew. "You cannot lead such a life without losing your moorings. Your grounding in basic values is lost in the relentless pursuit of the addiction."[8] Clearly the important point is that basic values must somehow be brought back into focus. It helps little to describe the underlying problem as an addiction, however.

The broader problem is not that people who work hard have abandoned other values. Indeed, it is clearly the opposite. People like Brad Diggins want it all. They are commited to their work and to the good life that money can buy; they also want more out of life. Indeed, when work and money are compared with other values in our society, they come out on top fairly infrequently. In my survey, for example, 29 percent of the labor force said their work was absolutely essential to their sense of personal worth, and only 15 percent said this about "making a lot of money." In comparison, 69 percent said their family was absolutely essential to their personal worth; 56 percent said this about their moral standards, 43 percent did so about taking care of themselves, and 39 percent did about their relationship to God. The study also shows that the minority who did say work and money were absolutely essential were actually *more* likely to value these other commitments, rather than less likely to value them.[9]

If something is wrong, it is that we want too much out of life, not too little. And yet to say that people want to spend time with their families, that they value their moral standards and their relationship to God, or that they want to serve the needy is surely not something to decry. The American Dream has always championed these other pursuits as part of what the good society should encourage its members to be doing. What has contributed to the difficulty of engaging in these pursuits in recent years is that social conditions and cultural understandings alike have been shifting rapidly. As a result, more and more people are having to think through their values in ways that were neither possible nor necessary in the past.

We shall want to consider the basis for claims such as this more carefully in subsequent chapters. For now, however, it is worth observing that most of the pressures and uncertainties surrounding economic commitments that we considered in the last chapter are in fact associated with the extent to which fundamental questions about values and priorities are being raised in our society. Feeling that one is working harder than before and wishing that one could work fewer hours, for example, are associated with a greater likelihood of thinking a lot about values and priorities in life. So are feeling burned out and feeling that one is not getting enough time for oneself. And so are feeling that one has a lot of financial obligations, worrying about how to fulfill these obligations, feeling that one is under a lot of pressure, and wanting more time for one's family. All these worries and concerns are associated with raising questions about one's values in general.

Fundamentally, then, the issue people like Brad Diggins are confronting is the need to make choices, of deciding when to say no, or even saying yes, but doing so in a way that keeps the material life in proper perspective. We are bombarded by the appeals of the leisure industry to spend more time relaxing and by the business world itself to do what we must to take care of our health. And yet the question remains whether there are principles other than self-interest, pleasure, and bodily preservation that should be factored into our thinking. The question is not simply how to rest up so we can be more productive at work the next day. The question is how to weigh the other priorities that have always characterized the human spirit against those to which the dollar sign can be affixed. Should we be willing to sacrifice an hour pursuing another business deal in order to visit a friend in the hospital? Or can we be content, as one writer discovered when he posed this question to a class of prospective MBAs at Harvard Business School, to regard such moral commitments as patently absurd?

Reforming the System

Historically, the most common way of placing limits around the economic system has been to invoke governmental restrictions. From early attempts to limit the workday, pass old-age- and disability-insurance measures, and promote greater safety in the workplace, to more recent efforts to outlaw discrimination and implement redistributive taxation schemes, legislation has been regarded as the principal means of combating the ill effects of the marketplace. One of the major axes around which modern political debate has revolved has thus been its position on how much or how little the state should intervene in economic matters.[10]

The reason why recourse to political means has so often been taken is that the state's powers seem the only measure strong enough to make a difference. Against the entrenchment of profit-motivated interests and the social influences of those in control of economic resources, only coercion can call a halt. Pragmatic arguments, indicating that political means have in fact accomplished much in terms of ameliorating the worst excesses of the marketplace, have often been advanced as well. Compared with schemes for overturning capitalism itself, these reformist measures have proven decidedly more attractive. Yet political solutions can go only so far in guiding and restraining economic life.

Government restrictions work best within a legitimating framework of fundamental human rights, including norms of justice and equal treatment before the law. They can help prevent the worst excesses of economic production and distribution, such as the exploitation of disadvantaged minorities, conditions injurious to health, or ones that pollute the environment. Government initiatives have sometimes been able to mitigate undesirable social conditions by encouraging long-range economic growth itself. Public expenditures on transportation systems, education, and basic research are often cited as examples. Where government restrictions cannot legitimately attempt to regulate economic life is in those realms deemed to lie within the domain of individual discretion.

Discretion to make fundamental decisions affecting the course and quality of individual life has come to be regarded as a culturally legitimate and constitutionally guaranteed manifestation of personal freedom. Government can pass legislation prohibiting an employer from dumping toxic waste on public land or from discriminating against racial minorities, but it cannot pass laws telling that employer to be at work by a certain hour in the morning, to spend Thursday evenings at home with the family, or to give $5,000 to charity rather than purchase a new wide-screen television set. All government can do in those areas is to provide gentle nudges in one direction or another. For example, it can encourage charitable contributions by making them tax deductible or it can discourage spending on luxury items by adding a surtax.

Anything further violates the individual freedoms so widely cherished in democratic societies. As efforts to legislate a thirty-hour work week, add new holidays to the national calendar, and mandate social service among the young all have demonstrated, it is extremely difficult for social reformers to legislate new conceptions of the American Dream, not only because of the costs of these programs, but because they can also be opposed on grounds of curbing fundamental human liberties.

The extent to which such opposition is present in the American population is clearly evident in opinion polls. Some questions, for example, suggest that the majority of Americans view government restrictions as an unwelcome intrusion in their lives, in much the same way that they dislike having to work in large bureaucracies or jostling through traffic jams on the way to their jobs. In one survey, two-thirds of the public expressed this dislike by saying government regulations were a serious or extremely serious problem in American society, while only 6 percent said they were not a problem.[11] Other questions indicate that part of the resistance to government intervention in the economy is that Americans simply do not feel such programs are effective. For example, in the same survey when people were asked whether spending more money on government welfare programs would help make America better, only 21 percent said it would help a lot, compared with 36 percent who thought it would help only a little, and 42 percent who said it would not help at all.

In contrast to these patterns, people are much more likely to think that economic solutions are the best way to deal with social problems. When asked how much it would help improve the society to keep our economy going at a steady rate, 71 percent said this would help a lot, compared with only 25 percent who said it would help a little, and 3 percent who said it would not help. Even when the issue is not so much income distribution or general well-being, but matters of social goals and priorities, the American public registers deep skepticism about government playing too large a role. One indication of this attitude is that 71 percent of the public thinks politicians have too much influence in shaping the nation's goals and values, whereas only 47 percent think this about business leaders.[12]

Social critics are correct in suggesting that much of the public's resistance to government intervention in the economy stems from raw self-interest instead of well-schooled conceptions of civic liberty. The critics also need to be taken seriously when they point out that civic responsibility requires people to press for government solutions to such problems as discrimination in the workplace, corporate greed, exploitation of the poor and the disadvantaged, fraud, and environmental destruction. But the same critics who voice these concerns have also come increasingly to recognize that government restrictions are unlikely to be instituted in the first place—or be effective—unless people are willing to subject themselves to some kind of moral restraint. In short, a society that places high responsibility on the individual must look not only to government to rein in its economic commitments, but to a better understanding of the ethics and values on which institutional and individual commitments are based.

THE GROWING ROLE OF DISCRETION

In advanced industrial societies individual discretion has become increasingly significant. Not only has it been championed in various ways by conservative and liberal political theoreticians; it is also built increasingly into the fabric of economic life itself. With late-modern levels of economic development, fewer people have to work from sunrise to sunset to eke out a subsistence living, nor do people spend as large a percentage of their earnings on food, shelter, clothing, and other necessities, thus leaving a larger share of their time and money available for discretionary uses. In the workplace itself greater emphasis is likely to be placed on autonomous decision making, with fewer tasks being mandated specifically by someone in authority. The choice of careers themselves and decisions about particular places of employment have increasingly become matters of personal discretion. Indeed, the very meaning of discretion, once connoting caution and prudence, has been subtly redefined to mean the exercise of choice.

Discretion is part of the normative order of most institutions as well. The individual is expected to make ethical decisions and to choose how he or she will achieve desired work goals. Greater discretion is expected of individuals in their private lives, from choosing sexual and marriage partners to deciding how to school their children. With nonworking hours being defined as free time involving a wide variety of options, people are expected to exercise discretion in allocating time to various leisure activities or to community service. They are expected to

exercise discretion in deciding how to allocate surplus financial resources among various consumer products and benevolent causes. All
these decisions have enormous implications for the economy itself and
for the quality of people's lives, but they are decisions over which most
people feel government has very little rightful control.

For Davis Reskin, 35, a middle manager in New York's garment district, it is precisely this ability to exercise discretion that makes him
glad he's alive. Like so many other people of his generation, he believes
the future holds whatever he decides to choose for himself. He has a
wife and one child but does not feel "encumbered" by his family the
way his parents did. Living in Manhattan, he picks and chooses his
friends, trying hard to be kind to them, but not getting himself bogged
down in community organizations like his mother did. He revels in
having enough cash to amuse himself in his spare time. At work, he
compares himself with the women he sees bent over their sewing ma-
chines ten hours a day stitching garments. He thanks his lucky stars
that he has the freedom to set his own pace. He likes the creativity and
artistry that his work requires. At the same time, he finds himself restless and ready to move on whenever the opportunity arises. "I'm very
open," he asserts. "I never close doors. Never say no. I'm interviewing
tomorrow as a matter of fact. Headhunters call me all the time and I
always go. I never say no. Only a fool would say that. I could do lots of
different things." He certainly does not want government telling him
what to do. In his view, that smacks of socialism, a system he believes
is rapidly becoming a thing of the past.

In the absence of guiding legal or coercive norms, discretionary behavior for millions of people like Davis Reskin has increasingly become
the domain in which economic influences are permitted to reign with
virtually unlimited authority. Individuals define themselves as economic decision makers, allocating time and financial resources to various services, leisure activities, and consumer goods. Economic institutions can rightfully try to influence these individual decisions through
marketing and advertising, or in the workplace, by offering financial
incentives. The individual is assumed to be free to make economic
choices, so no constitutional issues are at stake, and is regarded as
being motivated to participate in the marketplace as a consumer. Economic institutions are even said to have special claim to the individual
because they are, it is sometimes claimed, the source of this discretionary time and income in the first place.[13]

How Much Freedom Do We Have?

To those who have considered how much economic institutions shape our lives, the claim that people are increasingly free to do whatever they want is of course recognizably overstated. They know that even the relatively affluent professionals and managers who are said to enjoy the greatest freedoms often find themselves with little room to maneuver at all. Their corporations have a rigid set of expectations to which they must conform in order to survive and succeed. These may include everything from dress codes to formal objectives to unstated rules about how to greet the boss in the morning. Professionals who work in other settings may also be subjected to bureaucratic norms requiring them to perform efficiently, to meet fixed work schedules, and to participate in unrewarding gatherings of their peers.

Sociologist Robert Jackall, in an intensive study of the work lives of corporate managers, has provided a compelling account of how the bureaucracies in which most people now work shape their goals, their expectations, and their perceptions of themselves.[14] He argues that bureaucracy has fundamentally altered the rules by which people pursue the American Dream. From the outside, bureaucracies may appear as highly rational, hierarchically coordinated systems for getting the complex tasks of the modern economy done. From the inside, they appear more to be what Jackall appropriately terms "moral mazes." They encourage unwavering loyalty to bosses and patrons and divide people into floating alliances among coteries and cliques. Within these unstable networks, workers learn relativistic and often contradictory standards of trustworthiness. They turn to each other for behavioral cues, but what they experience is often too ambiguous to codify. Ethics and values take a back seat to yea-saying, pragmatism, and glib talk.

The result is that work gets done, but sooner or later most people begin to experience conflict between their work and the standards of value they perceive in other spheres of their lives. Jackall points especially to the tension that may arise between struggles for dominance in the bureaucracy and wider norms of friendship, honesty, and compassion. He also perceives tension between the standards of excellence that many individuals aspire to and the inevitable mediocrity that he feels plagues most organizations. Like other critics, he believes bureaucracy is fundamentally at odds with finding overall meaning at work because what is good for the organization may not be good for the individuals who work in it or for the wider society.

This line of analysis suggests that very little can be done to rectify the current situation. People may think they can exercise discretion, but this perception is fundamentally an allusion. Economic institutions not only operate according to their own laws, governing our workday and our pocketbook; they also determine the way we think. Furthermore, bureaucracies are unlikely to disappear anytime soon. In the meantime, we can delude ourselves by talking about the freedom we have, but we must realize that this apparent sense of control over our lives really operates to perpetuate the institutions that dominate modern society.

The trouble with this kind of analysis is that it attributes too much casual influence to the blind forces of which bureaucracy presumably consists. It buys too strongly into the kind of social structural determinism that sociologists have so often assumed they must defend in order to advance their own profession. Yet a more nuanced reading of studies like Jackall's reveals that "bureaucracy" is often little more than a metaphor for the patterns of language and behavior that are observed in the workplace. These patterns are not determined by something else; they are the stuff of which organizations are constituted. It is the conventional languages and norms that must be understood, not some deep force that exercises irresistible control over our lives.

Viewed this way, the same ambiguities that lead some observers to be cynical about the modern workplace provide small beacons of hope. If bureaucracy presents people with uncertainty rather than rigid structures, then there is indeed room for discretion after all. If most people make up their moral norms to satisfy each other, then these norms are by no means fixed from on high. Moreover, the assumption that economic institutions tie people down to the point that they despair of finding any meaning in their work flies in the face of evidence we have already considered. Perhaps people are simply deluded by the organizations for which they work. They may, however, find their work sufficiently meaningful that they would like to integrate it more effectively with the other parts of their lives. Only if they assume their choices are entirely free or entirely determined by the economic realm itself will they find it impossible to pursue this integration.

THE NEED FOR MORAL DISCOURSE

The individual is thus left to make an increasing number of decisions about how to use his or her resources largely without any government restrictions interfering with these decisions, and yet within a normative context in which he or she is defined as an economic actor subject only to the guiding hand of economic institutions and an ethos of economic interest maximization. But how is the individual to make these decisions? On the basis of what value orientations, conceptions of the good, ethical considerations, or moral commitments does the individual decide to participate or withdraw from participating in the marketplace? Economic considerations may specify a range of options and attach various costs and benefits to these options, but they neither exhaust the range of conceivable options nor provide standards of individual or social good to be weighed in selecting among various options.

For this reason, all societies have in fact encouraged conceptions of the good that in one way or another limit their members' participation in the economic realm and provide autonomous moral standards for the governance of behavior within this realm. In traditional societies a minority of the population generally opted out of the so-called productive vocations to pursue careers in monastic and religious orders. In many cases people of sufficient means abandoned the pursuit of ever greater wealth in order to engage in public service, cultivate the intellectual life of the salons and universities, or participate in the leisure activities of the court. In still other instances people restricted their economic ambitions in order to raise families or to care for aging relatives. Although these activities were sometimes mandated by the state, they were more often done voluntarily. Economic interest maximization was seldom a primary consideration. A commitment to values that were deemed more basic than economic pursuits erected moral limits around the economic life.

In modern societies, for reasons that include the declining salience of an all-embracing conception of cosmic order and the extension of rational decision-making processes to most matters of personal life, the concept of moral limits has largely been restricted to behaviors that have little to do with the economic realm. Morality has come to focus on such issues as sexual fidelity, honesty, and propriety in personal relations, rather than referring to a deeper sense of what is fundamentally good. Indeed, we might venture to say that economic thinking has itself penetrated the moral domain to the extent that technical solutions to the perplexing questions of personal life often seem preferable to old-fashioned conceptions of duty and obligation. British sociologist Bryan Wilson observes: "As for purely personal morality, that quaint concept, so vital to communities in the past, modern man might ask whether it has not become redundant. In modern language, to be moral is to be 'uptight'; to express moral attitudes is to inhibit people when they want—as modern men say that they have a right to want—'to do their own thing.'"[15]

But if morality connotes unwelcome strictures on personal behavior in general, it is likely to be all the more so conceived when these activities are defined simply as consumer preferences. When someone decides to purchase a new automobile instead of spending the money on an expensive vacation, it thus seems correct to speak of the decision as one of maximizing alternative utilities, but it would seem odd to say that certain moral understandings have been expressed. That we do make decisions about economic commitments that have broader moral overtones may still be beyond dispute, but exactly how we do this is less clear. It is thus to the realm of moral discourse that we must look if we are to gain a better understanding of how the deeper commitments of the human spirit relate to the economic realm.

THE NATURE OF MORAL DISCOURSE

Because it has so often been conceived narrowly, we need to consider just what moral discourse is and how in the best of all worlds it might be constructed in order to guide and curtail our economic pursuits in effective, satisfying, and meaningful ways. Moral discourse has been the subject of growing attention in recent years, especially among ethicists, but we must select judiciously from this literature.[16]

Ethical absolutes or moral truths of the kind "courage is a virtue" or "slavery is evil" will be of little concern. Ethicists worry a lot about such statements—and they think ordinary people should too—because they want to know how such claims can be defended and, if they cannot, fear there may be no basis for opposing fanatics and fools.

As one of these "ordinary people," I believe we often do not care much what ethicists have to say on these questions. The problem is not, as ethicists themselves will assert, that more compelling philosophical grounds need to be discovered for making these kinds of ethical claims. Most of us ordinary people, probably to ethicists' dismay, are quite willing to accept on faith that courage is good or slavery is evil and leave the fanatics and fools for others to dispute. The problem we sense with ethicists is that none of this has very much to do with the real questions we face in our ordinary lives.

Somewhere between the absolute good and the absolute evil with which ethics is concerned lie the questions we face routinely about what should be done, what is desirable or undesirable, and which of several options may be best for us to pursue. When a physician decides to take an afternoon to play golf, the issue is not one of absolute good or evil. Even though, by some larger calculation, there may be slightly more suffering—or even death—in the world than there might have been otherwise, we would not ordinarily consider this a question of virtue or vice. Nevertheless, there is a moral dimension to such a decision, and it is this broader moral dimension that should interest us here. How does a person decide when it is preferable to spend an afternoon playing golf instead of treating the sick?

Moral discourse in this sense is about preferences, but not strictly so, at least not in a way that suggests applying the various models of decision-making behavior that abound in the philosophical literature. In the present case, I am not really concerned with figuring out why one physician decides to quit working at 1 p.m. and another decides to continue working till 5:30. The moral dimension of importance is concerned with broader questions about the modes of reasoning and talking that define things as legitimate.

In his book *Theory of the Moral Life*, John Dewey framed a conception of moral reasoning that will be useful for us to incorporate into the present discussion.[17] First published in 1908, Dewey's arguments sometimes seem overly optimistic, placing too much faith in education, reason, and scientific progress to be credible in the more complex world of today. Yet there is still much to be learned from this book. Dewey's clear-headed, moderate style resonates far more deeply with the American experience than do many of the arguments that have been borrowed in recent decades from other traditions.

At the heart of Dewey's conception of morality is the distinction (to which we have already referred) between right and wrong, on the one hand, and value preferences, on the other hand. Citing the case of a man torn between his religiously inspired commitment to pacifism and his sense of civic responsibility, Dewey writes: "Now he has to make a choice between competing moral loyalties and convictions. The struggle is not between a good which is clear to him and something else which attracts him but which he knows to be wrong. It is between values each of which is an undoubted good in its place but which now get in each other's way. He is forced to reflect in order to come to a decision."[18]

This is precisely the kind of moral dilemma most people find themselves confronted with as they consider the relationship between their economic commitments and other values. The problem generally is not choosing between something good, like working hard, and something evil, like laying around the house all day in a drunken stupor. It is usually choosing between two activities of "undoubted good" that get in each other's way, such as working hard and taking one's children to the dentist, or serving people through one's profession and being a more responsible member of one's community. These, we recognize with Dewey, are often more difficult choices than making decisions between good and evil.

Dewey also draws a useful distinction between customary morality and reflective morality. The former depends on force of habit, on doing things the way they have always been done. It is the morality of the tribe, the ancestral home, the parental rules that have never been questioned. Reflective morality, in contrast, emerges from conscious deliberation. It "springs from the heart, from personal desires and affections, or from personal insight and rational choice."[19] It often requires criticizing existing customs and institutions from a new point of view.

Customary morality is of considerable importance because it often provides a reliable guide in matters of right and wrong. In principle at least, long-established norms about telling the truth, not stealing from one's neighbors, and the like still pertain appropriately to most people in most situations. Customary morality also serves a positive function in everyday life simply by permitting us to *avoid* thinking about some things. Dewey suggests there is something "sick" about a person who goes through life questioning the morality of everything. But customary morality becomes a negative force when people let institutionalized norms make their basic decisions for them. The economic realm can of course be a strong source of customary morality.

Reflective morality requires conscious effort on the part of the individual. It involves questioning one's behavior, knowing what options are available, thinking through the consequences of various choices, and recognizing one's responsibility to choose wisely. It comes into play most visibly when people are faced with choices about their basic values and how to realize these values in their daily lifes. Indeed, Dewey goes so far as to say that an immoral decision is one that has been made unreflectively, while a moral act takes the form of a well-considered judgment. Saying "I meant well" (when things turn out badly) is not a good excuse, Dewey asserts, because the person probably did not really pause to reflect on what he or she was about to do.

Unlike customary morality, which can often be articulated in simple moral dictums, reflective morality cannot be codified in terms of absolute rules. It is instead a matter of theory, process, and character. Theory—or, perhaps better, "outlook"—is a frame of reference, a set of beliefs and values that inform the individual's thinking. It includes a conception of individual freedom and responsibility, an understanding of the importance of reflection itself, and an awareness of the need to balance self-interest with the needs of others. Process is the ongoing act of reflection itself. It is not so much a matter of making air-tight, logical choices, but of bringing one's outlook into conscious engagement with one's experience and behavior. It requires individual soul searching, but is also a social activity, benefiting from formal education, reading, and interacting with others. "Character" signals the fact that reflective morality is integrally rooted in the self. This means moral worth is ascribed less to single, discrete activities than to longer-term patterns of behavior. It also means that morality and the self are fundamentally intertwined in a mutually reinforcing, and hopefully upward, spiral of development. In short, moral reflection is conducive to personal growth.[20]

In American society (probably in most societies), economic modes of moral argumentation command enormous respect. They do so because they are rooted in powerful institutions that compete to derive profits from the appropriation and deployment of scarce resources. These institutions provide the only places in which most people can find gainful employment, and these same institutions search constantly for new markets, attempting to define people as consumers and lure them into consumerist activities. The "lifeworld" in which people live is, as German sociologist Jürgen Habermas has put it, increasingly subject to the "colonizing" forces of these institutions.[21]

But economic demands stem as much from the ways in which people think as from the power of multinational corporations or commercial advertising agencies. The citizens of democratic societies may be ideologically opposed to Marxism, but they are nevertheless Marxists in practice, taking it for granted that economic considerations are fundamental. They talk about economic laws and principles as the determining features of human behavior, view the entire future more favorably when the economy is good than when it is bad, and simply assume that certain economic realities exist. They base their thinking on how much certain investments will earn, or how much certain items will cost, and throughout history they have been driven to war to protect the raw materials and transportation routes on which their way of life depends.

Economic thinking thus becomes a powerful form of legitimation. Even the most "scientific" arguments presented by economists generally go beyond mere descriptive statements to draw normative conclusions about what is right and good. "It is an extremely rare economist," writes sociologist Alan Wolfe, "who stops at the point of simply asserting the ethical benefits of self-interest; most continue on to make a point about obligations to others as well: because the pursuit of my self-interest contributes to some collective good . . . my obligation to you is to do what is best for me."[22] We have, in short, adopted a "market mentality," as Karl Polanyi termed it some years ago, that reifies the economic institutions we have created, turning them into forces we no longer believe we can control or even resist, but at the same time making of this necessity a moral virtue.[23]

Because of the enormous legitimating power of these economic assumptions, a reasonable place to begin in identifying the characteristics of an ideal moral discourse is to say that it must be capable of challenging economic norms and providing alternative ways of thinking. Moral discourse with this capacity may invoke a variety of substantive arguments, but these arguments should be based on something other than economic calculations or assumptions about economic laws alone. To carry authority, they are also likely to need institutional moorings. Thus, it would be more likely to find these moral languages in institutions such as families, neighborhoods, voluntary associations, public interest groups, universities, and religious communities than to imagine them existing simply in the abstract.[24] These are the institutions in which values are learned and reinforced voluntarily, as part of personal discretion, unlike political institutions that impose collective norms on individuals through coercion and principles of legality.

In saying that moral discourse should be capable of challenging economic assumptions, it should also be stated that moral restraint need not be inimical to hard work, material success, self-interest, or other canons of the economic life. It should only be understood, contrary to what economists have often argued, that moral conduct is not necessarily the same as, or always compatible with, these economic norms. For example, a value such as freedom is not necessarily contingent on economic growth, and hard work and material success do not necessarily indicate a life of moral virtue.

As long as moral discourse can be distinguished from economic norms, it can guide and constrain economic behavior in at least two ways. Internal to the economic realm itself, it can influence the norms governing economic behavior, causing these norms to be guided by ethical considerations as well as self-interest. Externally, it can establish the outer limits of the economic realm, showing where its assumptions and demands no longer apply. It can lead a parent, for instance, to spend time with a child, not as an "investment," but for the sake of the human relationship itself.

It is also worth remembering that morals and ethics have always (but perhaps especially so in modern societies) focused particular attention on the individual. This is because matters of right and wrong, and of what is more or less desirable, are understood to be matters of choice. For these choices to be legitimate, the individual must be able to make sense of them, giving reasons (if only in private) why something is an appropriate thing to do. Moral discourse is composed not so much of abstract principles but of personalized narratives, told to ourselves as much as to anyone else, to explain who we are, why we are good and decent human beings, and how we should respond to the choices we experience. Moreover, these choices have significant consequences for our lives, determining not only how time and energy are spent but also what values will be realized. Indeed, they play a significant role, as Dewey reminds us, in shaping the kind of self we will become. They involve the deepest longings and aspirations of the individual and are fundamentally concerned with how to live the good life. "Human spirit" is thus an appropriate reference for much of what moral discourse is about.

But moral discourse is also concerned with more than the individual, for implicit in it are assumptions about civil society. Individuals can make moral decisions only if civil society guarantees certain basic rights, such as respect for the individual and freedom of choice. Moreover, it is largely through the informal networks of association of which civil society is composed that the individual learns to practice reflective morality and finds ways to integrate these reflections with everyday behavior. At the same time, moral discourse generally assumes that the good life for the individual depends on sociality, friendship, and a sense of community. Hence, notions of responsibility to others and identification with the whole society in which one lives are also integral features of moral discourse.

For moral discourse to be effective, it must provide clear, unambiguous guidance about how to live individually and collectively. If it does not, people will be unable to make informed choices and in the face of uncertainty may well follow the dictates of unstated economic assumptions rather than consciously placing limits around these assumptions. But moral discourse should also provide room for a wide range of individual choices and lifestyles. Modern society is too diverse, too complex, too changeable for moral discourse to be codified as authoritative behavioral maxims. Communities of moral discourse function best when they provide opportunities for collective reflection and role models to emulate. Moral strictures may discourage greed and ambition as a general rule, yet provide arguments about individual talent or social service that legitimate exceptional endeavors for a few. Reasons for *not* following the rest of the herd, and stories of people who make a difference by leading alternative lives, may be one of the most beneficial functions moral discourse can provide.

In all this, it should also be evident that moral discourse, while terribly personal, must be a feature of the public life of any society. It must be codified in language, in the common stock of tradition and narrative, so that it can be communicated and provide a basis for shared understandings. Without this public dimension, moral discourse could not be transmitted intergenerationally or internalized to the point that it becomes taken for granted. This means that moral discourse, as discourse, matters in its own right and is distinguishable from ethical behavior. What people say about their lives—how they talk about greed and ambition—is at least as important as the implicit social norms that can be inferred from how they behave.

An ideal moral discourse, then, is one that can challenge, question, guide, and set limits around the economic sphere by giving voice to deeper considerations of what is good for the individual and the society. Rather than setting up an autonomous conception of morality that can be fulfilled entirely within the economic realm itself, it forces questions to be raised about the connections between this realm and broader conceptions of the human spirit. It provides a way of thinking and talking about what is legitimate that necessitates discussion of human values. In doing so, it makes room for diverse talents and interests but also defines broad categories in which thinking can take place and questions of good and bad—and, even more importantly, questions of better and best—can be deliberated.

Chapter Three

MORAL TRADITION: THE LOST AMBIVALENCE IN AMERICAN CULTURE

T HE IDEA THAT economic behavior can be regulated by moral restraint dates far back in history. It can be found in ancient religious texts and in the ethical writings of the Greeks and Romans. It was present in medieval religious injunctions against usury and was carried forward by the Protestant reformers' emphasis on stewardship and the Enlightenment philosophes' effort to derive principles of compassion and civic virtue from natural law. All these traditions came together to make the moralist literature in our own society particularly strong during the first half of the nineteenth century. Though eclipsed by the social and political theories of the later nineteenth century, questions of moral obligation were once an important part of our understandings of economic behavior. If we are to grasp the origins of our discontent with the material life, therefore, we must look beyond the current language of stress and overwork and seek to rediscover the moral ambivalence toward economic pursuits that lies deep within our own tradition.

Max Weber and the Question of Moral Limits

Nearly a century ago, Max Weber recognized the power of these value-based moral obligations when he asked how it was possible for people in the West to engage so enthusiastically in acquisitive capitalism. It was our ethical teachings, he argued, that encouraged a life of ascetic devotion to hard work, thrift, and the accumulation of wealth. But Western civilization was also distinctive, Weber argued, in not advancing absolute values that placed serious restrictions on the pursuit of wealth. In all other civilizations people had been taught to prefer honor to riches, happiness to wealth, salvation to material possessions. Only in western Europe, and then in America, did people strive continuously for economic gain as the ultimate end of their existence. Citing

Benjamin Franklin as the epitome of this incessant quest, Weber lamented, "Man is dominated by the making of money, by acquisition as the ultimate purpose of his life."[1]

If Weber's analysis is correct, we in the modern West are unique in having no values higher than that of material acquisition. Study after study has in fact followed Weber's lead in arguing that the values we do have largely encourage, rather than inhibit, economic pursuits. America is, after all, the land of the success ethic, the self-made man, the rags-to-riches hero. Benjamin Franklin was but one of numerous examples Weber could have chosen. Businessmen throughout our nation's history have extolled hard work as moral virtue, associated morality with wealth, and depicted themselves as contributors to the common good. And they have not been alone: politicians, writers, and religious leaders have all joined their cause. Their moral admonitions, these studies have concluded, only contributed to the American obsession with economic success. Apparently Weber was directly on target in claiming that we have made acquisition our ultimate end.[2]

But, as so often with Weber, we are only half right if we understand him this way. In addition to the ethic of acquisitive capitalism, there is a deep tradition of moral criticism in our culture that seeks to restrict the economic life. If the biblical precepts we inherited from the Puritans counseled a life of hard work, our moral tradition cautions against the material realm as well. The same nursery rhymes that warned little boys against idleness taught them that "all work and no play makes Jack a dull boy," and the lessons that instructed little girls to be "busy as a bee" also reminded them to be "gentle as a dove."[3] Weber was never unmindful of the complexities of such moral arguments, choosing only to focus on certain themes to the neglect of others in order to understand the origins of Western capitalism.

Ours in reality is a society conditioned by fundamental moral ambivalence toward the economic life. Evidence of this ambivalence is, in fact, present even in the figure of Benjamin Franklin. Despite all the admonitions from Franklin that Weber and others have cited—about time being money, waste resulting in want, and diligence leading to economic success—Franklin himself did not regard acquisition as the ultimate purpose of his life. He was the one who took two hours for lunch each day and quit working promptly at 6 p.m. in order to spend his evenings reading and thinking. Rather than devoting himself endlessly to the pursuit of economic gain, he retired from business at the early age of 42 and spent the last half of his life in public service and intellectual pursuits. He was, to be sure, disciplined, hard working, and well organized, but his economic pursuits knew strict moral restraints.

Like others of his day, Franklin was inspired by the republican ideal of civic virtue and by the Enlightenment's zeal for science, philosophy, and practical knowledge. As it was for a majority of Americans, the biblical tradition was an even more important source of teachings about the limits of economic pursuits. If that tradition was the source of Puritan discipline and frugality, it was also the origin of moral teachings that placed God above mammon. If it counseled believers to be diligent in their work, it also taught them to refrain from working on the Sabbath. It asserted that the love of money is the root of all evil, and that no man can love two masters, but must choose the spiritual life, being a devoted churchgoer and family member first and foremost, not a person bent single-mindedly on work and the acquisition of wealth. Having to labor for one's bread might be the expected state of humankind, but it was also part of Adam's curse, whereas spirituality was signaled by the Garden of Eden, the contemplative life, the heavenly realm. Love of God and love of neighbor were higher callings than mean, selfish, vulgar striving for economic gain. Work, money, and material possessions were all necessary aspects of the human condition, but their importance was hedged by a deeply held conviction that life was much more than these.

The ambivalence that many people express today toward economic pursuits is thus scarcely new. The same ambivalence can be found throughout our nation's history, and it is not simply the by-product, as news stories would sometimes lead us to believe, of undesirable working conditions and economic pressures of the moment. Burnout may be what we call it, but the desire to quit working and pursue other interests has a long history, as does our ambivalence toward money and material goods. We do not feel ambivalent toward the economic life simply because we grow weary of working and want a vacation, or because we are satiated by too many possessions, or even because we have become frustrated by being underpaid and underappreciated. These are simply the vocabularies most readily available for expressing our ambivalence. They tell us we have done enough and need to stop, just as Benjamin Franklin's daily schedule told him it was time to turn his attention to higher pursuits.

But the ambivalence Americans feel toward work and money speaks in an uncertain and wavering voice. Especially in comparison with the loud demands we hear to work harder, to be more productive, to get rich, and to buy more things, the opposing yearnings are often faint voices indeed. If we hear moral injunctions at all, they are the stern voices of the Puritans and their descendants, telling us to be more diligent, more dedicated to our work, and more successful economically. They encourage us to spend longer hours at the office, to induce our employees to do the same, to orient our children at an early age toward lucrative careers, and to accumulate enough wealth to do all the things wealth supposedly can buy. What we hear is a distorted, one-sided version of our moral tradition. What we need to rediscover is that other strand of our moral heritage that placed positive limitations on our economic striving. In this tradition, we did not limit our work or our wealth because we were too tired, stressed, lazy, or lacking in ambition, but because there were higher dimensions of human existence to be pursued.

THE TRADITION OF ASCETIC MORALISM

The moralist tradition that flourished so prominently in American culture during the first half of the nineteenth century drew heavily from biblical Christianity. Its leading figures were preachers, or sons of preachers who had received theological training before moving on to careers as academics and writers, and its popular expressions were often framed in the biblical language of hymns, religious tracts, and children's books. Moralist arguments varied in what they considered acceptable economic behavior, but a dominant strand of moralist thinking held the economic realm to be subject to strict moral obligations. It deplored what Jonathan Edwards in the previous century had described as the "niggardly, selfish spirit" prevalent in the land and counseled citizens to temper this spirit with Christian virtue.[4]

Like the earlier Puritan tradition that encouraged hard work and material acquisition, moralist arguments encouraged people to live an ascetic life of duty and sobriety. Morality, wrote Yale theologian Nathaniel Taylor, consists of rules derived from right principles that "govern the man" by enforcing a duty or obligation to engage in "right conduct toward our fellow men in all respects."[5] Ascetic duty in this tradition meant curbing material wants and even restricting one's devotion to gainful employment in order to pursue higher ends. For Taylor, the selfishness epitomized by the trader was the "very substance of moral degradation."[6] In contrast, he encouraged persons desiring to lead a virtuous life to "make some sacrifices of private interest for others' good by a largeness of liberality, and an extent of beneficence proportioned to your known ability" and to "leave no ground for the suspicion that you have not another and a better spirit than the world around you."[7]

Many of the ascetic moralists asserted the existence of divine laws that established the outer limits of acceptable economic practice and encouraged a Puritan-like obedience to the duties they implied. Stray beyond these limits and an individual or society would surely pay the consequences; abide by them and things would go well. "He who restricts his desires within the limit which these laws prescribe," proclaimed New England preacher Francis Wayland in a noted 1837 sermon on the subject, "will be free from unnecessary anxiety; he will be delivered from all temptation to coveting, envy, and over-reaching."[8]

Moralist teachings, like economic arguments today, often reflected the mood of their times. When the economy was flourishing, less attention was paid to the moral limits governing it than when times were bad. Wayland's discourse, for example, was prompted by the Crash of 1837. This debacle provided him an occasion to lecture his audience in Providence, Rhode Island, on the scourge of windfall profits and speculation. Underlying the moralists' specific arguments and injunctions, however, was a common core of assumptions about the limits of economic reality. Anything that violated the civil law, such as fraud, was clearly a breech of morality as well. Within these bounds there was considerable latitude, even positive support, for such virtues as hard work, frugality, and acquisitiveness. But the moralists also held in deep regard the human proclivity for vice (as in Wayland's reference to temptation). Ever present was the passion for an easy dollar, a quick profit, and an exceptional gain.

The basis for these teachings was a deeply rooted theological tradition in which virtue and vice constituted the core constructs of a universal ethical system. Virtue derived essentially from the two great commandments of the biblical tradition: love of God and love of neighbor. These were regarded as immutable rules revealed by divine inspiration to the writers of the Bible. They were often reinforced with references to the inscrutible wisdom of God and the need to live with the afterlife constantly in mind. "Act not as mere creatures of this life . . . but act as immortals" was familiar advice.[9]

But the rules of a virtuous life could also be translated in terms familiar to the growing emphasis on human life in the present world. To love God was to revere holiness, beauty, truth, and all goodness; to love one's neighbors was to cherish justice and benevolence and to avoid lying, fraud, and deceit. This commandment would "dispose to all suitable carriage between husbands and wives; and it would dispose children to obey their parents; parents not to provoke their children unto wrath; servants to be obedient to their masters, not with eye service, but in singleness of heart; and masters to exercise gentleness and goodness towards their servants," Jonathan Edwards had proclaimed in 1738.[10] A century later, theologians like Taylor and Wayland could add that these principles were consistent with reason and human happiness.

Consistent with the Protestant work ethic to which Weber had drawn attention, much of the moralists' concern was directed against the economic consequences of undercommitment, or idleness as it was commonly called. Schoolbooks and children's literature were particularly preoccupied with the immorality of such figures as "Lazy Slokins" and "Jacky Idle." An individual who worked hard for the wealth he accumulated could not be faulted, even if he worked exceptionally hard; the one who could be faulted was the person who wanted the same rewards but was unwilling to work or save and therefore engaged in deceit, speculation, and marginal financial schemes. But there was also a significant argument about the limits even of honest work and frugality.

Ascetic moralists were well aware that work was a necessary element of human life, but they regarded it as a means rather than an end in itself. Happiness depended on it, just as did the ability to achieve one's goals; increasingly, it became the way to avoid such weaknesses of the flesh as worry and depression as well. But this did not mean that an obsessive devotion to gainful employment was the way to live. A balanced life was the ideal. "Are we to be always at work [and] attend to our . . . labors all the day long?" queried one writer. "By no means!" In his view, "all work and no play would soon enfeeble both body and mind."[11]

Moreover, the nineteenth-century concept of work included much more than gainful employment in pursuit of material rewards. It also included the domestic labor involved in raising children properly, the time one might spend on public service or helping unfortunate neighbors, a student's quest for truth, an artist's search for beauty, or the disciplined activity that individuals like Benjamin Franklin devoted to improving their moral character. To say that there were few limits to work meant only that disciplined activity was enjoined as moral behavior, for even the kingdom of heaven was deemed to be a place where the saints "worked" in their service to God and worshipful endeavors. *How* one worked, and *to what* one's activities were devoted nevertheless constituted ethical restrictions on those activities concerned specifically with economic productivity. Substituting these mundane activities for the higher aims to which the human spirit was called meant subverting the divine law itself.

The point at which work came to be in positive violation of moral virtue was when it succumbed to excessive competitiveness. Normal competition in business was to be expected and was healthy for the economy, but individuals could also be tempted to overreach their neighbors, to work and save simply to show them up or to get the best of them. Even if a person was diligent in these activities the desire to overshadow someone else was a sign of moral deficiency. The problem with excessive competitiveness—indeed, the way to know if it was excessive—was that it substituted a wrong for a more rightful end. The proper end of economic activity was to contribute usefully to the good, or happiness, of all. When one did this, his or her own profit was justified, but excessive competitiveness replaced this proper end with the pursuit of one's own glory. Pride was the vice that made this a moral evil. Trying to accumulate wealth, simply to outshine a neighbor, meant one was concerned foremost with individual aggrandizement and display. The morally correct attitude, therefore, was to be diligent in one's work for the benefit of all and not to be seduced by fantasies of how well one was doing compared with others.

This argument gave some basis for moralist criticisms of what Thorstein Veblen would a century later label conspicuous consumption and even at the time reinforced popular skepticism toward the elite who lived ostentatiously on inherited wealth or riches derived from speculation. Citizens were admonished not to let their desires rise faster than their means, thus finding themselves with more than enough but still dissatisfied. "I am cursed with the gratification of all my wishes and the fruition of all my hopes," lamented the character in one tale. "I have wasted my life in the acquisition of riches that only awakened new desires. . . . I have everything I wish, yet enjoy nothing."[12]

Such laments occasioned admonitions directed especially toward those who seemed to value riches and material possessions more than the socially benevolent ends to which those means should be put. They encouraged people of wealth to contribute money to their churches and other charitable causes, or at least to plow profits back into their businesses, rather than spending them on luxury goods. "The richer . . . a man is," advised one writer in a typical formulation, "the greater is the obligation upon him to employ his gifts in lessening the sum of human misery."[13] For the vast middle and working classes, such advice may have done little to discourage hard work and monetary accumulation, and yet for them, keeping work in proper perspective as a means to higher ends was at least a way of relieving some of its drudgery and routine. "Once let a man convert his business into an instrument of honor, benevolence, and patriotism," Henry Ward Beecher advised, "and from that moment it is transfigured, and men judge its dignity and merit, not by what it externally is, but by what it has done, and can do."[14]

The moral limits restricting overzealousness in work and the pursuit of wealth also came from a different form of moralist argument. Less overtly, it was commonly assumed in moralist teachings of the period that the economic life was curbed by a host of other duties and responsibilities: to one's church, family, and community. In all these areas, responsibility was above all a matter of priority, an attitude, or proper way of thinking. The moralists cited biblical injunctions against the *love* of money to show that acquisitiveness could become an obsession. The proper attitude was to use one's time and talents wisely. If prosperity resulted, then so be it, but to worry about prosperity, or focus all one's attention on financial schemes, was to blind oneself to the other realms of life requiring one's attention.

A person's responsibility to the church consisted of the regular devotional duties needed to remind him or her of the moral law: daily prayer and Bible reading, communion with the saints, worship, assistance in the administration of church offices. All these took time away from work. Obedience to the Sabbath and the tithe was a concrete way of showing respect for God's ultimate dominion over, if not actual ownership of, the individual's time and money. The moralists also thought it of utmost importance to keep God at the center of one's mental priorities. The proper attitude was to apply one's time and talents responsibly in a chosen vocation—and trust God for the increase. Spending additional time scheming about the future or figuring out ways to achieve explicit monetary goals was to put too much trust in oneself. The result would be a preoccupation with the material at the expense of the spiritual. "When all that we possess is at the disposal of events which seem to depend upon second causes, and when our only resource is our own sagacity," Francis Wayland warned, "there is a special tendency to forgetfulness of God and to trusting exclusively to our own understanding. Hence, this mode of accumulation tends to render men morally thoughtless, and to foster presumption and practical atheism."[15]

Family was the next essential priority after one's commitment to God. If self-interest described the natural human attitude toward work and money, this attitude was to be curbed by the virtue commonly known as benevolence. And benevolence was expected to begin at home, if only because one was more likely to be mindful of the needs of one's family than of strangers. As Samuel Hopkins, a leading disciple of Jonathan Edwards, noted in an 1811 sermon: "[the] benevolent care of the members of the family to which he belongs, will be exercised in a higher degree, and more constantly, and with greater sensibility, than towards those of other families; especially if he be the head of it."[16] Family responsibilities included providing for the material needs of one's offspring but went beyond this to emphasize moral and spiritual tutelage.

In moralist discourse responsibility to the community also tempered economic behavior, even though the two were not incompatible. Through one's work and investments a person could create products beneficial to other people, but civic duty also required more. The responsible person had a duty to keep abreast of the needs of the community, to bear arms in its defense, and to participate in public meetings. Benevolence was to extend beyond one's family and temper the "prudence" of the individual who cared for his own interests, as one moral fable instructed, with the "good, amiable, sincere, and free" traits associated with generosity.[17] The generous person also had a special responsibility to the poor. Other than individual charity to help the poor, civic duty sometimes required little in the way of active community service, but moralist teachings were clear in their admonitions against anything that might contribute to the oppression of the poor. Anything from risky schemes that would artificially drive up the price of necessities to cut-throat business practices that sacrificed jobs for higher profits was morally reprehensible.

Besides specifying duties to family, church, and community, the ascetic moralists also recognized a responsibility to oneself. The human spirit, they argued, consisted of more than a pecuniary or physical need. Wealth should not be an end in itself, nor should one's time be devoted exclusively to the procurement of material benefits; there were higher pursuits to be cultivated, especially those that helped the individual to "subdue every sordid and selfish inclination."[18] People should thus strive to improve themselves, to gain wisdom by reading and meditating, and, in general, "to learn to prefer what is really good to what only appears so."[19] Moralist teachings recognized the value of pursuing the true, the good, and the beautiful, for these were the natural manifestations of God's glory, the handiwork that God had placed on Earth for the shared enjoyment of humankind. "I would be busy," intoned one of Isaac Watts's hymns, "in books, or words, or healthful play."[20] Especially the individual who gained the means to do so had a moral obligation—to God, to nature, to the moral law—to curtail the pursuit of additional gain and devote time to these other pursuits.

The logic of moralist discourse, then, was to restrict economic behavior primarily by setting up a conception of absolute ends that were worthy of the individual's highest devotion. Worship of God, responsibility toward family, benevolence, and self-improvement were among these ends. Work, money, and material possessions were regarded not as fundamental ends, but as necessary means to these ends. Governing these means, the dictates of conscience, of honesty, diligence, and an ethic of love also stood high on the list of moralist virtues. These were principles, set forth by God, but consistent also with reason and with what was good for the human spirit. As such, they were binding, placing duties and obligations upon the individual.

The Tradition of Expressive Moralism

In addition to the theologically oriented moralists who emphasized divinely mandated ethical obligations, a secondary tradition also emerged that, despite being less prominent, challenged the supremacy of mundane economic pursuits in an even more basic way. In this tradition, the needs of the human soul gained greater emphasis as legitimating arguments relative to conceptions of divine mandate alone. The natural longings of the human spirit were emphasized, as indeed was nature itself. Influenced by the British and Continental romanticists, it was advanced by prominent writers and academics, although it also shared visibly with the other tradition the pulpits of many New England and mid-Atlantic preachers. Rather than simply pointing up absolute values limiting the economic realm, its writers often questioned the basic meanings of work, wealth, well-being, and related concepts. Asceticism was by no means absent, but happiness, self-fulfillment, and play were more clearly in evidence here than in the other tradition.

This variant of nineteenth-century moralism also had deep roots in the biblical tradition. Jonathan Edwards, whose "Sinner in the Hands of an Angry God" would hardly make him a likely candidate to do so, had already provided a strong argument for the pursuit of personal happiness and self-fulfillment. "Self-love," he wrote, causes the person to become "little and ignoble"; but the Christian-spirited person lives in such a way that the self "is as it were extended and enlarged."[21] For Edwards, the problem was not one of loving yourself, seeking your own happiness, or pursuing your own interests. It was, rather, the relative importance one attached to these pursuits over a love of God and neighbor. Emphasizing the latter would help keep the former in perspective. Thinking about the happiness of others would guarantee one's own happiness, but the reverse was not true. He likened the relation to that of servant and master. With a strong master, a conscientious servant is a man to be admired, but if the master is absent or weak, the same conscientious servant may become too powerful.

More characteristic of this tradition than Edwards, though, were the works of Henry David Thoreau in literature and Horace Bushnell in theology. Writers with as diverse views as Ralph Waldo Emerson and Henry Ward Beecher, as well as many lesser-known literary figures and preachers, also contributed to the moralist critique of economic behavior. Their work drew inspiration both from the pietistic strand in American theology that was evident even in some of the Puritan writings and from the new literary influences that were beginning to be evident among American intellectuals, especially those associated with the Transcendentalist movement.[22] Although this tradition of moralist thought is often characterized as sentimental and idealistic, epitomized by Thoreau's retreat to Walden Pond, its leading writers were deeply concerned with such practical matters as how to think about work and money, just as Benjamin Franklin had been. Even the first, and longest, chapter of *Walden*, it will be recalled, is devoted to economics.

Well before the Civil War, the writers associated with this tradition were already concerned with the seeming lack of moral restrictions on economic life. "There are no bounds among us to the restless desire to be better off," asserted Henry W. Bellows in the inaugural issue of *American Review* in 1845.[23] Writers in this tradition were also beginning to argue that commercial activity as practiced in the United States was conditioned by social circumstances in a way that was unnatural to the human soul. The contrast drawn was between pressures in the cultural environment and what corresponded with nature. Unlike the ascetic moralists, references to the divine were generally absent in these arguments, recourse instead being made to the distinction that had arisen during the Enlightenment between civilization and nature, between man in the artificial surroundings imposed by society and man as he was intended to be prior to these corrupting influences.

In this literature economic activity to secure the basic necessities of life was considered desirable, or at least inevitable, but economic activity devoted to the pursuit of wealth or emanating from a desire to outdo one's peers was regarded as undesirable. On the one side fell happiness, cheerfulness, lightheartedness, and mental vigor; against these were pitted emaciation of health, wretched and demoralizing influences, excessive stimuli, becoming worn out, and having one's thoughts debased by focusing on low objects. Under the present system, work became a curse as the scriptures indicated it would after the fall of Adam. Individuals labored at everything, even the things they were supposed to be doing to have fun or to relax. Money became an end in itself, and people identified too closely with their possessions and judged each other according to material standards.

Those who contributed to these arguments already found much in the Puritan work ethic and the industrial revolution to denounce. It was time, they argued, for Americans to wake up to the excesses that had been ushered in by the eighteenth century. The nineteenth should follow a different path. Instead of continuing to pursue more and more wealth, becoming a nation of mere money changers, Americans should pause to take stock of what they had already accomplished and then rededicate their energies to the cultivation of the human spirit. Trade, these writers knew, would not cease, but their call was for trade to be placed in perspective. Instead of commercial society being the Promised Land, it should be seen as the Wilderness.

For all its affinity with the biblical tradition, the newer romanticist literature distinguished itself sharply from the older moralist interpretation of that tradition. Theological moralism, it claimed, was a Puritan perversion, giving a dour countenance to the human spirit. The most striking problem with moralism was its denial of play and of pleasure. Deny these, said a precursor of modern frustration-aggression theory, and the outcome will be wickedness and vice. "We are to conceive that the highest and complete state of man, that which his nature endeavors after, and in which only it fulfills its sublime instinct, is the state of play," reasoned the prominent Hartford clergyman Horace Bushnell.[24] Accordingly, human nature requires a healthy outlet for its playfulness.

When moralism, or business itself, becomes too serious, people will become morally bankrupt, barren, devoted only to the surface appearances of the moral life, but secretly obsessed with greed and ambition. Asked Bushnell: "Who that considers the ethereal nature of a soul can conceive that the doom of work is anything more than a temporary expedient, introduced or suffered to perfect our discipline? To imagine a human creature dragged along, or dragging himself along, under the perpetual friction of work, never to ascend above it; a creature in God's image, aching for God's liberty, beating ever vainly and with crippled wings, that he may lift himself into some freer, more congenial element; this, I say, were no better than quite to despair of man."[25]

Against a rigid morality, writers such as Bushnell argued for a clearer affirmation of the goodness to which human energy could be devoted. A life of conscience needed to be replaced by a commitment to the heart. The stale rules governing the respectable commercial class needed to be rethought from the ground up. Mercantile honesty was not the same thing as genuine honesty. More importantly, people should govern their lives not so much by the fear of evil but by a love of good. Meaning what? Less calculated righteousness and more spontaneous generosity. Less sobriety and more cheerfulness. Less deliberateness and more exuberance. Less propriety and more grace.

The assumption in this literature was of course that people could somehow escape the rigors of having to work constantly to earn a living. Its audience was the commercial middle class; its counsel to this class was to halt the incessant pursuit of more, and to use its economic resources to pursue life itself. Henry Bellows's admonition in this regard was clear: "Sooner than slave from morning to night at business, we would counsel any man conscious of inward resources, of the desire to cultivate his better nature, his social feelings, his tastes, his generous and cheerful sentiments, to give it up altogether as soon as the most moderate competency is secured; to seek the country—to occupy some of our rich western lands—to do any thing which will give him time to enjoy domestic pleasures, to rear his children, to acquaint himself with nature, to read, to meditate."[26]

But the tension in this strand of moralist thought was not so much between work and play, taken literally, as between conventional economic assumptions about life and a deeper vision of the human spirit. Thoreau probably expressed the contrast best when he asserted that "most of the luxuries, and many of the so-called comforts of life, are not only not indispensable, but positive hindrances to the elevation of mankind."[27] Unlike many of the other moralists, he refused to link economic behavior and higher values in a means-ends continuum. Instead, he argued for the necessity of taking a fresh perspective on economic life itself. Wealth was a burden, not an opportunity; work itself might be inescapable, but working at enjoying the sunset might be preferable to building a railroad.

Perhaps more than anything else, the literary force of this form of moralist writing challenged the reader to rethink the common classification scheme in which work and money were normally understood. Through such devices as terming the wealthy the most impoverished class of all or using business terms in alien contexts, as Thoreau did in saying he had sunk all his capital in trying to hear what was in the wind, writers called into question standard arguments about economic life.[28] Their purpose was not so much to denigrate the value of hard work, but to show that work and play were matters of perspective and definition. "There is a laborious ease, and even a laborious idleness," Horace Bushnell cautioned.[29] What people pursued as pleasure was often more work than what they did for a living. The important thing was to find some way to be impulsive, spontaneous, nonpurposive. These were the higher pursuits of the soul. Where one found them was likely to be variable, unpredictable. "What everybody echoes or in silence passes by as true today may turn out to be falsehood tomorrow, mere smoke of opinion, which some had trusted for a cloud that would sprinkle fertilizing rain on their fields," observed Thoreau.[30]

The Eclipse of Moral Discourse

The logic of the nineteenth-century moralists thus provided a basis for curbing the economic life. Mainstream moralist arguments invoked a means-ends continuum, limiting economic pursuits to the realm of means, always to be considered secondary to one's primary commitments to God, family, community, and self. Romanticist arguments were not dissimilar but paid greater attention to the natural needs of the human spirit, its affinity with nature, and its need for elevation, in contrast with the lower pursuits of commerce and trade. Both paid high tribute to the interior life of the soul and the pursuit of individual worth, the one emphasizing self-improvement, the other self-emancipation. But these arguments also contained formulations that weakened their effectiveness in curbing economic appetites, and as the nineteenth century progressed, moral considerations were gradually excluded from economic discussions.

Moralist arguments were at best ambiguous with respect to the relationship between morality and prosperity. Some writers asserted clearly that the purpose of leading a moral life was not to ensure one's material advancement. "Not by adding . . . does the moral sentiment help us," Emerson asserted, "no, but in quite another manner. It puts us in place. It centres, it concentrates us."[31] But others were more insistent upon demonstrating that moral virtue was not inconsistent with economic success and, in so arguing, often came close to suggesting that morality could indeed facilitate prosperity. From insisting that prosperity be seen as a means to higher ends, it was thus a short step to reversing this relation, making prosperity the end and morality the means.

In addition, equating morality with universal truth or divine reason, rather than private sentiment or intuition, subjected moral criticism to the growing claims of the new scientific disciplines, including economics, that sought to derive statements about morality from systematic reflection and social observation. Moral arguments gradually ceased being made on the aesthetic and idiosyncratic grounds of writers like Thoreau and were replaced by assertions about evidence from history and from social evolution. This transformation gradually resulted in moral claims being excluded entirely from utilitarian arguments rooted in statements about the common good.

Then, too, the moralists' claim that virtue was generally associated with the common good rather than private ends tended over time to subordinate arguments about individual needs to those asserting that the pursuit of self-interest contributed positively to the greatest good of the greatest number. Increasingly, utilitarian arguments that justified untrammeled economic ambitions overshadowed the limits that the moralists had tried to impose on economic life.

As moralist arguments were gradually excluded from debate about economic issues, the latter came to be regarded increasingly as a domain that happily regulated itself for the good of all. It was largely from the same intellectual context in which the moralists had worked that this new set of arguments about work and money emerged, eventually becoming much more prominent in American thought than either of the earlier two. The new arguments gained clearest expression in the emerging social science that referred to itself as political economy.

The central assumption on which political economists founded their arguments was that the human spirit is characterized by an unrestrainable drive for the accumulation of wealth, even beyond what is necessary for the immediate gratification of wants. This desire for wealth, they assumed, is in most cases unbounded; it is the principal reason why people work; and it results in competition. "It is a natural law," declared Boston business writer Henry Wood, "that any unusual opportunities for gain will call out seekers and competitors."[32] Nor was this drive regarded narrowly as a desire for money as such, but as a manifestation of the more fundamental human tendency toward ever-expanding wants and desires. "In contemplating the nature of man and the circumstances which surround him," observed George Opdyke in his 1851 treatise on political economy, "we discover the important fact that his wants and desires are ever in advance of the means at his command for satisfying them." So universal and invariable was this principle, Opdyke claimed, that it could be called "a fundamental law of human nature."[33] And to this law could be attributed the universal quest for wealth.

In this assumption the political economists were largely in agreement with the moralists. Adam Smith's emphasis on self-love differed little from Jonathan Edwards's. Where the two differed was in their evaluation of the human penchant for wealth. Many political economists admitted their subject matter was one of the lower interests of humanity. Some went so far as to describe these interests, in the words of political economist Francis Bowen, as "the lowest passions of mankind, ostentation and ambition, petty rivalry, the love of saving and the love of gain."[34] But whereas the moralists saw them as passions to be curbed, referring to them as greed, ambition, pride, and self-seeking, the political economists tended to assume that nothing was likely to change, that these were fixed characteristics of the human spirit beyond moral control; hence, they argued, take selfishness and greed as operating assumptions and see what the consequences might be.

In discussing the causes and consequences of this penchant for wealth, political economists also assumed it was necessary to bracket any consideration of other needs, aspects, or characteristics of the human spirit. In early writings on political economy (more so than in later renditions), authors recognized clearly that their subject matter constituted an abstraction from human reality, rather than an adequate depiction of that reality. John Stuart Mill framed the matter with characteristic clarity in discussing the intellectual presuppositions of political economy as a scientific discipline: "It supposes an arbitrary definition of a man, as a being who invariably does that by which he may obtain the greatest amount of necessaries, conveniences, and luxuries, with the smallest quantity of labor and physical self-denial with which they can be obtained in the existing state of knowledge." Moreover, he observed: "It makes entire abstraction of every other human passion or motive, except those which may be regarded as perpetually antagonizing principles to the desire of wealth,—namely, aversion to labor, and desire of the present enjoyment of costly indulgences." Noting that political economy regards humankind to be occupied solely with acquiring and consuming wealth, he also cautioned: "Not that any one was ever so absurd as to suppose that mankind are really thus constituted, but because this is the mode in which the science must proceed."[35]

Mill's argument was echoed widely among American political economists. Staking their claims on an analogy with the physical sciences, as so many social theorists of the nineteenth century did, political economists believed it necessary to view economic behavior as a kind of motion subject to its own law. They recognized that "economic man" was a theoretical fiction but still a useful invention, much as Newton's assumptions about an absence of friction in a vacuum were useful in understanding the law of gravity. In reality, no individual behaved only as economic man, and yet the line between theory and reality often became blurred as writers tried to apply the principles of political economy to the world around them. *New York Evening Post* editor E. L. Godkin, one of the most influential writers of his time on economics, insisted for example that the individual desires "to get as much of the world's goods as he can with the least possible expenditure of effort or energy on his own part."[36] In Godkin's view this desire was like a first law of motion for understanding economic behavior, but it also betrayed his understanding of the way in which rational individuals actually behaved.

Abstracting from reality in this way disallowed from consideration most of the arguments of the moralists. For Mill, the study of morals or ethics, the subject matter of which he considered to be "the affections, the conscience, or feeling of duty, and the love of approbation," was explicitly excluded from political economy because it was a separate science dealing with different laws of human nature.[37] In practice, this separation resulted in arguments that nevertheless focused on certain affections or duties at the exclusion of others. For example, Francis Bowen put forth this argument to illustrate for the uninitiated reader how wealth was created by being invested and allowed to circulate freely: "If the earnings of an artisan for a year have amounted to $300, he *may* expend them all upon food, clothing, and amusement. In this case, he spends them all *unproductively*,—that is, without expecting a return or replacement of them. At the year's end, all the advantage which *remains* to him from his year's labor is, that his strength, health, and spirits are renewed or replaced, so that he can now go to work and earn another year's wages."[38] Bowen went on to contrast this artisan with another who was "frugal and ambitious to grow rich" and for this reason drank nothing but water and gave up all his amusements. At the end of the year, the second artisan was able to save $100, which he invested, and after a year was able to see this investment grow to $104.50.

Bowen's purpose was not explicitly to favor the second artisan over the first, but his language betrays this preference by suggesting that the first used his wages "unproductively" and found himself with nothing left but his health and strength. These were meant to be value-neutral terms associated with the language of the political economist rather than moral indictments. What is more interesting, though, are the reasons why the first artisan does not save as much as the second. He is less frugal, less ambitious, given to spending his money on amusements, and, we are to suppose by the remark about the second drinking only water, a patron of taverns. He, in short, reflects the two negative factors that Mill admits may be of relevance to the political economist: a dislike of hard work, and a penchant for self-indulgence.

A moralist would have been able to think of other reasons why the first artisan might not have saved $100. To the ascetic moralist, legitimate reasons for not doing so would have included giving some of his earnings away in observance of the golden rule, spending the money to send one of his children to college, or restricting his workweek in order to devote more time to his family, church, or community. To a preacher like Bushnell or a writer such as Thoreau, legitimate reasons might have also included taking time to reflect on higher truths or to learn about nature.

Political economists defended their exclusive focus on wealth by considering it the essential means to all other ends. Francis Bowen also provides an example of this assumption: "I need not apologize for the science which treats of the creation of wealth, on the ground that it relates only to one of the lower interests of humanity, and that it is not of so much moment for an individual or a society to be rich, as it is to be wise, free, instructed, and virtuous. Wealth is that element of civilization which supports all the others, and that, without it, no progress, no refinement, no liberal art would be possible." He adds: "It is that which vivifies and maintains all the other elements and influences which dignify humanity and render life desirable."[39]

Like other political economists, Bowen agreed with writers in the moralist tradition that wealth is a means and not an end. And yet, by making it a necessary means, by bracketing consideration of anything else, and by proclaiming it to be a universal desire, he turned it into something more. The moralists paid explicit attention to what these other ends were and how they might conflict with the pursuit of wealth. In their more extreme statements, they regarded wealth not even as a means, but in Thoreau's words, a "positive hinderance" to the pursuit of wisdom, beauty, and an elevated life.[40]

Political economists also assumed that the pursuit of individual self-interest in economic matters necessarily led to the greatest good of the larger society. This argument basically took away one of the moralists' most serious criticisms. They argued that you should keep in mind serving others or else your work was wrong. In contrast, this argument said in effect, it does not matter what you think or what your motives may be; no matter how selfish you are, the common good will still be served. "When poets, philanthropists, and divines have said their worst of it, the love of personal acquisition remains the main-spring of most of the material good thus far achieved on this rugged, prosaic planet," Horace Greeley declared in his book on political economy in 1870.[41]

Self-interested pursuits were not only the means to common material good; they were also conducive to all the personal virtues advocated by the moralists. From Montesquieu to Adam Smith, a long tradition of European thought had pitted self-interest against the baser passions of human nature, describing the former as a way of restraining the latter.[42] Initially, self-interest alone was not regarded as the key to moral restraint; rather, a combination of the two was required for a society based on self-interest to function effectively. Even in the 1830s, when Alexis de Tocqueville made his historic visit to the United States, it was possible to proclaim, as Tocqueville did, that the secret of American strength was not simply self interest, but "self-interest rightly understood"; that is, pursued in the context of moral self-discipline and a sense of obligation to one's neighbors.[43] Gradually, however, the balance between self-interest and moral obligation shifted, so that political economists could increasingly argue that economic man was of necessity a person of moral cultivation as well. Wrote one economist: "Nothing sharpens the faculties and dispels prejudice as effectively as self interest."[44]

This argument also defied the political economists' own dictum about bracketing everything else in order to make political economy a science. Advocates of the new science could not resist the temptation to turn the tables on the moralists who worshiped God and God's handiwork in nature. Here, they said, was an even more profound demonstration of a divine law. Surely it was Providence that such willful individual behavior could result in collective good. "It is true, that men are usually selfish in the pursuit of wealth," Francis Bowen acknowledged, "but it is a wise and benevolent arrangement of Providence, that even those who are thinking only of their own credit and advantage are led, unconsciously but surely, to benefit others."[45]

In addition, the political economists chose to focus on government as the only likely form of intervention in the beneficent progress of the economic sphere. There is no mention in the writings of these political economists of the fact that other pursuits might get in the way of the market or cause people to work less or save less. Despite their belief that self-interest benefited the individual morally, their primary focus was on *social* betterment, on what might be good for the whole society rather than for the individual; hence, their concern about government. And the proper role of government, of course, was only to remove restrictions on free trade, protect the defenses of the country, and deal with crime and other overt vice.

In focusing entirely on the relative roles of government and the free market, political economists managed to exclude from consideration any concern for the ill effects of economic behavior for the individual. Bowen, for example, notes that the human passions for accumulation and consumption may "bring their own penalty upon the individual who unduly indulges them," but he does not consider these costs, only that the social benefit is still positive. Political economy was, thus, blind to the arguments of the moralists who asserted that economic pursuits, however beneficial they might be for the larger society, ran in ways fundamentally contrary to the needs and duties of the human spirit.

What the new science of political economy ushered in was essentially a conception of economic life as a morally benign self-governing system. Hard work and the selfish pursuit of wealth would result in social betterment as long as government stayed clear of the marketplace. Fears of the ill effects of unrestrained greed and selfishness were allayed by the argument that these traits harmed only the individual, not the society at large. Indeed, in this last argument lay the germ of an idea that was to become increasingly prominent in subsequent decades; namely, that morality and the pursuit of wealth enjoyed a kind of symbiotic relationship. By at first delimiting immorality to idleness and overindulgence, political economists were able to argue that immorality necessarily inhibited the successful pursuit of wealth, while moral behavior contributed positively to material achievement. Later, this argument was expanded in a way that absorbed many of the other moralist concerns as well. Dishonesty, paying too little heed to the needs of other people, and even excessive greed would also hinder the pursuit of wealth.

The Attainment of Closure

The economic realm thus became a kind of morally closed system. To the extent that moral concerns were acknowledged, they were considered, as historian Warren J. Samuels observes, as "nondeliberative forces"; that is, as restraints built into the fabric of ordinary social life, guaranteed by law and custom, and reinforced by the pursuit of wealth itself.[46] There was no need for moral preachments because wealth itself would be the reward for doing good, poverty the fruit of doing ill. People would simply toil away, driven by the desire for material goods, staying within the realm of common moral decency in order to better achieve these ends. Nothing need be said about other human ends that might conflict with the desire for wealth. Those could supposedly be purchased with the wealth one attained.

By the end of the nineteenth century, industrial growth coupled with social Darwinism and a deepening faith in scientific principles had done much to extend the assumptions of the political economists well beyond their own ranks. Survival of the fittest implied that individuals should work hard to succeed and that success could be taken as a sign of moral virtue as well as a contribution to the common good. Not everyone was content with the alleged benefits of wealth and hard work, but the American Dream was still cast largely in these terms for the millions of immigrants who streamed to the nation's shores. Preachers, journalists, and other moralists worried more about getting the lower classes to work harder than they did about greed and ambition among the middle classes. Increasingly, the economic realm was regarded as a separate domain impelled by its own incentives, conducive to human betterment for all who lived by its principles, and needing legal restrictions only to curb its worst excesses.

The exclusion of moral discourse from the economic realm was not entirely attributable to the advancing scientific arguments of classical economists, however, or even to the successes that were being achieved in the industrial sphere. A broad space—what we now refer to as "everyday life"—was being created by the gradual exclusion from it of all problems that heretofore had been especially conducive to moral and evaluative questions. Sickness, so long the condition that demonstrated the limits of the technical efficiency that governed ordinary life, was gradually being conquered through immunizations and better understanding of the human body. Death, still the ever-present foe of normal family life, came after the Civil War to be more and more the domain of hospitals and embalming parlors that removed it from view and sanitized it of its more fear-producing connotations. The mentally insane, once thought to exemplify the kind of moral weakness to which any individual could become victim, were now shielded from sight in asylums and treated as an entirely separate category of human beings. Even the poor, long the moral responsibility of families and local communities, were soon to be turned over to distinct programs and institutions. This "sequestration of experience," as social theorist Anthony Giddens has termed it, was the basis on which it became possible for the vast majority of middle-income people to live as if they could manage their lives securely and effectively through rational, technical mastery alone.[47]

If everyday life came to include most of what people did in their work lives, with their families, and in their spare time, it was nevertheless the economic sphere in which the sequestration of experience proved most effective. Of necessity, people still had to confront the prospect of their own death, but the dying were largely outside the workplace, and their survivors were increasingly shielded by life insurance and workman's compensation programs. The sick and the mentally insane were defined as economically unproductive categories of people. Within the world of work and money itself, means-ends calculations, technical efficiency, and planning for the future increasingly became the operative rules. The net effect of these developments, as Giddens has correctly argued, was to "repress a cluster of basic moral and existential components of human life."[48] Questions that once might have caused sufficient ruptures in the fabric of everyday life were now glossed over largely by the smoothness, efficiency, and continuity present in daily life itself. Answers to these question were supplied primarily by the "coherence of routines themselves."[49]

Understandings of work and money at the end of the twentieth century clearly owe much to this legacy. Despite the various waves of criticism and reform that have mounted assaults on mainstream economic thinking in the intervening decades, demands for a better society range more between the extremes of market growth and government regulation than toward the moral restraint of economic life itself. The moralists' arguments sound quaint and unscientific, if not overly pious and sentimental. Rather than attempting to regulate economic life with moral discourse, it now seems far more compelling to regulate moral life with applications of economic rationality. "After all, if, by time-and-motion studies, data retrieval systems, credit-ratings, conveyorbelts, and electronic eyes, we can regulate men's activities, and in particular their vital economic functions," asks Bryan Wilson, "then why burden ourselves with the harrowing, arduous, time-consuming weariness of eliciting moral behaviour?"[50] Absolute commitments are more likely to be viewed as personal decisions, requiring efforts to balance the marginal utilities of greater income against more free time. Benevolence and the pursuit of aesthetic interests have been subsumed under the rubric of various professional careers. Why people work and how they think about money are largely assumed to be questions answerable within an economic framework itself, rather than needing to be placed in a wider context.

And yet it has also been evident to social observers for some time that the economic sphere cannot answer all the questions people may raise about the meaning of their lives. Max Weber described the world of coherent routines as an "iron cage" devoid of larger meanings, internally stifling because it provided no connections between the daily lives people led and their place in the cosmos. More recently, social observers ask whether some of the malaise people are voicing about their economic lives is the residue of ancient questions about meaning and value that were buried during the nineteenth century, but not so deeply as to keep them inert forever. As Giddens observes, "The very routines that provide security mostly lack moral meaning and can either come to be experienced as 'empty' practices, or alternatively can seem to be overwhelming. When routines, for whatever reason, become radically disrupted, or where someone specifically sets out to achieve a greater reflexive control over her or his self-identity, existential crises are likely to occur."[51]

PART TWO
THE CULTURAL CONSTRUCTION OF
MATERIAL LIFE

Chapter Four

SHIFTING PERSPECTIVES: THE DECOUPLING
OF WORK AND MONEY

B Y THE MIDDLE of the nineteenth century, the moralist vision
that had provided a framework in which to think about economic behavior in relation to broader values was already losing
influence relative to the rising scientific claims of the political economists. Were we to trace these developments in greater detail, we would
see that the wider cultural movement of the nineteenth century was
toward a progressive narrowing of the framework in which public
discourse about work and money was located. To be sure, there was
still much at the popular level to link work and money with other
moral commitments: preachers talked about stewardship and community leaders encouraged civic participation as a token of respectability
among the rising middle classes. But expert opinion was becoming increasingly convinced that work and money needed to be understood in
a context by themselves. By the start of the twentieth century influential debate on these issues was set largely in the context of utilitarian
arguments concerning the connection between work and money. The
principles of scientific management advanced by Frederick Taylor and
so effectively operationalized by Henry Ford can perhaps be taken as
the apex of this development. Assigning monetary value to each motion the worker undertook, Taylor signaled not only the growing emphasis in American culture on efficiency but also its belief that everything could be transformed into dollars-and-cents calculations. For
worker, manager, and owner alike questions of cost, remuneration,
and profit had indeed become the bottom line.

As new immigrants arrived in the United States by the millions, the
American Dream itself came to be framed increasingly in terms of work
and money. Perhaps it was actually becoming more difficult for the
vast majority of Americans to achieve material success simply by working hard, suggests one of the leading historical studies of the period,
but the work ethic itself became all the more pronounced, and the reasons advanced for working hard were increasingly characterized in

purely economic terms.[1] Immigrants were said to have come to America in order to make money, and those who were willing to work hard could expect to succeed in this aspiration. How that quest might affect ethnic ties themselves, what it might do to families and to children, or what it meant for the communal life of the nation were questions better left to the few reformers concerned with such issues.

Today when the question arises, "Why work?" the common-sense answer is still overwhelmingly "To make money." Although there is a plethora of more sophisticated theories of work motivation in the academic literature, the common-sense view remains much in evidence. In a recent book on the subject, for example, a high-ranking business executive makes a compelling case for the argument that people work mainly to earn money by positing the outcome of removing various incentives. Take away lots of things and people would still work, he observes, but take away their salary and few would show up.[2] Management theorists themselves generally stress the same point. As one team concludes: "No other incentive or motivational technique comes even close to money with respect to its instrumental value."[3] This view is prevalent in other settings as well. When asked what they *thought* motivated other people to work hard, the leading answer given in a British survey, for example, was "greater financial reward."[4]

The common-sense view may even be regarded as the one that best fits developments in the economy itself. A century ago much of what people did was still outside the money economy; for example, the vast majority of women were not gainfully employed, many of the items that people consumed were homemade, and many of the services on which people relied, such as health care, fire protection, and old-age assistance, were provided voluntarily by relatives and neighbors. At the end of the twentieth century more and more of these activities have been subsumed by the money economy. To say that people work to earn money is thus a sensible view because we increasingly depend on having money for virtually everything we desire and need.

Support for the common-sense perspective can also be found by asking people directly why they work. In my labor force survey, for example, respondents were given a list of ten possible reasons for getting into their present line of work. The one chosen most often, both as an important reason and as the *most important* reason, was "the money."[5]

It follows from this perspective that how hard people work will be determined by how much they are getting paid or how badly they need the money. Extensive commitment to jobs and careers is thus a sign that people want or need money and that incentive systems are functioning effectively. There is, in other words, a direct relationship between the long hours many people are now working and the "golden handcuffs" that link them to their work financially. It also follows that economic decisions compose a self-contained system, operating in terms of reward-and-benefit calculations, while moral commitments and values constitute a separate realm. Work and money provide the material means for realizing higher values but are in themselves neutral with respect to the choice of these values. Money is in this view regarded as a universal exchange medium that translates labor into a commodity capable of being expended on any valued pursuit. We need to rethink the relationship between work and money, therefore, if we are to make a valid place for moral discourse to be considered.

WORKING FOR MONEY

Let us look more closely at the assumption that people work to make money. The adequacy of this assumption can best be assessed by considering several of its implications: that monetary rewards will rank high among people's job values, that people would not work if they were not paid, that people will work more if they are paid more, that career decisions depend largely on monetary considerations, and that job satisfaction will be closely associated with levels of remuneration.

If people worked for money, one clue that might indicate this possibility would be for people to value high pay in a job more than just about anything else, except possibly job security and short hours, both of which could easily be translated into monetary equivalents. When asked directly about the desirability of high pay versus other job characteristics, however, most Americans do not give priority to the monetary rewards. In one survey, for example, 91 percent agreed with the statement "it is better to work at a lower paying job that one enjoys than at a higher paying job that is not satisfying."[6] People in both the highest and lowest income brackets, and across all occupational strata and levels of education, agreed in about the same proportions. Another survey, in which people were asked to say what they most preferred in a job, showed that only 21 percent selected "high income," compared with 48 percent who chose "a feeling of accomplishment."[7]

Some studies, in which people do acknowledge that money is at least the reason why other people work, nevertheless indicate that this motive may be weaker in the United States than in other countries. One of the most interesting findings came from an eleven-nation survey in which young people age 18 to 24 were asked whether they thought people work mainly to earn money, as a duty to society, or to find self-fulfillment. Respondents in the seven advanced industrial societies were more likely than those in the four developing societies to say people worked to earn money, casting some doubt on the possibility that money is simply deemphasized in societies that have reached a comfortable standard of living. In all seven countries a majority selected this answer and did so each of the three times the survey was administered. And yet respondents in the United States were the *least likely* of those in any of the seven countries to give this response, and *most likely* to say people work to find self-fulfillment.[8]

Answers to survey questions like these might be dismissed for a variety of reasons, raising the possibility that less direct measures of the relationship between money and work might be better. For instance, if money is really the driving factor behind work, people who make more money should be more dedicated to their work. In fact, some evidence does show that people in higher income categories claim to feel a sense of dedication to their work more often than people at lower income levels.[9] But these differences are only a few percentage points—barely reaching statistical significance—and they are not as strong as those separating income groups on other characteristics of work. Dedication, it appears, may have much more to do with feeling one has a say in making important decisions—something that upper-income people experience much more often than lower-income people.[10]

If people worked for money, we would also expect wanting to earn more money to be one of the chief reasons given for quitting one job to pursue another. But in an analysis of 2,778 questionnaires submitted by employees leaving the federal government, only 10 percent listed the desire to earn more money among their reasons for resigning. Far more significant were reasons having to do with job satisfaction, the desire for more meaningful work, stress, wanting to make better use of one's talents, and conflicts with personal interests and lifestyles.[11]

If money is the reason people work, evidence might also demonstrate that how people feel about their finances is a strong predictor of how they feel about their work. Presumably those who feel better about their finances should also feel better about their work. Indeed, research does support this hypothesis. But it also shows that work satisfaction is much more closely associated with how a person feels about himself or herself than with that person's sense of financial well-being. For example, a multiple regression analysis of data from one national survey revealed that satisfaction with "your attempts to fulfill your potential as a person" predicted work satisfaction almost twice as well as satisfaction with "your financial well-being" when both factors were considered simultaneously.[12]

Some question about money as a reason for working is also raised by the fact that so many people continue to work in societies that provide a financial safety net through social welfare programs, or that give some people the opportunity to live off savings or family resources. Were money the chief motive, work hours should be decreasing in these societies as a result of government or private provision becoming more readily available. But few of the facts seem to correspond with this expectation. For example, the Swedish experiment in social welfare policies has been watched closely to see if it discourages people from working, and while the popular impression is that people do work less, this impression has not been supported by hard evidence. Quite the contrary. Despite the fact that Swedish law guarantees ample paid vacations, sick leaves for employees, leaves to cover parents' time spent tending sick children or newborns, and sabbaticals for study or union work, data show that most people do not use all their leave time, and the decline in official statistics on working hours is probably more than equaled by increases in work outside the official economy. Moreover, the proportion of Swedes employed has actually risen substantially during the same period in which these and other benefits providing for unemployment compensation and medical care were being extended.[13]

It may be that people keep working because their desire for a higher standard of living encourages them to do so, still suggesting the importance of a monetary motive. What makes this argument unsatisfactory, however, is the fact that when posed with the hypothetical situation of having all the money they need, people still say they would continue working. For example, one survey found that only 22 percent agreed with the statement "if I had enough money to live comfortably without working, I would not work," while 78 percent selected the option "even if I had enough money to live comfortably without working, I would still rather work."[14]

One conclusion suggested by data like these is that people are much more comfortable talking about working hard than they are talking about wanting a lot of money. For example, despite the stress and lack of free time that many people associate with working too hard, a relatively small minority of the American public say they would welcome less emphasis on working hard (24 percent in one survey). By comparison, a substantial majority (67 percent) say they would welcome less emphasis on money.[15] They may secretly work because they want lots of money, but if they do, they do not feel it acceptable to say so (an important possibility that we shall consider later). But even if people are merely reluctant to talk about money as a motive, they are then forced by this disjuncture in our culture to give other reasons for working besides money.

A growing body of evidence also suggests that in many parts of the world the link between work and money is being severed because people are questioning whether hard work is any guarantee of making more money. Japan supposedly does one of the best jobs of providing monetary incentives that encourage people to work hard, and yet a national survey of young adults in Japan showed that nearly half believe hard work is not rewarded.[16] In Great Britain, fewer than half the public believes it is possible to get ahead by working hard.[17] A national study conducted in France is even more telling. Three-fourths of those surveyed thought their efforts at work were unrewarded or compensated for, and even among executives this proportion was well over half.[18]

From a wide variety of perspectives, then, evidence seems to provide far less support for the argument that people work to make money than the common-sense view would suggest. None of this evidence can be taken to mean that people would still work if their bosses suddenly decided to cancel their paychecks. But the fact that the American public expends billions of hours each year on voluntary service activities does suggest that many kinds of work might continue if there were no pay involved at all. More importantly, the evidence suggests that whatever people may think when they are alone, there is something in the cultural tradition that makes it difficult for them to account for their work strictly in monetary terms.

THE POSTSCARCITY THESIS

Many observers of the workforce have been mindful that the connection between work and money is less than straightforward, but they argue that this disjuncture can be explained by a shift in economic con-

ditions themselves. Money, they argue, came to be the medium of exchange in industrial societies and was thus part of the distinct cultural
repertoire of the industrial era, rather than being simply a universal
want. In preindustrial societies people worked mainly to provide the
subsistence needs of their families, such as food, shelter, and clothing;
in industrial societies they worked for money, in most cases in the form
of wages needed to purchase the necessities of life that now could be
obtained only through the market, or in the case of the bourgeoisie as
profits that could be turned into capital investments. Money is now less
important, say these writers, because the twentieth century witnessed
a massive shift from industrial to postindustrial modes of production,
such as human services, the professions, information technology and
mass communication, as well as government and public administration. In these occupations, profit incentives are largely excluded, while
salaries are sufficiently high and secure to minimize the monetary concerns of the typical wage earner. As a result, values associated with
work shift increasingly toward emotional and intellectual gratification,
collegiality, and service.[19]

Some evidence supports this thesis; for example, a multinational survey conducted by Daniel Yankelovich and his associates revealed that
young people were less likely than older people in affluent societies to
choose material success as their core motive for working.[20] A question
asked in Japan also suggested that economic well-being itself may be
turning people's minds toward other values: posed with the statement
"since I have achieved some material wealth, I would like to improve
the spiritual aspects of my life," 50 percent of the Japanese public
agreed, compared with only 34 percent who agreed with the statement
"I want to improve the material aspects of life further."[21] The possibility that a deemphasis on money is associated with the changing occupational base of modern societies also finds some support. A national
study conducted in the United States, for example, demonstrated that
fewer people employed in the professions claimed to value "making a
lot of money" than did those employed either in managerial positions
or as skilled and semiskilled industrial workers.[22] As the professions
expand, this finding would also suggest a gradual decrease over time
in the value placed on money relative to other values.

But other evidence does not correspond well with the idea that
money is simply becoming devalued now as a result of culture shifts
associated with postscarcity. A national study conducted in Canada,

for example, found that young people were *more likely* to list high pay as a desirable job characteristic than were people over age 25.[23] In the United States, making a lot of money is also more likely to be valued by the young than by the old, and this proportion shows a steady decline with each successive age-group.[24] Annual surveys conducted in the United States among college freshmen have also documented an upward trend in the proportions who list being very well-off financially among their top values: from 39 percent who did so in 1970 to 71 percent in 1985.[25] An even stronger trend was evident in a study of French youth that documented a threefold increase over a six-year period in the percentages who chose money as one of the things most meaningful to them.[26] Comparisons of occupational groups do not entirely support the postscarcity thesis either. Differences between professionals and managers notwithstanding, American data show no overall tendency for money to be less highly valued among those in comfortable income brackets than among those with lower incomes, and persons employed in service occupations are *more likely* to value money than are people employed in industry.[27]

These patterns also point to an important caveat in considering the relation between money and work: as the evidence reviewed earlier suggests, people do not identify money as a primary reason for working, but they nevertheless continue to value money and the material comforts it buys. To some analysts, the logical conclusion is that people need to rediscover the work ethic if they are going to earn the money they want. But there is a deeper argument to be made as well: that how people understand their work, their money, and the relation between the two is a complex cultural matter. Instead of arguing simply that people work to make money, we need to pay closer attention to these cultural matters.

WORKING TO GIVE A LEGITIMATE ACCOUNT

In place of the work-for-money argument that seems to be of so little use in organizing any of the empirical evidence at our disposal, I want to suggest an alternative perspective: that people work in order to give a legitimate account of themselves. I am not altogether happy with this particular phrasing of the argument because it suggests a kind of teleological reasoning that I do not mean to imply. Different wordings that have certain advantages could include: people work if they can give a legitimate account of what they are doing, or in order to keep working people must be able to give a legitimate account of themselves, or that having a legitimate account of oneself makes it possible to work. But rather than rely on simple formulas, we need to consider what these words mean.

An account, following a still-valuable essay published some years ago, may be defined as "a linguistic device employed whenever an action is subjected to valuative inquiry."[28] Accounts are elements of conversation or discourse, things that people say to other people or to themselves to explain what they are doing.[29] A question like "Why do you work?" or "Why are you working at this?" is a valuative inquiry that, according to this definition, is likely to evoke an account. Calling it a "valuative inquiry" is helpful because this sort of question implies a connection between the subject at hand and some wider set of values or moral norms unlike, say, a question such as "Which way is the supermarket?" In adding the term "legitimate," I mean only to specify accounts that connect the particular act under question to values and ways of talking about values that are acceptable in a given social context. An individual might be able to answer the question "Why are you working?" in a number of ways (including "just because, now go away"), but only some of these accounts would be acceptable in particular situations.

Framed this way, the idea of accounts moves us very quickly into thinking about work as a *human* enterprise, rather than simply the activity of proverbial "economic man." It is often argued that work is a natural part of the human condition because it is the means by which we sustain ourselves. Such an argument has always offended humanists, though, because it misses the fact that we gain enjoyment from our work as well, derive pride from what we accomplish, and even recognize its artistic and spiritual qualities. To say that work is inherently connected with giving accounts of ourselves, however, is to suggest a different way in which it is fundamentally human. An account goes beyond the mere assertion that we desire (or do not desire) to work— perhaps because we need to eat or want to buy something nice for ourselves. An account provides a legitimate answer to the question, "Why is this desire of value?" It is the evaluative component of this question that most sets us off as a species. "We think of (at least higher) animals as having desires, even as having to choose between desires in some cases, or at least as inhibiting some desires for the sake of others," writes philosopher Charles Taylor.[30] "But what is distinctively human is the power to *evaluate* our desires, to regard some as desirable and others as undesirable." Accounts are in this sense part of our reflective capacity, part of what philosopher Harry Frankfurt has called "the formation of second-order desires," that are a common feature of human life.[31]

In terms that are perhaps more familiar among social scientists concerned with such matters, accounts are a vital element of the process by which we ascribe *meaning* to our behavior. Human action in this view is governed not simply by reward and punishment, or by utilitarian calculations of costs and benefits, but by the interpretations that actors give to their behavior. Max Weber, for example, took the process by which "the acting individual attaches a subjective meaning to his behavior" as the central issue with which social scientists should be concerned.[32] Others following this lead have insisted that human behavior nearly always takes place within a socially constructed definition of reality that not only makes specific actions meaningful but also guides actors in the behavior they choose to pursue.[33] A crucial assumption in this perspective is that there is a close relationship between meaning and motivation.[34] To say that one is motivated to do something is thus tantamount to saying that the person regards that particular action as meaningful. Indeed, motivation itself may be understood in terms of the ability to provide a meaningful account of one's behavior. Weber himself writes, for example, that an understanding of motivation consists "in placing the act in an intelligible and more inclusive context of meaning."[35]

There is, however, one special reason for emphasizing accounts, rather than suggesting simply that people try to give meaning to what they do. The subjective meaning an individual attaches to some activity may be largely hidden from view, perhaps even from that particular individual. An account, in contrast, is by definition something that occurs in public. We can observe it because it is spoken, written down, or acted out. But we must also be clear what it is we are observing. An account is a performance that people for some reason feel comfortable giving in public. In most circumstances people will attempt to give an account that is true to their own feelings and that reflects what they really believe. And yet it is doubtful that accounts reveal everything a person feels and believes. For example, if asked why I attend church regularly, I may say it is because I believe in God, but if pressed further (or asked by someone I know intimately) I might also reveal that I attend in order to meet prestigious people in my community. Accounts do not disclose the "real reason" why people do things (if any singular reason even existed). They fabricate an understanding that the speaker believes will be regarded, first of all, as reasonable, and secondly, as being compatible with certain widely shared background expectations. Accounts are thus an indication of what people believe to be socially acceptable and desirable.

It is perhaps easy to take a cynical view of accounts, regarding them only as window dressing that bears very little relationship to what really governs people's behavior. Yet in a society that values diversity and generally attaches importance to showing tolerance of individual diversity, there is considerable room for people to fabricate accounts that are actually to their personal liking. Whether a person might alter these accounts under extreme circumstances, as some observers emphasize, is not the issue. There are fairly widespread values that can be referenced with accounts that are specifically crafted for use under a wide variety of circumstances. Whether a particular account is honored by a particular listener is again not the issue. That speakers themselves honor their own accounts sufficiently to stay committed to a particular activity, to regard that activity as being meaningful, and to feel good about themselves when engaged in that activity is the point.

A Ragbag Theory of Accounts

Accounts make sense of an activity's relationship to the norms and expectations that exist within its social environment. Accounts are thus the connective tissue between activities and their social context. Their role or purpose is to render activities meaningful and legitimate in relation to certain features of their normative milieu. Accounts of work link this activity with some part of the culture in which it occurs.

But where do accounts come from? People do not for the most part make up stories about themselves from whole cloth. They make them up, it would be better to say, from the rag drawer. Rags have been used before, although quite often for a different purpose than the one to which they are about to be put. They are still usable as cloth, and this property renders them more useful for some purposes than for others.

To make something elaborate, such as a quilt, we also have to piece together our projects by using a variety of rags.

The rag drawer image is perhaps not as far fetched as it sounds. Others have likened the scripts and formulas that make up our everyday lives to repertoires and tool kits. The problem with repertoires is that they are always elaborate scores. The problem with tool kits is that they are used to make something, but a tool does not become part of the object itself. Rags are appealing because they have been around for a while. They are a bit worn, they have been used before. Often they are something else that is worn out. But this need not be the case. Looking around for a washcloth, I can find one in the rag drawer and still use it as a washcloth. Or I can use it to dust the furniture.

The fragments that make up our accounts are like this. The phrase "I love what you do for me" has been taken from other sources and been turned into a slogan for Toyota automobiles. We hear it on the television. Our memories put it in the rag drawer. Later, we may pull out the phrase again, but not in thinking about Toyotas at all. We may tell our spouse "I love what you do for me" and recognize only vaguely that the phrase has a familiar ring. Or we may decide to treat ourselves to a hot bubble bath and say something internally like "I like what I do for me." Accounts are also like fabrications from the rag drawer because they have a tangible existence. Somebody made them. "I love what you do for me" roams the backstreets of our memories because somebody made it up, put it to music, and paid for it to be broadcast on television.

An adequate understanding of work is, within this perspective, no different from an understanding of any other kind of behavior. People work, according to this view, because (or as long as) they are able to place this act within an interpretive context that gives it meaning. To say that one works in order to earn money is thus a way of constructing a meaningful account of one's action. But it is only one way of doing so. Other accounts might focus on a person's desire for self-fulfillment, helping to make the world a better place, or following some divine injunction to be productively engaged. Emphasizing the variety of possible accounts and the ways in which these are culturally constructed is thus to relativize the view that work is performed to earn money. It ceases to be an economic fact and becomes one facticity among many that can be constructed and legitimated.

The chief consequence of emphasizing legitimate accounts is that human action must then be understood primarily in terms of the social and cultural contexts in which it occurs, rather than being assumed to involve exchanges of goods, services, and other resources alone. The contrast has been seen vividly in studies of political behavior. Interest group theory, for example, argues that regimes stay in power primarily by producing results beneficial to certain constituencies who then trade their support in order to keep on receiving these benefits. Theories emphasizing legitimacy, in contrast, have asserted that regimes stay in power so long as they are able to give accounts of their actions that are deemed widely to be meaningful or legitimate.

Seeing work simply as a way to make money also places too much attention on the solitary individual, regarding him or her as a decision maker who calculates rationally how much to work, and what kind of work to do, in order to earn the desired amount of money. The alternative view regards work more as a social phenomenon, recognizing that workers may make monetary calculations in private but still engage in reasoning processes that reflect the subculture in which they live and are often tried out on fellow workers and members of their families and communities. The former view might be typified by the lonely breadwinner bent over his budget late at night trying to decide whether to take a new job or not. The alternative view puts this person in a community, shows him or her giving accounts to others, hearing their accounts in turn, and developing a personal story on that basis.

Although the desire for meaning and legitimacy may in this view be universal, the need to give accounts—or the questions evoking them—is nevertheless likely to be greater in some situations than in others. If I walk deliberately down the sidewalk using pretty much the same gait as everyone else, nobody is likely to come up to me and ask why I am doing this. But if I pace back and forth, pausing to hop three times on one foot every few steps, people will at least ask themselves what is going on. It is for this reason that accounts have sometimes been discussed with special reference to deviant social behavior, or have been thought to occur when normal behavior breaks down.[36] Under such circumstances, an account is likely to be given in a defensive posture, taking the form of either an excuse or a justification. I would like to broaden the idea, though, to suggest that accounts are more likely to be associated with any kind of uncertainty. Hopping on one foot creates uncertainty for bystanders because they can think of no immediate reason why I might be doing this. Telling off your host at a party may lead you to come back later and give an account of your behavior in order to patch up the relationship. Finding yourself wondering if your job is going to last, if you are likely to get a raise, or if you are really doing what will make you happy is also a kind of uncertainty that begs for an account. Giving accounts is likely to be prompted for the individual at times of uncertainty as far as one's work itself is concerned. But there are also times especially set apart in the wider society to reckon with such uncertainty by giving accounts in public.

To give a more concrete sense of what I mean by an account in the context of work and money, let us consider an actual case that comes from a recent commencement address given at a major university by the chairman of the board of a large multinational corporation.[37] After disabusing the graduating class of three supposedly common assumptions betraying the inveterate idealism of the young (the world cares about the young, the young will change civilization, and the young are forever young), the speaker asserted that a more realistic approach to life requires a focus on work, specifically, on doing good work. A series of accounts followed as the speaker attempted to indicate why work was indeed a legitimate emphasis. Included were arguments about glory, the essential humanness of work, its constructive dimension, and the communion, pride, and enjoyment to be derived from work.

The fact that these accounts were delivered in public as part of a commencement address should of course sensitize us to an important feature of such discourse and suggest to us the limits of generalizing too widely from this type of discourse. Public ceremonies such as college commencements are notorious for their rhetoric: the words are so embellished that few listeners would repeat them in other contexts (if they paid attention to them in the first place). Yet these ceremonies play an important cultural role, making explicit many of the higher values on which any society is based, and doing so at a time of transition in people's lives when the usual uncertainties associated with such times evoke rites of passage to instruct people in the roles they should play. An entirely different repertoire of accounts is likely to be drawn on when a recent graduate wakes one morning, still sleepy from the night before, and asks, "Why should I go to work today?" But the words delivered at commencement answer the same question at a broader level and do so in a way that will legitimate work in relation to some of the society's basic values.

We must pay close attention, if we are to understand accounts, to what exactly the speaker in this case is trying to accomplish. The key lies in his assertion, "Since work we must, like breathing in and out, let me share the greatest secret in the world with you. I tell you that good, first-rate work is glory." His account actually begins by acknowledging that work is a necessity. He is not, therefore, attempting (really) to explain why people must work. Rather, his account is concerned with raising that necessity to a higher level—much like Rousseau asserting that everywhere humanity is in chains, and asking, "What can render it legitimate?" The speaker wants his audience not simply to work, but to do "good, first-rate" work. He is concerned with legitimating not the necessity of work but its value, with providing his listeners an account that will encourage an intrinsic commitment to the value of work itself.

Why work?

1. "Good work separates humankind from the beasts."
2. "Good human work puts us all together."
3. "Good work builds."
4. "Good work adds to the sum of humanity."
5. "Good work pays."
6. "Good work makes us matter."
7. "Good work is fun."

These are the essential reasons, given briefly, compactly, with few intervening sentences, and then elaborated and illustrated in the course of the speech.

These reasons provide a legitimate account of work by linking it with widely shared social values and understandings—our humanity, our desire for community, wanting to contribute, and so on. It is important that multiple values are evoked, for different ones may appeal to different listeners, and in combination, their impact is likely to be greater. The embellishments are important too because they turn these abstract values into traditions deeply ingrained in the wider civilization: they include references to the Bible, to Enlightenment thought, to prehistoric man, to the business world, and to such recognizable figures as Beethoven, Michelangelo, and Dr. Martin Luther King.

It is also significant that money is not absent from these accounts but is placed in a proper perspective by the manner in which it is included. The first reference to money follows the speaker's assertion that good work pays: "In money. In the coin of communion. In the currency of satisfaction. It gives us pride in our talent and dedication." The reason for mentioning money at all, it appears, is almost to diminish it by turning it into a metaphor. It is not money as we commonly think of it that provides a reason to do good work; it is the communion and satisfaction. The only other reference to money in the speech is equally brief, and more pointedly negative: "Wealth tyrannizes."

What this case illustrates, then, is how an account that legitimates working may be constructed. The speaker not only presents this account during a rite of passage, but intentionally tries to evoke uncertainty in his listeners by challenging some of their youthful idealism. He then suggests the value of work and provides a virtual laundry list of reasons why it makes sense to hold work as a value. Among these reasons, money itself figures almost insignificantly.

ADDITIONAL CONSIDERATIONS

It should be evident that thinking about work and money in the context of how they are made meaningful and legitimate provides a natural bridge back into the questions of moral discourse that we have considered in previous chapters. If people do not work simply to earn money, but to provide themselves with a legitimate account of who they are and how they are spending their lives, then work and money cannot be considered part of a closed utilitarian system in the way economists have often envisioned it. Work especially must be understood in the context of other values and commitments that color our accounts of it and of ourselves. Insofar as we understand it this way, the kinds of moral discourse in which work was once embedded merit attention once again.

The relevance of moral discourse to considerations of work and money is all the more evident if we also recognize that people not only try to derive meaningful accounts of why they work but refer to their work in giving meaningful accounts of themselves. The simplest way of understanding this dual character of accounts is by observing that they always provide at least an implicit connection between the identity of the speaker and the action under question. Accounts do not provide answers to abstract questions, such as "why is there suffering in the world," or to purely informational questions, such as "how much does this cost," but to questions implying a motivational or volitional involvement on the part of the one being questioned, such as "why did you steal that car." To answer a question of this kind, the speaker must adopt some stance toward the action that either takes responsibility for it or suggests some other identity that separates the action from the actor. The same question can thus be forced more squarely on the speaker by asking "who do you think you are" or "how could you possibly do that." Something as central and as time consuming as work is thus likely to figure importantly in the way in which persons understand themselves. They will in a sense say to themselves, yes, I am a good and decent person because of the work I do, or yes, I am a good and decent person despite the work I do. But answers of this kind also suggest that the relevant frame of reference must include other commitments and facets of the person's identity. Contrary to many bureaucratic conceptions of work—which assume work is conditioned merely by characteristics of the job itself—this perspective, then, suggests that people will weigh the value of their work, and the value of themselves, in relation to a wider set of values, personal obligations, and perceptions of who they are.

If accounts of work bear a close relationship to how we understand the legitimacy of our behavior and of ourselves more generally, these accounts are nevertheless likely to differ depending on the situation that calls our behavior into question. In a useful essay drawing examples mainly from the ways in which people account for their love relationships, sociologist Ann Swidler suggests that accounts, maxims, personal narratives, and other formulaic cultural scripts function as a set of resources on which we can draw when we need to accomplish something in our social relationships.[38] She suggests that people utilize different scripts when their lives are settled than when things are unsettled. Thus, a romantic image of love may serve as the script of choice when people are trying to decide whether to get into or out of a love relationship (unsettled lives), while a more pragmatic orientation may dominate their day-to-day relationships with spouses (settled lives). By the same token, we might expect people's accounts of their work to be different when they are explaining why they chose a certain line of work in the first place (or why they decided to quit their job) from when they are explaining why they work hard or feel motivated on any given Wednesday morning.

The most critical possibility, however, is that people are unable to provide an account in either of these situations that is satisfactory to themselves—or convincing enough to those around them that these people are able to reinforce the speaker's sense that what he or she is doing is right. Under such circumstances, we would expect people either to quit their jobs and look for a different kind of work, if that were possible, or to express dissatisfaction with their work in any of a variety of ways. These might include saying their work was not fulfilling, denying that their work was making a contribution to their sense of personal worth, withdrawing commitment from their work, or feeling that the place of their work in their lives was somehow out of balance. According to this argument, the feelings of pressure, burnout, and overcommitment that many people in our society seem to be experiencing may be as much a result of not being able to give a satisfactory account of what they are doing as it is of economic circumstances themselves.

As one example of this possibility we might consider the extended autobiographical account of a young Wall Street broker presented in Michael Lewis's best-selling book, *Liar's Poker*.[39] Revealing early in the book that his father taught him to believe that how much money a person made was "the measure of a man," Lewis indicates that his own earnings rose within a short period to unbelievable heights, that he enjoyed the power of his position, and that he could have continued advancing rapidly up the corporate ladder. But Lewis also became increasingly dissatisfied with his career and after several years quit to become a journalist. The brevity with which he describes this decision, compared with the facility with language that characterizes the rest of his book, makes us think that part of his decision was simply that he no longer was able to provide himself with a convincing account of what he was doing. Indeed, he states: "Although there were many perfectly plausible reasons to jump ship, I left, I think, more because I didn't need to stay any longer."[40]

The importance of being able to give a legitimate account of ourselves has probably been heightened by the increased discretion to which I referred in chapter 2. At a time when everyone worked long hours simply to earn a subsistence living, and when most people earned their living pretty much in the same way as their ancestors and their neighbors, the need to arrive at an account for oneself was minimized by the fact that people could largely take their work life as a given. The contemporary world gives individuals much greater latitude in choosing their own careers, deciding to change careers, and even determining not to work at all. The postscarcity thesis captures some of why this change is important. But it is less that people are actually beyond working for money than it is that increasing discretion has greatly escalated the level of uncertainty we associate with work. While we may not have to worry about losing our jobs (although many people do), there is a plethora of questions about which career is best for me, whether I am doing what best makes use of my talents, how satisfied I am with my work, and whether I am devoting enough or too much of myself to it. Professions in which there is a high level of identification between the person and the job add to these uncertainties, as does salaried work involving high levels of discretion. The changes that have taken place in recent decades in the economy, such as the growth of new service occupations, and other developments, such as changing conceptions of gender and of family responsibilities, also heighten these uncertainties and thus place added importance on the ability to provide an adequate account of one's activities.

We must also come full circle and acknowledge that the commonsense view with which we began—that people work to make money—is actually less widely shared among specialists concerned with work motivation than is some version of the alternative perspective that I have tried to suggest here.[41] Work-motivation theory has come increasingly to focus on such personal attributes as the desire for personal fulfillment and the need to achieve, and on such environmental characteristics as recognition, support, and freedom to make decisions.[42] In the process, monetary rewards have been deemphasized, sometimes through neglect, but more often because it is assumed these are constrained by profit considerations or by the fact that workers are being paid according to standardized union contracts or as salaried professionals.[43] Money has also been deemphasized because it is taken to be an extrinsic reward and thus of less consequence than rewards more intrinsic to the job itself.[44] What separates most work-motivation theories from the present discussion is their tendency to reify both personal needs and environmental circumstances, regarding them only as realities in their own right, rather than recognizing the importance of speech and social interaction in the construction of these realities.[45] In the one view, manipulating the level of lighting in an office is assumed to have a direct effect on worker productivity; in the other, it is understood to have an effect because it helped supply workers with a new account of what they were doing and why they should be doing it. Nevertheless, the thrust of the present discussion is consistent with current work-motivation theories insofar as both emphasize the complexity of relationships between work and the broader needs, values, interests, and identities of the worker.[46]

The fact that work-motivation specialists have also increasingly recognized the need for meaning and legitimacy provides the critical next step that we must take in order to understand the simultaneous sense of commitment to work and being overburdened by it that we considered in chapter 1. Legitimate accounts of why people should work are not simply created in a vacuum. They are the products of institutions that have a stake in motivating people to work hard. Many of the accounts that we use to make sense of our work are in fact products of the workplace itself. As Marvin Scott and Sanford Lyman observe, "Organizations systematically provide accounts for their members in a variety of situations."[47] To understand why we are so committed to our work, and yet why these commitments are ultimately unsatisfactory, we must examine the ways in which individuals' accounts are influenced by the settings in which they work.

We shall consider how people account for their work in the next chapter, paying particular attention to the ways in which these accounts legitimate both the institutions in which they work and their own commitment to these institutions. Understanding these accounts will help us recognize how much our commitment to jobs and careers depends on wider cultural understandings rather than monetary pressures alone. We shall then be able in subsequent chapters to consider money and material possessions in the same light, asking about the accounts that sustain our commitment in these areas as well.

Chapter Five

ACCOUNTS: THE CHANGING MEANINGS
OF WHITE-COLLAR WORK

W HAT ARE YOU going to do with your life?" We ask this
question of our children and teach them to ask it of themselves. Generally we mean, "What kind of career are you
going to pursue?"[1] During high school or college, a legitimate way to
explain yourself is to say you are studying to become a ———. Later,
when asked who you are, it seems appropriate to respond by giving
your profession or describing the kind of work you do. Having chosen
one career out of the many possible, you also feel compelled to legitimate your choice in some way. The jokester's reply to someone's statement about their career—"Well, it's nasty work but I suppose someone's got to do it"—is funny because it isn't at all how we normally
think. We want to believe our work is something we enjoy doing because it fits our talents, makes a contribution to the world, gives us
freedom, and is a source of personal fulfillment. Being committed to
our work and feeling good about it depends on being able to supply
some account of this kind.

If we are to see how accounts maintain our commitment to our work,
and how they reopen the door to moral considerations, we must think
about where they come from, how they are shaped by the institutions
in which we work, and why they may leave us only partially satisfied.
To answer these questions we need to consider more carefully what
accounts do and listen to some people talking about their work to see
how their accounts are constructed. Doing so will help us understand
why most people feel deeply committed to their work and yet are
somehow able to dissociate it from the other values they hold dear.

We might expect the accounts people come up with to be so diverse
that few generalizations at all could be offered. Certainly corporate cultures vary in terms of the specific stories told about the boss or the
cautionary tales that warn new employees to work hard. But accounts
function in part to alleviate uncertainty, and one of the best ways to
provide certainty is by constructing messages that are familiar from

one setting to another.[2] Listening to people in a wide variety of settings talk about their work reveals that there are in fact some themes that surface again and again. These themes figure as fragments in the accounts people give of their work, demonstrating both the intensity with which most of us are committed to our work and the ways in which this commitment is channeled by the organizations for which we work.[3]

Writer Earl Shorris has suggested that these organizations fundamentally delude us into thinking we are happy when really we are not. "In the modern world," he writes, "a delusion about work and happiness enables people not only to endure oppression but to seek it and to believe that they are happier because of the very work that oppresses them. At the heart of this delusion lies the manager's definition of happiness: sweat and dirty hands signify oppression and a coat and tie signify happiness, freedom and a good life."[4] In short, the workplace provides a "moral home" that governs how people think about themselves.

Perhaps Shorris's assessment is overly harsh, but it has been expressed again and again by contemporary observers. It is one thing, however, to assert that people are shaped by the organizations for which they work; quite another to understand the specific ways in which our accounts reflect these organizations, tie us to them, and limit our moral horizons at the same time.

If there were an X-ray machine that allowed us to see into our souls with perfect clarity, most of us would probably find we are committed to our work for surprisingly complicated reasons (paying the mortgage, pleasing our mothers, getting out of the house). Any of these reasons, not to mention sheer inertia, may be enough to get us going most mornings. But sometimes we need more than that: a story to tell ourselves when things are going bad, an account to give when someone asks, "Why do you do that anyway?"[5]

THE STRENGTH OF WEAK REASONS[6]

Where we would expect to see people's broader values brought into closest connection with their work is in their accounts of how they chose their careers in the first place. Looking at other kinds of accounts, social scientists have concluded that people resort to high-blown arguments more when they are explaining some basic change in their lives than when they are talking about their daily routine. The reason for this seems to be that major decisions in life raise questions about fundamental values. What is the meaning of life? What do I cherish most? When people talk about their marriages, for example, they speak of romance, love, and compatibility to account for their decision to marry. They may speak of mortgages, child care, and inertia when they talk about the more routine aspects of their marriages.[7]

Mark Latham, whom we met in chapter 1, spoke in some detail about why he had chosen a career in high finance. Let us look closely at what he says: "I became involved in the work I'm doing because after being out of school about six months I found that I really didn't know what I wanted to do. I really had no qualifications to do anything. Usually I had just done things because I felt guilty if I was doing nothing." At this point he digresses for a few moments to tell a story about his father. Then he continues: "So I decided that I needed to get a job. I didn't know what I wanted to do. I said well, I'd do anything. So I found out there were a lot of local things going on. They didn't sound interesting. A lot of my friends were doing things in New York, and it just sounded more fun. They were making a fair amount of money. They were enjoying life." Likening a good company to a good school, he says he figured it would be easier to learn new things at a first-rate company. So he sent off his résumé. "I figured what the hell? I got into a program, and I picked the one I thought might compensate me more than the other ones, didn't have to do just one thing, wouldn't be locked into New York, and wouldn't require too much of my time. I figured it wouldn't be my whole life."

There is precious little here about Mark's basic values. We do of course learn by implication that he probably values his free time, having some variety in his life, and the opportunity to have fun. The overriding tone, however, is of a young man with fairly weak reasons for his choice of career. The tone is casual, breezy, detached. His account gives the sense of someone groping in the dark, being pushed at one point by his friends, at another by whatever seemed to be the course of least resistance, and at another by whatever program happened to accept him. If his career choice was a serious decision involving deep reflection on his basic values in life, he certainly fails to say so.

It is possible that Mark Latham is one of those exceptional young people who have so many options open to them that they really do not have to take their choices very seriously. He did have a good college education and he was talented enough, once he embarked on his career, to become enormously successful in just a few years. He may also be a person who enjoys having a good time so much he does not in fact reflect very seriously about his values. So let us consider another example.

Penelope Martin, 28, has worked as a special education teacher in Brooklyn for the past eight years, first in junior high and then in elementary school. During her first year of college she was planning on a career in accounting, so she has thought through a major change in career plans. We know from other things she says that she is a thoughtful person whose parents tried to instill in her a number of important values. Here is how she responded when asked why she had chosen a career in special education.

"I was a terrible student in accounting. I really didn't want accounting, but I didn't know what else to do. I just hated it, it wasn't for me. I decided to try an education course, and I really liked it. I was student teaching around the Brooklyn schools and I just really liked being with the kids. Now, of course, when you're in college they're going to put you in the best schools and make it seem like it's great. Then, my first real teaching experience was in junior high, mostly with delinquents, and I was really turned off to teaching. I thought I'd have a nervous breakdown. It was a shock to go from little gifted students in a head-start program to 17-year-old delinquents. I did that for seven years and then I moved down to elementary school. I used to work part time with brain-injured teenagers. On the weekends we would take them on trips and overnighters. That was fun, I had a good time. About five boys, myself, and another counselor. And we just really got along. We always had a good time."

Perhaps she assumes we can draw our own conclusions about the connection between her value of caring and her work in special education. Her account itself, however, is strikingly silent about this connection. In contrast with Mark Latham's narrative, hers suggests nothing of breeziness, vacillation, or simply doing what happens to be fun. Nevertheless, having a good time is the most recurrent theme in her account. She emphasizes this despite the fact that she nearly had a nervous breakdown. Her account is also more a description of *what* she did than an explanation of why she did it. It emphasizes the chronology of her decisions, showing her being pushed by likes and dislikes, but it does not reveal what influenced these preferences.

Neither of these accounts is entirely typical, but most accounts are similar in not referring explicitly to deeper values. One person spoke of being influenced by her brother. Another described a part-time job that gradually expanded into a full-time business. Some mentioned following in their parents' footsteps; some talked about wanting to pursue something different from their parents. Many emphasized simply being in the right place at the right time.

The most common narratives describe what happened when, rather than discussing the positive and negative considerations that lead people into a particular career. We might call these narratives *process-logic* stories. They essentially show that one thing follows another, taking the speaker through a number of critical turning points, showing that a decision occurs at each point. Process-logic stories are also characterized by the weakness of the reasons that are implied at each stage of the process. As Mark Latham did, many people go out of their way to say they did *not* know what they wanted to do. Like Penelope Martin, they point to likes and dislikes but diminish their importance by describing them simply as times of fun. Others emphasize the role of circumstances, thus denying that they really had a choice to make. Others lighten the weightiness of their decisions by saying they were made suddenly, without much thought. Many people suggest that their career decisions were made with youthful innocence or out of necessity, and these decisions are often described as being of little lasting consequence to what the person really wants out of life.

In the survey it was not possible to tease out such nuanced responses. It was evident, however, that many people believe their careers to have been guided either by circumstances or by such vague considerations that almost any line of work would have sufficed. For example, 41 percent selected the statement "circumstances just led me to it" as one of the most important reasons for getting into their line of work. "Knowing people in this line of work" was selected by 29 percent, and having a "parent or relative in this line of work" was mentioned by 13 percent. Generalized considerations that were frequently selected included "the opportunity to use my talents" (44 percent), "the challenge it presented me" (40 percent), and "wanting to grow as a person" (23 percent). The fact that many more people listed these as important than as decisive reasons is indicative of their weakness, as is the fact that many of these reasons were unrelated to respondents' overall commitment to their work.

Yet we know that people spend most of their waking hours at their jobs, and most people claim their jobs are personally fulfilling. What then is the significance of the weak reasons they give to explain how they chose these jobs? The strength of weak accounts is that they make room, as it were, for other themes that link people more directly to their work, also without raising questions about broader commitments and values. Weak reasons are strong because they seem to explain why someone chose a particular line of work without actually invoking any serious arguments about the nature and meaning of life. By not locating the eventual career decision in a larger web of significance, the narrator is then able to focus entirely on the work itself, letting the accounts voiced within the workplace and about it stand as the reasons for being committed to it. To understand why work is so engaging, and yet so detached from broader moral discourses, then, we need to examine these other, more specialized workplace narratives.

The Wonderful Sameness of Variety

One of the proverbial rewards for studying hard, then working hard, is the chance to move into a more "interesting" career. Especially in the professions people are taught to believe they can work at a more varied pace, do different things from day to day, and cultivate their own diverse interests. In contrast to the negative characterizations that once appeared in such books as *Babbit, White Collar,* and *The Organization Man,* managers have also been groomed to expect more variety in their work. Corporations try to give people command over a wider range of activities, often taking Volvo as their model because of its success in increasing worker satisfaction by altering the assembly process to include a greater variety of tasks. Recruitment brochures serve especially to get the message across that variety is a desirable feature of the working environment.[8]

Variety is in fact something most people say they like about their job. In the survey, for example, 76 percent said the statement "provides a lot of variety" describes their present work very well or fairly well. And those who said this registered significantly higher levels of job satisfaction than those who did not.[9] Equally telling are the spontaneous accounts people give of their jobs. Maxine Weingard, 48, a family therapist in Boston, observes: "I really enjoy my time with my clients.

I enjoy the creativity involved and the process of working with them. And I like the variety. I like the great variety of problems. And also the variety in ages." Other professionals, such as lawyers, doctors, and teachers, also emphasize the variety they experience in their jobs.[10] In other jobs that may seem predictable from the outside, people also emphasize variety. "I can be working on a half-million-dollar deal in the morning and handling a complaint about someone's checking account in the afternoon," explains Harold Bentley, 48, a banker in St. Paul. "It's the variety I like best." Melissa Schneider, 31, a Portland CPA, describes a typical day in similar language: "I guess one of the neat things about being a CPA is that there really isn't a typical day. Each project can be different. It is accounting, so it's typical in that sense. But you could be helping someone with deciding what software to buy, and in order to do that, you have to go out and learn what software's available. I'm doing that right now."

Variety is thus one strand of the rope that ties us so devotedly to our jobs. People who say they have a high degree of variety actually register more commitment to their jobs. In addition to being more satisfied with their work, for example, this group was also significantly more likely than average in the survey to say their work was absolutely essential to their sense of worth as a person and to devote more of their time each week to their jobs.[11]

If variety is something people seize on to explain their commitment to their work, their descriptions reveal it is nevertheless defined within very circumscribed limits. To work in a "varied" role is to have a portfolio of tasks that are still carefully prescribed by the organization for which one works. People also delimit what they mean by variety in the subtle ways they use language. Middle-class people frame their definition of variety by contrasting it with the most boring (often working-class) jobs they can think of.[12] By comparison, their own work seems enormously varied.[13] They contrast their present life with the rigid structure they had to put up with as children.[14] They mention rare instances—the exceptional deal, the unusual client, the business trip—as if to prove their point, but they fail to acknowledge how rare these instances are.[15] They talk about varying the time of their lunch breaks, teaching a new class, or learning a new computer program, but this variety all occurs within basically the same range of activities. They seldom speak of breaking out of this mold and experiencing variety on a totally different scale. In some instances, they admit that the variety they experience is restricted by the organizations for which they work, but they make a virtue of their situation by showing how they have adapted to it.[16]

Variety is thus the spice of life, helping to convince people that their work is really broad enough to fulfill the diverse needs of their complex personalities. Because it occurs within such a narrow range, however, people tend to define it as a virtue in itself, instead of perceiving it as a way of actually realizing other values. No sooner have they touted its importance than they reveal the lingering boredom they experience and the rigid rules to which they conform.[17] Many of them are like Bob Morelli, a New York restaurant manager who finds himself increasingly frustrated as time goes by. He says he likes the variety in his job, but he is beginning to recognize its limits. "After a while, you realize there's only so much variety. When something happens, it turns out to be pretty much the same sort of thing that's happened before."

MASTERS OF CHOICE

Choice is very much a part of the entrepreneurial image that has long been prominent in American culture. Over the years, the quest for freedom in one's work has led people to start their own businesses and to enter professional careers in which they could be their own boss. Observes Long Island shop owner Milt Walker, "I can create my own day. I'm totally my own boss and I dictate to myself what I do." Marcus Friedman, a New Jersey physician who operates his own clinic, says, "It's easier coming to work as your own boss compared with having someone tell you you'd better."[18]

People in less entrepreneurial jobs also say they like them because of opportunities to make their own decisions. What Irvine, California, attorney Steve Smith likes best about his work is the chance to deal with executives at a high level and to make decisions. Negotiating, persuading, analyzing are all important parts of his job. "Actually, what I like the best," he says, "is being the key individual on a transaction—when I'm the point person for the company and the client I represent, when I'm dealing with the other side and constantly having to try to evaluate what the other side is doing and saying, communicating that back to my client, taking my client's needs and communicating that back to the other side in a way that gets where I want to go."

Survey evidence gives some indication of just how widely freedom and choice are either valued or thought to be present in the American workplace. Thirty percent of the workforce listed "freedom to make my own decisions" as one of the important reasons for getting into their line of work, and among professionals and managers this proportion rose to 43 percent. In describing their work, 29 percent say they have a lot of freedom (36 percent among professionals and managers), and 69 percent altogether say a lot of freedom describes their work at least fairly well.[19]

Besides valuing choice for its own sake, people emphasize it as a way to exhibit the power and control they experience in their work. As Steve Smith's remarks suggest, having the capacity to make decisions means a person has earned a certain standing in the social hierarchy, the ability to tell others what to do, or at least not having others tell them what to do. It has to do with what Dr. Friedman calls the "prima donna" style among doctors, or what in his own case he prefers to label merely "a feeling of authority."[20] And the nice thing about this feeling is that it can be experienced at almost any level in the hierarchy.[21]

For the middle class, and for large segments of the working class, the belief that individuals are masters of choice is reinforced by social institutions from childhood on. The education system encourages children to explore a variety of subjects and then pick out a career suitable to their interests. The so-called job market further encourages this mentality: what is a job market, after all, but a kind of giant employment bulletin in which openings are advertised for which qualified individuals may choose to apply? Given adequate economic resources, individuals are then able to shop around, try one thing and then another, until eventually they come up with a job they like. The job they choose, moreover, may be one that has seduced them with messages like "design your own job," "choose what roles you'll play," "carve out your own niche."[22]

In reality, the process of choosing a job is guided by many factors beyond the individual's control. Not every job is listed in the giant employment bulletin, and those that are listed may be too few for the number of available applicants. Training, experience, talent, and luck all play a determining role. Getting a job, it is often observed, may depend more on a happenstance encounter on the street, and on being in the right place at the right time, than on a person's decision to "choose" a particular job. The new recruit who decides to design his or her own job, moreover, is likely to experience the formal limitations of the workplace head-on. In people's accounts of their work, choice is nevertheless a signal factor.

The main corollary of emphasizing choice of course is that work becomes something people do because it is satisfying. Work that people feel they *must* do can be complained about, but work that has been chosen must be described in positive terms. Otherwise, the question that lurks just beneath the surface is, "Well, why don't you switch into something you do like?" The same logic tells people they should be happy from day to day. As a St. Paul elementary school teacher explained, "In education the big buzzword right now is 'shared decision making.' We kind of dictate the situation we're working in. So if it's not good we have nobody to blame but ourselves."

Like variety, choice is not so much a feature of the work itself, however, as it is an account that people construct to show why they are as devoted to their work as they are. These accounts suggest choice in highly formulaic ways. They contrast the present with the past, in terms of both the evolution of an entire profession (such as nursing) and the job changes an individual has made.[23] In their stories, people especially like to show that they have it better than their parents because their parents had no opportunity to make their own choices.[24] They point to small areas of discretion, such as deciding when to take a coffee break, even if the larger work setting provides very little choice at all. When their discretion is limited, they attribute the problem to a temporary change in rules or some rigid individual, rather than the nature of the job itself, and they are optimistic about their chances for improvement and their ability to exercise discretion even in the face of constraint.[25] They also emphasize choice in talking about problem solving. All the problems may be posed by the system itself, but the individual exercises choice in figuring out how to solve those problems.[26]

Believing that work involves choice creates the condition for the problems people experience in limiting their work lives. There is an identification between the active part of people's lives, their decision-making center (what in Freudian terms would be termed their ego), and their work. The boundaries between work and personal life are thus blurred. People do not work simply to make a living, but as a way of fulfilling themselves. It becomes necessary not only to do a good job, but also to give oneself positive messages that the choices one makes are the right ones.

This form of commitment increases the importance of how people feel about their work. Self-reflection is required periodically to determine whether people still like their work. In addition to the physical or mental exertion that work has always required, people are thus placed in the position of having their work put a heavy load on their feelings as well. We must constantly reaffirm our work choices as the right ones by checking in with our feelings to make sure we are experiencing satisfaction and fulfillment.

Emphasizing choice also helps legitimate the organizations for which we work. When self-reflection leads people to ask why they make certain choices, our interviews show, they focus especially on instincts and other innate attributes of themselves.[27] They claim to be guided primarily by their own likes and dislikes, and after that by their talents and interests. The system, in contrast, is largely neutral as a determinant of their choices. It merely presents people with opportunities.[28] Indeed, these opportunities are often depicted as being so tempting that people hardly know which way to turn. The end result is that the system is probably good, at least benign, while people shoulder all the responsibility themselves for making choices that fit their likes and dislikes.[29]

PRIDE OF PERFORMANCE

If there is any single factor that work-motivation experts have championed in recent decades, it is the importance of people taking pride in their work itself. Motivation of this kind, say the experts, counts far more than monetary rewards, fringe benefits, time off, and other extrinsic factors. But, like variety and choice, high performance in the workplace is not just an abstract virtue that people define for themselves. It is channeled by—indeed, it depends on—the nature of the workplace itself. In case after case, people describe their performance not as a matter of achieving some goal they have set for themselves in life, but in narrowly specialized terms. Performance in fact seems to depend on specialization. It is possible to take pride in doing something well because we spend hours and years learning a particular set of tasks. These are the tasks that make up our jobs. They often bear little connection with the wider human values we have also been taught to cherish. Performance thus becomes an end in itself, rather than being part of the quest for beauty, truth, or goodness.

Dorothy Sizinski, 25, a customer service representative for a Los Angeles printing company, demonstrates the ambivalence many people feel when they talk candidly about the pride they take in their jobs. The detail in her responses about her work shows that she is deeply committed to it. She likes the challenges, the variety, and the responsibility. She quickly excuses the competitiveness and aggressiveness she experiences in her co-workers as being necessary to the job. Most of all, she says her work gives her a sense of fulfillment. She likens it to turning in a paper at school and getting a good grade on it. But she also recognizes the limits of this fulfillment. The deeper, more personal fulfillment (which she describes as "spiritual") is nourished by being an achiever but comes largely from other sources. She feels a need to make the world a better place and to serve people in need. She toys sometimes with the view that serving her customers is a way to do this, but she has difficulty drawing a strong connection between selling software manuals and realizing her higher ideals.

It isn't just that specialized expertise is somehow different—or separated—from wider values, though. The language of expert performances subtly transforms other values, turning them into a metaphor that points fundamentally to a different mode of valuation. Trust, for example, may be something valued for its own sake, simply as a feature of desirable human relationships. But in the language of expert performances, trust becomes a by-product of competence. The symmetrical metaphor of human bonding becomes an asymmetrical symbol of power. The human dimension is still there, but it becomes a rhetorical device to show that skills are the most desirable traits of all.

Observe what Stuart Cummings, the Chicago lawyer we met in chapter 1, says about trust: "I like the element of trust that you can build with a client." This sounds like a basic human bond. But without pausing, he continues: "It is very rewarding to have someone want your judgment on something—to want you to review a document and tell them what it means, or to have you tell them how they should handle a particular situation." From trust, the statement quickly moves to professional competence, and from there to power. "It's rewarding to be in charge of a transaction in which thirty people are involved, and you're the one who's scheduling it and coordinating it and getting it done. It's a nice feeling to know that a fifty-million-dollar acquisition of a company was accomplished because you're the one who was driving the ball. It's fun being viewed as a competent person who can get things done."

Performance that depends on doing specialized work also limits the quest for adventure that may be implicit in the yearning people have for variety in their jobs. Such yearning sometimes leads people to switch jobs and enter whole new careers. But the need to perform competently poses a serious check on such wanderings. Banker Harold Bentley explains: "I think everybody thinks about changing jobs, but you have to do what you know how to do best. When you do something else is usually when you get into trouble." Personalizing his observations, he adds, "There are a lot of related businesses I could get into. I don't rule those out. But just because I've been good at one thing doesn't mean I'd be good at something else."

Students of the American economy argue that one reason for its enormous success is that we have indeed championed job performance and found careful ways of measuring and rewarding it. But the ways in which people themselves describe the performance that binds them to their jobs belies this truism. Performance is scarcely part of a carefully calibrated system of means-ends rationality. It depends far more on winning symbolic victories and, perhaps even more than that, on being able to tell stories about these victories.

Laura Miner, a financial aid secretary at a midwestern university, provides a vivid example of the importance of being able to tell stories. She says it would be nice if she got a promotion. But recently she's decided it is better not to expect rewards to be geared closely to how well she does her job. Instead, she says, "I just remember this person that came in the first day and said, 'I have to go home because I can't pay for this; I just don't know what I'm going to do.' Then I said, 'Wait, just a minute; I'm sure we'll find a way.' That gives me a feeling that somebody did appreciate what I was trying to do after all."

If the modern workplace still operates on the basis of rational cost-benefit performance schedules, it has nevertheless become adept at manipulating the performances of its workers in other ways. If workers take pride in winning symbolic victories, then the workplace has been willing to accommodate. It provides ritualized occasions for these victories, giving people the chance to tell their stories. The only catch is that these stories are not entirely up to individuals to create. The workplace tells us at what intervals we must create them, schools us in acceptable scripts, and provides its own storytellers to help us emphasize some parts of the narrative more than others. "Excellent companies," write Thomas J. Peters and Robert H. Waterman, Jr., in their widely read book *In Search of Excellence*, "are unashamed collectors and tellers of stories, of legends and myths in support of their basic beliefs."[30] The workplace also channels our stories by providing us with standard résumés to fill out, by giving us job evaluations at appropriate intervals, and by training supervisors in how to applaud satisfactory performance.

What Pam Jones, 31, an Illinois-based software engineer, says about her job is quite typical, even mundane, and yet it reveals succinctly how much job satisfaction is channeled by the workplace itself: "I come well recommended, people think I do really good work, my supervisor told me that my test plan was the most thorough test plan he'd ever seen. Those kinds of things make me feel really good."

One way in which workplace culture shapes the stories we take pride in telling is simply by supplying a competitive mentality in the first place. Most people do not relish this competition for its own sake, but it provides the occasion, when they may happen to win, for them to tell stories about their symbolic victories. Being forced to engage in competition, they inevitably compare themselves with their co-workers and sometimes are able to accomplish something in a big way. Bigness itself becomes the measure of a good performance. The rationale for telling the story in the first place may be disguised under the rubric of bigness being an opportunity to do a job well, or making the work more interesting. But it is the bigness of the event that demonstrates why a person takes pride in it.

Stanton Haynes, 43, is a partner in a large Philadelphia law firm that specializes in securities litigation. What really draws him deeply to his work, he admits, is winning cases. He is a bit embarrassed to admit it, but the bigger the case, the sweeter it is to win. Although he couches the story he tells in the rhetoric of doing a job well, he clearly relishes the fact that the job was the biggest of its kind: "I like the size of the cases; I have cases that in monetary terms are significant, and because there is so much money involved I can spend adequate time in developing and prosecuting issues. One example would be the Wilkes Bond case where certain nuclear power plants defaulted on their obligations, and we brought in a fault action which resulted in a $750 million recovery—that was the largest case in the history of securities litigation in this country!"[31]

Because the workplace has come to emphasize occasions for storytelling so much, an unintended consequence is that we increasingly view ourselves as the characters in these stories, looking at ourselves more from the outside, as it were, than from the inside. Rather than actually taking pride in our work, we take pride in the fact that we are *viewed* as having done good work. We watch ourselves through a one-way mirror and are most gratified by the way in which other characters respond to that person.

There was a hint of this orientation in the words Stuart Cummings selected earlier to talk about competence. He did not say he enjoyed "being" competent; he said, "It's fun being *viewed* as a competent person." Minneapolis real-estate appraiser Norm Lündstrom, whom we met in chapter 1, makes a similar point in emphasizing how much he enjoys being *told* he is doing a good job. "It's the 'thank you, thank you,'" he says, that gives him the most pleasure. Another person shifted subtly from pride in the task to pride in how she is looked upon: "I like advising people. I like being looked at as an adviser, a counselor. That's a rewarding job."

What this language implies of course is that our accounts do link us with the roles we play and with the expectations of the system in which we play these roles. To be a character in a story may give us some distance from our roles (we apparently take some other stance in order to talk about ourselves). But letting the character take pride in how others respond, rather than from the intrinsic knowledge of having done a job well, is to place ourselves firmly in the grasp of the normative expectations of those around us. Statements that indicate so clearly how we enjoy living up to these expectations are vivid examples of the kinds of accounts we considered in the last chapter. They legitimate our work by providing a connective tissue between ourselves and the social norms of our environment.

Learning a job and doing it well is thus something people admit binds them to their work and makes their work intrinsically meaningful. But pride of performance does not imply that a thankful workforce has simply found a rewarding way in which to realize its deepest values. Instead, the performances in which people take pride have been defined so narrowly as part of the specialized work they do that achievement is largely segregated from their deepest values, becoming an end in itself. Organizations try hard to reinforce this end-in-itself conception and to set the rules by which it is pursued. They probably do this more effectively, our interviews suggest, by providing the larger context in which work is performed than by carefully rewarding specific levels of performance. People take greatest pride in improvising, in telling stories about the one great play they made, and in finding ways to bend the rules. It is as if they are trying hard to make the best of a situation that has largely been defined for them.

THE DEMONS WITHIN

We saw in chapter 1 that stress is widespread in the American workforce. In shouldering the responsibility to choose their jobs, to like them, and to perform well at them, people subject themselves to enormous pressures. The way they handle these pressures is mainly to accept full responsibility for them, thus contributing even further to the stress they experience. People objectify their feelings and focus on them. The formula they seem to live by is, "Don't try to change the situation or talk about external conditions; instead, work hard at managing your internal life, at cooling yourself out so you can keep on functioning."

Attorney Stanton Haynes is an instructive case. In his line of work, scheduling depends almost entirely on the judicial calendar, placing attorneys largely at the mercy of various judges. Because cases may be at various stages simultaneously, including pretrial and injunction hearings, plea bargaining, trial, or appeal, a lawyer sometimes has to work virtually around the clock to keep up. Haynes himself is frequently the victim of this system, the worst time being a recent period of ten days in which he had to work up thirteen depositions. And yet when asked specifically about these pressures, he argues that most of the pressure is "self-imposed."

Haynes's view is widely shared. "Pressure is generally created by the individual" is the way banker Harold Bentley puts it. He believes he alone is responsible for it. He tries to minimize it by "staying organized, making up lists, and doing things by the numbers." "It's all of my own choosing," declares Nancy Earnest, a woman who often puts in twenty-hour days writing advertising copy: "It's self-imposed pressure."[32] "An inner need to do the very best job I can" is the way pollster Daniel Yankelovich describes it, something his surveys show a majority of Americans (52 percent) say they have.[33] Successful people are especially driven by the sense that the pressures they experience are of their own choosing. They regard themselves as perfectionists, competitive, energetic, driven. They work hard because they feel it is just their nature to do so. They identify so closely with their work that having a satisfactory account of themselves requires putting this much pressure on themselves.[34]

In focusing so much on their internal drive to succeed, hard-working people make it seem as if they are entirely the masters of their own destinies. But do they simply make up these accounts from whole cloth, or have they bought into accounts provided them by the institutions in which they work? Much of the sense that pressure comes from within appears to develop through the schooling process. Everyone has experienced the performance-graded rewards, the competition, the recurrent testing, and even the subtle cues in schools that tell children they are worthy if they try hard and do well. It is not just "achievement" as an abstract value that is taught in the classroom. It is the capacity to push yourself, to interpret the pressure placed on you as coming from within instead of from outside, to believe that your successes and failures depend entirely on how much you exert yourself.

When people arrive at the workplace, they already have a strong sense that whatever pressure they experience is more of their own doing than anyone else's. But the workplace accentuates this perception. It provides the occasions for accounts that place the burden of responsibility on their own shoulders.[35] It may also subtly alter the meaning of internalized pressure. In school we basically work for ourselves, for our own improvement, and to create the kind of future we want for ourselves. We may be told on occasion that we need to work hard to make the teacher happy or to keep up the school's reputation in the community, but basically we know we are working for ourselves. In the workplace, however, our work is specifically intended to contribute to the benefit of the institution, helping it invent new products, earn profits, keep its clients from going elsewhere, and so on. But we are so used to the accounts we have learned in school that we fail to acknowledge this reality. Instead, we describe the pressure we feel as our own doing.

All organizations are greedy. Especially when they function in competitive markets, they try to secure as much commitment from their members as possible. Essentially they push us until we, ourselves, decide it is time to set limits on what we do. It is their job to ask, ours to refuse. In a sense, when we argue that our demons are from within, we recognize that it is indeed our job to refuse. The only problem is that most people do not carry their sense of responsibility this far. Instead

of recognizing the organizational sources of their feelings, they con-
clude that the feelings themselves are the problem, so they should
work on controlling or eradicating these feelings. They do not take the
feelings as an indication that it is time to say "no."

Pam Jones, the software engineer, reveals clearly how much the organizations in which we work can heighten the internalized pressures
we put on ourselves, and yet how hard it is for us to resist these pressures. Like most employees, she meets with her boss periodically for
feedback and evaluation. At each "priority feedback session" (PFS),
Pam's boss would try to help her set goals for herself by making suggestions and by determining if the energy expended over the past few
weeks had achieved the desired results. Innocent enough. But certainly
an important way in which Pam's own accounts of her work were
shaped to correspond with what the organization wanted her to accomplish. After a while Pam started calling them PMS, instead of PFS,
sessions because they always made her nervous, irritable, and upset.
"It was almost like going into confession," Pam recalls. "You'd know
that he'd think you hadn't achieved as much as he thought you were
going to achieve." She worried and worried trying to figure out what
the problem was. Blaming herself, she decided she was probably just a
perfectionist whose pattern was to feel pushed from within.

Only later did it dawn on Pam that everyone felt the same way
around her supervisor, leading her to recognize that he was adeptly
manipulating the pressure she was putting on herself. She also realized
that she had been trying to please him the same way she had her professors in college. Whereas they set limited workloads before her,
though, her current boss seemed always to expect more. She had been
out of college ten years when she finally realized, "No, he'll keep load-
ing me up with stuff until I say no! No! I hadn't realized it before, but
that was my job, to say no to him."

What makes it so hard for people to learn to say no is that the way we
talk about internalized pressure turns it into a higher morality. We do
not regard internalized pressure simply as different from organizational pressure; we regard it as better, more pure, ideal. Organizational
pressure seems petty, concerned with office politics and personalities,
whereas the demons within drive us to fulfill and improve ourselves
and indeed to get the job done in the most efficient way possible.[36] The
language we use has an anti-organizational tone that reflects the larger
negative sentiments we still harbor toward bureaucracies. Responding

to our own demons is better because at least these are the demons we have chosen. They connote our individuality; they represent promptings from our true selves. Thus it is not just the boss to whom we have to say no; it is something deep within ourselves that we have to train to speak in a different way.

Because they are internal, the demons guiding us have a powerful hold over us for several other reasons as well. One is that the standards they set may be so high as to be virtually unattainable. We may literally work ourselves to death trying. Another is that their voices speak in monologic tones, never subject to the counsel of others. What they require is ambiguous, consistent with the demand that we make our own choices, but still making it difficult to know when enough is enough. For people in jobs that actually involve a high level of ambiguity, the voice of these demons only adds to the uncertainty that enough may not be enough after all.[37] Their counsel is also unrelenting. Unlike the periodic review, they cannot be anticipated or forgotten. They may lurch at you in the middle of the night.

Dan Duryea, 29, works as a professional investor in Philadelphia. He acknowledges that there is an enormous amount of pressure in his line of work. Seeing it as entirely self-imposed, he is nevertheless candid about the reasons why it has such a hold on him: "I happen to be an individual who probably sets unrealistic or very challenging criteria to achieve." He describes the internal pressure as "fighting with yourself about what is it you're really capable of, can you live up to your own expectations, can you fulfill those responsibilities?" He recognizes these are not just questions about his work, but about an image of himself that he has created. "That's probably the greatest pressure." It is at least the most difficult to escape. "You don't go sit down with your boss and get a review. You sit down with yourself and review yourself, which may be at two o'clock in the morning, right when you don't want to be doing it."

It is probably fortunate that growing numbers of people are beginning to realize that the pressure they put on themselves is not entirely self inflicted. After a time, it becomes an expectation, a feature of their work, perhaps even a by-product of the success they have achieved. When the demons speak to them in the middle of night, these people are questioning whether these voices are entirely of their own creation or whether they represent pressures built into the structure of work itself.

Lawyer Stuart Cummings is one of the people who has begun asking these questions in recent years. "There's constant pressure," he admits. "When you're on the line over three months to get that fifty-million-dollar deal done, all everyone's going to know is whether or not you did it or not. And it's pressure that—I've used Rolaids over the last few years, which I never did before. And it is difficult to keep everything in perspective when there's that much pressure on you. It sometimes does not seem right. It does not seem consistent with the life I want to lead. I wake up at three in the morning worried about, oh, did we get that document filed, or oh, I've got to remember to talk to so-and-so tomorrow. That kind of pressure does not seem entirely healthy and is not really consistent with how I'd like to have my life structured."

THE MEANING OF SUCCESS

Striving for success has long been considered the primary reason why people devote themselves so wholeheartedly to their work. In the legends most of us learn as children, success is the reward of hard work. Like the rags-to-riches heroes popularized by Horatio Alger at the end of the last century, the heroes of today are admired because they have risen from obscurity to be corporation presidents, self-made millionaires, highly paid professional athletes, and movie stars.[38] It is still very much part of the American Dream to think that anyone who really wants to can climb the ladder of success. In survey after survey, people list the chance for advancement as one of the things they most desire in a job.[39] As we might well expect, sensing that possibilities for advancement are present is also closely associated with higher levels of job satisfaction.[40]

Organizations of course create incentive systems to encourage people to pursue success. Few words appear more often in corporate recruitment brochures than success and its synonyms—advancement, recognition, excellence, superiority, growth. The ladder that people are expected to climb is seldom distinguishable from the corporate hierarchy or the standards of success prescribed by particular professions. This does not mean that the old-fashioned ideal of attaining success simply by working hard and living right is still assumed to prevail. People in the modern workplace may recognize that being an adroit manipulator of people, a good talker, and a clever office politician may count most. The assumption nevertheless is that finding the key to success is uppermost in people's minds.[41] Understanding why people may become so committed to their work that they have trouble finding a place in their lives for other values, therefore, requires us to look closely at the role of success.

People seldom talk very long about their work without finding some way to mention success. Some people exemplify the success ethic in all its traditional trappings, talking about how they saw possibilities for upward mobility in the organization that hired them, discussing their climb up the corporate ladder, or revealing their desire for promotions or recognition. A lyricist in her early twenties who said she would like to be the "white Tracy Chapman," for example, admitted she would give almost anything to get her music before the public. She has considered sending it to someone like Prince or Sinead O'Connor. "I just wish someone out there would give me a chance," she says. Her view is most often shared by people who do not have organizational contexts in which to locate themselves or who (academics and writers are good examples) depend heavily on gaining individual reputations. Entrepreneurs and self-employed businesspeople are also among those who sometimes talk openly about individual success and failure. Brad Diggins, the travel agency owner, for example, says of his failures and successes, "I have nobody to blame but myself, because I have created the atmosphere, educated my staff, and taught them to reflect the image of the company." And yet when most people talk about success, they describe it quite differently from the way it has been depicted in the past.

As conventionally defined (creating wealth, winning in some competitive game, moving up in the world, doing something well), success appears to have shifted almost completely away from the individual. These meanings are still voiced frequently as people talk about their work, but they are used to describe *organizations* rather than individuals. A woman who works as a drug prevention counselor, for example, talks about her organization's success relative to similar programs. A man in broadcasting talks about why some communications schools are more successful in training students than others. A management consultant describes the strategies different companies use to gain success in selling their products.

It is understandable that these conventional meanings of success should be more closely associated with organizations than with individuals. Organizations have become the primary actors in the economic arena. Advertising campaigns describe the products of IBM,

Toyota, and General Foods, not the work of craftsperson X or Y. Even the "stars" whose success is still associated with individual performances are publicly described as being members of a certain athletic team, products of a public relations firm, or creations of the film industry.

The traditional view of success has also been redefined by the rise of the so-called service ethic.[42] People who admit being interested in success are much more willing to talk about it in terms of helping someone else be successful than in terms of advancing themselves. This view of success is especially evident among people who actually work in the helping professions. Teachers, therapists, and social workers, for example, all talk about the gratification they receive from seeing a student or a client become successful. People in managerial positions, though, often use the same language. A sales manager for a computer company, for example, says he likes it when he is able to make his customers look good because that helps them to advance in their own companies. By implication, people who help others succeed are also successful themselves. But service success is radically different from the self-made individual who rises simply by dint of his or her own wits and hard work. People who admit they are interested in success are also quick to say how this interest is tempered by other considerations. Being "on the make" is too blatant to be socially acceptable, so people tone it down by emphasizing some of the other themes we have considered. People are especially likely to subjectivize their definitions of success—and indeed the entire decision-making process—as a way of taking the rough edges off their accounts. A nurse in her mid-fifties who works in a supervisory capacity as a clinical evaluator in a New York hospital, for example, says she took the job because she was interested in professional advancement. Having said this, though, she immediately backpedals: "I guess I considered professional advancement as a constellation of factors. The position had to feel right for me. I had to be very interested in it. I had to feel that it wasn't just the right move, but that I would feel comfortable working with these colleagues." In emphasizing her own feelings, she thus gives the impression that professional advancement is not so much achieving standing in the profession itself, but doing something that she herself could consider important and worthwhile.

As this example suggests, the meaning of success has been greatly influenced by the turn inward that we have observed in people's views of performance and the demons that drive them to work hard. An elementary schoolteacher, for instance, says she generally feels successful at work, but she describes success as an "inner glow." She does not associate it with promotions or pay raises. A physician who runs a highly successful family practice refers to his interest in success obliquely in arguing that schools need to teach young people how to be successful. But what they should teach, he says, is "being happy, being loved, getting love, understanding God."

For most people, success is some combination of internal and externally defined standards.[43] They recognize that the environment in which they work encourages success, but the ladder they themselves climb is in considerable measure subjective. Consequently, they can experience ascent whether they receive pay raises, job promotions, and accolades from the boss or not. When these external rewards are in scarce supply, it is especially valuable that people can still feel they are making progress. This perception of success also strengthens the tie between individuals and their work. Having defined success for themselves, they can move up the ladder because they *want to*, not because they are being pushed and prodded by other people.

Consistent with this emphasis on subjective definitions, people also complain about external standards of success that their organizations try to impose on them. Real-estate appraiser Norm Lundström complains, for example, "My work requires me to measure everything in money. It bothers me that a lot of people I work with want everything to be measured in money. It's greed—needing and wanting and desiring and working for money. Sometimes I wish we could do things without money being involved, like live!" Brenda Kane, a history professor who recently received her Ph.D. degree from Harvard, observes a similar corrupting of basic human values in the academic world. Here, instead of money, intellectual snobbery becomes the name of the game. "It flows over in terms of how you deal with people," she admits. From being critical of ideas it is only a small step to "being short with people, being curt, and more quick to judge people on an intellectual basis. You say, 'Oh, that's a stupid argument,' and you write them off. It's horrible."

There is also a notable tendency to criticize the entire emphasis American culture places on success. A Nashville music publisher, for example, notes that he and his partner have enjoyed considerable success in the popular music world during the past five years, but the main lesson he has learned, he says, is that he does not like himself as well because he is compromising the kind of music he values most. A man in his sixties who has made a fortune managing various businesses in the entertainment world says he knows many people who epitomize the success ethic. But they repulse him because they see people as "expendable and usable." He believes this is too high a price to pay for success.

Other people admit they were interested in success when they were younger but say they now believe there are more important reasons to work hard. Teri Silver, the former Drexel Burnham systems analyst, says she always considered job openings in terms of "room for advancement," but now that she is approaching her thirtieth birthday she is more reflective. She says she has been thinking a lot more seriously about "where am I going" and "what do I want to do with my life." Sometimes these disclaimers come from people who are having to cope with not being as successful as they had hoped to be.[44] Just as evident, though, are highly successful people who believe success is no longer as important as it once was. For example, a man in his early forties who has achieved considerable success as a writer, editor, and publisher laments, "When I was growing up, it was extremely important to be successful in my studies and in other things. I didn't feel valued as a human being." He says he wants to provide a different kind of example for his own children.

Much has also been made of the language of games to describe the way in which Americans currently think about success. According to some analysts, success can no longer be defined in absolute terms, such as becoming a millionaire or finding a cure for cancer, so people contextualize it, likening themselves to players in a game. This metaphor emphasizes competition, encourages people to play hard, perhaps even gives them some tangible sense of winning, but ultimately demeans success by turning it into something played largely for its own sake instead of to achieve higher aims in life. The game mentality is thus a key to understanding how people can be committed to their work without associating it with their broader values.

When people discuss their work, they do sometimes talk about games. Their language, however, nearly always describes games in negative terms. A dentist, for example, looks back at the struggle he had to get into dental school and describes it as "a game I had to play." A young businesswoman who burned out at her job and quit says she was sometimes able to keep herself going by "making up games," but these did not keep her satisfied very long. A salesman says he can stand being rejected because "it's just part of the game." But he also realizes thinking of his work as a game is a defense mechanism that he would rather do without. Others talk about having to play "social games" or complain of the games their supervisors play, and a number of people explain career changes by saying they did not like playing the games they had to in their previous jobs.[45]

On balance, then, conventional views of success figure surprisingly little in the accounts people give of why they are committed to their work. This conclusion may appear contradictory to the fact that so many people in opinion surveys say promotions and advancement are important. It is nevertheless consistent with the *relative* importance people attach to these job characteristics. In one national study, for example, "chances for promotion" ranked third from the bottom in a list of sixteen characteristics people were asked to evaluate.[46] In my own survey, it ranked eighth (out of ten) as an important reason for getting into one's line of work.[47] This does not of course mean that success is unimportant in absolute terms. Like money, it probably is one of the background conditions that helps keep people tethered to their jobs.[48] The fact that people are virtually silent about it, at least as conventionally defined, though, is significant in itself. People do not want to feel they are driven by forces that may be beyond their control, such as an eventual promotion or pay raise. They want even less to think they are simply part of the vulgar, success-driven culture they read about in the newspapers. Instead, they define their own standards of success and associate these with features of their work, such as service to others or feeling good about themselves. This way of defining success allows some people to bring their wider values to bear on how they think about their work. For many, however, internally defined success is still very much an end in itself. It defines a relationship between persons and their jobs yet provides little in the way of language to talk about the wider commitments in which that relationship is situated.

WORK WITH A HUMAN FACE

To hear most people tell it, the best thing about their work is that it resembles the cozy, hearth-lit general store depicted in a Norman Rockwell painting. Contrary to what critics have said, the modern workplace is apparently not a vast bureaucracy with mindless drones chewing up paper in their respective cubbyholes. No matter how large their organization may be, people insist they work in a warm, congenial environment. The human touch is so much in evidence that they like their work and feel deeply committed to it.

In the folklore of American corporations, increasing importance has indeed been placed on turning the workplace into a family-like atmosphere. "Companies are coming back to the family thing," says Mel Thompson, a businessman whose work takes him to dozens of major companies both in the United States and abroad each year. He says the idea is to acquaint employees with each other's personal habits so they can work together more effectively. Company parties, monthly picnics, and activities that bring workers' families to the office are being initiated for this purpose. Managers believe that making people feel more at home, Thompson explains, enables them to feel freer about making suggestions, increases their loyalty to the organization, and makes work more enjoyable overall. He thinks American companies have been influenced to move increasingly in this direction because of Japanese competition. "The Japanese have forced a lot down our throats, which at the beginning I thought was bad," he admits, "but now I think it's the best thing that's ever happened."

Thompson's view appears to be widely shared. In the extensive interviews conducted among top brass of "America's best-run corporations," Peters and Waterman discovered frequent attempts to depict these organizations as "extended families." Mega-bureaucracies such as IBM, Wal-Mart, McDonald's, Delta Airlines, Hewlett Packard, Kodak, and Procter & Gamble all insisted they functioned more like the local neighborhood picnic than billion-dollar enterprises.[49] People in other settings often express the same view.

"The atmosphere here is very collegial," says Stanton Haynes. The law firm he works for includes more than forty partners, fifteen paralegals, and seventy-five support staffers. But in his view it still functions like an intimate family: "We're all on a first-name basis and anybody in the firm is free to ask anybody else in the firm for advice or contribute their thoughts." Harold Bentley works for an interstate banking firm that operates thirty-two branch offices in the Twin Cities area alone. His company does not seem like a huge bureaucracy to him either. He describes it more as a family. "You don't treat people so much as employees as you do as co-workers, and you develop the small family ties and, yes, I know who their kids are and who their wives are."

How can people who work in large bureaucracies maintain the belief that their organizations are like families? By focusing on the few individuals who happen to treat them right, while ignoring the larger and more impersonal hierarchy in which they work. They become "local" in their thinking, as it were, much in the same way that people who live in vast urban jungles manage to block out the impersonality and anonymity of these places by huddling together with a few of their closest friends. Sheathed in the protective safety of their own enclave, they feel more powerful than if they had to confront the entire world.

Dorothy Sizinski recognizes that the printing company she works for is a large, well-established firm that puts its employees under a lot of stress and requires them to be "high-power individuals" if they are going to survive. But she is able to block out much of that pressure by focusing on her own immediate department. "Fortunately, I work with people that understand that it is high stress and can break the tension with humor. It's a team atmosphere. No one ever feels out on a limb. We all kind of run it. If we want to make changes, we can make changes."[50]

As they do in other kinds of accounts, people also put a human face on their work environment by telling exemplary, ritualized stories. These stories focus so much on exceptional episodes that they turn life into a succession of crises and celebrations rather than the daily routine of which most of it consists. Stuart Cummings, for example, says the lawyers in his firm are strong, competitive individualists who look out for themselves and get their work done. But he hastens to add that they "are also supportive and are genuinely happy for you when something happens positively in your life." He is convinced the people he works with care about him as a person. What makes him think so? He tells a story: "My uncle seemed to be sick with some sort of cancer a couple of years ago, and one of my senior partners who was chairman of the Board of Trustees at the University of Chicago Hospital went to bat for us. There were no holds barred in lining up the best doctors available immediately to help my uncle." It was a rare case, but Stuart is quick to generalize from it: "I know that if I ask my partners to help me out in a pinch, they would be more than glad to help me out."[51]

These stories stand out in people's memories only partly because they stem from crisis events. They also become part of the corporate culture of the workplace. People tell them to their co-workers because this is the way things are *supposed* to be. Bosses want to think their employees are part of a satisfied little family. Management mythology emphasizes a connection between warmth and productivity. Management experts insist this is indeed the way it should be. As one consultant explains, "Effective organization design has to do with love and respect for people no matter where they stand in the hierarchy; organizations that are able to do that do magical things, really exciting things."[52]

Companies often try to project this image directly to their employees. Peters and Waterman, for example, found frequent mention of it in corporations' annual reports. The family image may also be projected in advertising and in recruiting brochures. It is likely to be communicated by personnel managers who carefully evoke pledges of loyalty from employees and repeat these pledges in initiation rites involving new recruits. As the personnel manager of a large California department-store chain observes, "In the training I do, I emphasize that you're not a number here, people know you by name. There are a lot of companies out there that really don't care about you that much. You're there to make money for them and that's all."

The mom-and-pop image also helps people believe their work makes a difference. The service ethic is often at odds with other requirements of the workplace, particularly its need for bottom-line efficiency. Just how much customers and clients have actually been helped is often difficult to measure as well. But holding forth exemplary cases of people being helped is a way of demonstrating that our work indeed has a human face. If we have invested something of ourselves, and if we know our coworkers well enough to sense that their motives are pure, then so much the better.

When people feel their work is part of a *human* enterprise, rather than just a cold bureaucracy, they generally do feel better about themselves. They work harder and commit more of their personal identity to their place of work. This is in part because the mom-and-pop image helps overcome the sense of inauthenticity that has become such a feature of the marketplace. The feeling that one cannot truly be who one is has been reinforced by the salesperson motif and by the glitzy, "image is everything" character of advertising and the mass media. People feel that selling themselves in the marketplace requires them to put up a false front. But most people insist they do not really have to sell themselves. The warm atmosphere in which they work allows them to be themselves. They feel authentic because the workplace draws in more of their personal talents, traits, and peculiarities.

Like other themes, then, work with a human face is an account that helps people explain why they feel committed to their work. It shows that work ultimately cannot be compartmentalized in an economic category operating according to its own laws. Even when people talk only about their work, they invoke implicit assumptions about themselves and their lives. The workplace channels these accounts, helping people to focus on the few people who treat them with respect, rather than the bureaucracy that knows them only by number, providing ritual occasions for telling stories about caring, and integrating family and service orientations into corporate mythology. The commitment that results is thus a connection between work and *self*, not simply a type of role behavior. When intimacy, warmth, and family can all be experienced at work, little reason exists for people to set limits on that part of their lives. Yet, in reality, people lead richer lives and have deeper needs than these workplace definitions of the self are able to fulfill.

PUTTING IT ALL TOGETHER

On the whole, the accounts people give of their work reveal that it is, in most cases, meaningful to them. The reason they feel committed to their work and expend so much energy on it is that they feel right about it, and it in turn makes them feel right about themselves. Everybody has moments of doubt when they wonder if they are pursuing the right career, and they know their current job is by no means perfect. Being able to tell stories to themselves and to their acquaintances, however, sustains them from day to day. We fail to understand the significance of these accounts if we assume, as much of the published literature does, that people somehow start out their adult lives with a certain set of values, search the labor markets until they find some line of work consistent with these values, and then live happily ever after.

Staying committed to one's work is an ongoing process (which is why people burn out, become discouraged, and make career changes). What sustains commitment in this ongoing way is not so much the monthly paycheck or the annual promotion, but the ability to call up stories about why we are doing what we do. These stories forge links between our work and our personal lives, our biographies, including especially our sense of who we are and where our talents lie.

They may do so in quite selective ways, showing how one side of our selves is reflected in one aspect of our work. Countering this tendency toward narrowness, however, our accounts also emphasize the great variety we experience in our work. By implication, they suggest that our work is as rich as a full conception of our total personality would require. In this sense, the very narrowness of our specialized jobs is the reason we emphasize variety as much as we do.

Our stories also legitimate the work we do and our conceptions of ourselves by emphasizing the active, willful role we play in deciding how best to accomplish it. A self is many things, not the least of which are those supposedly innate traits and dispositions over which we have little control. Were we simply to emphasize those characteristics, we might view our work as a kind of destiny to which we needed merely to resign ourselves. By emphasizing the ongoing reality of choice in our work, we force ourselves, as it were, to accept responsibility for its meaning and value.

Doing the job well may also be regarded as nothing more than living out the perfectionism of our parents, or doing what we must in order to stay employed. Talking about the feelings of accomplishment we derive from our work, though, is a way of saying that it does contribute to our sense of being good, decent, worthy individuals. The self not only gives of itself (in the sense of expending energy), but receives as a result of the work it does.

When we describe our compulsion to do well as an inner voice, we merely complete the circle, showing that we are responding to more than external conditions. These voices, as our interviews have indicated, rise up, not just from the surface promptings of our conscience, but from *deep* within ourselves. People describe them as long-standing, enduring voices that they have known all their lives, as voices powerful enough to awaken them in the middle of the night, even as voices they sometimes wish they could escape.

How all this emphasis in our accounts on the role of the self can be reconciled with the fact that we actually work in complex organizations that present us with so many things not of our own choosing is a significant question. We resolve this problem by creating a kind of interpersonal space within these complex working environments. People recognize the structures and norms that govern their places of employment but speak of them in remote, abstract terms. The perceptual space in which they actually work appears to be a kind of antistructure—what anthropologist Victor Turner has called "communitas"—peopled by warm, caring individuals who get along well with each other, and who often get the job done *despite*, rather than because of, the larger structures in which they work.[53] Not surprisingly, people give negative affect to these larger structures, compared with the positive affect they associate with their immediate communitas.

What they especially dislike, to the point that it often figures in accounts of job switching, is someone in this immediate space who violates its human qualities. Co-workers who act like "snots," as one woman put it, or who compete too aggressively, and supervisors who do not share the values of their workers are frequently cited examples. Even when such negative presences are part of the communitas, though, workers are often able to retain their sense of the essential humanness of this space by attributing problems to personality deficits or to external pressures.

Within this human space, workers are thus able to feel that they themselves are able to act as complete persons, rather than simply having to act out a role. Being able to do so is consistent with their sense of being in control, of listening to their own voices, and of being persons who are doing the right thing.

WHEN E. F. HUTTON SPEAKS

The greatest irony of the savings-and-loan scandals of 1989 and 1990 is that E. F. Hutton kept its morally bankrupt empire alive by running frequent television commercials announcing to the world that when it spoke, people listened. But the commercial should have given the public a clue to the vacuity of the empire they were being asked to trust. For when people turned to listen, the commercial went silent.

The same is true of the accounts people give of their economic behavior. More can often be learned from their silence than from what they say. People believe that what is best for them is best for everybody. They do not see themselves as greedy and ruthless, or even as overly aggressive and ambitious. They see themselves as caring, responsible individuals, pursuing the good life simply by working hard, doing their best, and enjoying the choices set before them. But listening closely to their accounts, as we have tried to do in this chapter, reveals that the stories they tell follow certain formulaic patterns. They depict variety, choice, achievement, responsibility, and even caring, but in ways that reflect workplace definitions of these values. Little is said about broader horizons, wider varieties of choice, deeper meanings of human achievement, or the ways in which economic institutions delimit the actions of caring individuals.

Best-selling books written for aspiring corporate moguls have come increasingly in recent years to emphasize values. It may be that these books will effect a new managerial revolution that overcomes the present separation between work and broader human values. More likely, however, is the possibility that middle-level bureaucrats will simply become more adept at manipulating corporate cultures to give the *appearance* of talking about values when the real message is still silence. One can wade through much hyperbole about "values and beliefs" in a book like Peters and Waterman's, for example, before finding any substantive definition of what these values and beliefs might be. When one is finally presented, moreover, it sounds strikingly similar to the well-bounded workplace accounts we have just considered. Being the best, taking pride in executing high-quality work, stimulating internalized individual motivation, promoting informal communication in the office, providing for variety and creativity—these are the "basic values" from which people are supposed to find meaning and purpose for their lives.[54]

People are also silent about how they set limits on their work. So much of what they say focuses on the relationship between what they do and their inner selves that their accounts do not lead to statements about obligations toward family or community that might limit their work by setting it in a larger context. The fact that work traits translate so subtly into personality characteristics also makes it hard for people to say how their work may *not* nourish other parts of their selves. People do have ways, as we shall see in later chapters, of limiting their work commitments. Their inability to integrate these other commitments into their accounts of work itself, however, is often a source of the stress, guilt, and ambivalence that accompanies the otherwise positive feelings they have about their jobs.[55]

The irony in all this is that American capitalism sustains itself as much (if not more) through its culture as it does through its economic functions. Despite the fact that critics and defenders alike have focused on its capacity to generate profits and to lure workers economically, it is the accounts capitalism provides that serve as its most powerful tools. They tell us that working hard is a good thing because it brings variety to our lives and lets us exercise choice, even if this variety and choice amount to very little in the wider scheme of things. Our accounts provide us with symbolic victories in which we take pride, even if the occasion for these victories is carefully orchestrated and interpreted by the organizations for which we work. When pressures mount, we do not try to change the conditions of our work; we try to change ourselves, taking responsibility for our feelings, telling ourselves that the trouble lies within. In consequence, capitalism functions less as a taskmaster, forcing us to do something we would rather not, and more as an alluring siren, compelling us with stories of its wonders and its irresistible charms.

Capitalism certainly renews itself by generating profits. It sustains itself, as observers point out, by establishing bureaucratic norms to which people feel compelled to conform—norms of dress, corporate etiquette, teamwork, self control, and public propriety. Much deeper than these norms, however, are the legitimating accounts that tell us *why* it is good to be committed to our work. These accounts are cultural constructions—stories we find printed in the schoolbooks we read, voiced in the organizations for which we work, and eventually repeated in the echo chambers of our own minds. Insofar as they invoke fundamental definitions of reality, insofar as they suggest conceptions of the good, insofar as they tell us how to behave—they are fundamentally *moral* rather than economic. Yet they have been appropriated and shaped by economic institutions to the point that they seldom show any connection to the larger moral traditions that make up our cultural birthright.

Chapter Six

(NOT) TALKING ABOUT MONEY:

THE SOCIAL SOURCES AND PERSONAL

CONSEQUENCES OF SUBJECTIVIZATION

ONEY IS ONE of our deepest passions. Loved, sought after, sometimes ridiculed and despised, it has always been considered fundamental to the lives of individuals and of societies. Following customs nearly three millennia old, printed currencies carry the faces of public figures who symbolize the commonweal. The great age of exploration that led to the founding of our own nation was prompted in no small measure by the belief that bullion and power went hand in hand. Even the radical social reformers of the nineteenth century, so often critical of the economic arrangements of their day, believed money to be a singular force in the shaping of modern life. Shakespeare had written that it would "lug your priests and servants from your sides [and] pluck stout men's pillows from below their heads." But it was Marx who quoted these lines in support of his own argument that money was the quintessential "omnipotent being."[1]

The view that money marches through history of its own accord, "tempting the soul" with its innocence and simplicity (as sociologist Georg Simmel once declared), has been widely challenged in recent years.[2] Realizing that money is too important to be left entirely to economists, scholars in sociology, anthropology, and history have begun to examine the cultural meanings of money.[3] In the current view, society exerts a reciprocal influence on money, rather than being shaped only by the all-transforming power of money itself. Moral, social, and religious values all need to be considered. My colleague Viviana Zelizer, for example, has shown that "special monies" such as household pin money and children's allowances have often carried quite different meanings from the currencies of the wider marketplace.[4]

The recent view is a much-needed corrective to simplistic economic thinking about money, but in trying to relate money more closely with cultural understandings some interpreters lose sight of one of the vital contributions of the earlier work. In the writings of Marx, Simmel, and others of their day, the essential *conflict* between money and other human values was always emphasized. Zelizer in fact summarizes these arguments in a way that illustrates how strongly this conflict was emphasized: "A sharp dichotomy is established between money and nonpecuniary values. Money in modern society is defined as essentially profane and utilitarian in contrast to noninstrumental values. Money is qualitatively neutral; personal, social, and sacred values are qualitatively distinct, unexchangeable, and indivisible."[5]

We must retain this insight and try to understand better how it contributes to our present predicament. It is not enough to recognize that money takes on different meanings in different situations. Anyone can plainly see that a dollar placed in the offering plate Sunday morning means something different from one placed on the horses Saturday night. Nothing of great importance derives from this insight. Why a fundamental dichotomy exists in our culture between money and nonpecuniary values is a far more troubling question. It goes to the heart of the problems we face in relating our economic commitments to the other parts of our lives.

Once this question is taken seriously, the newer perspectives on money can prove enormously helpful in directing our thinking toward creative solutions. The political economists of the nineteenth century largely assumed that money was distinguishable from other values because of some intrinsic property of money itself. They advanced arguments about its inherent neutrality with respect to its uses, the significance of its divisibility in quantitative gradations, and its seeming tendency to reproduce itself. The newer perspectives require us to think of money as a product of culture. Why it is separated from other human values is, in this view, a function of the cultural patterns that shape our thinking. To understand these patterns we must pry into some of our most commonsensical, widely taken-for-granted assumptions about money.

The nineteenth-century writers who criticized the social role of money made another significant contribution that should remain in the forefront of our thinking. Zelizer also provides a succinct summary of this argument: "Monetary concerns are seen as constantly enlarging, quantifying, and often corrupting all areas of life."[6] This too is a tendency that rings true in the experience of many Americans. They feel constantly pressured by the need for money, by rising prices, and by their own desire to have more money than they do. But why? Is it just the so-called spiral of inflation that causes this pressure? Does money contain a hidden energy that causes it inexorably to expand? Or does its enlargement and corrosiveness depend in some way on how our culture encourages us to think about money?

THE AMERICAN TABOO

Anthropologists have long recognized that a key to understanding cultural systems is to focus on those things that are considered taboo. First brought to the attention of Europeans by Captain James Cook's observations of Polynesian rules against touching the dead, taboo has gradually come to be recognized as a feature of all societies. It is associated with something so sacred, so powerful, that to touch it or even to talk about it is to expose oneself to considerable danger. The taboos among the ancient Israelites against entering the Holy of Holies, touching the Ark of the Covenant, or uttering the name of Y—H provide vivid examples. Freud's contention that taboos are the public manifestation of deep-seated psychological repression and anxiety also merits serious, if qualified, consideration.[7] The Victorian taboo on public discussions of sexuality (giving rise to many of Freud's own contributions) is perhaps the most frequently cited example. Of significance, too, are numerous studies pointing to the *positive* role played by taboo in maintaining the status quo of established social patterns.[8]

Over the past century countless taboos, once guarding features of American life deemed too inviolable even to be discussed, have been exposed and shattered. Victorian prohibitions against sexuality have been replaced by candid educational, commercial, and artistic portrayals of nearly all aspects of this topic. Taboos that once made it virtually impossible for persons of one race to marry persons of another race have largely been eradicated. Other forbidden behaviors, such as women participating in electoral politics or intellectuals subscribing to heterodox political views, have gradually come under the protection of civil liberties legislation. But if anthropologists are correct in arguing that all societies have taboos, we must ask where the deepest taboos in our own society are now to be found. Money is perhaps the topic that remains most subject to deep norms of stricture and taboo. More than sex, health, death, or any other aspect of personal life, it is the one most difficult for us to discuss in public.

This claim may at first glance strike some readers as peculiar. Surely anyone even casually acquainted with American culture would argue precisely the opposite. Foreign visitors, for example, typically observe that buying, selling, price tags, advertising, and dollar signs seem to be everywhere. Virtually every newspaper includes a business section filled with long lists of stock quotations and discussions of currency rates. Television programs and magazines have carved out significant markets by specializing in money. The number of periodical articles dealing with money has risen steadily in recent decades, as have the number of advice books on this subject and the number of people who earn their living as brokers, accountants, and financial advisers.

The public visibility of particular topics, however, is seldom a good barometer of how much these same topics may or may not be couched in taboo. Indeed, a compelling argument can be made that precisely the same power arrangements may lead both to public visibility and to popular prohibitions. Among the ancient Israelites, for example, the gradual establishment of a powerful priestly class resulted both in more elaborate public rituals of worship and in stricter taboos governing private moral and religious behavior.[9] Or, for another example, what has commonly been recognized as a strong taboo against discussions of death in Western culture can generally be understood in the same way. This taboo was in effect strengthened by the growth of hospitals, funeral homes, and professional occupations devoted to the care of the dying. Within these institutional settings, discussions of illness and death became ever more common, technical, and scientific, while a pall of silence on these topics fell increasingly over the general population.[10]

Despite the highly technical discussions of money markets, currency rates, and other financial wisdom that appear in specialized public media, the American public is almost completely mute on the subject of money. When asked if they ever discuss money or personal finances with friends, family, or anyone else, most people flatly say "no" or else qualify their answers to indicate that these discussions occur infrequently, avoid sensitive topics, and require special levels of trust. A typical response is like the one given by a Chicago insurance broker. Although he deals with money questions every day in his work, he says he never tells anybody in his personal life what he makes, how much money he has saved up, or what his investments are. Asked why not, he admits, "I don't know why; I just think it's taboo."

As people reflect on this taboo, we discover just how deeply rooted it is in our understandings of what constitutes appropriate behavior. Stuart Cummings, whose friends are mostly wealthy, says it is just plain rude to talk about money. People who do, he thinks, are trying to show how much they have. A New Jersey dentist who earns a moderate income says he gets along better with his friends when he keeps his mouth closed about any kind of financial matters. A young man in Washington, D.C., who is still struggling to get established in his profession, says he keeps quiet about money because people he associates with then think he has more than he really does. A senior banking official in Chicago says the taboo exists without exception in his company because there would be an epidemic of jealously and complaints if people knew each other's salaries.[11] This was the same lesson Michael Lewis, author of *Liar's Poker*, learned during his short career on Wall Street: "investment bankers didn't like to talk about money."[12]

Working women are a bit more likely than men to admit they have had conversations about money. But many say they learned very quickly to monitor themselves. A clergywoman in California, for example, admits one of her parishioners became quite offended one day when she innocently inquired about his personal finances. A Washington-based therapist says she and her fellow workers used to talk about finances when they were first starting out, but soon quit doing so because they all realized the discussions were taking a competitive turn.

The blackout on discussions of money is not absolute, of course, but what people say they *do* and *do not* talk about is also very revealing. A woman in Philadelphia says she sometimes talks with her friends about tuition at the private school where she and her friends send their children, but this is about all she is willing to discuss. "I wouldn't talk about how much my husband makes. I wouldn't tell anybody how much we owe on credit cards or our home equity loan, or even how much our mortgage payment is. There's just a strong feeling that that's a tacky thing to do." Another woman talks occasionally with her friends about the price of automobiles or how rent costs are rising. She says the discussion, though, is usually at a very general level, like how high prices are, rather than anything touching on specific problems. A number of people say their discussions arise when they are trying to decide on a major purchase, such as an automobile or a new home. In these cases, they often feel free to seek advice from a parent or close sibling; yet it is also common for people to shield these discussions from other members of their family whom they have learned not to trust.[13]

These examples suggest that people will talk about money when the ice has somehow been broken. They are most likely to discuss prices of consumer goods and other standard household budget items that have been advertised. In these cases, advertising makes general price levels public, so people feel they are revealing less in discussing these prices.[14] Occasionally, people are able to discuss financial matters that might not otherwise be in the public domain because they all find themselves in the same situation. Waiting to pick children up from the same private school may be such an occasion. Another example came from a woman who found she was able to discuss home repair costs because everyone in her neighborhood happened to be making the same repairs at about the same time. What people are most reluctant to discuss are their salaries, their personal net worth, and their debts. These are more purely financial or monetary, rather than being associated with marketable goods, and as such they are protected in a cloud of secrecy.[15]

The other context in which people find it possible to talk about money is when professional norms are present. A small percentage of people, for example, say they seek advice from financial advisers, brokers, and accountants. A few people we talked to also said they had found ways to obtain such advice informally from friends and co-workers.[16] The way in which people talk about these encounters, however, reveals that they function best when certain conventions are respected and that even under the best circumstances people often feel awkward and embarrassed. An air force officer who had recently been forced to declare personal bankruptcy sought advice from an attorney; he admits, however, that he found it very embarrassing to talk about his finances even in this professional relationship. A minister who regularly seeks advice from an accountant says he hesitates to do so because he feels he should be more competent himself in dealing with money questions. A sales representative who often receives valuable advice on stocks and investments from his co-workers acknowledges that these discussions work because nobody actually reveals how much they are planning to invest or specific amounts they have earned or lost. He also says he limits these discussions to the few co-workers who have positions and lifestyles most similar to his own.

The few people who say they talk freely with friends and family about their personal finances also demonstrate that the taboo on money talk is a cultural norm rather than a kind of censorship that individuals simply develop on their own. It is a norm that most people accept, yet it is clearly a phenomenon largely of the American middle class. It is much less widespread among the underprivileged, in the working class, and among ethnic groups that retain a strong sense of family and community identity.[17] When asked if he ever discusses his personal finances with friends and family, a Hispanic man in Los Angeles, for example, replies, "Sure, it's part of my life!" He says this is not unusual in the Hispanic community. Others who said they talked about money on a regular basis included a Minneapolis priest who discusses personal finances with others in his priests' support group, a banker who had just returned from an assignment in China where he discovered there was much more openness about personal finances, and an air force electrician who says people talk more freely about money in the military because salary levels associated with each rank are public information.[18]

As anthropologists who study other kinds of taboo have discovered, the rules underlying deeply held social prohibitions are often best revealed when people violate these rules. Some of the examples just considered show that violations of the money taboo subject people to personal discomfort and even criticism. The people who find special circumstances in which to talk about money reveal that taboos depend on institutional arrangements. They also depend on cultural understandings that supercharge money with extra meaning, power, perhaps even a kind of sacredness. The few people who tried successfully to overcome norms against talking about money were those who consciously adopted a different stance toward it. One woman, for example, says she has been able to talk more frankly with her parents in recent years about personal finances because they have learned to joke about these issues. Bringing humor into the conversation strips money of its gravity. Another woman tries to talk openly about family finances with her children to help them understand better why she and her husband make certain decisions. The language she uses is much like the language people adopted when sex was first becoming a subject of family discussion. Money, she says, is not something special or mysterious. It shouldn't be turned into something more than it is. "It isn't so precious that it needs to be hidden or kept secret; it is just like anything else, just a fact of life."

Most parents, however, do not treat money with this degree of candor. Indeed, one of the reasons many people find it so hard to talk about money is that during their formative years they never heard their parents discuss it. Some parents intentionally shield their children from discussions of money because they fear it will generate insecurity. Others believe money, like sex, is an adult subject that children cannot understand.[19] They talk about children being innocent and pure, whereas money is complicated and dirty, an "adult" subject.

Barb Gimelli, 40, a single mother who owns a management consulting firm, is more open about her personal finances than most people. She participates in a support group for working women that frequently gets into candid discussions of such matters. As a single woman, she also has some friends she confides in. But, like others, she sets limits on these conversations. She claims not to understand exactly why she does this, but somehow she feels such discussions are not appropriate, especially in the context of children. "My kids ask me sometimes, 'How much money do you make, mom?' And I tell them the same thing my parents always told me, 'That's not something I should share with you.' And I always think that maybe that's sort of weird. I don't know why I say that. It's sort of an automatic response, but I guess I think that it's a little crass or I don't really like talking about, oh, I make X dollars or something. Yeah, I wouldn't talk about that."

But the main reason children do not learn about money from their parents is that contemporary family patterns simply do not encourage that major financial decisions be made in the presence of children. With work being geographically separated from the home, and with mortgages being negotiated in bankers' offices and bills being paid by electronic transfers, children can grow up without having direct access to any of their parents' monetary thinking. It then becomes easier for parents to enforce the taboo against talking about money because the subject is shielded from view.

It was not always like this. In an earlier era children worked alongside parents on the family farm or in the family business. Prohibitions against idle talk about money often kept parents from discussing their deepest fears and fantasies with children. The day-to-day handling of money, however, was likely to be conducted in the presence of, and sometimes with the active participation of, children. As a result, children learned more of the reasoning behind their parents' decisions. They saw that money was not just a means of paying the bills, but an integral feature of life itself.

The significance of such interaction is clearly illustrated by an older woman, Lydia Kramer, who spoke with us about her childhood. Born in the 1920s, she lived most of her childhood during the Great Depression. Lydia's parents owned a farm in Pennsylvania. Times were hard, but her father managed to turn scarcity into a relatively comfortable living. Realizing that his dairy herd could produce more than milk alone, he started adding butter and cottage cheese to his delivery route. Relying mostly on family labor, he was able to sell these products inexpensively. Ice cream was becoming more popular, so Lydia's father experimented with that, too. It proved difficult to sell on the delivery route, however, so the family moved to town and opened a small store, still keeping the family farm. To cover costs at the store, they soon added sandwiches, butchering their own livestock to supply the meat. With additional cheap labor, mostly from family members (seven of her father's eleven siblings worked in the store), they added other items as well, such as homemade pies, and kept the store open longer hours. From the time she was nine years old, Lydia worked in the family store.

She remembers vividly one of the lessons she learned about money from this experience. "Whenever my friends came in, I felt they should have free ice cream. But my father said, 'That sounds all right if you are the only one working here and want to give free ice cream. But this is a business and you cannot make a profit if everything is free. So if you want to give something free, you put in a nickel for every ice cream you give your friends, and I'll do the same thing.'" Later, when she was a teenager, her father taught her all the other jobs in the store and gradually included her in more of the decisions he was making. She especially remembers him talking with her about the importance of knowing how hard people have to work for their money. When customers were being laid off and couldn't pay their bills, she also saw him struggling to balance compassion and keeping the business afloat. When she went away to college, she not only had skills that helped pay her way but knew how to negotiate for the best positions. She also believed firmly that helping people was more important than earning an extra dollar.

Younger people who grow up in the suburbs seldom learn what their parents think about money in such detail. They often know it is extremely important to their parents, but they have to try to guess what their parents' values are by looking at the goods they purchase or from hearing an occasional argument in the middle of the night. Sometimes they assimilate their parents' habits of spending money freely or of being extremely frugal, only to discover later that they have little understanding of *why* their parents behaved as they did. When asked what their parents actually taught them, they are caught short, realizing, as one young man in New York put it, "I'm not sure what they thought about money; I don't feel I was taught anything specific about money."

For those whose parents did talk more openly about money, the main lesson often is still that this subject should be kept under wraps. The reasons why have deep roots in American culture, linking present understandings with vestiges of the moralist arguments we considered earlier. From the ascetic moralists comes the idea that money is not as important as family, neighbors, or God. An example of this idea is given by a woman in Los Angeles who remembers seeing pictures of the saints in their robes at the Catholic church her parents attended when she was a girl and concluding that it was wrong to worry about money. From the romantic moralists the view is still prevalent in some quarters that money is crass and unsophisticated, compared with intellectual and artistic interests. Other views hark back to the aristocratic notions held by some of the founders of our society, men and women of comfortable means who thought it beneath them to discuss financial matters. In this view people who are so concerned about money that they cannot refrain from discussing it in public are shallow, boorish. In the absence of frank discussions in the home, however, these traditions have become transmuted into simple dictums that say little more than "don't talk about it."

The Privatization of Money

The taboo against talking about money is significant in its own right, making it difficult for people to understand why their parents behaved the way they did, leaving them uncertain about how to make financial decisions of their own, and cutting them off from informal support that might come from friends and family. It becomes especially hard for people to think through the relationship between money and nonpecuniary values when they never hear anyone else discussing this relationship. Not talking about money is, however, only one of the ways in which this topic is retreating increasingly into the private recesses of individual life.

The richness of personal life, marked by intensely important memories, feelings, hopes, and aspirations, seems so familiar that it is difficult to imagine life being lived in any other way. Yet there is considerable agreement among students of society that private life was not always such a vivid feature of human existence. Although conceptions of individual identity and the inner life can be found far back in history, especially in most of the ancient religious traditions, modern notions of private life became evident only in the eighteenth century.[20] The growth of cities in this period allowed people for the first time to lead anonymous personal lives that were largely separated from their public roles. This dichotomy was reinforced by the growth of specialized, bureaucratic organizations in the public arena, particularly those performing governmental and economic functions, and by the development of newspapers and publishing houses.[21] Both within and among organizations, specialized tasks could now be coordinated without involving the entire life of those who performed these tasks. As the public sphere gradually expanded and became more complex, personal life correlatively became more fully autonomous and private. In literature new conceptions of the person became evident in the rise of the epistolary novel, in the use of deception and mistaken identity as a literary device, in gender conceptions that contrasted female characterizations of the private realm with male characterizations of the public realm, and in portrayals of the self as being more changeable, subjectively defined, and concerned with problems of identity.[22]

The process that social scientists have labeled *privatization* refers to the ongoing extension of this separation of personal life from the large-scale organizations that make up the public life of modern societies.[23] It is an umbrella term that shelters a variety of more specific developments generally thought to be characteristic of contemporary life. One of these is a sense of subjective alienation, sometimes associated with behavioral withdrawal, from the larger, seemingly impersonal organizations that dominate public life. Skepticism and passivity on the part of ordinary citizens toward political institutions are often cited as examples. It should not be supposed that alienation and withdrawal are necessarily negative in their social consequences, however. Public institutions may actually function more efficiently when individuals do not expect to have a voice in the routine affairs of these organizations. A second development connoted by privatization is that individuals increasingly focus on subjective beliefs and understandings rather than presuming there to be objective realities to which they must pay heed. Subjectivity means that beliefs become more free floating and malleable, rather than being rooted in stable institutions over which individuals have little control. And third, these subjective beliefs and understandings take on added meaning because they figure more directly into the personal identities of individuals. As creator of subjective beliefs, the individual must take greater responsibility for his or her own outlook on life. As a person whose identity is not conferred by larger institutions, interior beliefs become more fundamentally constitutive of the self.

The effects of privatization have been considered most often with respect to religious commitment, and to a lesser extent in relation to the changes that have been observed in definitions of family life and leisure time. These activities indeed are said to constitute the key ingredients of the private sphere. Money, in contrast, is a less obvious candidate to be considered in the same way. It is, if anything, an integral feature of the massive institutions that make up the public sphere in modern societies. State bureaus, for-profit firms, labor unions, professional associations, and even educational institutions are intensely concerned with the attainment and distribution of money. Stock markets, international currency exchanges, brokerage firms, banks, investment columns in newspapers, and most of the other social arrangements that deal specifically with money are in fact closely associated with the functioning of large-scale public institutions. What is generally neglected in treatments of these institutions, however, is that their growth in the public arena has been accompanied by an equally significant expansion in the private meanings and functioning of money.[24]

Part of what gives money its "objective" quality is that it has been highly institutionalized in the public arena.[25] Standardized national currencies are but one example. "Functional rationality" adds to the facticity with which money is generally perceived insofar as money is widely assumed to facilitate the exchange of goods and services. Prices framed in standard currencies thus contribute to the belief that money is not simply a subjective phenomenon. Increasingly, money is also given objectivity by "procedural rationality"; namely, the establishment of money supply levels, interest rates, and terms of international exchange by formalized agencies established for this purpose. It may thus be known that money supply is not simply a fact of nature, and yet the procedures used by the Federal Reserve Board in regulating money supply suggest to people that this phenomenon is neither arbitrary nor under their own control.[26]

The objectivity of money in the public arena is, however, reinforced as well by a countervailing tendency to regard it subjectively in the private arena. From the standpoint of the individual, money in public settings seems to be a hard, immutable fact because it is determined in rational ways that the individual does not understand and in settings that are far removed from the individual's own experience. These objective realities become a part of the alienated consciousness of the individual, remote, distant from the lived experience of everyday life. Death and taxes, as it is said, are indeed alike, not only because both are inevitable, but because both are bracketed from daily experience. The meaning of money that seems more vibrant to the life of the individual is that which arises in personal life. It is largely a private construction that focuses on consumption, lifestyle, personal identity, and individual freedom. All these are accentuated by their exclusion from the meanings of money in public life.[27]

In contrast to its objective facticity in public life, money tends to be understood as a subjective phenomenon in the private realm.[28] This is not to suggest that people think they can pay their bills with anything but hard currency. But people do believe money is as much how you think about it as it is how much or how little you have. The current emphasis in scholarly circles on the *meanings* of money is itself symptomatic of the growing tendency to view money as an artifact of culture, much like people's views of sex or their attitudes toward religion, rather than a feature of the external world alone. At the popular level, people worry not only about having money but also about the fact that they are worried in the first place. They wonder if their fears and anxieties are justified, or whether they may be living in a fantasy world of their own creation. Not knowing quite why their parents behaved as they did, people feel that perhaps their own attitudes were shaped arbitrarily by personality quirks and personal experiences. Feeling that they have little control over the forces shaping money in the public arena, they say the main way to exercise control in their own lives is by thinking right and paying close attention to their feelings.

Manny Hernandez, 33, a Chicago insurance salesman, says he worries about money all the time. He constantly feels insecure. On the surface, it appears that he and his wife earn a good living. They own their home and, other than the mortgage, are free of debts. Although he is still young, Manny's deepest worry is not having enough money for retirement. He knows the Social Security program is supposed to take care of older people, but he does not understand it and fears it will go bankrupt before he qualifies to receive benefits. In his case, the extreme distance he senses between his personal life and the larger institutions that deal with money objectively is thus an important source of the fear that characterizes his subjective orientation toward money.

Dane Golished, a 41-year-old schoolteacher in Philadelphia, also emphasizes the subjective meaning of money. He says, "We're comfortable, all our needs are met, and we have enough income to meet our expenses." When he tries to think objectively about money, he isn't sure he needs more or would even want more. But still, he admits, money is something he worries about all the time. He feels he needs to get a better perspective on it. In the meantime, it absorbs his attention and adds stress to his life.

In both these cases, money is such a private matter that neither man talks about it openly with his friends. Indeed, both men have argued about money enough with their wives that they feel they cannot always discuss it with them either. As a result, both men are terribly vulnerable to the smallest tidbits of external information. Manny Hernandez hears someone mention Social Security and it sets his fears in motion. Dane Golished reads a newspaper article about children's allowances and begins fretting about his personal finances. Both are at least dimly aware that their feelings about money are not entirely consonant with their financial situation. But the feelings are something they take very seriously anyway. They realize these feelings are a source of stress and anxiety. In the absence of any way to talk out these feelings, neither man is able to move beyond them.

Part of what the privatization of money entails, therefore, is a sense of being radically alone. People have probably worried about money in all times and places. By some objective standard, there is probably less reason for people to worry now than at most times in the past. But people continue to worry and to feel vulnerable and insecure. Moreover, they now locate these worries more purely in their private life. Talking about them would make these worries more of a collective phenomenon. Keeping quiet about them makes people think of them as an extension of their personality. It is never quite clear to people when these worries are justified. The very definition of "enough" becomes harder to pin down.

Besides being a matter of personal anxiety, money is subjectivized in several other ways. One derives from the fact that there are no agreed-upon, objective standards for thinking about money. Advertisers encourage people to spend their money; other norms encourage stark frugality. Within the home, parents often take these extreme views. It is as if children are being raised by devout fundamentalists married to equally dogmatic atheists. The result is that attitudes toward money become a matter of personal choice, just as one's religious opinions do.[29] The choice itself is likely to be warranted as an arbitrary personal proclivity, such as taste, because none of the competing public warrants is grounded in a firm sense of absolute reality. Indeed, cynicism toward the claims of public institutions concerned with money is likely to reinforce the conviction that individual treatments of money depend largely on arbitrary preferences. Because they are private, moreover, norms of civility surround these choices.[30] One learns not to judge the way other people spend their money, treating their choices as functions of lifestyle, upbringing, or disposable income itself. The taboo against money-talk reflects these norms of civility. Money is also subjectivized by virtue of being hidden from public view. In the proverbial struggle between God and mammon, the two have come increasingly to resemble each other. Any objective sense of either is sufficiently mysterious that their existence must be taken largely on faith. To the outside viewer, it may be assumed that a person "has money" (knows God), but the evidence comes from observing externalized activities, such as buying things (going to church). The phenomenon itself is associated with the most intimate parts of a person's private life.

In the case of religion, privatization is associated with the tendency for individuals to think of faith primarily as a means of resolving questions about personal identity. This orientation is by no means recent, having roots in questions of personal meaning that were evident in many of the earliest religious texts, but it has been accentuated both by the seeming inefficacy of religion to deal with more collective issues and by the increasingly problematic character of self-identity itself. In the case of money, connections with self-identity can also be found historically. Speaking critically, the earliest religious leaders also cautioned that money could be an idol from which people derived all their sense of meaning and purpose. The contemporary links between money and self-identity, however, extend well beyond notions of this kind.

Money is subjectively linked with self-identity because individuals take on ultimate responsibility for their own financial well-being. We will see more clearly, as already suggested in the last chapter, that individuals no longer define this responsibility primarily in terms of working hard in order to earn money. And yet despite widespread claims that Americans are looking increasingly to social programs of various kinds to take care of them, individual responsibility for personal finances is probably more pervasive, and associated with deeper levels of the self, than at any time in our nation's history. Many of the older conceptions of fiscal individualism remain, while newer ideas have been added. Most people deny (appropriately, it appears) that their sense of self-worth is determined to a very significant degree by how much money they have. But there is still a strong belief that individuals are ultimately responsible for paying their own bills, supporting themselves and their families, and making their own economic decisions. At a time when some evidence points toward people depending more on family support systems to make ends meet, other evidence suggests that the breakdown of extended families, the rising number of people who live alone, and changing gender roles, among other developments, are imposing an even greater sense of fiscal responsibility on individuals. In addition, the subjectivization of money is itself a source of increasing responsibility, for individuals now must not only pay their bills but also decide how they are going to think about these bills.

In *Habits of the Heart*, Robert Bellah and his coauthors write of the importance of "leaving home" as a sign of independence in American culture.[31] Young adults have traditionally been encouraged to separate geographically from their parents, sometimes to settle the open frontier or to move from rural villages to the city. In preparation for leaving home, children are encouraged to seek independence from their parents at an early age, and teenagers heighten this process by undergoing a period of "adolescent rebellion." The mature adult is supposed to be, as Emerson argued long ago, "self reliant"—in choice of occupation, in habitat, in religious preference, and in outlook on life. In recent years, according to Bellah and his associates, the self-reliant individual is also expected to shun commitments that might prove constraining and to shoulder responsibility for feeling good about oneself.[32]

In our interviews, people overwhelmingly associated having money with greater individuality, with freedom to be themselves. This attitude reflects the value Americans place on leaving home. Indeed, when asked what they would do if they had more money, many people spoke literally about "leaving home." Many said they would get away by going on long trips. Others said they would get rid of their current home and build a new residence, perhaps several new residences in different parts of the world, so they could go from one to the others. Hardly anyone thought having more money would tie them down, nor did they fantasize about uses that would create, rather than loosen, social obligations. They did not, for example, talk about bringing their families to live closer to them, starting a business, or working on community improvement projects. Instead, they talked about getting away, being free of obligations, debts, bosses, neighbors, and children.

In less fanciful ways, leaving home has always meant, among other things, "getting on one's feet" financially. Usually this has been taken to mean earning your own way in life so that you are no longer an economic burden to your parents. Financial independence, however, is much more about self-identity than it is about putting bread on the table. Most of the people we talked to said they lacked for very little while they were growing up. Their parents may not have had much, but there was always money for food and clothing, school trips, movies, gum, and other childhood essentials. As these children got older, their needs and wants expanded, but in most cases the parental purse still provided. And yet, what these young people resented most were the "strings attached" to the money they received. They got what they wanted, but they had to defend their choices to their parents. They wanted not to have to talk with their parents about money, just get it and spend it. Their freedom was being stifled and they were being treated like children.

Charles Greenwood, the sales manager we met briefly in the last chapter, describes his parents as frugal, middle-class people who managed their money very closely so they could afford the big-ticket items they wanted, such as owning a nice home. They gave him spending money, but he found early in life that his own views toward money seemed to differ from his parents'. Indeed, being able to differentiate and express his views about money became one of the ways in which he "found himself" during adolescence. He came to the realization that "I enjoy spending money to satisfy my interests, whatever they might be at the time. I also have a need to be independent in a financial sense from others, so my attitude was to make my own money so that I could spend it the way I wanted." To make his own money at age 10, he started growing vegetables in the backyard, taking them around the neighborhood in his little red wagon. A few years later he got a job at a local nursery doing weeding. On weekends he caddied at a country club, and then in high school he worked as a stocker and bagger at the grocery store.

Like it has for many other people, Charles Greenwood's quest for financial independence has proven to be never-ending. At age 50 he admits it is still an "ever-present consideration." The reason it is for so many people is that finding oneself is much more difficult than simply moving away from one's parents. Once money becomes linked with self-identity, then the definition of "financial independence" becomes much more subjective, and therefore subject to constant redefinition. It becomes, as Bellah observes, attached to conceptions of the "life course," each developmental stage requiring a new declaration of independence. For Charles Greenwood, it meant growing vegetables at one stage, leaving home for a career in the military at another stage, and now amassing enough capital that he can buy his freedom from his employer.

With rising divorce rates, changing views of gender, and increasing numbers of women in the labor force, the idea of "leaving home" has also been extended significantly in recent years to include the relationships between husbands and wives. For women in the past, leaving home generally meant moving out of their parents' household but becoming financially dependent on their husbands. Today, many married women are capable of earning their own living, and leaving home means finding a career capable of sustaining themselves, rather than seeking a spouse to do so. One symbol of this new meaning of self reliance is that a significant minority of married couples now keep separate bank accounts. The reasons for this are varied, including protecting assets that each spouse may have brought to the marriage from previous earnings or previous marriages, especially in the event of divorce. But separate accounts also serve a deeper function: they enhance the individual's personal autonomy, giving her or him greater control in the handling of personal finances. The link between self-identity and money is thus strengthened. Ostensibly, the reason for separate accounts may be that it simplifies married life by taking away a source of conflict. Yet the language people use also suggests that the underlying assumptions have to do with personal freedom, self-expression, and individuality.

Mindy Griscomb, 31, a Chicago audiologist, says she has followed her mother's example in keeping a separate bank account. Despite the fact that she and her husband operate their own business as partners, Mindy believes firmly in the importance of keeping her money and his separate. She points out that the reason has nothing to do with not trusting her husband, and that separate accounts would do little in the event of a divorce since each carries both their names. The reason she prefers to have her own money is simply that "if I decide to do something with it, I don't want to talk about it or argue about it." For her, how you spend money is largely a matter of taste. There are no hard-and-fast rules. People just have different styles: she enjoys buying things; her husband is a tightwad. So having separate accounts lets her express herself more freely. Even more deeply, she associates this freedom with personal autonomy. Generalizing, she says, "I think everybody needs that [autonomy] just so they don't feel completely dependent on somebody." She says she would not want an allowance from her husband. But the reason she feels this way is not that she might then lack for food or money to buy the children's clothes. The reason is that she would feel demeaned as a person. Her self-identity would be compromised by having to adjust her tastes to his.

MONEY AND WORK

The concept of privatization helps us understand better why money seems problematic to so many people in our society. The trouble is not just that people are caught in an "economic squeeze" involving higher prices and modest salary increases. The problem is that money has increasingly become a subjective phenomenon, located in our private lives, linked to our self-identity, and separated from the objective realities of large-scale social institutions. As a result, the financial responsibilities that our society has always expected individuals to bear have been greatly increased. People now seek financial independence as part of their quest for self-identity but find that the definition of "enough" is always elusive. They are not sure their financial worries are grounded in any external reality, so they worry about the very fact that they experience anxiety. They respect the taboo against talking about money, not because money is unimportant, but because it is too private, too dangerous to discuss. Being materially linked to someone in a way that requires discussion and negotiation puts our individuality at risk.

To say that money has become privatized is to suggest that this development also has roots in certain institutional characteristics of our society. One of these is the increasing dominance of public life by large-scale, bureaucratic organizations. Public discourse about money, usually couched in the rationalistic vocabulary of economic analysis, focuses to a large extent on these institutional settings. Alienation from these institutions, in the sense of regarding them as distant, impenetrable, impersonal, and impossible to understand, forces an increasing share of individuals' attention toward private life. In this sphere, money takes on the characteristics we have just considered. And yet to attribute these characteristics only to the growth of large-scale institutions is to neglect the more immediate social conditions that have contributed to the present situation.

Understanding why money in personal life has become, as it were, "subjectively defined" requires us to look again at its relationship with work. One of the principal ways in which money in personal life has traditionally been anchored in some sort of objective reality is by connecting it closely with work. In simplest terms, work was conceived as a means of earning money; money was thus an end to be achieved by working. This conception served two important functions: it put money in a determinate relationship with something else, and that "something else" was something over which the individual generally was able to exercise some control.[33] Money, we might say, was thus linked in a relatively stable way to an individual's life. People could make more money by spending more time working or by working harder.

This same conception also gave rise to many of the broader social programs and concerns that are still familiar today. If work was the means of making money, then three concerns in particular needed to be addressed. The efficacy of work itself should be maximized by providing people with the necessary tools, skills, and education, and by bringing their labor into an appropriate relationship with other "factors of production," such as management and capital. If work was the means of making money, then attention also had to be paid to mechanisms ensuring social justice. Wage rates on the whole needed to be commensurate with the amount of labor expended, and within categories of the labor force, fair treatment, equitable rates of remuneration, and nondiscrimination were all ideals to be upheld. In addition, social policies were deemed necessary to ensure that opportunities for people to work were available. Full employment became an aspiration to be realized. The work-money nexus was thus not only a stabilizing force in the private lives of individuals but also a way in which the same conceptions governing individual life could be linked systematically to the larger institutions (business firms, labor unions, and government agencies) of the wider society.[34]

The view that work and money are linked closely with each other is by no means absent in our society. Despite being perplexed about their parents' ideas on money, many people say their parents taught them to work hard for the money they earned. Lou Candela, the Boston man who teaches high school woodworking classes, says his father never talked to him about money; but Lou learned by example. Supporting twelve children on a plumber's income, Lou's father worked early and late. Lou had to do the same. He recalls, "If I ever had any money, it's because I went and shoveled snow or went to cut someone's lawn or worked for some neighbor doing some job for them. That's where we got money. It was never given to us. We always had to go out and earn it." Jena Forsythe, the Wall Street broker, also says her parents didn't talk much about money, but they had strict rules and encouraged her to work. In fact, when she started babysitting at age eleven, her parents required her to save a fourth of everything she earned. Later, when she asked to attend a private high school, they told her she would have to pay a certain percentage of the tuition herself. As she reflects, she says working to make money and saving for the future were the basic values, "not good things, just part of life, like eating and sleeping."

Much of what we have considered in the previous two chapters, however, suggests that the connection between work and money is becoming increasingly tenuous.[35] Work-compensation specialists focus increasingly on incentives other than money in order to motivate people to do well in their work. The accounts people themselves give of their work describe it either as an end in itself or as a means to achieve such nonpecuniary rewards as variety, freedom of choice, and a sense

of accomplishment. Surveys also cast doubt on the relationship between work and money. In a 1982 study, only 9 percent of the U.S. workforce said their view of work was captured by the statement "work is
a business transaction—the more I get paid, the more I do," while 52
percent selected the statement "I have an inner need to do the very best
I can, regardless of pay." Another study gave somewhat greater cre-
dence to the role of money but still found that only 45 percent of the
public would work harder in order to receive "good pay." According
to other studies, the belief that "hard work always pays off" has declined from being held by a majority a generation ago to about a third
of the American public today.[36]

Additional evidence that the relationship between work and money
is not a dominant factor in contemporary understandings comes from
the ways in which people perceive their chances of having more money
than they do now. Most people say they would like to have more
money; in fact, it became common in the interviews for people to question the question, asking if anyone ever said "no" (a few did). When
asked to say how they would get this money and what they would do
with it, most people resort immediately to the possibility of winning
the lottery. Some speculate about winning the Publishers' Clearing-
house Sweepstakes, and a few imagine inheriting money from an un-
known relative. Nobody talks about landing a more lucrative job or
even about gradually working into the upper echelons of the salary
scale. Indeed, when asked specifically what they would *not* be willing
to do to make more money, people mention being unwilling to work
harder or take a job they enjoy less in order to earn a higher income.

A 36-year-old dentist explains with particular clarity the relationship
he sees between working harder and making more money. He admits
he would like to have a reasonably higher income than he does now,
simply because he wants to buy a boat and still save enough to pay for
his children's education. He realizes some dentists earn more than he
does, either by working longer weekdays and Saturdays, or by learning new techniques that bring higher fees. He knows he could also
increase his net worth by spending more time monitoring his investments. He doesn't do any of these things, though, because his work is
more or less defined in a hermetic space of its own. Although it is his
livelihood, it is not so much a means he can manipulate for financial
ends, but a familiar routine, a big chunk of his lifestyle that he prefers
to take for granted. He says, "I don't think I could make a lot more than

I'm making now. I'm kind of a 'go in the office and grind it out' type of person. That's where I was trained and that's where I feel most comfortable earning my money."

Although his parents taught him the basic connection between work and money, he now keeps the two in largely separate spheres of his thinking. Other people seem never to have learned the relationship in the first place. Teri Silver, the systems analyst, claims her parents never had a lot of money, but she admits she and her sister "never lacked for anything." They had nice clothes and were given riding lessons. Her parents never gave her a fixed allowance or expected her to live within a budget. They simply gave her money whenever she asked for it. Later, when she began getting part-time jobs, she spent the money impulsively on luxury items, rather than saving any of it. Even now, in her late twenties, she sees very little connection between work and money. She thinks of work mainly in terms of personal enjoyment. Living with her boyfriend, she has few bills to pay. And when she thinks about the possibility of being rich, she pins her hopes on the lottery, which she plays regularly.

The degree to which work and money have been dissociated in our society can also be observed clearly in contemporary attitudes toward the rich. Throughout most of our nation's history people took pride in working for their money and for this reason resented rich people who had inherited their money or obtained it through speculation. Even now, this attitude persists, especially among older people who have worked hard all their lives. A vivid example of this attitude comes from a midwesterner, Rob McHugh, who recognized it clearly in his father: "My dad was very proud that he worked hard, and in some ways he was almost proud that he got relatively little for how hard he worked. He was proud that he was still willing to work that hard. And my dad definitely looked down on people who didn't work for their money. People who inherited their money, or the money just kind of fell into their hands."

But there is also a newer attitude. Michael Lewis expresses it well in describing how he felt the day he started working at Solomon Brothers. "I didn't really imagine I was going to work, more as if I were going to collect lottery winnings."[37] Rob McHugh, at 32, doesn't see his job teaching elementary school quite that way. But he clearly distances himself from his father's view. "What's the use of working two jobs, like my father did, only to die at 57?" he argues. He believes rich people are no worse, and no better, than himself. The bottom line is that everybody should get as much pleasure as possible from the money they have. He hopes Ed McMahon will come knocking at his door, but meanwhile he isn't going to kill himself trying to earn more money.

This attitude is voiced repeatedly as people reflect on what it would be like to be rich. They seldom express any dislike for those who have money but have not worked for it. In privatizing money, they make it such a personal matter that no room is left to judge whether someone obtains it in the proper manner or not. Norms of civility prevent them from criticizing the rich. Instead, they mostly indicate admiration for the good fortune that some people happen to experience in life. If the goddess of good fortune happens to smile on them too, then so much the better.

Further insight can also be gained by looking more closely at the rare instances in which people bring up money in discussing their work. They do admit there is (can be or has been) a connection between working and earning money, but they also state explicit reasons why this connection should not be taken seriously or at face value. Before Barb Gimelli started her consulting firm, she operated a bakery and then taught classes in business at the local community college for several years. She calls herself a "risk junky" who likes to live on the edge, always running at a frenetic pace just to see if she can do it. Asked what motivates her most in her work, she replies, "I need the money." But without hesitating she goes on: "No, that's not it. I could be making a lot more doing something else. I love the world of ideas. That's what I love." She elaborates, saying she enjoys constructing things in her head, working out proposals, presenting them to her clients, and convincing them to think about things her way. She loves the freedom to create and the satisfaction she derives from this process. We should not discount the fact that she acknowledges working for money. Her pattern of speech allows her to admit this, but then, as if feeling something is not quite accurate about that explanation, she hastens to provide additional reasons.

Several other examples are worth considering because they illustrate different ways of discounting the relationship between work and money. Amy Oldenburg, the 39-year-old Los Angeles nurse, admits she pursued her career because she had always been taught to be responsible and to work hard, but she says graduating from college at the height of the counterculture in the early 1970s undermined the legitimacy of working in order to earn money. Tony Arno, a Chicago photographer who is exactly the same age, has a similar view of money. He isn't sure if it was the counterculture or having relatives who were artistic, but he specifically denies that money had anything to do with becoming a photographer. Teri Silver is a decade younger. She admits money was a big issue when she first began looking for jobs. But she now attributes that interest to immaturity. She says she came to realize that money was nothing alongside happiness. An exact contemporary of hers, Doug Hill, who works in New York City as a copier salesman, makes a similar point. A few years ago, he says, people in his organization were trying hard to make a lot of money. But now their focus has turned more to "values," even though they still work hard.

The denials people offer about working for money provide significant indicators of the norms governing this topic in our culture. The reasons given to dissociate money from work are precisely the same reasons people give for not talking about it in other contexts. Money is crass compared with the pursuit of other values. It is not quite right to admit one works to make money. To say so would open up embarrassing questions about how much one earns and why one does not pursue a more lucrative career. Keeping money in proper perspective is a sign of maturity. Emphasizing it too much smacks of unsophistication.

Certainly there are limits to these denials. If there were none, people would argue they could be just as happy earning little or nothing. Recognizing this is not the case also helps us put the relationship between work and money in perspective. A woman who ran her own business for two years says she was working seventy-hour weeks and making no money, so she gave up the business and pursued a different line of work. Barb Gimelli, with income of about $70,000 a year, says more money would not make her any happier. But she also explains that if she were only making $12,000 a year, additional income would indeed increase her happiness. "I have been really broke before in my life and having to get food stamps, not being able to get my teeth filled, not being able to take my kids to get glasses. That kind of stuff eats me alive. I can't stand that. I couldn't be happy like that. I think that the difference between 12K a year and 30K a year made me happier. The difference between 30K a year and 70K a year, I don't think has made me any happier."

By their own admission, then, separating money from work is something middle-class people can do because they feel they are no longer at a subsistance level where every extra dollar makes a difference. Within the broad income range that defines their comfort zone, however, they prefer to think of money in other ways than simply the result of working. Doing so is a significant factor in the privatization of money. Were money linked closely with work, it would also be connected solidly to such realities of life as how much energy a person is willing to expend working, how many hours in the day can be devoted to the job, how well one's corporation is faring, and whether or not the economy is functioning at full tilt. Most of these are limiting realities over which the individual has little control. In being separated from these realities, money can become more squarely a feature of private life, particularly those discretionary realms that include one's leisure activities, one's spending habits, and one's attitudes.

Grandchildren of the Great Depression

In addition to its separation from work, money in our society is further removed from the objective realities that once anchored it by virtue of specific historical circumstances. People are now uncertain about the meaning of money because an increasing number are what we might call grandchildren of the Great Depression. An older generation (their parents) was fundamentally shaped by the Depression, not directly, for even they were generally too young to have lived through it, but because of the way *their parents* raised them. People who were children during the 1930s and 1940s were often raised by parents who had been deeply influenced by the Depression. Having had to work hard, save carefully, and live on a very meager income, the Depression generation believed it was sheer economic necessity to take money very seriously. They trained their children to think the same way. Money was something you worked hard for and treated with cautious respect. The only problem was that these children of the Depression mostly experienced prosperity during the 1950s and 1960s. To their children, the Depression grandchildren, the attitudes they saw their parents expressing toward money thus seemed arbitrary. Frugality, for example, seemed not to be an economic necessity, but a personal idiosyncracy of one's father or mother.

John Phelps, the Minneapolis businessman we first met in chapter 1, provides a clear example of the attitudes that characterize many grandchildren of the Depression. Born in 1960, he spent his formative childhood years mostly during prosperous times. His father was an attorney, so the family actually had plenty of money. John's father, though, had been born in 1932 and thus had been raised by parents who knew firsthand what the Depression was like. John's mother grew up in a similar environment. As a result, his parents were extremely frugal, even though times had changed considerably by the 1960s. But to John their orientation was, and remains, difficult to appreciate. He describes his parents as "cheapskates" and says they often drove him nuts. "We knew my dad made fairly good money as an attorney," he explains. "We could've lived on the other side of town, like the more upscale, affluent part of town." But his parents never moved. They doled out small monthly allowances to John and his sister, which John feels in retrospect pretty much covered all his needs. And yet John found their attitude oppressive. With his parents always "squirreling away their pennies," John found it difficult to understand exactly what the appropriate relationship should be between money and his own attitudes toward it. As he has matured, he distances himself increasingly from his parents' views, especially by regarding them as "views." He relativizes these views by attributing them to unique historical circumstances. Summarizing his understanding of his parents' views, he concludes, "I think it all goes back to them coming out of the Depression."

The contrast between grandchildren and children of the Depression emerges clearly when we consider how the children themselves were influenced. Mary Cavenah, now a marriage counselor in San Francisco, is a child of the Depression. Born in 1937, she was too young when the Depression ended to have direct memories of it. But she is still experiencing its effects on her family. In 1929 her paternal grandfather, a wealthy Los Angeles businessman, lost everything and committed suicide. Her maternal grandparents had also been wealthy but lost most of their wealth in the Depression and spent the rest on alcohol. Her own parents struggled to provide the basic necessities for Mary and her brother. She recalls her mother making lampshades, reupholstering the worn-out furniture, and never buying a new coat. Both parents were extremely frugal and always believed in paying cash. Even in the 1950s, when Mary was in her teens, her parents watched every penny. In part, they had to. Her father supported his widowed mother. Her other grandmother depended heavily on her mother for financial support. Then, a few years later, her own father died, leaving Mary with the responsibility of partially supporting her mother. The effect of all this, Mary says, is to leave her feeling extremely insecure about money. She associates money primarily with security but believes firmly that there will never be enough. Her husband has actually provided her with a comfortable suburban home. But Mary is still afraid to spend any money on herself. She fears she too may be "left in the lurch" as she grows old.

Estelle Cavenah is Mary Cavenah's daughter. Born in 1961, she gives us a direct look at the differences between grandchildren and children of the Depression in the same family. She says she realized as a child that her parents always treated money as if it were terribly important, but she never understood exactly why. They seemed to have plenty of it; at least she and her sister never seemed to lack for anything. Still, it seemed her parents were always fretting. Even today, they ask her if the modest income she makes working at a public health clinic in Los Angeles is really as good as she can do for herself. They seem to comment too often on the things she buys or does not buy, and they set up invidious financial comparisons between her and her sister. For Estelle, none of these worries has roots in the economic conditions her mother talks about. Money is instead something she scarcely tries to understand as an object in itself. She admits, for example, that she had no sense growing up of what you had to pay for and what you didn't. Even now, she lives modestly enough that she seldom confronts difficult financial questions. To her, money itself is much less important than her own attitudes. "Getting it in perspective" is what interests her most.

We must be cautious in drawing generalizations from these examples, of course. Despite its devastating effects on the economy as a whole, the Great Depression touched some families far more deeply than it did others. There are also large segments of our society that have not experienced the more recent prosperity as fully as people like John Phelps and Estelle Cavenah. It is more difficult for them to view their parents' cautious attitudes with misgiving. The important point, nevertheless, is that some of the current tendency to privatize and subjectivize our views toward money can be attributed directly to the historical circumstances in which we live. More than half a century later, the Depression is still a significant factor in our thinking. Knowing how it shaped the attitudes of their parents and grandparents, many people today make reference to it as a way of relativizing these attitudes. They can believe people at one time thought of money as an objective fact of life, conditioned directly by economic circumstances. But their own experience, growing up in more prosperous times, is that attitudes toward money often do not bear a close connection with external reality. They attribute these attitudes instead to personality traits and to idiosyncratic psychological orientations. They thus come to emphasize attitudes themselves much more and to believe it is the individual's responsibility to define these attitudes.

THE DUBIOUS PLEASURES OF MONEY

The tendency to make money so private that we never talk about it in public has far-reaching consequences for our society and for our personal lives. We assume great responsibility for our money, but we receive little support from other people of the kind that might help us make better decisions or feel more confident about the decisions we do make. Consequently, we worry in private and feel guilty about spending too little or too much. We may live frugally, but we no longer know exactly why we do. Without the capacity to compare our thoughts and feelings with those of our peers, both our fantasies and our fears often run wild.

The ultimate indicator of how far removed our subjective sense of money is from anything concrete is the fact that people in our society seem capable of terrorizing themselves with deep-seated financial worries, no matter how much money they have. They know, perhaps from hearing about the financial misfortune of a friend, or even from personal experience, that money is always uncertain. They then turn this uncertainty into an obsession that far outweighs any material advantages they may enjoy. Karen Kelsey, the Washington-based therapist we met in chapter 1, experienced this kind of fear firsthand in the life of her mother. She recalls, "I remember how Mom used to lay on her bed and sob because she thought they were going to become impoverished. But we were living in a house in Beverly Hills on Rodeo Drive, and we had horses, and we had apartment buildings, and we had nice silver and jewelry, just endless amounts of material things. But I grew up always in terror that the next day we would be out on the street, impoverished, because my mother always believed that. She had no sense of what was a reasonable amount of money, of what you needed to survive, or even of what loss was."

By the same token, our ability to fantasize about preposterous sums of money seems no longer to bear any relation to how much or how little money we actually have either. It used to be that studies of material fantasies found people reluctant to think very broadly beyond their actual standard of living. A typical example would be someone earning $10,000 a year who said it would be nice to earn $12,000. But now, as we have seen, people's minds turn to winning the lottery. Even self-styled spendthrifts say it would be nice to have "just enough," like an annual income of $200,000 or a net worth of several million.

Advertising must of course be blamed for some of the fears and fantasies that plague our imaginations. Life insurance companies play up the worst-case senarios, while cruise companies, airlines, and game shows all provide glimpses of what it must be like to enjoy the "lifestyles of the rich and famous." We know from careful studies of the effects of advertising that most people adopt an appropriately cynical view of these appeals to their fears and fantasies. So all the blame cannot be placed on advertising alone. It is the nature of our personal lives themselves that is much more to blame. Abiding so faithfully by the taboo against discussing money with our friends and families, we are left at the mercy of our own imaginations.

Extreme fantasies and fears about money, however, represent only the least significant of the ways in which money can take possession of our personal lives. Because we have relatively few anchors in the external world for our thoughts about money, we sense that it makes incessant demands on our personal time and energy. Despite relatively high incomes, many people feel they need even more money to solve their problems. A lack of money symbolizes constraint; the way to gain freedom is thus to have more. Prosperity appears as a psychological fix, even though the desire for it magnifies our sense that things are not sufficient as they are.

Not talking about money is, in the final analysis, both a source and a consequence of the dubious pleasures we derive from it. Part of our cultural heritage tells us money can never be a source of true happiness. Handling money is just a grubby business, more detail to worry about in our personal lives. It makes no more sense to talk about it than it would to hold forth about brushing our teeth. But not verbalizing what we think about money also makes it possible to entertain private beliefs of a very different sort. We may have learned somewhere that money cannot buy happiness, but at a deeper level we believe it can. There is thus an internal contradiction in the way we think about money, one that leads us to want more and more, and yet to deny that this is what we really want at all. The result is a heightened sense of pressure in our personal lives, as if we are trying to break free of something we cannot fully identify. This pressure is also increased by a pervasive cultural view about the relationship between money and material goods.

Chapter Seven

GETTING AND SPENDING:

THE MAINTENANCE AND VIOLATION OF

SYMBOLIC BOUNDARIES

IF MONEY is so personal that people often feel at sea in thinking about it, there are nevertheless highly institutionalized frameworks in our culture that guide our conceptions of money most of the time. I suggested in the last chapter that money is *both* subjective and objective, a feature of private life and a matter of public record. Great psychological distance often separates the two. And yet the two are inextricably connected. We must now try to understand what these connections are.

My argument will go something like this: Having been severed to a considerable extent from work (as we have seen), money in personal life is now conceived primarily in relationship to spending. The material uses to which it can be put largely constitute the mental frames or "horizon" in which we now think about money. Within this horizon a kind of instrumental rationality predominates. It manifests itself chiefly as a way of coordinating means and ends within the rather limited confines of comparative pricing. Broader values, in the form of absolute or ultimate ends, are generally bracketed from these considerations. The result comes close to what has sometimes been called a "consumerist" mentality. It might be supposed, given the apparent rationality of cost-benefit calculations, that personal money would thus be handled in a highly rational manner. Other characteristics of personal money (such as its "privatization"), however, suggest that symbolic rituals may play a greater role than rational calculation. A comparison of these rituals with those we have already considered in the workplace will yield a clearer understanding of the meanings and functioning of money in personal life.

I then extend the argument to show how money is culturally constructed by negative example. If the logic of consumption provides rules concerning the "internal" construction of money, then sharp cultural boundaries drawn between money and human relationships help to define it "externally." I argue that these boundaries are consonant with the privatization of money, that they derive from the personal experiences of children and adults, and that they figure prominently in cultural understandings of *ambiguous* cases (i.e., ones that create confusion over the boundary between money and human relationships), such as norms governing the making of personal loans and the giving of gifts. Finally, I suggest that these understandings of loans and gifts play a significant role in undermining the legitimacy of social institutions, such as religious organizations and charitable associations, that might otherwise provide nonmarket settings in which to engage in collective discourse about the relationships between money and human values.

MATERIAL HORIZONS

In many ways, every part of life is connected with every other part. Nowhere is this truism more evident than in our thinking about what constitutes means and ends. When work is seen as a means, money might be taken as the end being accomplished by that means. But if buying a new house is the end a person is seeking, money then becomes one of the means of realizing that end. To complicate matters further, a new house itself might be regarded only as a means for achieving, say, the goal of living in a good school district, in order to send one's children to a good school, so that they can have opportunities open to them as they grow up, all of which may contribute to their parents' happiness. Means-ends chains of this kind become linked with other such chains as well, adding to the complexity of deciding how to think and behave in specific situations. Buying a new house, for example, may seem to be associated negatively with teaching one's children to be concerned about standards of social equality and economic justice, and so, to alleviate the guilt that violating these standards might engender, the parents may try to become active in community service projects in their new neighborhood.

Being able to think through complicated means-ends sequences like this is a way of constructing meaning. What difference does it make if I have $5 or $10, we might hear a child say, if I can't spend it? The money has no meaning because it seems to have no connection with any other aspect of life. Enlarging the range of perceivable connections is generally a way of enhancing the meaning of any specific object or activity. As the example of people contemplating their reasons for buying a new house suggests, however, wider considerations can also become so internally complicated that the additional meaning gained from them begins to seem counterproductive. Rather than work out all the possible meaning-enhancing means-ends connections, therefore, most of us are content to bracket some considerations out of our thinking.

This tendency toward bracketing has been described in various terms, such as "framing," "multiple realities," and "spheres of relevance." Most of these terms imply something both about cognitive perception and about evaluation. The game of tennis, for example, constitutes a delimited framework that literally forces a player to focus his or her attention on certain activities and objects, and to evaluate them in terms of relevance and quality (the ball is relevant; where one hits it makes a qualitative difference to how one evaluates the game). Some of these terms also suggest the role of language in constructing partial realities but often place less emphasis on it than on the presumed psychological states of the individual. I shall employ the term "horizon," as developed chiefly in the work of M. M. Bakhtin, because it points primarily to the importance of discourse.

Much of what I said about money in the last chapter has already set the stage for thinking that there are specific horizons in which the meaning of money is generally constructed. I suggested that money in personal life is often placed in a category or framework that bears little connection with the discussions of it we find in the financial section of the newspaper and that this subjective framework is partially mapped out by connections drawn with personal responsibility, independence, freedom, and private fears and fantasies. The Bakhtinian concept of horizon helps us to understand better what "subjectivity" may mean in this context. It does not necessarily mean that money exists as a set of beliefs or deep inner dispositions within the individual's consciousness (although that may be the case). It does mean that common discourse about money associates it with terms such as "belief," "worry," and "feeling," and with individuating notions of freedom and responsibility, all of which are sometimes summarized with umbrella terms such as "subjective" or "private."

What we have considered thus far, however, is only a partial statement of what constitutes the horizon in which money is commonly framed in individual life. People may say they have beliefs about their money or indicate that "having money" conjures up images of greater freedom. But what are they referring to exactly? When people do open up and talk about money, they have to frame it in a certain vocabulary in order to communicate what they mean. Explaining what "having" or "not having" money involves, for example, requires them to use additional words. My question, then, is what are these other words? And what do they tell us about popular conceptions of money?

Let us consider the following example. Lynn Rothman, 43, is a single mother of two who works as an executive assistant in a large Oregon law firm. Between her salary and the child-support payments she receives from her former husband, she manages to pay the bills. She owns a home, drives a practical car, and is able to do most of the things middle-class Americans aspire to in their leisure time. For example, she takes the children out to eat once in awhile, sees her friends, and occasionally goes shopping just for fun. Like most people, she thinks about money a lot, but she seldom discusses it with anyone. What exactly does "money" mean to her?

She says it mostly means being comfortable and not having to worry. These are two sides of the same coin. They define, within a fairly narrow range, the upper and lower limits of what money connotes. "Comfort" is having just enough money to feel some pleasure in the way one lives. For example, her present house is practical, meeting the necessities of her family, but it is not "comfortable" because she did not have quite enough money when she bought it to get one she really liked. She would like to have either a new house that she could design herself or an old house with some added charm, like a nice kitchen or a utility room with a built-in ironing board. She insists she would not want to live extravagantly, just comfortably. "Worrying," in contrast, means being in a situation where the money may not even be sufficient to cover necessities. For example, she had a couple of unexpected bills this month and has had to call the bank to make sure she doesn't overdraw before the end of the month.

We can understand more clearly what "comfortable" and "worry" mean by considering the rest of what Lynn Rothman says about them. The level of comfort she has in mind involves being able to buy an $80 blouse or a $250 suit at one of the main department stores in town. That would be comfortable because she wouldn't have to worry whether she was spending too much. She admits that "by some standards" spending that much on clothing seems "outrageous." But she quickly diverts attention away from such standards by arguing that it is "not unusual" to pay this for a suit. She also suggests that spending a lot more, say $1,000, would be "extravagant." Altogether, she figures it would probably take an annual income of between $100,000 and $150,000 for her to feel comfortable. Again, she insists "extravagant is not me," but comfort is something she feels is a legitimate aspiration.

This example suggests in a preliminary way how the culture in which we live sets the moral context for our considerations about money. I say "moral context" because there is a sense of right and wrong, of justice and injustice, in these comments about comfort and worry. It is reasonable to think a person should live comfortably and not have to worry all the time about money. It is not reasonable for an ordinary person to want to live extravagantly (although they might fantasize about it). What these words mean, however, is defined chiefly by the marketplace. When the going price for department-store blouses is $80, then being able to buy one of these becomes a legitimate use of money. We take it for granted that the good life, financially, will consist of expenditures in this range. The meaning of money is thus subjective, in the sense that each individual must develop his or her own standards of what is reasonable, but this subjectivity is in turn deeply influenced by the more objective standards that prevail in the marketplace.

But how far does this example take us toward understanding *why* money is constructed culturally the way it is? And where are we in terms of understanding what money has to do with broader questions of meaning and value? Once it is suggested that money is a way of paying our bills, this suggestion seems so commonplace that it overwhelms almost any other thinking we might wish to do on the topic. This, nevertheless, is the place to start because it establishes the crucial context in which money must be considered. It helps substantiate that we are looking in the right place when we try to understand the meaning of money by considering how people spend it.

It seems especially important, too, to observe that this same context emerges when we look more closely at how people describe their childhood memories of money. As we have seen, people often express uncertainty about their parents' actual *views* of money because their parents said so little on the subject. But children are keen observers. They pay remarkably close attention to the nuances of the marketplace and, in the absence of other information, draw their own conclusions about money on that basis. Even much later, when they reflect on their childhood memories, adults are able to recall in vivid detail many of the specific expenditures that shaped their own views of money. One man (who says his parents were not very open about money), for example, remembers at age 4 going from dealer to dealer with his dad to look for a new automobile. The car they purchased, he recalls, had none of the "extras" he wished they could have gotten. He also remembers that when color television became popular his family didn't get one. Nor did they remodel the house or buy a new stove, like some of the neighbors. Other people speak with equal vividness about their childhood impressions of money. They remember that their mother bought them clothing at one store rather than another or that they got a new bicycle but not the specific brand for which they had hoped. They do not remember any reasons being given for these decisions, only that they came away with a sense that money was tight, plentiful, or somewhere in between. The implicit message, nevertheless, is that the right (only?) way to think about money is in terms of what it can buy.

Starting with these initial observations, we can turn then to the more specific questions that must be addressed in order to locate money within this material horizon. One obvious path to follow, still as a point of departure, is the literature on consumer behavior. For our purposes, we must, however, focus on the guiding assumptions of this literature, rather than on the more substantive arguments that are made once these assumptions are taken for granted. The consumerist model actually conceptualizes money as having a direct relation to an individual's basic life values. It assumes, in most formulations, that people fundamentally want to be happy. The specific ways in which they pursue happiness are likely to vary (depending on background and circumstances) but may include such goals as health, security, being loved, being a member of a supportive community, beauty, knowledge, and relaxation. Consumer goods provide the specific means of attaining these goals. Money takes on meaning primarily as the wherewithal for purchasing these goods. This way of understanding money clearly gets around the concern I have voiced about values being bracketed out of people's thinking about their finances.

A surface reading of the argument, though, tends to be misleading. Several additional assumptions substantially weaken the connection between money and values. One is that the typical consumer is only vaguely and partially aware of his or her specific values. Another is that all the values to which people are likely to be oriented tend to be positive (for example, health as opposed to illness); consequently, the greater the *number* of these values that can be attained, the happier a person will be (by implication, therefore, the more money one has, the better off one is). A third assumption is that all values can be pursued meaningfully through the expenditure of money on material goods and services. And a final assumption is that choices among specific values are likely to reflect individual or cultural preferences that lie outside the model itself. In combination, these assumptions give little reason to believe the average consumer actually takes his or her values very much into account in making decisions about the expenditure of money.

They also provide a strong basis for arguing that the taboo against talking about money and the material horizon in which money is subjectively framed by the average consumer are connected in more than a casual way. The literature on consumer behavior generally acknowledges that human values, including their implications for the uses of money, can be influenced by conscious reflection and collective deliberation. The reason it assumes this is that any effort to mold consumer behavior (for example, through advertising) depends on its malleability. The same literature argues that these efforts are not only possible but desirable as well, *because people often feel they lack sources of advice on how best to live their lives.*[1] In short, not talking about money in personal life makes a place for advertisers to exercise their definitional craft.

We come, then, to a fuller exposition of the claim made in the last chapter, at that point largely by analogy, about the connection between institutionalized control over public life and the strength of taboos in private life. What might be termed "privileged" or "hegemonic" discourse in the realm of consumer behavior is strengthened by the fact (or assumption thereof) that people do not know how to connect their own values with their uses of money in private life. It thus becomes the advertisers' role to establish this connection, presumably by convincing the prospective consumer of a causal relationship between an expenditure on product X and the realization of value Y. Taking the consumer behavior literature at face value, we might even assume that the advertiser's role, therefore, is to perform a positive, value-clarifying function. What might give pause to accepting this argument at face value, however, is the possibility of conceptual bracketing that was raised earlier. Clearly, any hope of settling the matter requires us to consider some empirical evidence.

Though the consumer behavior literature itself is replete with empirical studies, it behooves us to take people's own accounts of their behavior seriously, rather than relying on inferential evidence about the supposed connections between purchases and values. Again, talk is not simply a fallible indicator of deeper psychological dispositions but a constitutive feature of values themselves. How people talk about their purchases provides a way of gauging the material horizons within which they frame their discussions.

The consumerist orientation is particularly evident when people talk about relatively small, discretionary items. "I just look at it as kind of a trade-off between getting something of high quality and yet not spending more than I felt I can afford," is the way one man describes his decision to buy a stereo. A woman talking about buying a nice dress for herself uses some of the same language. "Mostly the price," she volunteers. "Am I getting my money's worth? I knew if it didn't turn out, I could return it, of course. But it wasn't exorbitant; I knew I could afford it." We might think these discretionary purchases would need to be linked more closely with personal values than items more easily legitimated in terms of necessity. Instead, people appear to think of them as goods that everyone has; thus, the question is not so much "why should I get one of these?" as it is which brand is the best buy.

Many such items may of course be casual, even impulsive purchases that do not require significant thinking about the uses of one's money. But people who admit they scrimp and save in order to make purchases about which they reflect deeply also tend largely to talk in the language of the marketplace. "I had to save my speaking fees and Christmas money for two solid years," says Audrey Cole, a highly conscientious woman, age 43, who directs a nonprofit organization in the Midwest. She is talking about buying a personal computer. "I only had so much money so I couldn't just go out and buy any old machine I wanted. I had to spend a lot of time shopping. I didn't know much about them. I had to talk to a lot of sales people. And it just so happened that I got lucky because they accidentally mispriced the unit. So I basically got the monitor for free." Asked specifically to say *why* she bought the machine (and to talk about her motivation), she continues to frame her account, as it were, within the context of the computer store itself. "It was the right price; price had to do with a lot of it. A lot of the IBMs were priced over my budget. I didn't want a cheap machine. I had certain specifications. So, when I went into Sears and he quoted me this price, I just said I'll take it." Pressed further to talk about any other feelings or considerations that may have been important, she begins to sound even more as if she is being asked to do a commercial. "Sears is a well-known company. We deal with Sears a lot. You can get these service contracts." She concludes, "I was pretty proud of the deal I had made and the price I had gotten and the machine that I ended up with."

The largest single financial decision most people ever make is purchasing a house. Here we would expect all the larger questions money implies to come rushing to the surface. Not only does the financial obligation incurred in purchasing a house commit one to a certain lifestyle; the house itself defines a considerable portion of that lifestyle. If people are too busy to examine their values every time they buy a new article of clothing, the same cannot be said of buying a house. Most people buy one infrequently and put a great deal of effort into the process. What are their main considerations?

Davis Reskin had recently purchased a house in West Chester, so the issues he had considered were still fresh in his mind. The main questions, he recalls, were, "Are we choosing the best area? Is the house in good condition, not just cosmetically, but the pipes, the electrical wiring, the whole bit? What can go wrong? Are we getting the best deal possible for the money?" Charles Greenwood had also made the decision to buy a house not long ago. He observes, "The primary issue in making that purchase was the ability to meet the monthly obligation— basically the initial cost of making the acquisition and then carrying the acquisition in the sense of how secure my income was and whether there was enough income and how much income I could devote to that particular acquisition." Asked to elaborate on any other considerations, he explains, "It also represents a way to avoid expenses, rental expenses or living expenses. In the long term it would be a cheaper, less costly way to fulfill the need of having a place to live."

These statements are not atypical. Most of the people we talked to discussed purchases of houses, cars, boats, and other major items in terms of financial considerations alone. They took for granted that such expenditures are legitimate personal needs. Trade-offs among various needs or wants were not discussed. Instead, people started from the unspoken assumption that they were already "in the market" for an item and then proceeded to explain why one selection was a "better buy" than another. Being "in the market" is decisive because it brackets out of consideration any of the reasons that might have placed one in that context in the first place.[2]

The consumerist framework is so common to the way people talk about their purchases that we might ask whether it even makes sense to suggest there may be reasonable alternatives. Does *anybody* bring a wider range of considerations into their decisions about spending their money? Let us listen to Pam Jones, the Illinois software engineer whom we have heard from several times in previous chapters, as she describes how she and her husband decided to purchase a house. "Bill and I had a pretty high income, and I felt like it was a real waste of money to be paying rent all the time. I wanted to build up some equity. I also felt like it'd be good to lower our taxes, by being able to deduct the interest on a house. I was ready to settle down, too. So it was mainly just personal preference for a lifestyle, the tax issue, and making good financial sense."

Her account sounds very much like the consumerist framework most people invoke. It is interesting, however, that she also mentions something about lifestyle. This notion is thrown in almost as an afterthought, with such brevity that it can almost be missed, especially as she reiterates the importance of taxes and financial considerations. The consumerist framework, it appears, is the one she knows most readily how to put into words. She seems most comfortable talking to the interviewer in these public, commonly accepted terms. Her use of the phrase "personal preference" in conjunction with lifestyle suggests that there may be a deeper meaning she feels may be less appropriate to discuss. Fortunately, she continues.

"We probably could've gotten something a lot more expensive," she explains. "I think this is where our sense of lifestyle came in. We didn't want to be tied down to really expensive monthly payments. We wanted something that we could pay for with only one of us working, or maybe both of us working half-day jobs. So when it came to choosing the house, those factors came into play. And then, we wanted a big enough living room that we could have friends over. Also, we do a lot of our visiting in the kitchen, so for us we wanted either a large kitchen or a kitchen with the family room right next to it."

As she discusses their decision in greater detail, Pam reveals that she and her husband included their deepest personal values quite explicitly in their deliberations. At first, her remarks about friends seem to express little more than the usual desire to entertain. But closer consideration reveals there is a matter of principle involved as well. "We've talked a lot, Bill and I, about living in more of a community setting. We've talked about how much our need for privacy would balance against our desire to live more equitably, to live better, to live more in a community. In fact, Bill had a problem with buying a house at all because he feels it doesn't make sense for the Earth as a whole for everybody to have their own little houses, or everybody to have their own little lawn mower. Why don't we share stuff? Why don't we live more in community? So he's real excited that there is a community organization, a neighborhood block organization. We've also talked about the possibility of having refugees live in the basement. Or even converting the big room downstairs into a bedroom for us and then the other upstairs room we could share with whoever needed it. In fact, my password is 'to share' because I felt like that's the purpose of the house."

From these comments we see that values other than sheer financial considerations were indeed highly important to Pam and her husband. Even though they could have afforded a more expensive home, they decided to restrict their financial obligations. Their sense of friendliness and community responsibility played an important role as well. Some of these considerations, in fact, may strike readers as being quite understandable. And yet three things are important to observe. First, Pam Jones is the exception rather than the rule. Most people, including the ones who talked at greatest length about their purchases, had difficulty saying anything about considerations other than price, brand, comparable worth, and the like. Second, Pam herself drastically relativizes the role of values in her account by talking, at least initially, in the language of lifestyles and personal preferences. Somehow, her values were strong enough to restrain the materialism evident in many people's comments, but on the surface these values have no more cultural authority than those driving other people to express a "lifestyle preference" for luxury goods and ostentatious living. And third, Pam's account demonstrates clearly how the privatization of both money and personal values inhibits public discourse that might serve better to integrate the two. She has discussed this relationship at great length in the intimate confidences she shares with her husband. But it is as if she is revealing a personal secret when she discusses them with us.

We can see more clearly where the relationship between expenditures and values is located in Pam Jones's map of the world if we pause to hear what follows immediately after the portion of her account that we have just considered. "Another thing that's related to this is Bill and I are not legally married. That's because it's cheaper. You pay more taxes as a married couple than you do as two single people." Conservative, religious, and family oriented as she is, this is an important revelation for Pam to make. She realizes herself that it might not have come out in the interview had she not volunteered it. Opening up, revealing the more intimate details of her thoughts about money and values, has prompted her to make this admission as well. But is she really meaning to say that she and her husband stayed "single" for purely monetary reasons? Yes and no. The surface reason is to save money on taxes. The deeper reason, she reveals, is that she is a pacifist who refuses to pay the "military portion" of her taxes. "I'm willing to withhold taxes and get in trouble for it, and have it garnished off my wages and taken out of my IRA account," she explains. "This is a legal thing I can do to reduce that."

It is evident from someone like Pam Jones, then, that spending money can be intricately tied up with a wide range of deeper human values that stand largely outside the marketplace. Trying to integrate these values into one's thinking about money can lead to a reduced level of expenditures on material purchases and to other decisions meant to nurture these values. Such considerations are often complicated, requiring husbands and wives or (as in the case of Pam and Bill) other supportive friends to reflect seriously on how best to make these decisions. Most people find it easier to bracket such considerations out of conscious deliberation by focusing only on the economic aspects of their purchases.

An additional reason for bracketing out broader considerations is that decisions to spend money, like thoughts about money itself, are subject to a wide variety of fears and anxieties. Making so many of these decisions, as we do, in private, we wonder if we are doing the right thing. It is difficult to know because few of the purchases we make can be justified entirely in terms of necessity. Having a car, for example, may be considered a necessity, but whether to pay $3,000 extra for options becomes a matter of judgment. Facing the full implications of our purchases also puts us in contact with moral dictums that arouse anxiety and yet are too vague to be of much help. People talk, for example, about feeling guilty after they make a purchase because they have been taught that frugality is a virtue and materialism a vice.[3] Good salespeople, of course, realize this and make sure they say something affirming about our purchase before we leave the store.[4] Framing our thoughts in purely market terms also helps reduce our anxiety. Instead of wondering whether we should have made the purchase in the first place, or how it really fits in with our values, we can concentrate on the price. Comparing the item we bought with one we did not buy limits our attention to the specific merits of our purchase.

THE FAMILY BUDGET

Conventional economic wisdom suggests that framing our thinking about money in purely materialistic terms has one redeeming virtue: at least we can then think rationally about it. The logic behind this argument goes like this: The subject of human values is a murky area, filled with lots of anxiety-producing uncertainty. Much of the connection between money and values must indeed be personal and subjective. The individual, however, can exercise control over the choices he or she makes by paying careful attention to the ways he or she spends money. A well-planned, closely monitored budget may be the best solution.

The family budget, therefore, merits special consideration. If people do not talk much about their money, they may nevertheless be more judicious in its use than we have thus far suggested. In following a budget, they may in effect translate vague personal goals into numeric calculations, weigh the various options, and make rational choices. If so, several possible implications of immediate relevance to our argument are likely to follow. One possibility is that the family budget substitutes in a negative way for the value-laden discussions that might help people escape the cycle of consumerism in which they find themselves. This possibility implies that budgets, like comparative shopping, force so much attention onto specific economic considerations that broader goals are neglected. A different possibility is that the family budget, rather than moral discourse, can be an effective way of guiding and restraining the financial commitments that add pressure to people's lives. In this scenario, getting more people to budget their money would be the best way to curtail excessive spending and the anxieties associated with it. There is also the possibility that budgets themselves contribute to these pressures and anxieties. In other words, budgets reveal the facts of the matter, that really not having enough money is the problem, not the ways in which people think about their money. All of these possibilities, it should be noted, also suggest that money is not as subjective or free-floating as I have argued but is part of an objective, rational system of personal finances.

None of the possibilities just mentioned seems credible, however. The reason is that most people either do not have family budgets or, if they do, seldom try to follow them. Most of the people we talked to actually regarded budgets more as a nuisance than as something they *should* follow, if only they were disciplined enough to do so.[5] They felt this way for a variety of reasons, ranging from having enough money that they didn't have to worry, to having too little to worry about. A common attitude, though, was that budgets are unessential because expenditures mostly fall into two categories in the first place: those over which you have no control anyway (such as rent and utilities), and those that are discretionary, but okay as long as you don't write bad checks or find yourself unable to pay your bills.[6] Some people regarded balancing their checkbooks as a more convenient way, after the fact, of keeping tabs on their expenditures. But even this method was too bothersome for a number of people. One man, for example, explained, "I haven't balanced my checkbook in over a year. I just know there's money there, I don't know how much is there." In other cases, people admitted they didn't follow a budget because trying to do so had forced them to talk about their money, the result of which seemed to be marital discord.[7] This sensitivity to the mixing of money and human relationships is also a more general concern that we shall consider later in the chapter.

It is perhaps not surprising that so few people follow budgets, but the importance of this fact cannot be understood enough. One of the standing arguments in favor of the modern money economy is that it has made rational economic, means-ends calculations possible. Organizations devise budgets for precisely this reason. The models of economic virtue to which we look in our nation's history advocated careful budgeting in personal life as well. From Benjamin Franklin to Andrew Carnegie, and from the Puritan divines to contemporary self-

help manuals, the message has been that a well-disciplined life involves following a precise personal budget. If the passions guiding the
human spirit were unruly and untamed, at least the realm of personal
finances could be subjected to a more rational mode of governance.

The evidence suggests, however, that within the material horizon of
personal finance itself, things are generally more uncertain than the
economic model would like to admit. Instead of planning one's expected expenditures ahead of time, like an organization producing
goods might do, consumers spend their discretionary income without
any preconceived plan. Paying the bills is their method, after the fact,
of aligning these expenditures with their income. Consumerism is thus
an even more pervasive characteristic of personal finances than the accounts we considered earlier might have led us to believe. In the absence of a budget, comparative pricing and advertisers' reassurances
become all the more important. It is little wonder that the subjective
correlate of this consumer orientation is the feeling that more money
would solve everything. Purchasing decisions dictated by the outer
limits of one's economic resources exert constant pressure to extend
beyond these limits.

Consumer Rituals

How, then, do people make their decisions about spending money?
Can we learn something more from these decisions that will help us
understand the nature of economic commitments better—why they
seem less rational than they should be, why they seem disconnected
from other parts of life, and why they seem so difficult to restrain?
What we have considered thus far about consumerism and the lack of
family budgets provides a valuable clue. Most people do not structure
their money and spending habits by engaging in planning, systematic
calculations, and keeping rational budgets. Instead, they engage in
symbolic acts, "consumer rituals," that signal implicit, behavioral connections between their money and some of the values they hold dear.
If they believe it is a good thing to be frugal, for example, they find
token ways in which to demonstrate this value by denying themselves
certain material pleasures. They may also find ways of getting around
the value of frugality by ritually redefining certain activities so that
they "don't count."

In calling these activities "rituals," I follow conventional understandings of this term in the social sciences. Ritual is symbolic-expressive behavior that communicates something about social relations, often in a relatively dramatic or formal manner.[8] In the present case, I am suggesting that certain activities, such as the purchase of a consumer item, convey special meaning beyond whatever material gratification they may provide. That money and material goods have a symbolic dimension has, of course, long been recognized. A new car, for example, symbolizes status in the community as well as being a mere means of transportation. Here, however, I want to focus on a more restrictive kind of symbolism. Some consumer activities, I shall argue, are formally and dramaturgically set apart in a way that not only makes them special, but gives them special meaning as markers of appropriate consumer behavior itself. In other words, these activities take on special significance because they define the outer boundaries of the material sphere in which the individual resides. Consumer rituals do this largely by establishing special relationships between the individual and some material object acquired through an expenditure of money. We shall see that loans and gifts also perform this function, but in a different way. Understanding what consumer rituals are, and how they function, will require us to consider some specific examples and to contrast them with some of the activities we saw earlier in considering accounts of work.

Consumer rituals come mainly in two varieties: those that define appropriate spending behavior by erring on the side of frugality, and those that define it by providing examples of splurging. An example of the former would be lawyer Stanton Haynes's obsession with turning out the lights. Although he earns a six-digit salary and luxuriates in the "ambience" he has created with fine furnishings in his apartment, turning out the lights helps him think of himself as a frugal person. In contrast, a ritual that defines splurging would be appraiser Norm Lundström's policy of setting no limits on the amount of orange juice his family consumes. Frugal in many other ways, he sees this particular activity as evidence that he also knows how to be extravagant.

By most indications, behavior like this is so trivial that it deserves little more than passing attention. Yet boundary-defining activity of this kind is precisely what anthropologists consider the key to understanding cultural systems. The behavior itself may be of little consequence economically, but it takes on special significance because it transgresses established cultural demarcations. There is power in these demarcations because they provide order, regularity, in social life.[9] Activity that crosses them acquires some of this power. In the present case, consumer rituals are much like the hypothetical examples Lynn Rothman used in explaining the differences among worry, comfort, and extravagance. Comfort, we can now say, is an appropriate level of spending, the upper and lower boundaries of which are defined by rituals of frugality and splurging. Turning off the lights is voluntary behavior that reminds one what it might be like actually to worry that one's utility bill could not be paid. Extravagant consumption of orange juice is token behavior that points toward genuine (costly) extravagance, such as purchasing a $1,000 dress or having a second home in the Bahamas.[10] The specific behavior that serves these ritual functions may of course be quite different from one person to the next. In both the examples just given, we know why the particular behavior is significant, however. In Stanton Haynes's case, his father always made an issue of turning out the lights, even though Stanton felt as a child (and feels even more strongly today) that a few kilowatts here and there were scarcely significant. Norm Lundström's orange-juice extravagance also ties back to his upbringing. His mother always rationed the orange juice; not rationing it is his way of being a spendthrift.

A few other examples will illustrate the variety of consumer rituals. Like turning out the lights or consuming orange juice, many represent relatively insignificant items for the average, middle-class household: going to matinees instead of evening movies, paying cash to avoid credit-card interest, or keeping the thermostat set two degrees below the comfort level, all on the side of frugality, or taking the kids out for dinner once a week, splurging on favorite compact discs, or treating oneself to a massage, on the side of extravagance. Many of these activities have acquired ritual significance because they are the subject of advertising campaigns and financial advice columns. Other consumer rituals may be considerably more costly but also frequently represent conformity with, or a retreat from, the consumer appeals evident in the wider culture. *Not* buying a new BMW (but getting a used one) can thus be a ritual of frugality.

One type of consumer ritual came up so often in our interviews that it deserves special mention. Middle-class men and women who otherwise led reasonably conservative lives in their consumer behavior routinely admitted to having purchased something they considered extravagant in recent months. One person mentioned a new pair of skis; another, a wide-screen television set; another, an airplane; many, a new stereo system; others, a sportier-than-average automobile, a computer, or expensive sports equipment. Their way of justifying these purchases, against what appeared to be a slight case of guilt, was to describe them as "adult toys." This of course is a term that marketing experts have coined, applying it to entire stores that specialize in such items. But I believe there is also a deeper reason why it rolls so easily from people's tongues. Appropriate consumer behavior is associated with adult roles and responsibilities. A way of dramatizing the outer edges of this behavior is to act like a child. Some married men and women, for example, claimed they were completely unconcerned about money but revealed they could be because their spouse made all the decisions. They were, in a sense, adult children. The term "adult toys" carries similar connotations. It mixes registers, thus symbolizing perfectly the boundary between adult responsibility and childhood indulgence. Temporary regression into the role of child allows adults to do things they otherwise would not do. But labeling this regression as such also limits it. Purchasing adult toys is a consumer ritual that helps define responsible behavior by temporarily abandoning it.

Though common, consumer rituals are peculiar in one respect. They suggest, like the other evidence we have considered, that the world of money, as most people experience it, is far less rational than we might imagine from listening to economists. Ritual may convey its own sense of rationality. But it mostly takes us away from contemporary notions of this term and places us squarely in the midst of primordial societies in which ritual and symbolism is everything. To understand the significance of ritual, we must then consider the functions it has always performed in such settings.

Rituals acquire special meaning in a world of uncertainty. They help people make sense of their lives when conditions seem out of control, beyond comprehension. They may be institutionalized, observed at regular intervals, or even mandated by law. But their purpose is clearest when they help people through times of transition, when they clarify ambiguous relationships, and when they give structure to moments of awe. They tell people how to behave when the situations they face defy systematic forethought and calculation.

Consumer rituals provide ways of responding to the economic uncertainty that pervades private life in modern societies. We may try to plan out our lives, but we seldom know with any assurance whether our planning will pay off or not. This is especially true in the short run. While it may be true that nothing is more certain than death and taxes, monthly expenses can fluctuate wildly. Health insurance may save individuals from bankruptcy, but an unanticipated visit to the doctor can wreck havoc with family finances. Uncertainties brought on by fears of losing one's job, fluctuations in the stock market, instability of retirement programs, and difficulties in predicting the cost of higher education aggravate the problem. Faced with these uncertainties, people do symbolic things, like turning off the lights or refusing to scrimp on orange juice. These rituals make them feel better about themselves. In the absence of more objective criteria, feelings become important indeed.

We can grasp the importance of consumer rituals better by distinguishing more carefully among the types of uncertainty that characterize economic life. In the workplace, large bureaucracies and rationalized performance criteria make things fairly structured and predictable but often restrict the flow of information sufficiently that knowing exactly what one's contribution has been is difficult to gauge. The problem tends to be *ambiguity*. For the individual in such settings, uncertainty is likely to be experienced chiefly as doubt about the relationship between one's limited, specialized efforts and the wider goals of the organization. Workplace rituals, as we have seen, reduce this doubt by focusing on the relationship between one's activities and the self or an immediate community of co-workers or by magnifying the scope and variety of one's tasks. Consumer rituals respond to a vastly different sort of uncertainty. Unlike the workplace, where things may be all too predictable, the typical consumer is faced with a high degree of *unpredictability*. Serious risks may again be reduced by large-scale institutions, such as the social security system or life insurance programs, but the degree to which any specific activity can be predicted to achieve its desired goal may be relatively low. This is because the individual or household is relatively weak compared with the larger institutions and economic forces governing social life. It is also a function of the lack of training most individuals feel they have received in understanding the relationship between work and money, between saving and spending, or in thinking about the role of money in achieving broader human goals such as happiness.

There is thus a link between consumer rituals and the broader issue of how money and human values should be understood. The unpredictability that generates consumer rituals in the first place occurs largely because money is actually a function of our behavior as whole persons, not as the narrowly defined occupants of social roles. Role performance can be prescribed; the behavior of whole persons cannot be. In the workplace, for example, an executive can predict with a high degree of certainty that his or her secretary will send out the letters he or she writes. The same person, as consumer, is subject to much more uncertainty because he or she cannot predict very well whether one child will wreck the family car, another child will decide to attend an expensive college, or his or her spouse will sue for divorce. In short, unpredictability is a feature of human communities, whereas ambiguity is a function of organizations.

The best way to reduce unpredictability in human communities is to encourage greater communication, especially discussion that clarifies the relationship between means and ends, between action and values. But faced with the taboo that prohibits talking about money, individuals engage in consumer rituals instead. These rituals function like grunts and hand signals, telling others (and oneself) in a vague way that it is good not to be too frugal or too extravagant. They permit specific decisions about money to be made largely on the basis of cues received from advertisers and marketing campaigns. But they serve poorly to communicate more exact messages about how to relate to other human beings.

Money and Human Relationships

Besides the taboos and rituals that give money its peculiarly delimited location in American culture, there are also strong boundaries that separate it from human relationships. Money has to be kept in its place, we say, because it corrupts these relationships. What does this mean? How do we maintain these distinctions? How do they further prevent us from considering money in a less delimited way?

Were an anthropologist from another society to observe the relationship in American culture between money and human relationships, that person would undoubtedly recognize its centrality to the way our culture is organized. Activities and objects are placed in different categories, depending on whether they are viewed as monetary concerns or as human concerns. An anthropologist would also notice that the human category is often thought to be corrupted or contaminated by too much exposure to the monetary category. The possibility of such contamination is a danger that people worry about in American society. The reason they do so is that money seems to expand into new arenas where it has not been evident before. When such expansion is perceived to occur, it generates a sense of unease, a feeling that things are somehow askew and need to be set aright. Why it seems this way, and what can be done about it—whether moral discourse can be mobilized to protect human relationships from further contamination—are the questions that require attention.

A prior issue, however, is what exactly it means in this context to talk about "human relationships." The transaction that constitutes a human relationship may be with a real estate agent who has been retained to sell a person's house. During the process, the parties involved may exchange pleasantries about a wide variety of topics and may even develop a level of trust between them. When money is exchanged at closing, however, one is unlikely to hear anyone complain that this relationship has been corrupted. Consummation of the deal is, in fact, likely to terminate the relationship entirely, but neither party complains because it is known from the start that money is the basis of their interaction. It may be worth noting, however, that the actual transfer of money takes place with some solemnity (an exchange of formal papers, checks placed in envelopes, situated in an attorney's office) that allows casual conversation to continue with only implicit acknowledgment of the monetary dimension of the occasion.

The type of relationship most likely to evoke fear of being corrupted by money is one founded on some other basis (especially kinship) and presumed to involve the whole person or a large number of roles, rather than one delimited role. "Intimacy" is the test characteristic of such relationships, but clarity about the meaning of intimacy must be established. Despite the fact that intimacy is often used to indicate the physical dimension of relationships, it should be evident that this dimension is seldom the one that arouses concern about the role of money. One expects to pay a doctor, masseuse, or prostitute for the physical services they provide. Intimacy is better understood in terms of the scope and depth of a relationship. Sharing emotions or dreams and aspirations that lie at the core of one's being is said to indicate "depth" in a relationship. Sharing a wide variety of experiences (child rearing, house buying, tennis) and ones that may extend through different stages of a person's life cycle constitutes intimacy because of the scope of the roles that are included.

What is at issue, then, is the fear that money corrupts something fundamentally *human*. Intimacy, depth, scope are at risk, not simply any kind of social interaction. What is at risk is the sense that something of intrinsic value will be transformed when it is brought into contact with money. It is the same fear that prompts people to say that a work of art is "priceless" or that no monetary value can be attached to one's health, to one's spouse or children, or to love. This moreover is why intimate human relationships that cannot literally be kept free of monetary implications are often surrounded with special rituals that help keep the separation intact symbolically. Marriage, for example, always establishes a legal relationship involving fundamental economic commitments (such as agreeing to share property equally or file tax returns jointly). But these commitments are carefully shielded from view during the wedding ceremony itself. Norms may even function to keep the material gifts that well-wishers bring at some distance from the ceremony itself. For example, some traditions require that these be brought to the bride's house before the ceremony; some, to the reception (which is likely to be held at a different place); and some, to be given in cash, but anonymously, in a special envelope.[11]

It is easy, in a general sense, to understand why the boundary separating money from human relationships is so important. The problem of mixing the two is that the ability to price something unique is implied. To say only that something precious is *like* money does not raise this problem. For example, when the Hebrew scriptures proclaim, "I have rejoiced in the path of your instruction as one rejoices over wealth,"analogy is presented, but nothing more. In contrast, it would seem problematic for someone to say, "My wife is worth $10 million; how much is yours worth?" The reason is that placing a specific monetary value on an object implies a market for that object. But the very notion of a market suggests universal standards of evaluation, interchangeability among equally valued objects, and the possibility of transferring objects from one party to another. Something valued because of the unique relationship between it and a person cannot adequately be subjected to the pricing mechanism of the market.

There are, of course, abundant examples of precisely this kind of pricing taking place. People may be unique, but they still take out insurance that attaches a monetary value to their life. They may build their own home and fill it with their own unique memories, and yet be able to agree on a price for it when they have to move. But in both these examples the market mechanism does not accomplish a complete con-version of something unique into a monetary value. Life insurance is not intended to replace the person, but simply to cover some of the costs that might be borne by that person's survivors. Virtually any amount can be purchased; the pricing mechanism applies only to the cost of premiums, which are determined largely on the basis of actuar-ial statistics. The price of a house is determined by local market condi-tions, as evidenced in recent sales prices of comparable houses and on standard appraisal guidelines for square footage, acreage, number of rooms, improvements, and so on. What is unique (e.g., personal memo-ries) or difficult to price in the local market (e.g., expensive Chinese wallpaper) is likely to be omitted from the calculations.

In most cases, the boundary separating money from human relation-ships serves a more specific purpose, however. The relationship be-tween parents and children can be taken as an example. Although a parent might in extreme circumstances be forced to place a monetary value on the life of a child (perhaps in a court settlement involving accidental death), it would be much more common for money to enter the relationship in less holistic ways. Parents, for example, routinely give their children allowances, reward them monetarily for making good grades in school, pay them to do household chores, and so on. In these cases it is even possible to say that a kind of spot market often exists to determine the amounts of money involved. Children, for in-stance, may compare allowances with their classmates to determine appropriate levels or adopt collective bargaining practices with their siblings to drive up the price of carrying out the trash. The difficulties and limitations of these everyday monetary transactions point to some of the most important functions of drawing lines between money and human relationships. One is that true market conditions do not prevail. A child dissatisfied with the allowance offered by his or her parents cannot simply go to another set of parents in hopes of receiving more. Another is that the "memory" of these limited markets is likely to de-pend more on standards of justice external to market considerations than on market characteristics themselves. A younger sibling may de-mand the same wages for doing household chores as an older sibling receives, as a matter of principle, even though the level of performance may not be equivalent at all.[12] A third factor, compounded by the other two, is that the transaction costs involved in attaching monetary value to particular activities may become a limiting consideration in them-

selves. Buying a newspaper at a fixed price of fifty cents illustrates minimal transaction costs. Paying a child to go buy the newspaper would
likely involve a great deal more time and energy because no external
mechanism is available to dictate the going price and because a whole
range of "personal" considerations are likely to be taken into account
(such as the weather, the child's age, how badly the child needs money,
what siblings have been paid for comparable tasks, etc.). If these transactions are sporadic, necessitating renegotiation each time, the relative
costs will be even higher.

Because of the limited applicability of true market mechanisms in
these situations, the following norms are likely to be followed, all of
which help restrict the degree to which monetary transactions interfuse
ordinary human relationships. First, what might be called "global"
agreements will be resorted to, rather than engaging in specific negotiations about the price of particular activities. Spouses agree to pool
their money as long as they are married, for example, instead of paying
each other on a daily basis for making the bed, driving the children to
school, and so forth.[13] Parents pay children a standard monthly allowance, rather than negotiating a piece-rate system for particular household chores. Second, those transactions to which monetary value is attached are likely to be restricted either to rare, substantial events or to
easily calculated, routine events.[14] Spouses may have prenuptial agreements that cover the distribution of assets upon divorce, as an example
of the former. Parents may pay children for good grades because a
fixed price scale can be specified and there is relatively little ambiguity
involved. Third, much of what makes the relationship "human" is
likely to be excluded from monetary transactions, either because the
costs are deemed too high or because having to establish a price in the
first place would significantly alter the nature of the exchange. It might
be possible, for example, to establish a system of monetary rewards to
encourage such activities as smiling, saying nice things to one's siblings, or being "helpful." Behaviorists have tried to do precisely that.
But for most people, the difficulty of deciding exactly what smiling,
saying nice things, and being helpful are renders a system of this kind
unworkable. And fourth, attempts to reduce transaction costs may include withholding valuable information from some of the parties involved. Children bargaining with their parents for higher allowances,
for example, may not reveal the fact that their friends are receiving
substantially less. Parents may also withhold relevant information; for

example, about their salary, to prevent this from becoming a factor in the negotiations. This, of course, is one of the practical functions served by the taboo against talking about money with children and close friends.

These norms help reinforce the boundaries separating money from human relationships. But they tell us more about the consequences of these boundaries than they do about their sources. Somehow, people learn that money corrupts human relationships, and they learn this lesson well enough to keep the two separate. How? Functional explanations of the kind just considered focus chiefly on efficiency. Cultural explanations reveal more about the actual understandings, the language, that people use to justify the deeper sense they have that money and human relationships have a corrosive effect on each other.

Our interviews revealed clearly that people learn early in life that money and human relationships, like oil and water, do not mix. Amy Oldenburg, the Los Angeles hospital chaplain whom we have heard from before, provided one of the clearest answers on this subject. She described her father as "a very, very poor preacher's kid" whose clothes were generally "hand-me-downs" from the neighbors ("he used to have to fight sometimes to keep them on his back, or so he told us"). Her mother, in contrast, was "a very, very rich little girl" whose father owned a huge lumber mill in Oregon ("she never wanted for anything"). Amy's own upbringing, she explains, occurred in a relatively affluent setting. Her father was a "self-made man" who had done well in the insurance business. But her experience of money as a child, she believes, placed her in a difficult double bind. "I think my dad would always get nervous when my mother was spending the money, but they really did have it for her to spend. So, the double bind came with us kids thinking, well, gosh, we have it here, it's around us, and yet they're always fighting and arguing about it. It was a very tense issue."

The conflict Amy saw between her parents has deeply influenced her view of money as an adult. "Today," she says, "I feel very insecure about money matters." She fears money because she isn't quite sure of its appropriate place. On the one hand, "it seemed to be the thing that caused a lot of unhappiness and division within my family." But on the other hand, "it seemed to be the thing that also made for a good time, or made life seem comfortable and secure." Valuing it positively, and yet worrying (like her father) that it might disappear, she has often experienced what she describes as "panic" when the subject of money is discussed. She handles these feelings chiefly by separating money from her thinking about human relationships. Whenever she accumulates some extra cash, she goes out and spends it. That way, at least, she is able to enjoy it for a little while. Part of her believes more money would make her happier because she could go shopping more often and not worry as much about paying the bills. But another part of her views money with suspicion. It "messed up" her home life, and she would like to experience an intimate relationship with someone now that was simply free of any considerations about money.

Many of the people we talked to explained that they had learned to separate money from human relationships by seeing their parents fight about it.[15] This was especially true in instances where their parents held widely differing views about money, a situation made more common by the high level of upward social mobility that characterized American society during the 1940s and 1950s. With working-class people entering the middle class in growing numbers, some (like Amy Oldenburg's father) were bound to marry into more affluent families and thus find themselves linked with someone whose views about spending were markedly different. In other cases, upward social mobility itself caused material circumstances to outpace attitudes toward spending, thereby increasing the likelihood that family arguments about money could not easily be settled by economic logic alone. Exogamy across ethnic and religious lines also added to the likelihood of marital disagreements in some cases. When parents were divorced, children were especially likely to feel money had tainted their relationships, perhaps because the divorce itself had forced financial issues to the surface. In many other instances, people described conflict with their own spouse over questions of personal finance. Feeling they had no clear guidelines, or even ways of discussing it reasonably, they resolved the question of money by putting it in a different mental category from their thinking about relationships.

Two additional arguments have emerged during the past two decades to reinforce the view that money can have a corrupting influence on human relationships. One has arisen in conjunction with alimony and child-support suits and has been voiced particularly in women's-rights literature. It emphasizes the economic dimension of family relationships, often pointing out their conflictual nature, and the contrast between these conflicts and ideals of intimacy, nurture, and caring.[16]

The second surfaced in our interviews mainly among people who had been deeply exposed to therapeutic perspectives on human relationships. Besides leading to arguments, these people suggested, money becomes a means of power, control, and manipulation. It creates asymmetries between parents and children or between men and women that can interfere with personal autonomy, self-expression, and frank considerations of emotions and feelings. In both views, money appears increasingly as a corrupting influence.

With strong cultural norms, as well as practical reasons, for keeping money and human relationships apart, the question arises, then, of why money seems to expand into realms where it has not been present before. The issue can be framed as one of stasis versus dynamism. A static understanding of American materialism would emphasize that people have good reasons to keep money in its place, and generally do so, if only because the transaction costs of extending it into the human realm become prohibitive.[17] A dynamic understanding, in contrast, emphasizes the fact that people nevertheless perceive it to be difficult to keep money restrained. Sensing that money can be a corrosive feature in their lives, they go ahead to worry that it is in fact having a corrupting influence. Why?

The growing penetration of money into other realms of personal existence is rooted in the dynamics of modern society itself. The fleeting, mobile relationships with strangers that have replaced more enduring forms of interaction in many parts of modern society contribute to the rising influence of money. They do so because there is no secure way of reciprocating in these relationships. Long-term neighbors, for example, can provide meals to each other in their own homes, knowing that over a period of years many opportunities will arise for reciprocity; strangers who may meet for a business lunch are more likely to pay cash because they will never see each other again. Uncertainty about the longevity of marriage is an even more striking example. Monetary considerations become more important because each spouse may have collateral from previous marriages and realistically anticipate dissolution of the current partnership sometime before death. Child-rearing patterns have also shifted toward increasing involvement in market relations. Although child labor has always raised economic considerations in families, the provision of goods to children in traditional societies generally took place outside the market, depending heavily on homegrown food, homemade clothing, and education through apprenticeship. At present, nearly everything children require, from food and clothing to medical care and college tuition, involves monetary transactions. In both cases, what appears to be an increasingly problematic role of money is also rooted in the fact that egalitarian norms are opening new possibilities for those formerly excluded from decision making (wives and children) to negotiate matters of family finance. Another major development that has reinforced the monetarization of human relationships is the growth of professions. Child care, care of the sick and elderly, away-from-home lodging, cooking, moving, home repairs, lawn mowing, and trash hauling are only some of the activities now done by professionals on a for-pay basis that were once performed largely by family members, neighbors, friends, and volunteers.

These societal developments, however, do not occur simply as a result of lawlike evolutionary trends. They are furthered by the institutional competition built into the market system itself. Corporations selling goods and services can often increase their profits most effectively by enlarging existing markets or by creating new markets. Existing markets are enlarged significantly when people who have previously done things on their own are in some way drawn into the marketplace. The classic historical example is the success experienced by colonizing powers of drawing traditional communities into the Western market for spices, rum, and finished cloth.[18] Gandhi's attempt to return India to homespun cloth was thus an effort to extricate his people from dependence on British markets. New markets are created by inventing new products and by finding a way to distribute goods and services that have formerly been outside the pricing system. Chains of for-profit nursery schools, for example, have subjected a realm of personal life to the market that once was defined almost exclusively as a family matter.

The main consequence of market expansion is to bring monetary considerations into an increasing number of areas that were formerly categorized as human relationships. In many ways, this is not an ominous development at all. Hiring a professional to mow one's lawn is likely to be more efficient, at least in terms of transaction costs, than attempting to coerce labor from, or negotiate an equitable spot market involving, one's children. For-profit nursery schools may provide higher-quality professional care than could be given by older siblings, grandparents, or busy parents. Were these activities evaluated strictly in economic terms, there might well be sufficient reasons to consider the expansion of monetary relations beneficial or benign. And yet what has already been said about the cultural construction of money suggests that something important may be endangered by this expansion.

First, the quality of human relationships changes significantly when money becomes their underlying principle. Spouses become "wage earners" or "investments"; children become "subcontractors"; parents become "deep pockets"; friends become "business contacts." More significant than these labels, however, are the norms that rise to prominence in fiduciary relations. Money's lack of memory replaces trust with transience. Bargaining becomes more important than sharing. People calculate what to do chiefly in terms of costs and payoffs. The consequences have been documented clearly in experimental psychological research involving children. Observing that young children generally perform acts of kindness and helping naturally, spontaneously, researchers have tried to discover what happens when efforts are made to reinforce this behavior with monetary rewards. Children consistently respond to such rewards by performing good deeds at higher (but only slightly higher) levels than they did before. But when the incentives are removed, the behavior also ceases. Money teaches them that good deeds should not be done spontaneously after all.[19]

Second, market dependence leads to a significant "deskilling" of the population. The term has been popularized mainly in studies of the working class, showing how standardization and mass production have systematically narrowed the range and depth of artisanal skills that workers once had. The same process operates among middle-class and working-class people alike when monetary transactions take over new realms of human interaction. A working mother in Chicago provided a vivid example. In a recent conversation with other working mothers, all highly trained professionals employed in careers such as law, social work, and higher education, she discovered that everyone shared some misgivings about the "care givers" they were paying to raise their children. In one case a child had actually been abused in the name of punishment. Yet despite their considerable advantages in formal education, none of the mothers was willing to intervene. The reason was that they felt incompetent to do so. They had read little about child rearing, felt inexperienced as mothers, believed they could not deal adequately with their children, and doubted that their children trusted them.

Third, market expansion may contribute significantly to the breakdown of communities in which basic values are shaped, shared, and supported. Monetary transactions, coupled with mass-media promotions of marketable goods and services, encourage individuals to make choices on their own, following personal needs and tastes, but with the mass market itself as a primary reference group. Going to Disney World, flying United, taking a Princess cruise, shopping at Sears, and eating at McDonalds become activities that anyone can do, regardless of race, color, or creed (or ethnic origin, gender, region, or age). Money permits the individual to decide on one or another of these options, whether or not anyone else in his or her community happens to share the same impulse at the same time or not. Many people, of course, are likely to make the same decision, but their choices are nearly always made in private. In contrast, something like an ethnic festival is both more difficult to subject to purely monetary relationships and more heavily dependent on shared values and communal interaction.

Fourth, the increased amount of money required by greater participation in the marketplace is likely to shift individual utility functions significantly in the direction of income as opposed to free time. Just the opposite has been suggested by some proponents of the concept of an emerging "leisure" society. But their argument is belied by the fact that people are actually working more hours, rather than fewer, spending a greater share of the higher levels of income they receive on services, and complaining more about their lack of free time. Despite the fact that having more money is generally regarded as a source of greater individual freedom, the reality of the situation is that the need to secure this money actually gives people less free time to do what they want and to pursue activities that might not involve the marketplace at all.

Fifth, and not without some basis in reality, subjective attachment to money is likely to increase as a result of its being seen as a solution to conflict in human relationships. Most of the people who talked to us about marital conflicts (their own or their parents') seemed to believe, as George Bernard Shaw once said, that "the *lack* of money is the root of all evil."[20] Consequently, they thought the simplest way to avoid such conflicts was to have a more abundant supply of money. That way, they felt there would be no need to argue. Furthermore, dependence on others would be reduced, and each person would be better able to express his or her own desires. By their own accounts, having money in abundance had not always deterred their parents from fighting about it. Yet even though they worried that money was a corrupting factor in their own relationships, they saw money itself as the way of fixing the problem. In short, they were caught up in a vicious cycle, money being both cause and solution to their worries.

Two additional consequences associated with the perception that money is corrupting larger and larger areas of human life merit somewhat fuller consideration. One is the ambiguous status in which loans and gifts have been placed by the expansion of monetary relations. The other is the tension that surrounds public perceptions of charitable organizations. Both bear special significance to the question of how possible it may be to encourage greater discussion of personal and public values in contemporary society.

LOANS AND GIFTS

It is a mistake to think that traditional societies cultivated tight-knit communities, including the values supported by these communities, entirely in the absence of monetary transactions. Through godparentage systems, landlords were often morally (if not legally) obligated to loan money to serfs when crops failed or when the number of children multiplied too rapidly. The church was another important source of emergency assistance, as were low-interest loans and gifts among family members themselves. But with the growing monetarization of life in modern societies, these informal means of assistance have become increasingly problematic. Not that they have by any means disappeared. But they have been transformed in ways that draw a firmer line between the monetary realm and human relationships.

Loans to family members and friends have become particularly problematic because these transactions necessarily invite confusion between the norms governing money and those pertaining to intimate relationships. In the marketplace, loans are contractual arrangements involving a temporary transfer of funds from one party to another party, in return for periodic payments of interest and a repayment of principal on a specified date. Among friends and family members, however, loans are generally based on need, compassion, and a sense of obligation to help someone with whom a relationship already exists for other than economic reasons alone. Consequently, interest payments may be nonexistent or at lower-than-market rates, a repayment date may not be firmly established, and the entire transaction is likely to be conducted without legal supervision. As a result, people frequently report having had frustrating experiences in making personal loans, express fear that loans currently outstanding will never be repaid, and point to "hard lessons" that make them reluctant to enter into such relationships in the future. Many have refused to make loans to needy friends and relatives at all, arguing that people should stand on their own feet and not expect financial help from anyone. Others have made loans on rare exceptions but have done so through third parties so as to keep the relationship as anonymous and as much at "arm's length" as possible. Rather than personal loans becoming an occasion for deeper interaction or for reflection about the role of nonmarket values in the use of money, therefore, they have simply been minimized in importance.

Paying close attention to the language people use in talking about loans reveals an underlying assumption that relationships cannot truly be genuine when money is involved. One woman, explaining why she preferred to loan money anonymously, said she feared the recipient would be embarrassed and that the relationship would be altered if she helped someone in person. Part of her reasoning was that recipients would feel she was "one up" on them. She did not want someone feeling indebted to her. There was also something deeper, though, that she could only express by saying "they couldn't be themselves with me anymore."

Why not? Apparently because genuine relationships should be based on shared values rather than competing interests. Somebody who loans money has an interest in getting it back. Somebody who borrows money has an interest in *not* having to pay it back. This tension results in strained relationships involving anything from suspicion and avoidance to deference and condescension.[21] More comfortable dimensions of interaction, such as intimacy, caring, and interdependence, are crowded out. Under the circumstances, most people prefer to distance themselves from the relationship by turning it into something closer to a market transaction.[22] They keep their relationships pure but also restrict them to a narrower circle of family and friends.[23]

Gifts have in many respects become even more problematic than loans. They fall more squarely on the human side of the equation. Their monetary value is not supposed to be an important issue. Unlike loans, they seldom become the subject of legal contracts and are never supposed to be repaid according to some formalized schedule. Their purpose is to solidify relationships among friends and family members. They express what people value; hence, we say it is "the thought that counts." But everybody knows equally well that the thought is not *all* that counts. In most settings, gift giving is governed by a powerful underlying expectation of reciprocity. To give is to expect something in return. And in modern society, where nearly all gifts are purchased in the marketplace, it becomes all the more pertinent to translate this norm into an expectation of "equal value," meaning comparable price. As a result, people worry, just as they do with loans, that gifts are becoming too commercialized, that there is actually a conflict between their monetary nature and the human values they are supposed to reinforce. Some succumb to the temptation of thinking about gifts in monetary or in utilitarian terms entirely. Others try to find ways to protect gifts from being regarded in the same terms as ordinary goods and services. Making gifts by hand is still a preferred way to keep market considerations at bay. Because of the assumption that individuals' tastes are entirely idiosyncratic, however, money itself is often given instead, despite the fact that people often express negative views toward such gifts.[24] When it is, ritualistic mechanisms may be introduced to distance it from ordinary currency: for example, giving uncirculated bills, placing it in sealed envelopes, or giving gift certificates instead. Increasingly, people also try to emphasize the human dimension in their giving by seeking out esoteric goods (such as "adult toys") that are exchanged only in limited, specialized markets and that demonstrate special thought, expertise, technical know-how, or cultivated taste on the part of the giver.

Many of the people we talked to said gift giving was becoming problematic for them. They found they were spending too much money or felt their gifts were somehow not "special." They were having trouble keeping the human dimension unsullied by the market element—the sense that all gifts are mass-produced and for this reason alike, the sense that people pay too much attention to how much they spend rather than what they buy, and the difficulty of finding something to give that the recipient has not already purchased as an ordinary consumer good. Some people expressed their concerns by saying they wanted to "simplify" their gift giving. This seldom meant spending less time or money on gifts, though. It meant finding a way of removing them from a market orientation. One woman simplified her gift giving by making rugs from rags and plastic bags. The idea that these rugs were also a way of protecting the environment (by recycling) helped her feel good about them.[25] Other people gave gourmet coffee, flowers, books, and other items that involved specialized "taste," that helped to "personalize" the gift or tailor it to the particular relationship between giver and recipient (going together to a favorite restaurant was a common example), or that showed the giver knew the "right" places to find interesting things.[26] Some stressed giving "quality" gifts, as if to distinguish what they gave to people they loved from things produced for the masses (that thus "fall apart"). Family trips, theater tickets, movies, concerts, and sports outings seemed to fulfill a similar function: they could be regarded as sources of "experience" or of "memories," rather than mere commodities. A few people actually distinguished self-consciously between "material" gifts and "symbolic" gifts. Having seen people give and receive for the monetary benefit of the gift alone, they said they were trying to be different. They wanted to give gifts, as one man said, that "have a different meaning, that somehow reflect who I am, maybe even ones that are a little strange."

Most people may manage reasonably well to protect their gift giving from being tainted by the marketplace, but the effort it takes to do this adds to their sense that economic life is becoming more difficult, more expensive, and more time-consuming. Even though they deny that the monetary value of gifts is important, they acknowledge that they have to pay a lot to find presents that are really "meaningful." They also talk about limiting their gift giving to a very small circle of family and friends. This helps keeps the cost down, of course, but it is rooted even more in the sense that gift giving has become an ambiguous, even dangerous, enterprise. Someone you already know well will forgive you for getting the wrong thing. Knowing them well also increases your chances of getting something they will consider "special." For a slightly wider circle of acquaintances, you have to depend more on the market for your cues and thus may offend them or not help your relationship with them by giving a gift. Insofar as gift giving may be a nonverbal means of making up for some of the lack of talking about money that most people experience, then, even this form of interaction seems to be limited increasingly to a small circle of intimate acquaintances, rather than binding people in wider ways to their communities.[27]

IMPLICATIONS FOR CHARITIES

The perception that money is constantly expanding into new areas is of special significance to charities and philanthropic organizations. Like private gifts and loans, the donations given to these organizations are an ambiguous commodity, symbolizing both money itself and human values such as a concern for the needy or an interest in art. In traditional settings, the predecessors of contemporary voluntary associations followed time-honored observances that helped to keep these two realms apart. For example, Taoist shamans in rural China often earn considerable wealth performing healing rites in their villages, but their activities are never "monetarized" by charging an actual fee; instead, their clients donate a *gift* to the gods, from which the shamans then deduct a percentage.[28] Many conservative religious bodies in the United States follow similar practices. In other settings, the anonymous donation or the physical separation of fund-raising galas from the actual work of the organization may help to maintain a vital symbolic distinction. But tax laws, competition, and the sheer magnitude of many nonprofit organizations now makes it harder for them to remain unsullied by the taint of money.

Public attitudes toward nonprofit organizations are for the most part favorable.[29] In the United States, billions of dollars are taken in by these organizations each year. But most Americans also harbor some misgivings about the purely monetary side of these organizations. People worry, for example, that too much energy is being devoted to fundraising. They question the motives of wealthy donors. They believe many people make donations just to receive tax deductions. Large numbers believe corrupt foundation officials are lining their own pockets. Telethons and direct-mail solicitations have become topics of particular distaste. Most people also exhibit greater respect for those who give of themselves, donating their *time* to volunteer for social service activities, than for those who only give money.[30]

There are many idiosyncratic reasons for these various misgivings. Some people actually know firsthand of corruption in charities; others have had their evening meals interrupted once too often by phone calls from their alma mater. The underlying problem in all these misgivings, however, is the sense that money is once again endangering some dearly cherished aspect of human life. What was once a cup of cold water is now a $1,000 check. The Good Samaritan has been replaced by a multi-billion-dollar industry. Impersonality, utilitarianism, and an emphasis on efficiency are the perceived consequences. Like Sherman marching to the sea, money destroys everything in its path.

Whether these fears are well- or ill-founded is not the immediate issue. The problem is that charitable organizations *as a source of values* are left considerably weakened. Consider the small, community-based voluntary associations that impressed Tocqueville when he visited the United States early in the nineteenth century. Those associations functioned largely outside the marketplace. Money was not an issue. They brought people together, gave them a place in which to discuss their collective values, and, as Tocqueville recognized, empowered people to bring those values into the public life of the nation. In many ways, voluntary associations still perform these functions. Local churches and synagogues, volunteer fire departments, parent-teacher organizations, clubs, and the like provide a space in which to preserve such values as kindness, compassion, community service, and civic responsibility. They could also (and sometimes do) provide an important forum in which to relate these values to the ways people think about their money. But because of the long-standing belief that money and values are like oil and water, these organizations are often reluctant to do so. They skirt the issue, encouraging donors to give anonymously. When they do speak about money, they frame the issue in narrow economic terms, paying heed to the complaints they receive about "always talking about money." And they justify their programs, much as a business enterprise would, in terms of cost-benefit analyses. It is not surprising, then, that much of the public views these as *service* organizations, functioning mainly to perform some unprofitable social function, rather than recognizing their potential to instruct the public in how better to think about values.

THE QUESTION OF VALUES

As American culture searches for its soul, is it, then, possible for human values to be brought back more squarely into the picture, even to inform our thinking about money and about our consumer behavior? Or is it more likely that the two will remain separate realms? From what we have considered, the prospects for integration do not seem bright. Not talking about money is a powerful tradition. Like the taboo on sex that prevailed in Victorian England, it would have to be attacked frontally to be undermined. It in many ways serves us well. So does the new mentality that regards money chiefly as a subjective item grounded only in the inner life of the individual. Keeping money out of circulation in our dealings with family members, compartmentalizing our thinking about gifts, and engaging in consumer rituals we don't quite understand also serve us well. We can make decisions largely the way advertisers tell us to, reducing our transaction costs, and getting through life with a minimum of difficulty.

But these mechanisms are rapidly beginning to be undermined by changes taking place in the economic realm itself. Money has not been content to sit quietly in the back room while interesting discussions of other topics were taking place in the parlor. Its roots in the marketplace have made it increasingly restless. As it tiptoes down the hall, and now enters the parlor itself, we are having to confront our misgivings about it. The choices are becoming clear. Either we let it make the decisions for us, or we learn how to think through our values and relate them consciously to our economic behavior. Taking the latter route may be less efficient, because it would require us to examine our spending habits more carefully than we would like. The former is in many ways easier because it has functioned well to keep the economic system itself in charge of our lives. And yet the personal strains have been considerable. As we have seen, fears and fantasies, uncertainty and doubt, and much concern about interpersonal conflict are all rooted in our refusal to face the issue of money head-on. Increasingly, this refusal is likely to have negative consequences even for the public life of our nation. Certainly, the environmental crisis that has deepened in recent decades requires deliberation, rather than continued herdlike grazing in the defoliated pastures of consumerism. Corporations themselves are also realizing that marketing oriented toward stable human values may be more profitable than simply catering to the vagaries of rumor and whim. For the new white-collar class, whose thinking about money has largely been disconnected from its thinking about work, it will thus be especially important to find ways of anchoring its perceptions in deep moral commitments. For the working class, despite the pressures that render it more vulnerable to the marketplace itself, the question of values also surfaces with considerable importance.

Chapter Eight

THE WORKING CLASS: CHANGING CONDITIONS
AND CONVERGING PERSPECTIVES

AT FOUR-YEAR INTERVALS the American political system tries to rejuvenate itself from the bottom up. In the process, seekers of high office make ritual pilgrimages back to the nation's roots: its working class. Here they expect to find earthy homespun wisdom. America's workers are the proverbial keepers of its moral values, the bedrock of common decency, the heartland, where the dream still resonates loudly. They are characteristically thought to be unsullied by the intellectual pretensions of the better educated and uncorrupted by the conspicuous glamour-grubbing of the affluent upper middle class.

I have to this point deliberately said little about class divisions in Americans' understandings of their work, their money, and their material possessions. As a people we are, in fact, reluctant to speak about class differences at all. At least most of us prefer to think we are part of the "middle class." We find it awkward to talk about the "lower class" or even the "working class," preferring to lump ourselves together in one big, classless society. As Richard Trumka, United Mine Workers president, suggests: "Ninety-nine point nine percent of the people in this country think they're middle class."[1] Yet it clearly must be acknowledged that class divisions matter enormously.

We know this instinctively whenever we think about the one-seventh (or so) of the population who live below the poverty line. But even among Americans privileged enough to be working full time, about a third work in blue-collar, skilled or semiskilled, or clerical occupations, have little or no education beyond high school, and earn incomes substantially below the national mean. They may consider themselves part of the middle class, but they are able to reap far fewer of the benefits of middle-class life than those who work in professional and managerial occupations, who have college or graduate degrees, and who earn incomes substantially above the mean.[2]

Such differences are likely to have enormous consequences for the ways in which work and money are understood. Differences in the nature of work and the level of prosperity are, after all, largely what we mean by class divisions. If there are signs of erosion in cherished conceptions of the American Dream, then we must, like seekers of high office, try to discern whether the soil remains solid at lower levels of the social substrata, or whether it too is beginning to shift.

Much of what we have considered in previous chapters might well be understood in terms of what social scientists at one time referred to as "the anomie of affluence."[3] Work, made meaningful by its variety, can certainly be considered the luxury of those who no longer take jobs from sheer necessity. Working to give a legitimate account of oneself is an interesting idea, but perhaps one that does not apply to lower-income families. By the same token, scarcely anyone would doubt that anxieties about *feelings* toward money, replacing anxieties about money itself, signal a threshold of material comfort already having been achieved.

But I want to suggest caution toward accepting such generalizations. America's working class has also been undergoing deep changes in recent decades. Its very identity has become blurred. Characterizations of its work, drawn from studies of heavy industry and of assembly lines, no longer apply. Nor do many assumptions about how its values and aspirations differ from those of the affluent. We need to consider how the composition of the working class itself has been changing; then consider how these changes are stirring up questions and uncertainties common to Americans at all levels in the social hierarchy.

THE CHANGING COMPOSITION OF THE WORKING CLASS

In 1946, when sociologist Ely Chinoy set out to examine the American Dream among Detroit's working class, the natural site for such a study was the city's auto industry.[4] Only the naive would now look to that location as a window on blue-collar America. In the intervening half-century heavy manufacturing has diminished dramatically in importance, while a vast array of service industries has risen. Wholesale and retail employment have expanded. And a new layer of technical and clerical work has been added. Even heavy industry has been transformed by automation, by a huge influx of immigrant workers, and by new modes of management and organization.

The most striking change in the American working class since World War II has clearly been the decline of blue-collar occupations and their replacement by so-called lower white-collar jobs. Different occupational classifications yield slightly different assessments of this change, but even the simplest comparisons reveal how dramatic it has been. In 1950 blue-collar occupations composed approximately two-thirds of all working-class jobs. Four decades later only about half of the working class held blue-collar jobs.[5] The most significant declines in blue-collar jobs occurred in manufacturing, especially of durable goods, in low-tech industries, in mining and construction, but also in transportation and agriculture. In contrast, employment increased in clerical and sales jobs, in retailing, and in a wide variety of services, particularly finance, education, health, and government.[6]

A correlative trend, most evident since 1960, has been the erosion of organized labor. Prior to that date, union membership had held nearly constant for several decades as a proportion of employment in working-class occupations, but since then it has declined in virtually all sectors.[7] As a proportion of privately employed workers, union membership in fact shrunk from a high of 35 percent in 1958 to a mere 13 percent in 1990, one of the lowest proportions in any advanced industrial society.[8] In manufacturing the decline has come about as a result of shrinkage in heavily unionized industries, such as steel and automobiles, and the rise of new industries, such as electronics and computers, as well as some relocation of plants to new areas. In addition, service occupations have generally been less subject to unionization in recent years than manufacturing. To some extent, corporations acquiring services from independent subcontractors and from temporary or part-time workers have also undercut the organizing capacity of labor unions.

The other major trend has been an increase in gainful employment among women. Although working-class families have always relied on women's economic contributions, these have come more often in the past from domestic activities, such as canning and sewing, whereas now an increasing share of these contributions comes from gainful employment outside the home. At present working-class employment is divided almost evenly between men and women, although more women (especially those with children) than men are employed part time. The shift from heavy industry to sales, clerical, and service occupations has of course resulted in large numbers of women being employed in the latter.

These trends have all conspired to perpetuate class divisions in American society. Average wages in service occupations are generally lower than those in manufacturing and heavy industry. The demise of labor unions has left increasing numbers of blue-collar workers in poorer bargaining positions with their employers; in recent years, blue-collar incomes have thus fallen at a rate approximately twice that of white-collar incomes.[9] And job-for-job, women are still paid less than men. Despite its continuing commitment to equal opportunity and to upward mobility, therefore, the American economic system has by no means created a vast, homogeneous middle class strictly in terms of average incomes or levels of wealth; indeed, during the 1980s, disparities increased between upper and lower segments of American society in terms of income and wealth alike.

One route into the working class that remains important is of course to be born into it. Mike Kominski, 34, a Teamster who earns his living driving a cement truck, typifies this segment of the blue-collar workforce. His dad (Mike likens him to Archie Bunker) was the classic second-generation Polish father, loyal to his church, a veteran, a volunteer fireman, and, above all, a union member. Growing up, Mike seldom associated with anyone who wasn't blue collar. Today, his primary loyalties are still to the working-class community in which he lives. Several years working as a garage mechanic and a few plant closings and layoffs have taught him to value the hourly wage and the seniority he enjoys after a decade in the union.

But men like this make up a diminishing share of the working class. Ed Butler, 38, illustrates what has become an all-too-familiar story of entry into the working class. He was scheduled to participate fully in the American Dream. His parents gained a foothold in the middle class by dint of hard work and ingenuity. Dad owned a flourishing restaurant and did some farming on the side. Mom was among the growing number of women in her generation who brought in a second income. She worked as a nurse. Ed's aspiration was to become a teacher. But somehow it never worked out. One reason was that the family was too large for even two incomes to guarantee opportunities for all the children. Ed was second youngest of seven. Another was that Ed's father died when Ed was only seventeen. Working part-time jobs and not really believing he could realize his dreams, Ed made only average grades in high school. His teachers tracked him into a vocational-technical program, rather than encouraging him to prepare for college. Working as a dishwasher at one of the local restaurants, Ed decided to shape his vocational training in that direction. Most of his high school courses were geared toward learning how to cook. After graduation, he went to culinary school for a year. And now, after several assistant-chef and assistant-baker jobs, he's working as head baker—back at the same place he worked in high school. He wonders when he will get on his feet financially, and whether he and his wife will ever own a home.

Jack Paretti is another casualty as far as the American Dream is concerned. His grandparents were hard-working immigrants who managed to send all their children to college. Jack's father earned a B.S. degree in accounting and got a job at a large pharmaceuticals company. He brought in enough money to support a family of six (Mrs. Paretti never worked outside the home). But when Jack was 16 his parents split up. Jack, furious with both of them, moved into an apartment of his own. He could have finished high school, could have gone to college. But he didn't care to. His father had never been happy. Why should he devote himself to a career? For a while Jack mowed people's lawns; then he worked for a landscaping company. He'd learned some printing in high school. Spent some time doing that. Quit to go on tour with a small-time rock band he played guitar in. Came back, working part time in printing and a few other jobs as well. For the past eight years (ever since he got married) he's worked the graveyard shift at the print shop he first went to when he quit high school.

Joan Larsen is one of the many women who now make up the American working class. She describes herself as a "child bride" who, like many southern girls from working-class families (her father worked in a mill), got married out of high school and soon discovered she was pregnant. Small children kept her occupied till she was 27, but then her husband divorced her and she was forced into the labor market. Working first as an office assistant and then for a while selling real estate, she eventually remarried, had another child, and moved to a different part of the country. That marriage also fell apart. Now, married for the third time, she has held a steady job as a secretary in a California law firm for more than a decade. She enjoys the work, has been able to assume more responsibilities in recent years, and feels she is well paid. Like many of her ("baby boomer") generation, she also feels the squeeze of economic and family obligations. Her parents are old enough that they need her care. Her youngest child, after a personal crisis and losing his job, is now living at home again. She keeps herself trim, rising at 5:30 every morning to exercise, and she takes time to participate in a church group. She also dreams of finishing her education and launching a new career. But at 51, she knows those possibilities are limited.

Women like Joan Larsen illustrate the upper echelon of the working class, where jobs are fairly secure and family relationships, if unpredictable, nevertheless contribute positively to their financial well-being. For Murial Johnson, 35, a Chicago woman heading a single-parent household with four small children, working as hard as she can is necessary just to keep one hand clinging to the bottom rung of the working-class ladder. Growing up in one of the city's poorest neighborhoods, she has experienced both overt racial discrimination and the devastating problems of underfunded inner-city schools, crime, and a lack of attractive jobs. In a way, she was lucky. After high school, the Board of Education hired her as a camp counselor because she had been a leader among her peers. Since then she's worked as a crossing guard, sold Avon, Tupperware, and insurance, driven a truck, and worked at the post office. Right now she has three part-time jobs and is training to be a police officer. She wants no sympathy and no handouts. But she also wants nobody else depending on her. Her children are enough. She fears that having a husband would just add to her financial troubles. As long as her health holds up, she figures she can fend for herself.

On the surface, there is little to question about characterizations of the working class that emphasize its changing composition. That significant changes have been taking place is scarcely at issue. Yet the implications that are drawn after the fact often turn out to be more problematic. Indeed, two lines of argumentation can be identified in recent discussions of the working class, neither of which is entirely satisfactory upon more careful reflection. One attributes the declining position of the working class to short-sighted, if not genuinely malicious, policies on the part of the capitalist ruling class. In their quest for quicker and higher gains, American capitalists have allegedly robbed the U.S. economy of jobs by investing in speculative ventures, rather than recapitalizing productive operations. The implied solution is thus to bring in different policy makers who will be more attentive to working-class interests, including investments in infrastructure and social programs. The other perspective stresses that structural changes adversely affecting the American working class are built into the world economy itself. All advanced industrial societies are observed to be shifting increasingly toward services (and quasi-professional or technical occupations), while heavy industry and other unskilled, labor-intensive enterprises are shifting increasingly to lower-paid labor-markets in the underdeveloped world. Moreover, this shift appears more likely to occur in goods-producing industries, especially as transportation costs diminish, leaving a larger share of domestic working-class jobs in harder-to-export service occupations. The implication of this analysis is that little can be done for the working class, other than continue to encourage unionization, to spur free trade in hopes of promoting new jobs, and to provide condolences (or perhaps some social benefits) to make up for shattered dreams.

The weakness of both arguments lies in an overly simplistic view of what the American Dream has meant to American workers and of what changing economic expectations may be doing to this dream. Both perspectives focus almost entirely on a narrow material interpretation of the American Dream. The challenge posed by changing economic conditions is thus defined by diminished chances of upward job mobility for the working class, poorer chances of gaining a higher or more equitable family income, and frustration in attaining some of the more tangible manifestations of the American Dream, particularly homeownership. To make the American Dream into nothing more than material aspirations, however, is to demean the moral depth of the American working class. The American Dream has meant more than job opportunities and affordable housing. At the same time, difficulties in attaining these material amenities do more than simply make it harder to put food on the table; they generate uncertainties about the relationships between economic behavior and other cherished human values that have always been part of the American Dream.

We will need to consider how working men and women talk about their work and money in order to understand these issues better. First, however, we must confront more directly the question of whether structural changes in the working class have simply widened the gap separating this class from more affluent Americans, or whether there have also been changes that may be generating cultural convergence in the ways in which work and money are understood. In the event that such convergence is evident, it will also help us to understand how the American Dream may be undergoing a subtle redefinition.

THE PROFESSIONALIZATION OF EVERYONE?

Writing in more prosperous, or at least optimistic, times, social scientists of the 1950s predicted a homogenization of American culture resulting from trends that would render the working class more similar to the middle class.[10] With rising levels of education and greater dependence on advanced technology, the American worker was expected to become more highly skilled. Expertise and greater job complexity would in turn make room for more control over the labor process itself, in part because workers could take their expertise with them if new employment opportunities proved more interesting than their current ones. Workers would thus begin to think of themselves as having careers; in short, they would become professionalized, like lawyers and doctors.

Sober-minded analysts of the situation, even at the time, realized there was far more to becoming a professional than simply having expertise, and they cautioned against the likelihood of plumbers and electricians forming professional associations such as the American Medical Association.[11] Yet there were trends afoot that have largely been forgotten in the recent spate of literature about plant closings, deskilling, and deindustrialization. The American working class has been subject to changes that have indeed produced downward mobility and perpetuated income inequality between it and higher strata in the labor force. But these and other trends must also be examined for culturally homogenizing effects, rather than the production of a radically separate working-class culture.

If the shift from manufacturing to services is again taken as a starting point, it is important to recognize that both the ethos and the organization of service occupations are likely to share a great deal with professional and managerial occupations. In both settings an ethic of service is likely to be emphasized as an ideal, and even as a goal of the workplace, and working with people is likely to take precedence over working with things. Moreover, service work is seldom easy to divide into highly specialized tasks that can be routinized in assembly-line fashion but require a high level of employee discretion. In addition, clerical, sales, and service work more often place employees in direct contact with professionals and managers, thus exposing them to similar workplace cultures.

The alleged deskilling of work would perhaps militate against any tendencies toward professionalization. Yet training requirements and credentials have, if anything, become more important in blue-collar and lower white-collar occupations, just as they have in professional and managerial positions. Nearly a quarter of all full-time working-class people now have at least some college training, and among younger members of the working class the vast majority have graduated from high school. The institutionalization of vocational counseling, standardized testing, and career guidance programs in high schools has also created a new way of forging common understandings of work.

Much attention has of course been devoted in recent years to downward mobility from the middle class into the working class, and from better-paid working-class occupations to poorly paid jobs. Although the psychological results (characterized in such phrases as "falling from grace," "fear of falling," and "worlds of pain") are indeed serious, what has been missed is the fact that downward mobility also implies some level of exposure to middle-class values and expectations. Economic determinists might argue that downward mobility would totally subvert these values and expectations. But it would seem more realistic, given what we know about other kinds of socialization, that whatever understandings of work and money were picked up in middle-class homes would continue to exercise an effect on this segment of the working class.

Generational factors have had a deep impact on the working class as well. For working-class men like Mike Kominski's father, "America, right or wrong" was often a fitting slogan. Immigrant parents had taught them to value the land of opportunity. Distancing themselves from their ethnic roots, they sometimes tried all the harder to be "truly American." The Great Depression may have delayed their economic ascent, but at least everything after that was an improvement. Except the war, which gave those who survived it an even deeper faith in the virtue of their country. Their children, however, experienced something rather different. Vietnam shattered their innocence. Unlike their college-based peers, they may have been less exposed to the ideological turmoil of the 1960s. Yet the turmoil was so pervasive they could not escape it entirely. Mike Kominski remembers reading about the war, talking to his friends in school, and thinking how terribly dated ("unhip") his parents had become.

The 1970s widened the generational rupture. Only part of it had to do with Vietnam, drugs, and the sexual revolution. For many young people a quieter realization began to set in. They were not going to fulfill their parents' version of the American Dream. The steady growth in average family incomes of the previous two decades was beginning to falter. They were not going to be the first generation in their families to go to college. Or if they were, they were not going to graduate and land jobs in the managerial sector. In other cases, they were not going to match their parents' educational and occupational achievements. Their values shifted, perhaps ever so slightly, to make sense of these changes. They didn't believe as strongly in the American Dream. At least not in a dream of upward job mobility and income advancement. They began talking more about family values and personal freedom. If they were not as successful economically as their fathers, it was because they wanted to spend more time with their children. Their parents' values seemed too narrow, too rigid; in contrast, they felt the need to be more relaxed, to have time for themselves, and to rediscover some of the simpler pleasures that money couldn't buy.

Enumerating the potential sources of common understandings of work and money also requires mention of the powerful effects of television, advertising, and the media of mass consumption. To be sure, professionals and managers may shop at different department stores from working-class men and women, and the two may have different tastes in art and music. There has, however, been an enormous increase over the past half-century in the means of communicating common messages to the American public regardless of class divisions. During the Watergate hearings in the early 1970s, for example, millions of working-class families gained an inside look at the daily work habits and thought patterns of an elite circle of government bureaucrats whose lives would have been shielded from view in earlier periods. Fictionalized portrayals of work, say, on situation comedies or in movies, are often quite sparse on technical details of jobs themselves but give clear messages of what may constitute more- or less-interesting work. Television advertising may communicate some of the "corporate culture" to a wider public that large firms may try to convey to their own employees; it certainly exposes viewers to common messages about consumer goods.

It would be rash to think that work and money might be understood in exactly the same ways by working-class men and women as by professionals and managers. The possibility of considerable overlap, however, is at least conceivable. If work is pursued not only for money but because of legitimating accounts, then working-class cultures may be just as likely to give hints about values and about moral restraint as those of higher occupational status. Let us consider the evidence.

WORK: ANOTHER LOOK AT ITS DISCONTENTS

Academicians interested in the plight of the American working class have grudgingly acknowledged that many aspects of life in the workplace have improved dramatically over the past century. Safety standards have improved. Some headway has been made toward cleaning up chemical pollutants to which workers were once routinely exposed. Child-labor laws have greatly reduced the exploitation of children. Disability insurance has mitigated the fear of workplace injuries. Automation has taken the sheer physical effort that once was required out of many manual-labor occupations. And if jobs are still insecure and family budgets tight, wages have at least increased enough to make many material amenities possible for today's working class that were much more difficult for an earlier generation to attain: whereas only one home in two was owner-occupied at the close of World War II, that figure today is closer to two-thirds; over the same period, car ownership has risen from 200 per 1,000 people to nearly 600; a radio that took 23 hours of labor to pay for in 1952 took only 5 hours in 1992; and a long-distance telephone call that would have taken an hour and a half to pay for then required only 4 minutes of labor time to purchase.[12]

But the literature on working-class labor is correct in emphasizing other sources of discontent. Too often, work is still boringly repetitive. Employees have little opportunity to learn new skills that might lead to higher-paying jobs. Control over one's schedule, pace, and daily decisions may be minimal. Power is exercised by supervisors in a way that diminishes the self-esteem of employees and sometimes subjects them to blatant episodes of harassment or discrimination. For all these reasons, job satisfaction is considerably lower among working-class people than it is among professionals and managers.[13]

The extent of such differences should not be overdrawn, however. Although measures of job satisfaction and of other desirable job characteristics are decidedly lower than average among poorly paid working-class employees, the more striking fact is how many of these employees nevertheless express positive views of their work on these measures.[14] Two out of three, for example, characterize their work as providing a lot of variety. Three-fourths say it suits their personalities. An equal proportion say their co-workers care about them. Six out of ten say their jobs pay very well. And more than half describe their work as mentally stimulating and say it provides a lot of freedom in making their own decisions.[15] These views are, of course, conditioned by the changing composition of the workforce itself. For example, workers in service occupations are more likely than those in manual occupations to say they can control their own schedules and set their own goals.[16] Yet some views may have less to do with specific working conditions than with broader cultural understandings. Saying variety is characteristic of one's work, for example, varies little from one occupation to the next.[17]

Ed Butler, the baker, reveals how such characterizations translate into language that legitimates work, explaining why it is interesting and fulfilling. Asked to describe a typical day, he says, "I generally make the donuts. We cut those out. From that point on, I'll decorate a few cakes, if necessary, for early morning cakes. And then I'll start making pies. And we try to get all our pies done for not only the restaurant, but for the store, before eleven o'clock, because that's when our general business mostly for that type of item is. And then I will generally get things like finish the rest of my cakes for the day and then look around and see if there's things like fillings that have to be made or things like icings or whipped cream or clean fresh fruit and things like that, getting that kind of stuff ready. After that, it's a matter of just cleaning up, going to the next day." But if all this sounds pretty routine, that isn't the way Ed sees it. He concludes his account by asserting emphatically, "Every day is different for me."

Jack Paretti speaks a similar language. He schedules printing jobs every day, making sure they go through the various processes and get finished on time. If it sounds routine, he denies it. "Typical day? If you've ever been in this business, you know there's no typical day."

What he means is that each order has its own set of problems. He also means he can do all the various jobs that may come up. Ordinarily he supervises six people: three press operators, a typesetter, an artist, and a clerk. But if any one of them calls in sick, or goes on vacation, Jack just fills in. For Mike Kominski, variety is also the spice of life. Driving a cement truck every day could become very boring, but not for him. His attitude toward work depends on being able to tell stories about the unusual job, the spectacle. "Sometimes we'll go do big jobs," he remarks. "I've done a lot of work in Atlantic City for the casinos. I've done a lot of work down at the Oyster Creek nuclear power plant, and that's like a neat kind of thing because it's very different, and when you go do a job as big as a nuclear power plant, I mean it's very impressive to watch something like that work."

Besides variety, these men like the fact that their work involves a sense of caring. They are in part inspired by the service ethic that has come to pervade so much of the working class. They are also aided by not working in large or highly bureaucratized settings or having to deal with too many people in their work, all traits that are significantly more common among professionals and managers than in working-class occupations.[18] Ed Butler says he loves his job as a baker. The reason is the "one-to-one communication" he can have with his customers. Even though most of his time is spent baking, he says it is the human contact he cherishes. He compares his position with that of being a chef. "The chef just stays in the back all the time. Never sees a customer. I come out. I ask how they liked the dessert. I take an order for an anniversary cake. That sort of thing. It means a lot." For Jack Paretti, the best part of his job is his boss and the six people he works with. He says "it doesn't matter to me what the work is, just as long as I get along with the people." And he does. They all started about the same time. "We've sorta just grew up together."[19]

Whether it is "the professionalization of everyone" or just a cultural script, taking pride in one's work is also a common way of talking about it. Part of the pride comes from having specialized expertise. For instance, Joan Larsen says she enjoys the "detail work" because it gives her "a sense of self-worth" knowing that the lawyers she works for can depend on her to get the routine information they need. But it is more typical, just as we saw in chapter 5, for working-class people to tell stories, not about routine mastery, but about unusual episodes in which things fell into place to give them a special sense of accomplishment. Ed Butler recalls that "It was a wedding cake [that] was really different. I never did it before. It was a real challenge. A real challenge. The decoration part was really different. I never did it before and I just had a picture to work from. I took it out and set it up. It took me about an hour to set it up. The lady came back today, the mother of the bride, and she just couldn't thank me enough about how happy she was about the cake, not only the flavor of the cake, the taste of the cake, the decoration was exactly what they wanted. The colors that were on the cake that were exactly what they wanted. And as much as I hated to do that cake, as much as I didn't like doing the cake, and as much as it gave me a headache, because I thought it was a very difficult cake to do, it basically erased all the problems that I had with it, when I heard that."[20]

Ed Butler actually describes his job as a "profession" and prides himself on being "professional" in the way he behaves.[21] Murial Johnson does not. But the same ethic pervades her discussion. Of her three jobs, working as a security guard at the city convention center (her evening job) takes up most of her time. The reason she is especially committed to it, she says, is that she has been able to do well at it. She says she has earned the "respect and liking" of other employees to the point that she is often called on to serve in a supervisory capacity. She takes pride in having organizational skills. When a big event takes place, or when there is a special crisis (she tells about a time when she was very short staffed), she can be counted on to make things work.

Professionals and managers, wielding the reins of power as they do, would seem more likely to find meaning in their work by drawing connections between it and the wider world (making the world a better place). But a large majority of working-class people also feel they are contributing to the betterment of the world.[22] In fact, they are *more likely* to say this in personal interviews than in anonymous surveys. Cynicism, it appears, is not pervasive because their expectations are not so inflated in the first place. Thinking it is enough just to make a small difference, they are happy to be doing what they can.

Ed Butler again provides a revealing illustration. Making donuts and pies and cakes all day, he might be the first to feel his job contributes little to the betterment of humanity. Indeed, he admits people could get along without his desserts. But that thought occurs to him only when pressed. Uppermost in his mind is the view that he contributes simply by having a good attitude and by working hard. Others, he feels, will see his example and be inspired to do better themselves.

He also believes deeply that his work is helping to bring families closer together. When someone comes in for a cake that will serve twenty-five or thirty people, he says, it gives him a good feeling just thinking "a family is coming back together." It's a small thing. But it connects his work to an ideal he cherishes deeply.

These descriptions, then, bear a striking resemblance to the accounts professionals and managers give of their work. The similarities are also clearly evident in discussions of what people *do not like* about their work. The reason levels of job satisfaction are lower among working-class people than among professionals and managers is seldom frustration about one's career, long-term goals, ability to realize broader values, or position in the social hierarchy. For people in both categories, the source of dissatisfaction is usually associated with specific people, quirky personalities, bad tempers, muggy weather, and the like. This is not to say that satisfaction is immune to bad working conditions. Statistical analysis, in fact, reveals that satisfaction is lower when work is perceived as being boring or emotionally draining or involving too much pressure, and that it is higher when perceived to pay well, suit one's personality, and be mentally stimulating.[23] Many of these characteristics are of course "structural" in the sense of being built into the job itself or the work environment. But accounts alter these conditions, linking people to them in ways that seem less determinant.

Working, as they typically do, in bureaucratic organizations, professionals and managers tend to blame unpleasant working conditions on bureaucracy itself, red tape, cumbersome procedures, and especially on the personal traits of middle-level supervisors themselves. They tell stories of their bosses behaving irrationally, staying out too late, bringing personal problems to the job, and having bad days. Working-class employees do some of this as well. But they are less likely too, partly because of the simple fact that fewer of them work in such settings. Indeed, bureaucracy also provides some of them with a powerful symbol, but as a way of saying what they like about their job. They like it because it is free of bureaucracy. Joan Larsen, for example, says she's very glad to be working in a small law office rather than a large firm; she has more control over her own schedule and is able to do a variety of tasks because there is no one else to do them.[24]

What serves the same function as managers' gripes about quirky supervisors are stories about hard-to-please customers, snafus with materials and supplies, and contingencies that simply could not be foreseen. A story told by Jack Paretti will illustrate. "There's a customer whose daughter was killed. She lived out in California. These people are elderly people and they were sending out a memorial mailing to 500 people. They brought all this stuff in. We typeset it, set it up like they wanted. They proofed it. They approved everything. We printed it. They hated it. They complained that it wasn't what they were told it was going to be, even though we had signed proofs and color charts and everything. So we did it again, and they hated it. This went back and forth like three and four times. They were just completely unreasonable. I mean I thought this was ridiculous. I mean they were sending out this like ten-page letter about their daughter's history. There had been a problem between them and their daughter, and they were trying to rectify it after she had died. It could be very annoying. This went on for like two weeks. They would call every day. I used to dread their call, because they weren't happy with anything."

One implication of such stories is that there is nothing intrinsic to the job itself that can (or should) be fixed; the problems are random occurrences. Another implication is that some of the pressure and frustration comes from within. Working-class people generally do not have the rich repertoires to describe these internal demons that professionals and managers do. But there are simple slogans that make the same point. For example, Ed Butler says, "I just like to do a good job; I hate to see sloppy work." Similarly, Jack Paretti explains, "Put out a good job. It just makes you feel good." In short, some of the discontent they experience with their work is self-induced.[25]

It could be, of course, that accounts such as these matter less to the average worker than the sheer economics of the job. Driven more by economic necessity, working-class men and women might well be more inclined to admit they work for money, whereas professionals and managers would have the luxury to claim other motives linked to allegedly "higher" values. There is in fact evidence to support this claim.[26] Yet it is nevertheless revealing that only one working-class person in three lists "money" as the primary reason for choosing his or her current line of work. Many of them provide weak reasons having to do mainly with circumstances, all the while still finding ways of emphasizing choice. Many others express personal goals, such as wanting to make use of their talents, desiring to grow as a person, being challenged by the job, or seeing it as a means of attaining personal success or freedom.

On the whole, the reasons working-class people give for getting into their work actually resemble those of professionals and managers quite closely, especially because the reasons are weak, offering a haphazard chronology of circumstances, events, and half-choices. The main difference is there are fewer options. Consequently, the element of choice is much less evident in blue-collar workers' accounts of their work than it is among professionals and managers. They emphasize being in the right place at the right time, knowing somebody who helped them get a job, and simply being out of work and needing something. But circumstances also played a prominent role in the accounts of professionals and managers. The difference is that those accounts emphasized circumstances in order to keep from seeming vain about their accomplishments. Working-class accounts are much more matter-of-fact. There is no implicit message about having the right talents or being especially clever.

It is wrong, however, to think that working-class accounts are filled with despair or even a sense of inevitability. They resemble white-collar accounts in showing how individuals challenged the system (often winning). One man talked about refusing to fill in all the information required on personnel forms. Another beats the system by taking any job available, just to get his foot in the door, and then transfering as quickly as possible to a better position. Several admitted they had defied immigration laws or minimum age restrictions. Many emphasized going against their parents' wishes. And many asserted they had courageously taken jobs for which they were not qualified. Accounts that otherwise sound quite ordinary are thus occasions for affirming the meaning of work, reasons for being committed to it, and even the fact that choice was by no means absent. Listen to what Jack Paretti says.

Q: Tell me how and why you became involved in this kind of work.
A: When I was still in school, there was a pretty good graphics program which I got into. I enjoyed it, and I had known my boss since I was little because she had been kind of like a family friend.
Q: This is the woman who owns the shop?
A: Uh huh.
Q: What's her name?
A: Mildred. She had a part-time opening in the summer.

Q: She was a friend of the family, right?

A: Yeah. My dad had known her through business and what not, because he also had his own accounting business. I got hired there one summer, and I've been there ever since.

Q: You started working before you were out of high school for her?

A: Yes, one summer.

Q: What did you start doing?

A: Just basic bindery work. Something simple like folding brochures or fold-your-own jobs, real simple stuff. That was about it. I did it in school, and I enjoyed it, and I still do.

Reading this account closely suggests that the assertion at the end about enjoying the job comes as a non sequitur. Yet the rest of the account actually sets the stage for this assertion. The circumstances involved in getting the job show a strong element of uncertainty, almost randomness, involving times and places and people. Implicitly, the search could have continued, resulting in other outcomes. The fact that Jack Paretti has stayed with this work is thus testimony to his own choice, and to the fact that he likes the work well enough to stay.[27]

Such accounts generally take the role of money for granted. In anonymous surveys, working-class people are of course more likely than professionals and managers to say they took their present job because of the money. But in personal interviews they seldom emphasize money as a primary motive. When it is mentioned at all, it is wedged into the conversation as a kind of afterthought, sometimes with a note of pride that comes with feeling one's job pays well. But just as often, money is dismissed as an important consideration, almost apologetically. Implicitly, the message is "I could be earning a lot more than I am now, but I didn't think that far ahead," or "I wanted to get married at the time," or "a baby came along," or "I just didn't want that kind of pressure."

For most working-class people, then, work is understood by framing it in personal accounts that have less to do with money, or even the nature of the job, than with the person's values and interests. But, just as with professionals and managers, these accounts follow well-thumbed scripts that lead to shallower, rather than deeper, understandings of the place of work in one's life. Even when people open up and talk at great length about their work, their values, their philosophy of life, and their sources of personal identity and gratification, they have trouble situating work among the rest of their commitments on the basis of these scripts.

One of the scripts that repeatedly surfaced reflects the vocational guidance many younger- to middle-aged working-class people received in high school. This was the last time they had received any explicit advice about how to think about work, so it stuck in their memories, perhaps even more so than for white-collar workers who had received additional messages in college and from their professions or employers. For example, Jack Paretti also says he likes his work because it fits his personality. He can be himself, he doesn't have to be somebody else. This is a revealing comment that comes up frequently in working-class accounts. It is the kind of account that probably comes from high school, the idea from vocational counseling that a job should fit one's personality. It by no means describes work as a calling that gives higher responsibilities; it simply makes one content. It also does not raise questions about one's values. Happiness in the job is a subjective feeling that confirms one is doing the right thing. Personality means some innate and hard to understand disposition, like how patient or irritated one gets, how much pressure one can withstand, whether one has a need to achieve, and the like. For the working class, there often is not as much of a sense of having shopped around, or feeling that any number of jobs could suit one's personality, or thinking that one should grow through a job, or use one's talents. It's more that this is the job I happened to find, that the job I ended up with is okay because among other things I'm reasonably happy and that means it must suit my personality.

Another script articulated frequently in working-class discussions of work draws heavily on family metaphors. Like Jack Paretti's earlier comments, it emphasizes family connections, or in other cases focuses on parental expectations (if only to defy them), the desire to get married, or the need to earn a better income to support one's family. But both of these scripts function best to tell people why they should be (and generally are) content with their present work. They do not offer strong reasons about why one is doing a particular kind of work, what the value of that work is, how much of one's time and energy should be devoted to it, or on what basis one might decide that enough is enough.

The family script is particularly problematic because it has traditionally been central in the American Dream and of course has undergone significant changes in recent years (which we shall consider in the next chapter). American working men and women have always tempered their commitment to the workplace (or tried to) by viewing work as a means to achieving some goal for their family. Or repeating bravely the adage that "nothing matters more than family." The one often balanced the other. Yet that balance now seems out of kilter as working-class men and women talk about the two. Seldom (and less so for men than for women) is work described as service to one's family. Children's futures, for example, are rarely mentioned as a reason for working hard. Instead, family obligations rear ugly heads, connoting sources of inevitable conflict with work that have no way of being happily resolved. A man says he could get into something more interesting that also paid better, but his family has grown used to a certain lifestyle and he wouldn't feel right depriving them of that to make the switch. A parent says I feel bad having to work when my son is having a soccer game. Yet the feeling is too weak to dictate actually taking the time off.

We have of course come to the point of taking these conflicts for granted. We cannot work less because we would lose our jobs. We cannot excuse ourselves from feeling bad about not attending the soccer game because doing so would be admitting to callousness as a parent. We cannot consider a different career because our family is living from month to month and couldn't make the transition. These conditions rise up as inevitable features of contemporary life. Yet they are not so familiar that we take them entirely for granted. We recall a time when things were different (or think they were), so we refuse at some level to believe they are inevitable. Nor are we able to rearrange our priorities, or our thinking about means and ends, to put things back to rights.

What all this demonstrates, then, is that working-class men and women also work, not just to earn money, but to give a legitimate account of themselves. Their understandings of work are anchored in stories that imply conceptions of the desirable, personal goals, and culturally accepted values. They do not think of themselves as being driven by necessity, but as having choices to make, and having made choices already about how to spend their time and energy. Their work is grounded in a moral context. It is, at least in principle, subject to moral restraint. Ideas drawn from school, vocational counseling, training sessions, and the workplace itself render working a legitimate, personally meaningful enterprise. But these ideas, like those evident among professionals and managers, often fail to place work in an even larger context. As work has become better institutionalized culturally, its relationships with other parts of life are thus more difficult to grasp. This is true even of its relationship with money.

The Social Grounding of Money

If money is nothing more than the wherewithal to pay for things, those who have less of it should be quite different from those who have more. But if money indeed has meaning—if it is embedded in cultural frameworks—then it is far less clear how understandings of it may vary with levels of affluence. To be sure, the working class is no less likely to make a virtue of its having less than professionals and managers are of their having more. Yet the story is complicated by the fact that there are also common cultural traditions on which to draw.

The taboo against discussing money is clearly one such tradition. At the top, circumspection may be dictated by considerations of modesty. At the bottom, it is more deeply rooted in the fierce, independent pride that has always characterized American workers. But, in either case, the norms are powerful.[28] Ed Butler says money was "very seldom ever discussed" when he was growing up. He follows the same pattern. "My salary, I wouldn't discuss that. That's personal, I feel. My contribution to churches. I think that's personal. My debts." Jack Paretti had the same experience. "I really wasn't taught anything about money at all," he admits. To discuss money, he feels, is to give up some of one's privacy. He doesn't discuss any of his financial dealings with anyone other than his wife, certainly not family, or people at work. Why not? "I just don't think it's really any of their business. I don't see where it would matter to them or to anybody else really what I make or what I do with my money." A feisty sense of independence also characterizes Mike Kominski's reasons for keeping money matters to himself. "My money is my business," he asserts. "If I ever had difficulty and needed assistance from somebody, then I would [discuss it]. But as far as general chitchat, as far as, you know, 'Oh, I've got $100,000 in the bank,' or something like that, never. I would never, ever do that."

These views are widely shared by working-class women as well.[29] Though they may have a trusted friend with whom they can share intimate details of their lives, they think it inappropriate to disclose economic facts. "I don't think I was ever taught anything about money," Joan Larsen recalls. Part of the reason, as she looks back, is that her father didn't even discuss money very openly with her mother. There was a distinct gender division; money was not for women and children (especially girls) to be worried about. Joan hopes she is setting a different example for her own children. Yet she finds it difficult. Now that her children are grown, they sometimes ask her if she is doing okay or not. "But to get down to details about my finances or how much I make or whatever else," she says, "I don't like to do that."

Murial Johnson reveals yet another reason why working-class women may be reluctant to discuss personal finances. Keeping this information to herself is, in her view, the best way to avoid arguments. Contemplating marriage, for example, she says, "I can't see committing my life to having to fight over the right to make a decision whether or not to spend my money. No, I can't handle that. I can't be controlled that way." Like Joan Larsen, she says she wasn't taught anything about money as a child, and she hopes to give her own children better training. Yet it is hard for her to discuss money even with her own family. "Everybody's in competition," she admits, "especially the women against the men." So she's worried that giving away information will result in yielding some of her independence.

There is also at least one indication that the taboo against discussing money is even more prominent in working-class families than it is in more affluent families. Working-class parents, it appears, are more likely to withhold financial information from their children in order to protect them from worrying, and in other cases to shield themselves from embarrassment or criticism that might come their way from children spreading news about family finances among friends and neighbors. As a result, people who say their parents were "hard up" financially are much less likely to say they had a clear idea of how their parents made financial decisions than people whose parents were "well off."[30] Working-class parents are also more likely than professionals and managers to say parents should not discuss finances in the presence of their children.

Working-class men and women, just as professionals and managers, are thus left to their own devices in trying to figure out what to think about money.[31] Being closer to the margin financially, they understandably worry more—about paying their bills, to be sure, but also about whether or not they are making the right decisions, and feeling guilty about their purchases.[32] Having enough in the bank to pay the rent at the end of the month, or being able to buy a new tire if one goes out, these are what matter most. In Jack Paretti's case, for example, it has been the sudden, unexpected bills that have caused the most grief. His job doesn't provide medical insurance, so when one of the children gets sick it really hurts. "Yeh," he says, "I worry a lot." Yet, with few exceptions, these worries are shouldered alone. "Most of the time when my financial situation is bad, I just concentrate on the best way for me to get out of it," says Murial Johnson. Telling her family would be the last thing she'd do. "I rarely tell people about any of my [money] problems," says another person. "Because they're my problems. And I found out through life, most people have their own problems. You know, why do they need to know mine?"

Money is thus like work in the sense of being driven by demons within. Despite all the so-called objective conditions that economists and social theorists write about, working-class Americans overwhelmingly feel themselves to be responsible for their own economic affairs. Just as professionals and managers, they recognize limits to their ability to control their earnings or their family's spending habits. But one thing they can control is their attitudes toward money.[33] Personal finances have meaning, not just as the wherewithal to buy goods, but as signals about how to think about one's well-being and sense of worth.[34] Money is thus doubly problematic: for its cultural as well as its economic significance.[35]

Working-class Americans also find it difficult to know how to think about money because it is increasingly severed from work. Most of the ones we talked to had been taught to work as children. Having a little money to spend had always depended on work. Ed Butler, for example, said he always had little odd jobs to do around his dad's restaurant and chores to do on the farm. "You always put your chit in." Yet people who had held jobs as children still complained frequently of not developing a solid understanding of the worth of money or how to use it wisely. Ed Butler knew his mother saved every penny. His dad didn't. Ed figured it was just a difference in personalities. As for himself, money generally went through his fingers like water. Only later did he begin to realize he'd have to start thinking more carefully about it. Moreover, the connection between work and money is often rooted more firmly in childhood teachings than in the reality of adult life. Eight out of ten in fact deny that those who work hardest in their line of work generally get paid the best. Conversely, only one in eight says there is a close relationship in their own jobs between working harder and getting more money.[36]

It's not just that disconnecting money from work makes it harder for working-class people to know how to obtain money. Rather, it is that two essential components of the American Dream have now become more difficult to reconcile with each other. On the one hand, the dream of working hard and becoming financially successful is still widely cherished. Even more than among professionals and managers, working-class men and women are likely to admire those who work hard and make a lot of money.[37] Yet, on the other hand, the chance that hard work will actually yield higher incomes appears to be so low that the effort may not appear worth it. Indeed, only a third of the working class say they would be willing to work longer hours in hopes of making more money, and even fewer express willingness to take a less interesting job, subject themselves to more pressure, or move to a new location.[38]

Little wonder, then, that making money seems like winning at roulette—an intriguing fantasy, but largely beyond the realm of realistic possibilities. Jack Paretti, for example, says his wife pressures him to try to make more money, but he doesn't feel he can. He knows he would need more education to get into something better. And he says he can't do that because he has a family to feed and it would mean starting over and taking a long time just to get back where he is now. So hard work anchors money in one sense: realistically, he knows that he works for his money, and that if he didn't work he wouldn't have money. But hard work is also not seen as the way to make more money, because of structural constraints, such as needing education but also having a family to feed.

Consumerism is the other cultural influence to which upper-, middle-, and lower-income people alike have become increasingly exposed in the past half-century.[39] Working-class men and women do bring some distinctive perspectives to bear on consumer goods. For professionals and managers, consumer purchases are often framed entirely in terms of use-value, quality, price, and personal gratification. For working-class people, a stronger connection between work and purchases—between production and consumption—is still evident in some cases. Ed Butler made this connection in talking about a new addition to his house. "I felt good about doing it because I felt like I worked for it; we put our minds on to it and we did it the way we wanted to do it; I got a lot of self-satisfaction in doing it because I also helped work on it."

Economic necessity also provides working-class men and women with a language to justify their purchases. For instance, Jack Paretti recently purchased a new car. He says they had to because they had "a broken out piece-of-garbage station wagon that just died." He and his wife thought about getting along with one car, what the monthly payments would be, and how much their insurance would go up. But in the end they felt good about their decision: "It was a necessity. We basically thought we had to do it."

What constitutes an appropriate use of money is, however, defined more by rituals and symbols than by anything else. Working-class people talk about buying a cheaper brand of cereal as evidence that they are not extravagant, or say they splurge sometimes (perhaps buying "adult toys").[40] Often the sacrifices are less than purely ritualistic, of course, arising more from necessity, like they do for Jack Paretti, who says his family goes hiking and camping because they can't afford any other kind of recreational activity.[41] The purchases, or splurges, though, are probably more ritualistic, like having special toys, such as cars or musical instruments. In the absence of strict family budgets (fewer than one in eight has one), these rituals provide a general sense of order for the working-class consumer.[42] Moreover, their content is deeply influenced by frames of reference supplied through advertising and sales appeals. Being frugal, for example, may be defined as purchasing a wide-screen stereophonic color television but forgoing four-channel simultaneous display; yet spending $400 on the cheaper model can be conceived of as economizing only because a salesperson has been pushing the more expensive model.[43]

Unlike professionals and managers, working-class men and women are also likely to view the law as a symbolic way of setting outer limits around their economic activities. They worry about making purchases that might be "hot" or that might get them in trouble with the bank. "Don't spend above your head" was the way Ed Butler expressed it. He said this was a saying he'd heard many times growing up from his dad. It came in the same breath as "stay out of trouble with the law." Living in poor neighborhoods where street crime is often all too visible, working-class people also use legality as a way of setting themselves off from this undesirable element in their communities.[44] As one man who barely earns a minimum wage observed, "I want more money, a lot more, but I worry, that's greedy, I don't want to get into wanting dirty money." Even those who lived in middle-class neighborhoods some-times raised this specter, as one man did in describing the kids next door, who he said were both rude and materialistic. "We don't let them over here any more because they're headed for a life of crime."

But the most important symbolic distinction is the one drawn be-tween material goods and human relationships. Having less discre-tionary income, they find it especially reassuring to think that money cannot buy true love or happiness. Indeed, they believe wealth is asso-ciated with unhappiness more than with happiness, and they argue that they could have attained more money only by sacrificing cher-ished relationships with their families.[45] Having never discussed money very openly with their families, they can point readily to those few times when money was discussed as proof that it does damage close relationships.

Ed Butler's most vivid memory concerning financial issues was when his sister went away to college. It caused a lot of friction between his parents and between her and her siblings. Nobody could agree on what the proper amount was to spend on a college education. It made his sister feel so bad she never came home again. Jack Paretti remem-bers his mother and father fighting every time they went over the bills together. Like professionals and managers, working-class people are also reluctant to mix money and family relationships if they can avoid it. Loans to family members may be more common because of financial necessity, but they are still regarded with skepticism. Paretti, for exam-ple, borrowed money from his grandmother once, and he will never do it again, it seems, because money means independence to him, wanting to be free, whereas the loan tied him down, gave her control over him, at least to lecture him about being responsible. He felt demeaned. "That's the year I was cutting grass," he recalls, "so I was working. I was working that summer. I just didn't have the full amount [I needed] so I asked her. She's not rich by any means, but I knew she had some money put away. She was like one step short of pulling out a loan agreement, and I got this massive lecture about financial responsibility. It was just like you shouldn't borrow money. You shouldn't buy any-thing unless you have the money in hand. Like this whole negative angle. Then she gave me the money anyway. I was just like, man, it's not worth going through that for $400, whatever it was!"[46]

What has sometimes entered political debate as an emphasis on "family values" can also be understood in this context. Working-class men and women talk vehemently about the value of family ties because doing so provides an account of why they have not pursued more lucrative careers. It is thus understandable that political discussions of family values should hold appeal for working-class families, especially during economic downturns. Joan Larsen, for example, remarks, "I agree with the Republicans. They're trying to get back to the family, and I agree with that, because society now is just saying 'everything's okay.' I mean, even the Nike commercials are saying 'just do it.' Anything goes now, and I don't agree with that. There should be a lot of rules and boundaries. Anybody can live with anybody, you can marry anybody. It doesn't matter at this point. And I don't want my kids growing up to believe that. That's garbage. You're a girl, and you marry a guy, and you have children, and you keep it that way. I don't want to see all this other stuff going on now. And that's on TV and everything they're picking up these ideas that it's all okay. I don't agree with that."

Working-class people depict family values as being wholesome and in keeping with the natural order of things, rather than artificial, but also as a legitimate reason for not working longer hours, not trying to earn more money, or not spending money in more extravagant ways. One man who has had to rely on financial aid from his church for help during a slack season, for example, says, "Sure, I could get another job and maybe earn $200 more a week. But then I'd never get to spend time with my family. What would be the point?" Another man explains that camping is not only cheap, but better: "It's a family thing. We don't need things to entertain us. Those things just cost money."

The symbolic boundary between material goods and human relationships also has a sharp vertical dimension for working-class people that is generally absent among professionals and managers. Money doesn't just turn people's heads away from their friends and family. It makes them feel superior. And those who don't have as much, in consequence, are made to feel inferior, even though another side of them says they are just as good as anyone else. For the working class, then, materialism is a social problem because it connotes corruption among the wealthy. What they dislike about the rich is their apparent eagerness to put things ahead of people. The illustrations they think of when talking about materialism usually imply some sense of being looked down on by the rich. Ed Butler says, "I know people who think the more money they have, the more powerful they are." Jack Paretti observes, "It just seems the upper echelon of the earners, the Donald

Trumps, are idolized." But, he argues, "I don't see the point; they're just people." Another man asserts, "I'll never take the back seat to someone who has a million dollars, or a hundred million. They're no better than me."[47] By the same token, the wealthy can be excused for their position in society if they overcome the tendency of things to stand in the way of people. Thus, wealthy people who have been known personally are generally thought to be okay because they were just regular guys who didn't try to show off and who treated working-class people with respect. Asked to describe some rich person he knew personally, for example, Ed Butler's first remark was "He always treated me well." Another man said he had known several millionaires, and he was happy to say "they were always very respectful to me, very nice to me."

In most ways, though, the similarities between working-class and professional or managerial understandings of work and money outweigh the differences. Despite more severe economic concerns, working-class men and women generally formulate accounts of their work that legitimate it in terms other than money. They consider it enormously meaningful, and for the most part satisfying, because they can tell stories about its variety, the challenges it provides, and how it suits their personalities. They keep their financial worries to themselves, taking responsibility for their feelings about money, and they frame their consumer purchases less in strict economic calculations than with symbols and rituals that supply implicit understandings of how much is enough. In all these ways the economic sphere of their lives is clearly subject to cultural processes. It is a legitimate sphere of activity, not simply because of economic necessity, but because it has meaning and order.

Yet the order that draws working-class people deeply into their work and their quest for material goods is limited, just as it is for professionals and managers. Whereas the American Dream once legitimated work as a means to achieving long-term ends, such as a better life for one's children, work is now framed more nearly within the workplace itself. It is engrossing as long as tales can be told about its variety or about some minor victory or an instance of camaraderie. How it connects to the rest of life is less clear. Consumer goods are neither a means to an end, nor an end in themselves, but a necessary evil, one that borders on obsession at the same time it requires constant vigilance (with attendant guilt). The pursuit of these goods is bounded by a clear sense that human relationships and happiness, symbolized especially by family, are of greater fundamental worth. Yet the two realms stand in contradistinction, posing as antagonists, rather than being conceptually linked.

There is thus much cause for concern about the American Dream in the working class, just as there is in the more affluent sectors of American society. Income divisions between the have-it-alls and the don't-quite-have-its continue. But a service ethic, professionalism, common schooling experiences, and uniform exposure to mass culture have contributed to a standardization of assumptions about work and money. For most working-class families the American Dream means something more than newspaper depictions characterizing it simply as the quest for more material goods. But these depictions are themselves possible because the other moral meanings once implicit in the American Dream have become fragmented.

THE NEW IMMIGRANTS

The American working class is of course being transformed in yet another way that we have thus far not considered directly: by a new wave of immigration that is virtually unprecedented, even for a country founded by immigrants. In the 1980s alone, some 8.7 million people streamed to the United States, matching the record number who came just after the turn of the century. With native-born birthrates down, immigration has been producing a steadily higher share of overall population growth, rising from only 11 percent of total growth in the 1960s to 39 percent in the 1980s. The recent wave also differs from its predecessors in origin. Nearly half come from Mexico, the Caribbean, and Latin America. More than a third come from Asia. Only 12 percent are European.[48]

The new immigrants are by no means contributing only to the reshaping of the working class. About as many male immigrants are college educated, for example, as among native-born Americans. Yet a significantly higher proportion (about a third) are high school dropouts than in the general population. Those with college degrees are often forced into underemployment situations because of language barriers. And, besides documented immigration, as many as 200,000 illegal immigrants arrive each year seeking employment, largely in unskilled positions.

Immigration and the American Dream have always been closely associated in the popular mind. People came to America seeking a better, freer, more affluent life. That was the dream. And if native-born Americans have lost clarity about this vision, there still may be hope of it being revitalized by new immigrants themselves. "It is still those 'huddled masses yearning to breathe free' who will keep the American dream burning bright for most of us," declare one team of journalists.[49] And most nonimmigrants at least seem to agree. Despite fears that immigrants may be taking scarce jobs, surveys show that immigrants are generally regarded as hard working, and a majority of the public feels "the American dream of middle-class prosperity" is still a realistic goal for new immigrants.[50]

But talking with immigrants themselves yields a more ambiguous picture. They know what the American Dream is: it means simply the hope for a more prosperous life. It means work, making money to support your family. Many say they have made great sacrifices to come to America because they want a better life for their children. They would do it again, if they had to decide. Yet they also sense that things are no longer what they used to be. Juan Ysidro, 46, has been a sheet-metal worker since coming to the United States from Ecuador in 1970. He's raised his family here. He says the American Dream "hasn't happened." He doesn't mean just for himself, but for the whole society. He wants to go back. "Twenty years ago," he says, "the U.S. was a good, good country." But "right now, the U.S. has got a lot of problems."

Slower economic growth, coupled with stiffer competition for jobs, has been part of the reason for such misgivings (Juan had recently suffered a six-month layoff before being rehired). Like many of their predecessors, recent immigrants without education or job skills are often forced to endure sweatshop conditions with little hope of climbing the occupational ladder. How much harder it is to be near the bottom than on a higher rung of the social ladder is clearly evident in the case of Jesu Tejeda, 23, a machinist in a New York sweater factory. Growing up in the Dominican Republic, he heard from his mother time and time again to "work hard and get an education." But the words meant something different than they do to most Americans. Translated, hard work meant starting work in a cheese factory when Jesu was 10. And get an education meant take it slow instead of going in for instant cash, like his brother, who wound up losing a leg in a high-speed truck chase. By the time he was 20, Jesu had worked in a grocery store, done construction in Puerto Rico as an illegal alien, painted houses in New Mexico, and worked as a janitor. He feels lucky to be earning $3.80 an hour at his present job, even if it means working eleven-hour days with only two ten-minute breaks and a half hour for lunch. He also wonders if he will ever make enough to support a family—or even get a vacation.

Yet it is not only those at the bottom who express concern about the American Dream. They worry about false hopes, the values their children are learning in school, the pace of life, relating to their neighbors, and the possibility of regaining what they once thought America was all about. Rina Patna, 40, came from India seventeen years ago. Her husband has had steady work in a company owned by his brother. She has been able to stay home with her two children. She knows she has improved her life economically by coming to America. She has also talked to many other immigrants about their dreams. The problem, she says, is that "people thought they were coming to heaven," but now they find themselves "in a very bad situation." They've given up their friends and the respect they had in their communities and found little to replace it. She feels success needs to be redefined. She says it should mean "good children, good husband, good living situation, good friends."

If new immigrants have doubts about the American Dream, it is nevertheless mistaken to think that previous generations of immigrants believed in a dream composed of nothing more than material prosperity. Their parents taught them to work hard, often by example, more than by what they said. Their parents wanted them to have opportunities. But how they realized these opportunities was up to them. They didn't feel they had to graduate from college and become successful lawyers or doctors to please their parents. Being able to pay their bills was often enough. Or pursuing a trade. Or having children. The values they learned focused more on *how* to live than on *what* life to lead. They were told to do a job well, not which job to do. They learned to work hard, at whatever they did. Honesty was important. So was respect. And family.

Many grew up with a taken-for-granted division of labor between their parents. Dad worked very hard to earn money. They seldom saw him but had no doubts that his reason for working hard was to support the family. Mom stayed home. There was no question about her having a career. But she contributed economically nonetheless. She took the paycheck, did the shopping, and paid the bills. She also wiped runny noses and bandaged scraped knees. She was less insistent that her children succeed than that they know the difference between right and wrong. The American Dream was thus one is which people at the bottom could feel they were good and decent citizens, worthy of respect whether they became prosperous or not.

Searching for a Script

These values are still prominent in working America. If the American Dream is being rewritten, it is not becoming a script about money at the expense of everything else. Nor is it a story of diminished expectations. The changes are deeper, rooted in the shifting character of working-class work itself. And they are more subtle in their consequences.

American workers at the end of the twentieth century are not simply pursuing a dream their parents only partly realized. They are redefining the dream to mean more of an emphasis on family values as an antidote to materialistic expectations, to mean happiness regardless of one's position in the occupational structure, to mean fathers devoting more time to their children, and to mean wives having a career and a life of their own. The dream is also being redefined negatively: not to be as compulsive and rigid about achievement as their parents, but still to have a comfortable life, whether that means a car that doesn't break down, or separate bedrooms for their children.

Yet in any process of redefinition there is uncertainty. Employers are anxious to encourage workers to spend more time at the job, and advertisers would like nothing better than to see working-class people spending more of their money on new consumer items. The American working class has by no means lost touch with the moral meanings of life. But it, like the professional and managerial class, is having to rethink how work and money connect with family, with community, and with other sources of basic human values. Whether these institutions are up to the challenge is thus a question to be considered seriously.

PART THREE

THE PRECARIOUS SOURCES OF

HUMAN VALUES

Chapter Nine

FAMILY LIFE: THE NEW CHALLENGES OF

BALANCING MULTIPLE COMMITMENTS

NEWCASTERS AND POLLSTERS have trained the American public to think of economic commitments and family life as trade-offs: working too hard or being too interested in money focuses attention away from the family; lightening up on these commitments gives more time to focus on family values. Individuals can be more devoted to one or the other. The whole culture can also tip from side to side. "Americans are placing increasing importance on family values and turning away from materialism" is thus a formulaic lead for a newspaper story about public opinion.[1]

The trade-off between economic commitments and family life can be taken as a good starting point for considering the sorts of human values that may be capable of imposing moral restraint on our material needs and desires. The family is often pictured as the cradle of human values, nurturing the human spirit deeply and affectionately. Embodied in the family are such primordial values as respect for authority, moral obligation, interdependence, and loyalty—all of which seem remote from the marketplace. Devotion on the family side suggests strength to endure economic deprivation, the ability to rise above self-interest, and a commitment to the future, to the training of the young, and to the preservation of values cherished more deeply in the past.

But is this really the way it is? Hasn't the family also been a source of the work ethic? Isn't the family itself an economic unit? Don't family obligations make people work harder and want money all the more, encouraging them to be good breadwinners, to send their children to good colleges where their economic fortunes will be furthered, to live in fine neighborhoods that are the envy of their parents and siblings, and to pass on a respectable inheritance to their descendants? Haven't economic commitments been deeply implicated in the very values around which the family has traditionally been organized? How is it, then, that we have in recent years come to regard family values as an *alternative* to American materialism?[2]

To answer these questions, we need to take a giant step back, putting ourselves at a greater distance from the present, in order to see it more clearly. Instead of simply assuming the trade-off between materialism and family values to be inevitable, "the way it is," we must ask why we have come to this view in the first place. Taking this perception as our starting point, we can put it in a wider perspective. We can ask what it tells us about the changes currently taking place in our culture, and with those changes in mind, we can then evaluate more objectively whether the family really is a strong source of moral restraint on the economic life, or whether its role needs to be reconsidered and refurbished.

The argument I wish to consider is that the perceived trade-off between materialism and family values is symptomatic of the more fundamental breakdown in our way of thinking about the American Dream. My contention is that the American Dream traditionally included two primary assumptions about the family: that the male would function as chief breadwinner, and that the female would be the chief agent for the preservation and transmission of noneconomic values. These assumptions worked fairly well to unify (create complementarity between) materialism and the human spirit. In the normal course of affairs, gender differences provided a way of mapping the distinction between economic commitments and human values, but the two could for the most part be regarded as being in equilibrium, or as not being problematic. This was especially true in expansive economic periods (such as the 1950s) when added effort in the economic sphere actually produced enough resources that time and money could be devoted to the cultivation of family values. As market pressures increased, though, the division between the two realms actually became more pronounced. Working longer hours and feeling themselves under greater economic pressures, men devoted more of themselves to the material sphere and separated themselves psychologically (if not physically) from the realm of human values. Then, as married women themselves began to enter the labor force in growing numbers, the division also became more problematic. The material world outside the family came to be seen less as a resource and more as a threat.

No longer could children be launched into the world to pursue their parents' vision of the American Dream. Children themselves became problematic, as did the question of what values to teach them. These changes have also produced different modes of adaptation among men and women. The legacy of the earlier division is still very much in evidence among men, where compartmentalization between work and family provides a favored mechanism for managing multiple commitments. Among working women, however, extreme compartmentalization is neither as feasible nor considered as desirable. The larger debate about values in American life is thus deeply imbued with gender connotations. The most far-reaching attempts actually to bring values to bear on economic decisions, rather than simply to compartmentalize the two, have come from working women. To substantiate this argument, it will be necessary to consider, first, evidence on the changing relationship of the nuclear family as a whole to economic commitments, second, the problematic relationships between parents and children, third, the "tug of war" in which men typically engage to manage the relationship between economic commitments and family life, and fourth, the alternative mechanisms that have emerged among working women.

The Nuclear Family as "Haven"

It has become commonplace among students of the family to point out that the "traditional" family, as we know it, is anything but traditional. The "Leave It to Beaver" family, composed of mother, father, and two children living in spendid isolation in the suburbs, tells us more about the 1950s than about the family at any time previously.[3] And yet it is this nuclear family that we must take as a starting point, if only to inquire more deeply into the sources of its vulnerability.[4]

The distinguishing feature of the nuclear family is its relative autonomy from wider networks of kin.[5] It is a product of the idea that young people must "leave home," moving away from their parents—geographically, economically, and emotionally—to start a home of their own. It contrasts sharply with the family patterns evident in tribal societies, where children may be raised by their mother's siblings, and it is radically different even from the settlement patterns of a century ago, in which adult children often took over a portion of the family farm and raised their own offspring in close proximity to grandparents, aunts and uncles, and cousins. Understood this way, the nuclear family is still very much the dominant feature of private life in America today. Single-parent families, parents who are divorced and remarried, and couples without children may, as some observers have suggested, be "postmodern" compared with the Cleavers, but their members for the most part remain separate from wider kinship networks.[6] The families that deviate most from the nuclear pattern at present are the extended families that prevail in some sectors of the Hispanic, African American, and white working-class populations.[7]

The extended family mediated between the individual and the material realm. Taking over part of the family farm was a common way in which parents helped their children "get a start." So was incorporating sons into the family business and marrying daughters to prosperous neighbors. In return, parents expected their offspring to provide for them when they grew old. If a breadwinner became ill, his family could count on siblings and cousins to take up the slack. Hard times in one segment of the wider economy could be withstood better because relatives employed across a variety of industries could pool their resources. Gifts and personal loans provided a line of defense against bankruptcy and starvation. As consumers, extended families also mediated the needs of individual members. Scarce commodities, such as an automobile with good tires or a house big enough to hold a wedding, could be shared. The family also established norms of consumption, collectively defining the differences between "comfort" and "extravagance," and legitimating tastes in food, clothing, and household furnishings that might be different from those in the wider society. Even when it did not function as an economic unit, the extended family served too as a source of emotional support. Work and money might be individual responsibilities, but they could be integrated with the values of one's family in daily conversation.

The nuclear family, in contrast, has functioned as an emotional escape, a haven, from the external realities of economic life. Having gone out to an unseen destination to conduct business in the marketplace, Ward Cleaver returns home to kick off his shoes, eat a nourishing meal, engage in good-humored banter with his sons, and relax in front of the television. His family has been shielded entirely from the marketplace, spending their day interacting with the neighbors, going to school, working on crafts, and enjoying themselves. Even in the less romanticized lives of actual people in the 1960s and 1970s, the nuclear family continued to be understood in this way. It was a place where children could (or should) grow up with the warmth and security they were not likely to experience later in the dog-eat-dog world of business. It was where romantic love, intimacy, and personal caring should predominate, in sharp contrast to the self-interest and impersonality of the workplace.[8]

The American Dream of the late-nineteenth to mid-twentieth centuries articulated the dominant understanding of how the nuclear family should relate to the wider economy.[9] Economic self-sufficiency was one of its ideals. This meant that the nuclear family should not expect material help, either from kin networks or from government. Success, however, was something for which the nuclear family should strive. The breadwinner should try to be financially successful by working hard. His spouse was to facilitate this effort by managing the family budget with care, providing emotional support, and perhaps presenting an appearance of material success to neighbors and friends. She was also supposed to encourage the children to be successful. To this end, they too were to work hard, doing their homework, learning the value of money, and cultivating such virtues as honesty and personal integrity. The pursuit of success was thus linked quite closely with a concept of intergenerational transmission. It did not have to be achieved in one generation. What was passed on need not be wealth itself, but simply the material means to provide the next generation with opportunities to climb a notch higher on the ladder. Human values and material life were closely integrated within the nuclear family itself: good values, such as hard work and honesty, led to material success, which in turn was the basis both of personal happiness and of the ability to transmit these values to the next generation.

But the nuclear family could never in actuality provide a safe haven against the full fury of economic forces unleashed against it.[10] Working-class families were never able to shield themselves fully from the stark realities of unemployment. Those that succeeded in realizing the American Dream to a modest extent saw their children turn their backs on the family values they had been taught.[11] Middle-class families found their own safe havens invaded by television commercials drawing them into a vicious cycle of higher expenditures and harder work. Separated increasingly from the ethnic subcultures and family financial support on which previous generations had depended, they also found it harder to achieve economic stability on their own, to know how to think about work and money, and to pass on essential values to their children.

BESIEGED BY MATERIALISM

Having retreated into itself, the nuclear family is now perceived as a weak, embattled, but sometimes heroic combatant faced with insuperable forces from the outside world.[12] Except for drugs and crime, the fears of people we talked to focused more on the effects of materialism on their families than anything else. They worry that too much attention to material pursuits inevitably corrupts family life, much the way they see money corrupting all intimate human relationships. They believe their children are particularly susceptible to this corruption. They want to protect them from it, but they often harbor a more complex, ambivalent orientation toward their children as well.

"Materialism prevents people from realizing deeper values in life" is the underlying theme in people's comments about its effects on their families. Most of them do not blame it for specific problems, such as being in debt, having to work hard, arguing with their spouse, or suffering broken family relationships. They see it more as a distraction, like a titillating picture that keeps them from enjoying something more valuable in their lives. "It keeps people from seeing the real issues." "We get so wrapped up in it that we don't stop to smell the roses." "It's a very selfish way to live." "Materialism makes people insensitive."

Most Americans believe materialism penetrates the far corners of their society. Nine out of ten, for example, agree that "our society is much too materialistic."[13] But television provides them with the most vivid examples. Dietician Lydia Kramer thought immediately of the message presented in soap operas. "Everybody has a new dress on every day, every house is glamorous." The problem, she feels, is that these implicit messages "make life unrealistic." Personal problems are always cured in a few episodes. Poor people are never shown. People are put into strata; everything becomes "us and them," and "we all try to come out better than someone else." Materialism is thus not simply about having things, but a source of conflict in human relationships. "It has to do with our values," Lydia explains.[14]

The reason people perceive a trade-off between materialism and their families is that materialism stands for everything that is (or might be) wrong in their lives. Family, in contrast, symbolizes everything that is right (even when facts belie this assumption). If we only had a surer sense of who we are, it would be unnecessary to find happiness in material pursuits. But advertising, career aspirations, and job pressures stack the odds against the family to the point that people cannot find serenity there. Children cannot learn what is truly important in life. Parents don't have time to relax. Couples don't have time to nurture each other.

But feeling that one's family is besieged by materialism, perhaps paradoxically, can actually increase, rather than reduce, the economic commitments people are willing to undertake. The reasoning appears to be similar to that underlying the way in which people select gifts for their close friends and family members. Wanting to escape the sense that money and market pressures reduce everything to a least-common denominator level, they search for one-of-a-kind products, quality goods. To set their home apart, they try to incorporate similar "values" into their decorating and personal accoutrements. They add personal touches, even though these require considerable time and money to put together.

Collecting antiques is how Stanton Haynes, the Philadelphia attorney, creates a "home environment" for himself. He feels these items, produced in an era when materialism was less rampant than it is today, embody direct contact between the producer and the person for whom he or she was producing. This provides him with a greater sense of "intimacy" in his environment. Mass-produced goods, in contrast, symbolize the impersonality of the marketplace ("produced for people you'll never meet"). He worries that those goods lead to an "artificial construction of values." He also worries that the "quality" of those goods is often "disappointing." Buying antiques brings him into personal contact with people who really know what they are doing. He even imagines that he is contributing to the re-creation of a kind of old-fashioned artisanal community. When he decided to remodel his kitchen, for example, he found it especially enjoyable to feel that he was "supporting people who are trying to do something correctly and in the old way, and just bringing people together who might not have met otherwise."

The rich have always carved out personal enclaves like this to distance themselves from the "crass materialism" of the majority. But distancing is always relative. Boutiques and specialty shops now make it possible for members of the middle class to differentiate themselves from one another in the same way, but at a price. Their homes become a haven constructed of expensive antiques, collections, hobbies, and travel mementos, all of which define a symbolic boundary between the standardized, impersonal world "out there" and the human spirit that is uniquely "in here."

An important corollary of this orientation among the well-to-do is that materialism also provides a way of blaming the poor for their own problems. Taking the view that materialism is something any knowledgeable person can simply "rise above" leads easily to the conclusion that the poor should simply resist the shallow values of the marketplace and go after "quality" in their family lives. Fashion manager Davis Reskin, for example, takes a cavalier attitude toward materialism in his own life. He recognizes the temptations are "out there," but he figures he can resist them. (He says he doesn't need twenty Rolex watches; one will do.) The problem, as he sees it, is that materialism is corrupting American society from the bottom up, as it were, by subverting the values of the poor. "Those are probably the people that have the hardest time in life and find it most difficult to exercise control. They're slightly out of control to begin with and they're malleable by the media." The result, he says, is "very shallow values." What he means is people sitting there watching "the bowling alley league woman" and "those soap operas and the values in the soap operas." Materialism, in his view, is precisely what Stanton Haynes says it is. "My God," declares Reskin, "the stuff isn't even quality."

The fact that "quality goods" cannot be used by everyone to set up expensive symbolic barriers, however, means that marked tension between materialism and the family continues to be a common perception in our culture. We want our homes not only to be a reflection of our personal values, but also to be more authentic than the world we see around us. That world seems to be without values (artificial) because it is materialistic, alien, externally produced, threatening. When it penetrates our homes, it makes us think things are no longer quite right. We use words like "misplaced," "misguided," "superficial," "shallow," and "off course." Talking about materialism is thus primarily a way of saying that something has gone awry with our values.

CHILDREN: THE ENEMY WITHIN

Anxiety about materialism can be free floating, but generally it seeks out a specific target with which to associate itself. Often this target is the television set because it brings the temptations of the marketplace vividly into the quiet sanctity of the home. As such, it symbolizes a breach in the fortress wall. It connotes special danger. But even more dangerous are the children who watch it. "Children today," agree nine people out of ten, "want too many material things."[15] They become active agents of materialism within the family itself. They become the enemy within.

"Kids today have the 'gimmes,'" complain a number of the people we interviewed. "Gimme this, gimme that." "I'm always having to tell them 'no.'" "They're always demanding more; it just never ends." "It really bothers me, especially after the way I scrimped and saved." "What do they expect anyway?" Such remarks are often tinged with anger and fear. Parents are unsure whose side their children are on: theirs or the forces of evil.

Stuart Cummings sees himself as a bulwark of restraint who seldom lets money or material desires worry him. But he admits, "I worry about my kids. It's a very consumer-oriented era for our kids. They grow up watching TV, they see things they want, every commercial is like beckoning them in. And so I worry about [materialism] on their level. I'd like to rein things in." His worries reflect the broader image in our culture that portrays children both as especially powerful (holding the key to the future) and as particularly vulnerable (innocent).

Psychologically, the enemy within is particularly disturbing because it reflects deep ambivalence within ourselves. At one time, the American Dream told parents it was desirable to make almost any sacrifice on behalf of their children. Most important was the belief that one's children should have more opportunities and a better life than their parents. That view, while still accorded lip service, has begun to erode significantly. During the 1980s Americans ran up a huge national deficit that may seriously curtail the nation's prosperity for future generations. In more subtle ways, children are being robbed of the privileges they once enjoyed as a result of rejected tax initiatives for better schools or simply from parents failing to take time to read to their children or encourage them with their homework. "Adult rights to self-fulfillment may well have gotten out of hand in contemporary America," writes economist Sylvia Ann Hewlett. "We might not quite be ready to sell our children, but we are almost there."[16]

Focusing on the materialism of children can be a way of deflecting criticism from ourselves. Even those who seem to have children's interests at heart convey a mixed message when they speak as if children have become the agents of undesirable economic forces. Theater director Dick Stonefield does not have children of his own, but as a close observer of the media he worries that children are being exploited to bring materialism into the family. "Film and television are being dictated by kids because kids are the ones who watch TV and who the commercials are geared for. The kids get their parents to buy this particular cereal, or this particular brand of whatever. 'Oh, please, let's try this.' The mother's like, all right, maybe I'll try it. I mean, basically, these commercials make you think that you need to have this. It's something that you need to have and, obviously, in most cases, you don't need to have it, but when it reaches this kid it's like, you know, everybody has one of these. I should have one or I'll feel left out." In his view, children are thus the enemy in two ways. They subvert a parent's good judgment by clamoring for consumer products they see advertised on television. They also symbolize weakness in the adult world itself. The "adult child" responds to the infantalizing concerns expressed in advertisements.[17]

Parents typically put themselves on the side of wholesome family values in the struggle they see between their children and materialism. Clearly, however, they are the role models from which some of this materialism emanates. San Francisco psychiatrist Saul Feldman says he sees this pattern all the time in his family-counseling practice. Just recently, he recalls a youngster complaining to him, "Gee, Daddy only got the model XJ6 Jaguar, and *we* thought he should have gotten this other one, it was only $20,000 more." Feldman believes the damage indicated by this kind of perspective goes far beyond materialism alone. It isn't just that children are innocent *and then* become susceptible to the appeals of the marketplace. The process actually works back on itself, Feldman argues. These appeals make it *harder* for young people to develop psychologically and emotionally. They need to be discovering who they are and learning what to value in life. Instead, their attention is constantly being drawn away from themselves toward some feature of the material environment.

NEW PERSPECTIVES ON VALUES

This is the context in which new concerns have arisen in recent years about the transmission of values to children. When the old consensus was in place, parents could feel they were passing on wholesome values to their children with relative ease. Hard work and honesty were

simple enough that parents could concentrate their attention on reinforcing these values, both in what they said to their children and in the
way in which they themselves lived. Other values could be considered
matters of individual preference, choices that the child made largely on
the basis of taste, with the opportunities hard work and honesty created. For those who still think this way, instilling values is relatively
straightforward. "I just want them to work hard and be honest and
ethical," says Norm Lundström. He tries to do this the old-fashioned
way: "Mostly just by example; it's not really teaching at all." These
values make sense to him because they "engender success in whatever
you do." "After all, that's the way to be happy, isn't it?" he asks. But
with materialism knocking at the door, and with many parents no
longer as sure that hard work pays off in human happiness, the kinds
of values needing to be transmitted to children are becoming much
more problematic. Indeed, only one person in two claims to be "very
sure" of the values they would want their own children to learn. As a
society, say half of respondents, we are doing a poor job of raising our
children; and of the remaining half, fewer than one in five thinks we are
doing a good or excellent job.[18]

Few people are as articulate about these changes as Mike Kominski,
the truck driver we met in the last chapter. "You learned a different set
of values back then," he says, describing how things probably were in
the 1920s and 1930s. "You learned the work ethic back then and you
definitely learned to take care of your family." For the past several
decades, though, "people have had to work so hard just to maintain
their standard of living (the way costs have gone) that they're not available for their family." In the earlier period, he says, people worked
from morning till night, but then "went home and stayed home." Nowadays, "everybody's become yuppies and workaholics." They don't
spend any time with their families, so they buy them things instead,
like a Nintendo game. He figures children understand when their parents are working hard just to pay the electric bill, but they don't understand when their parents seem to be working hard for no good reason.
"To the kid, it just looks like the parents have something better to do
than be with me."

It all comes back to materialism. The parents are no longer earning a
living for their family; they're trying to get ahead, trying to advance
themselves, both directly and vicariously through their children. "I
hear that you now have yuppie parents," says Kominski, "who are
reading their kids advanced books when they're in the crib, hoping

that their evolving brain cells will take some of this in and give them a head start in school, which will give them a head start in college, which will give them a head start in business." This shouldn't be the purpose of life, but it is. Parents don't have time just to sit around with their children, letting them absorb good habits. But even if the time was available, it isn't clear what values the children would learn.

If most parents are not the mindless yuppies Mike Kominski thinks they are, they nevertheless wonder what exactly their roles should be. Questions are now being asked about each premise of the American Dream, the net result of which is to generate heightened uncertainty about the relationship between economic factors and child-rearing values. Fathers and mothers may still work hard, but if that effort becomes more of a burden than a way of realizing the American Dream, then what sort of message is being given to the children? "If we bring up our children today seeing fathers unhappy and grousing and groaning and complaining about their jobs, that is an example that will be very bad for the future," observed one woman. "If mother comes home harassed from her job," she added, "why should this young person want to be a working mother?" If the relationship between success and happiness falls into question, children's values may become problematic in yet another way. Frustrated parents will try to achieve happiness vicariously through their children. Parents themselves, however, are likely to feel deeply ambivalent about their children's interest in material success. It thus becomes harder for parents simply to teach their children by setting a good example for them. Values no longer emerge naturally from children observing their parents live their lives. Instead, parents must consciously try to "create experiences" for their children, discuss their own mistakes, make periodic reassessments, resist what comes naturally, do things differently from their own parents, and take into account the kinds of "yesterdays" they are creating for their children.

Ben and Sarah Arkwright know what it's like to raise children in uncertain times. Both are administrators at a prestigious midwestern university. They earn less than they could in the private sector, but they like the fact that they can send their children to a "lab school" run by the university. Their daughter Beth is there now. Their son Jeremy graduated two years ago and is now doing well at an elite university in New England. Ben and Sarah feel like they have been fighting materialism all their lives. They own a television set but have always had strict rules against the children turning it on. Sarah says she becomes "totally hysterical" if she comes home and finds the television on. They have refused to get cable hooked up, and they pride themselves on never having seen some of the popular shows. They've had a running battle with Beth ever since she was little about using the telephone instead of doing her homework. They've also been disturbed by the designer sneakers, the leather jackets, and the Rolex watches their kids wanted because their friends at the lab school had them.

The Arkwrights still believe a good chunk of the American Dream. Their children are bright, so doing well in school seems like a good way to succeed. But the Arkwrights don't define success in material terms. They want their children to become "intellectuals" who value ideas for their own sake, not just as a means of obtaining wealth. Being "intellectual" is their way of talking about alternative values. These values, however, are filled with internal contradictions. For example, Ben and Sarah have revived one of the ideals of an earlier time that said children learn best by getting practical experience ("you grow up with your feet"). But they also realize their children have spent so much time on schoolwork that they really haven't gotten any practical experience. They also believe being an intellectual means thinking on your own. But they have had to impose so many rules on their children that they figure Jeremy and Beth haven't yet learned to think for themselves. They know children have to work hard to excel in school. But they worry that Jeremy especially has tried "too hard to be good" and may be suffering emotional burn out as a result. They want their children to be interested in volunteer work and philanthropy but find little support for those values in the lab school. Sarah is especially anxious to be a good "working mom" role model for Beth, but she also thinks women should spend more time at home with their children than they do. So raising children has not been easy for the Arkwrights. They admit they have had constant battles with the children and with each other. They think, on the whole, that American society is doing "a terrible job" with its children. Sometimes they aren't even sure anymore of their own values. Still priding themselves on being "extreme 60s liberals," they find themselves "very, very conservative" in many ways. "Isn't that sad?" Sarah laments.

Raising children at a time when the old consensus has broken down takes added time and emotional energy. Everything has to be thought through from the ground up. Giving mixed signals creates interpersonal conflict that requires effort to resolve. Uncertainty about what values to teach and how to instill them causes anxiety and guilt. Ironically, then, the conflicts that many people feel between their work and their families are aggravated not simply by the demands of their jobs, but by the broader uncertainties these demands place on their roles as parents. These uncertainties are aggravated further by the fact that working men and working women juggle multiple commitments in different ways, thereby adding to the pressures experienced in their relationships with each other.

Working Men: The Great Tug-of-War

In addition to the questions that have arisen concerning the training of children, the collapse of the old consensus has widened the gap between economic commitments and family values for adults themselves. It has done so for both men and women, provoking new concerns for how to live as individuals and as couples. But the manner in which men and women have responded has been markedly different. Although common experiences in the workforce have generated some convergence, men and women have been conditioned to respond differently to these experiences by the fundamental conceptions of gender roles that were built into the American Dream. Among working men, what was initially a gendered division of labor between themselves as breadwinners and their wives as nurturers of values has now been stretched into a more extreme division within their own sense of themselves.

Defining their economic commitments mainly in terms of work, most men try to keep their work in bounds by compartmentalizing it completely from family: come home, do odd jobs, relax, but leave the duties of work at the office. Minneapolis banker Harold Bentley explains it this way: "I rarely, rarely bring something home. I don't make a phone call from home to work. That rarely happens unless there's an emergency at work, something broke down, or somebody will be asking how do you handle this, but that's extremely rare. I try to keep complete separation between the two."

Compartmentalization is the word that springs most readily to mind. An orderly life is a life divided into separate spheres. Having a strong commitment to family is thus a way of setting limits on one's economic commitments. But the trouble with this metaphor is that it is too static. Compartments connote cubicles found on trains or cubbyholes inside a rolltop desk. Although the individual moves from one pigeonhole to another, the pigeonholes themselves stay where they are. Such fixity, however, is no longer the experience of an increasing number of people. As work and money pressures have escalated and become more subjective, people find themselves torn between conflicting forces, pulled in opposite directions by forces that overlap, wax and wane, or cry out ever more loudly for attention. A tug-of-war would be a better metaphor. Two groups of people line up along a rope and pull in opposite directions, each struggling to get more of the rope on their side of some midpoint. The rope stands for the individual who is being pulled in different directions by various commitments. These commitments take on life as the muscular figures poised along the rope. One set represents commitments to work and the earning of money; the other set, commitments to family.

For men, the pressures pulling in the direction of work are often so intense that an incredibly strong counterpressure must be exerted from the other side. For some men, this counterpressure has taken the form suggested by the traditional American Dream and extended it to the point that it has now become a matter of extreme loyalty to wife and children. In this conception, the man's primary roles outside of work become those of protector, lover, provider, and father, all heightened in importance by the nuclear family's emphasis on warmth and intimacy. When he is not working, he stays at home, seldom goes out with friends, coddles his loved ones, and seldom initiates a divorce or separation. But this pattern is being replaced with a more subtle and dynamic form of counterpressure.

The contemporary working man cannot count on having a wife and children who stay at home waiting to be coddled.[19] And if he does, the economic pressures to provide a high standard of living may pull strongly toward the workplace anyway. He balances these pressures essentially by dividing his identity. He becomes, as it were, a split personality. Everything he is at work must be balanced by its *exact opposite* at home. If work is mental, as it is for a majority, he marks his nonworking self by intense physical exercise. Hiking, jogging, bicycling, playing tennis, lifting weights all help to define an alternative, nonmental self. If work requires him to be dutiful and responsible, he "vegges out" when he is at home, sitting like a mindless "couch potato" in front of the television.[20] If work requires him to exercise a great deal of discretion, he becomes completely incapable of deciding what to do with himself at home. If he feels like the master of the universe at work, he grovels in weakness and insecurity at home. If at work he is an adult; at home he becomes a child, watching television, playing with his children, or enjoying his toys.

Trying in this way to keep the tug-of-war even, the contemporary man must be viewed in a completely new light. He does not shirk doing housework simply because he is a male chauvinist or is blind to dirty dishes. He shirks housework because the intense pressure he feels to be responsible at work requires him to find balance by being a shirker in some other part of his life. He shirks because he, in fact, needs to be a shirker. By the same token, he leaves his work at the office, refusing to say anything about it at home, not to protect his wife, but to protect himself. He wants his family to be different, to provide him with a nonworking frame of reference, because the pressures from work demand a powerful opposing force. Getting him to do his share of the housework, or of child care, is thus a matter of bringing about a different understanding of the whole relationship between his economic commitments and his values.

A few examples will illustrate how the male tug-of-war influences men's behavior in personal life. Stuart Cummings says that playing with his children in the evening is an instant release because it forces him to play and be a kid. He also says, "Being a doer during the week, I do not want to be a doer on the weekend. I want to be as little like myself on weekends as I am during the week." Harold Bentley says the best "outlet" for pressures he experiences at the bank is bicycling. He rides about 2,500 miles a year. The trade-off between physical and mental activity is direct: tiring himself out exercising one day makes his mind sharper the next day. He also releases tension by "changing the pace": at the bank he goes full speed, at home he likes to "just putz around." Photographer Tony Arno puts balance back into his life by altering both space and time. He quit the insurance business because he always felt couped up in the office; even taking pictures, say, at a wedding leaves him feeling cramped. So he gets in his car and drives, maybe two or three hours at a time. The open road expands his horizons. He especially likes to do this late at night. Working all day (worrying a lot about lighting), he associates pleasure and freedom with the darkness. Housing-project director Jim Joyner also makes the late-night hours his own. He likes to put his mind in neutral and just sit in front of the television doing nothing. Fritz Kahler, a Chicago minister, does the same thing. He admits he sits and aimlessly flips through the channels, intentionally turning himself into a zombie. Other men found ways to build symbolic dividers into their lives that were even more pronounced: one man who works with people all day comes home and spends three hours in the shower; another works thirty-six hours straight and then sleeps as long as he likes; another man buys himself flowers and cooks a gourmet meal.

To someone from a different culture, the surprising thing about these habits would probably be the fact that many men are able to maintain them with relative ease. Despite the changes that have occurred in gender role concepts, men are still relatively unlikely to perceive serious conflicts between their work commitments and their families.[21] Partly this is because they physically remove themselves from the home environment much of the time. For the growing number of men who are single or married but without children, how they manage their free time is very much their own choice. The intrinsic meaning that work provides keeps them from having to regard it as a means to realizing the American Dream for their family. They can simply pare their personal time down to the bare essentials, coping with job stress by working harder, like one man who likened himself to an oil slick: "I just keep spreading myself thinner and thinner; that's what I do." When the home ceases to be a comforting haven, they can merely withdraw their emotional energy from it and devote more of their attention to their work. In addition, the lingering image in the American Dream of "relationships" essentially being women's work means that men can more easily shift the blame for trouble in the home to their spouses.

The male-as-provider image still blends readily into the ruggedly masculine role that considers it soft or feminine to want the security of a close family relationship at all. Real men can live on the road and enjoy the hardships of long hours in strange places, so it is their female partner's fault if any domestic conflicts arise. Steed Wellman is a case in point. Often traveling five days a week, he is sometimes unable to come home on the weekends as well. But as far as he is concerned, this is not a problem. If anyone has a problem, he explains, it is his girlfriend. "She doesn't like me traveling." But then in his view, this is not so much because he is away much of the time, but because she is "extremely protective." It is "missing me" and "that kind of stuff," he says, "girly stuff."

The other way in which men keep the tug-of-war between work and family even is by keeping mum.[22] Many, of course, talk over their work with their wives or girlfriends; some even work together. But they find it difficult to treat their wives as co-workers, fellow professionals, or co-equals in the labor force.[23] They do not share their feelings about work, not because they don't have them or because they don't know how to talk about these feelings, but because bringing work problems into the household contaminates it. They dislike listening to their wives' work problems for the same reason. Wanting hearth to be a refuge from the material world, they expect their wives to be playmates and lovers, mothers, servants, pleasure seekers, and fellow putzers. They do not want their wives to be weak or economically dependent, but neither do they want them to be June Cleavers, preoccupied with cooking, doing volunteer work, helping the neighbors, and mothering the boys. Those are recognizably too much like work itself to provide the symbolic diversions men feel they need. Instead, women should be available to go with them to a movie or on a weekend outing, or they should be able to spar intelligently about politics and ideas, or they should be interested in tennis and football. They should be available for "quality time when they're not thinking about their work," as one man put it.

It is worth noting that one gains the impression from listening to men talk about their home life that they are scarcely working themselves to death. They may be putting in long hours, but they still find time to do lots of things for themselves. The pressure they talk about is real, but it is also built into the way they understand their lives. It is what legitimates their free-time activities. The strain of working hard must be balanced by doing nothing very strenuous at home. The one sphere does not merge easily into the other. Instead, one is maintained by being the mirror opposite of the other. The tension between the two is always present. Work seems to tug constantly at one end of the rope, and one has to pull just as hard at the other end to keep life in balance.

Working Women: From Composure to Composing

The contemporary working woman sometimes plays the work-and-family game the same way men do. For instance, women too say they set boundaries around the mental work they do by exercising to blow off steam and clear out the cobwebs. Others escape into a good novel, do gardening, or putter around the house. But women basically play the game differently from men. The strong pressures they experience at work may keep them as preoccupied as men, generating the same long hours and intense commitment to jobs and careers. Working women, however, are more likely to say they feel responsible at home as well. Rather than putzing or vegging out, they do the household chores.[24] Faced with a sick child or a stack of dirty dishes, they let the rope that had been pulled more toward the workplace be pulled radically back in the other direction. Or in other cases, they feel a strong responsibility to themselves and to their friends and, in a growing number of cases, to aging parents.[25] As a result, they more often feel compelled to say no when job opportunities beckon.[26] Unlike men, they are less likely to manifest split identities that are the mirror opposites of each other. They are instead pulled back and forth, depending on the priorities of the moment, or what one woman described as an "internal clock" (its pendulum swinging back and forth), and they thus feel the ambiguity among conflicting commitments more acutely.

The reasons for this difference are varied. Still shouldering a disproportionate share of the emotional nurturing of the family, women with children find it impossible to shunt these needs into predictable time slots.[27] A crying child needs attention at the moment rather than next Saturday. For the larger proportion of women than of men who work part-time, jobs and household responsibilities are also more likely to be mixed on a daily basis. "You've planned to take your kid to a hockey game," one working mother explained, "but then a client calls up, so you wind up taking the client with you to the game." Thus, a substantial number of women say they have experienced difficulties with their work because of issues such as child care and getting household chores done.[28]

Some have argued that the reason is essentially one of differential power between males and females. Having found the better (or easier) way to construct their lives, men pressure women into adopting the less desirable mode. Others have suggested that long centuries in human evolution led to a differential pattern that may even be genetically imprinted. As hunters, men learned to focus their attention on one task for long periods of time, while as gatherers women learned to shift their attention more easily from one task to another (such as weeding, nursing, and cooking). Whatever the reasons, the more pressing issue is how working women are managing to balance their multiple commitments. Desirable or not, how is it possible? And what does this pattern contribute to our understanding of the present relationships between economic commitments and the quest for values?

The answer to the first question is that working women often manage their dual responsibilities at work and at home only at great cost to themselves. Meg Allen, 42, is a married mother of three who works full-time managing a day-care center in Nashville. She explains, "I don't have much free time at all. Any free time I have is devoted to my children. I really don't stop. I just have to learn to deal with my exhaustion." Sleep is what refreshes her, but sometimes she is too "stressed out" even for that. "I think it was 3:30 this morning and I was still wide awake, coming from a budget meeting where we'd been pleading our cause. You'd think, when you've been up since a quarter of five that morning, you'd just toddle right off to sleep. But it revs me up. Probably tonight I'll die at 10 o'clock."

The physical exhaustion, nevertheless, is only a part of the story. Whereas men talk about physical and mental exhaustion, women are more likely to say they experience emotional exhaustion ("sucks away my emotional energy," one woman said).[29] The difference is partly terminological, but it is also symptomatic of the way in which the boundary between work and other commitments is maintained. If men experience a sharper contrast between the two ends of their rope, women's experience involves more buffeting and daily wear-and-tear as a result of being jerked back and forth in each direction. They require, as it were, more repair to keep themselves intact.[30] They worry more about what they should be doing at each moment of the day, and they are less sure that the choices they are making are the right ones. Because of their multiple commitments, they often find it hard to stop thinking about work when they are at home, or about personal and family matters when they are at work. Their identities are not so simply divided—blue on one end, red on the other—but require more frequent redefinition and reconstruction. To solve this problem, especially in the presence of spouses who find it necessary to bracket such issues (or who diminish the importance of their spouse's work), women turn to other women for support.[31] Talk-therapy becomes the way to renegotiate a satisfactory identity.

"Just in the last six months," says Meg Allen, "I have started going out with a couple of girlfriends maybe one night a month, on a Friday night, we'll go out to eat or go to a show. That has helped tremendously. We just talk about each other and what we're doing, and I found that to be a great relief." Before this, she had been using her teenage daughter as a confidante, but felt it wasn't fair to cast her daughter in that role. Meg and her girlfriends have also talked about bringing their husbands along on their Friday night outings sometime. But they worry that this might ruin its effectiveness.

The reason Meg Allen turns to her girlfriends for support is not so much that she is a more communal person than her husband but that she needs to talk out the day-to-day decisions she has to make and her feelings about them. She provides a vivid example of how she struggles with these decisions. "Last night my 15-year-old son was trying to catch up on his biology homework that he had neglected for several weeks. My husband was at the vet with the cat, and I had to walk out. I had to go to this court hearing for the day-care center. I was gone three-and-a-half hours. And that's hard. That's something I have really had to work on. Something is not right. This job has come first a lot of times, before my family. And I don't really mean to do that, but I take it so seriously, and I view what I do as so important that there are times I walk out on responsibilities. I should have been at home last night pushing my son through his homework. I should have been at home with my 10-year-old who was crying about the cat. And I wasn't. So there are times that you have to make trade-offs. And it's just hard to know what you need to trade off."

In some cases, working women have been able to develop quasi-formalized support groups to give them the help they need.[32] These can be as informal as Meg's outings with her girlfriends or as formal as a therapy group or debriefing session. Mary Cavenah, the Los Angeles counselor, for example, says she and her co-workers have established a special table in the rear of the building where they can go and generally find someone with whom to talk over their problems. "I really like the nurturing and the support," she says. Being able to talk about things gives her reassurance in the face of uncertainty ("there are never any right and wrong answers"). It also helps her get rid of what's bothering her so she doesn't have to take it home.

Besides the chance to vent feelings and receive reassurance, talking with friends and participating in informal support groups provides valuable information on how to tie the pieces of one's life together. Graphic designer Ruth Cardeau says she and her girlfriends exchange tips on how to prepare a quick meal while talking to a client on the telephone and helping the children with their homework. Teri Silver says she and her co-workers talk a lot about what they did on weekends. She feels her own interests have broadened as a result. With fewer boundaries between their personal lives and their work lives, women are also more likely than men to say they discuss "private" matters with their co-workers. Doing so is sometimes a way to "vent their spleen" about something that has made them resentful at home. In these cases, work rather than family functions as a haven.

The daily buffeting that comes from juggling multiple commitments has also resulted in an emerging redefinition of the ideal woman. In the American Dream that prevailed from the Victorian era to the 1950s, the ideal woman was sufficiently protected from the marketplace by her husband that she could strive for a life of composure. Keeping the house neat, making sure the children were well-mannered and even-tempered, providing well-balanced meals for her family, and maintaining her spiritual and emotional health in order to provide an anchor in the storm for her husband and children were all part of this ideal. But few women nowadays would say that ideal is attainable. "There's just too many things to get done," complains one working mother. "I get nuts and start yelling, and then everybody goes nuts!"

At present, the ideal pattern is expressed much better by the phrase "composing a life." As anthropologist Mary Catherine Bateson explains in a book by this title, the contemporary woman is faced with too many demands to be a model of composure. But these demands also provide her with expanded opportunities. She can combine activities in ways that lead to creative new insights about her world and about herself. "Perhaps Kierkegaard was wrong when he said that 'purity is to will one thing,'" Bateson writes. "Perhaps the issue is not a fixed knowledge of the good [but] a kind of attention that is open, not focused on a single point. Instead of concentration on a transcendent ideal, sustained attention to diversity and interdependence may offer a different clarity of vision, one that is sensitive to ecological complexity, to the multiple rather than the singular. Perhaps we can discern in women honoring multiple commitments a new level of productivity and new possibilities of learning."[33]

Composing a life, however, means that the question of values becomes much more important than it was when female roles were more clearly defined.[34] "I'm afraid I'm not the happy homemaker," admits Naomi Rose, 40, a self-employed businesswoman in Portland. "I'm not happily running my husband's shirts to the laundry and giving great birthday parties for my children." Instead of following any stereotypical model that always puts her family first, or her work first, she says she's "picking and choosing what I do." This means thinking through her values and setting priorities. It also means paying more attention to how she feels and what she wants to do at each particular moment. Sometimes it involves spending more time with her children; at other times it may mean devoting a weekend to doing volunteer work for a Jewish women's group. Deciding what to do isn't always easy, especially because her preferences often differ from her husband's. Mostly, she is having to face up to the big questions that are raised by the little decisions in her life: What do I really want in life? What's important to me? What do I believe in? What gives me fulfillment and makes me grow?

Moral Restraint

If changing understandings of work and money have resulted in greater tension between economic commitments and family life for both men and women, this tension is at least one of the ways in which people are being forced to ask questions about the moral limits of their economic pursuits. To be sure, important policy questions are being raised as well, especially those focusing on child care, employee benefits, and family-leave requirements. But the moral issues must not be neglected. Even if vast new legislation were enacted, American workers would be confronted with daily decisions about how best to reconcile their economic interests with the needs of their families. Much that the home stands for in American culture still symbolizes the importance of limiting economic commitments. Feeling it necessary to separate their work from the time they spend at home provides men with a way of saying enough is enough: I don't need to work any harder or earn any more money; having time for my family and for myself is more important. Taking time to talk about their feelings and gaining support from their friends is a way for women to say enough is enough: I'm stressed out and feeling like I'm juggling too many commitments; I need to express my feelings and receive some reassurance about who I am and what I am doing.

Neither of these patterns is entirely satisfactory. Materialism still beckons for more of the family dollar, family obligations encourage people to work longer hours, rather than actually spending time with their families, and parents wonder if they are setting a good enough example for their children.[35] Men get away with relaxing in front of the television because their wives are doing the housework. Women struggle to find the time to keep their support networks intact. The tug-of-war in which men engage reinforces a split in their lives but does not necessarily tell them how to order their values, and the composing in which women engage does not necessarily lead to composure. Growing numbers of working women are experimenting with the compartmentalization that men have tried, and a sizable number of men are seeking ways to share their feelings and to find emotional support. And yet these patterns are terribly important, not simply because they are common in our society, but because they point toward something larger.

The tug-of-war between work and family is reminiscent of the ascetic moralism of the early nineteenth century. The desire to express feelings is reminiscent of the expressive moralism of the same period. Both traditions are being rediscovered, at least in the ways men and women are living their lives. Both traditions are also being redefined to fit better with contemporary economic conditions. We will want to consider how these current manifestations are beginning to provide a new sense of moral restraint on economic behavior. Before doing that, however, we must consider several other ways in which Americans are currently seeking values that limit their material pursuits.

Chapter Ten

REDISCOVERING COMMUNITY:

THE CULTURAL POTENTIAL OF

CARING BEHAVIOR

AND VOLUNTARY SERVICE

THROUGHOUT our nation's history, being involved in the community has been another value that forced people to set limits on their economic pursuits.[1] People took time off from work to help sick neighbors with theirs. They paused from the daily routine to attend the weddings and funerals of their neighbors and kin. Sometimes they set work aside to form vigilante committees for the physical protection of their communities. They devoted evenings and weekends to community events, and they donated a portion of their earnings to local relief chests. Marveling at the extent of these activities in the 1830s, Alexis de Tocqueville placed them high on the list of virtues he linked to the survival of American democracy itself.[2] In the century following, they probably increased, growing as the population expanded and diversified.[3] These commitments signaled benevolence and camaraderie, a conviction that life was better when the community was strong. In tempering the restless pursuit of material gain, citizens transformed naked self-interest into something more communal and more civilized, something that Tocqueville could applaud as self-interest *rightly understood*.

If community involvement restrained individual greed and ambition, the structure of small-town and village life nevertheless made it easier for people to reconcile these commitments with their economic pursuits. Time spent helping a sick neighbor might well be repaid tomorrow when the tables were turned. The same American Dream that prodded people to desire a home of their own recognized that volunteer fire companies were essential to protecting these homes. Traditional gender conceptions favored a similar complementarity. Women shouldered many of the responsibilities to provide neighborly assistance while their husbands devoted full attention to earning a living. In addition, male involvement in community affairs helped establish trust and created a public image that was conducive to business. Even the poor were obliged to make meeting their needs a more natural part of community life. Until the middle of the twentieth century, in fact, a majority of poor families lived in rural areas where village norms of caring could still provide a sheltering umbrella.

Doing things for the community shaved the sharp edges off the questions that have arisen so abruptly in recent years about volunteer work: What are my motives? Am I doing it for someone else or for me? Is it altruism? Or is it really egoism? How can I find time to be a volunteer when my work and my family take all my energy? How does it fit with my career? Questions of this kind made no sense when the recipient was one's community: sure, something other than yourself benefited, but so did you, because you were a part of this larger entity. Caring for others was neither altruistic nor egoistic; it was mutually beneficial. People helped their neighbors as they had always done because a norm of reciprocity prevailed: favors done for someone else became an implicit bond; you could count on them (or their family) to return the favor when you were in need. What went around came around. The circle was complete.[4]

The moral logic of caring for others was thus deeply embedded in the realities of community life. To be sure, moralist arguments drew the contrast between material pursuits and service to others.[5] Distinguishing the two had always been part of the cultural tradition. Familiar Bible stories, such as the New Testament tale of the widow's mite, taught that it was better to be generous than to hoard one's possessions. Folklore underscored the same distinction. If caring implied a moral alternative to work and money, the two nevertheless played in harmony, rather than striking discordant notes. Fairy tales demonstrated that generous villagers often became the recipients of unexpected material rewards. Community service could be regarded legitimately as "self-interest rightly understood" because recognizing their interdependence would in the long run make individuals more successful as well. So interwoven were material interests and caring for others that it actually made sense to speak of a "moral economy," as students of traditional societies have suggested, rather than regarding the very notion as an oxymoron.[6]

In our own society, we still find traces of this logic in the caring behavior of people who live in close-knit communities. Ellen Montgomery, a woman in her seventies, lives in a neat but badly run-down duplex in a predominantly African-American section of Philadelphia. She has lived here all her life. Her grandmother, freed from slavery at age 6 by the Civil War, purchased the house in 1920. After her grandmother's death, Ellen and two sisters kept the house, eventually raising six children in its tiny rooms. The "neighborhood" surrounds the house about five blocks in each direction. Only in the past few years, as white students have come in search of inexpensive dwellings, has its sense of neighborliness begun to erode. A large woman whose very presence is commanding, Ellen has always been active in the community. Despite long hours working as a maid in the suburbs and time devoted to her children and grandchildren, helping others has been her way of life. "It's normal; just natural," she says. "If I know you're sick over there, I mean, I'll go over and see if there's anything I can do for you. If I saw you coming down the Pike or waiting on a bus or something, I mean, I'd pick you up. Or we'd call each other if we needed to go to the doctor." Stressing what a beautiful community it is, she emphasizes again that caring is just "the normal thing." She knows her neighbors; they know her. There is a common bond.

If Ellen Montgomery is right, the key to understanding caring for others is the structure of community life. When community is strong, caring will seem natural, even if it takes time away from the business of making ends meet for ourselves and our families. Seeming natural, it can happen with less thinking, less introspection, less deliberation.[7] When this sense of community is lacking, the relationship between material pursuits and caring behavior is likely to be strained. Helping the needy may still be possible, but it will seem less natural. Rather than being merely distinct from work and money, it will stand in sharper contrast to these activities. It will be regarded as a trade-off, rather than playing a complementary role in the moral economy of interpersonal relations, and it will require more effort and planning. Being a caring person will thus carry more symbolic importance, distancing people from their work and material interests, at the same time that it becomes more problematic. So will the needy themselves, as they shoulder the responsibility of providing an animus to the materialism of contemporary life.

From Community to Volunteer Organizations

The happy (perhaps mythical) communities of yesteryear in which everyone helped everyone else have, as we know, faded largely into the dim recesses of our collective imaginations. The typical surburban neighborhood owes its very existence to the fact that too many jobs grew up in one part of the city for everyone to live nearby. At one time, many of these neighborhoods may have been like company towns, sending their breadwinners off to the same steel plant, automobile assembly line, or commuter train. After a generation of plant relocations, outmigration, and selective geographic mobility, however, most of these neighborhoods have become settlements of people who have little in common besides their gas grills and lawn mowers. Of course backyard barbecues can revive a communal spirit in the suburbs. But true needs are unlikely to be shared on such occasions—indeed, the truly needy are unlikely to be invited at all.[8] They live some distance away in an urban slum that seems remote and forbidding. Within the surburban enclave itself, life may remain (as it was once described) "remarkably tactful."[9] But media images provide constant reminders of deeper needs outside the community.

The more recent shift from heavy industry toward a service economy has been widely hailed as a way to revive the communal spirit of the suburbs. The faceless white concrete office buildings that have sprung up in suburban office parks, however, generate little of the civic spirit that once characterized the shopkeepers who earned their livings in the public square. If anything, the service economy has actually contributed to the further depeopling of the suburbs. June Cleaver is no longer at home all day to inquire about the comings and goings of her neighbors. Child care is less likely to be the responsibility of the lady next door than that of a for-profit day-care center located somewhere along the route to work. Even the legendary paperboy, cycling through the neighborhood with the local news, is likely to have been replaced by an anonymous van speeding through the streets in predawn hours with papers printed by laser signals from distant satellite stations.

The changing character of community has had profound consequences for the ways in which Americans express concern for the needy. Volunteer efforts, most studies show, continue to be widespread. According to recent estimates, approximately 98 million Americans engage in some type of volunteer activity on a regular basis, collectively donating more than 20 billion hours of their time each year.[10] Rather than diminishing with the increasing anonymity of contemporary life, these efforts appear to be holding relatively stable and, if anything, may be enlisting the commitment of more people today than a decade or two ago. Even with increasing numbers of people in the labor force, and with many people working longer hours, volunteer efforts remain strong.[11] Yet the most important, and frequently overlooked, feature of these volunteer efforts is that their relationship to the local community has shifted decisively away from the model described by Tocqueville and so many of his successors.

Volunteer work has come increasingly to mean a donation of time to some formally incorporated, tax-exempt, nonprofit organization. Slogans about "community service" notwithstanding, helping one's neighbors has shifted largely away from activities performed as an integral part of community life toward ones orchestrated by specialized organizations whose aim is to draw people out of their regular routines into some other type of service-oriented behavior. Indeed, current estimates suggest that nearly three-quarters of all voluntary helping behavior in the United States takes place in conjunction with such organizations, whereas only a quarter consists of "informal" activities such as helping a neighbor or friend on an ad hoc basis.[12]

Other research demonstrates clearly how much of a disjuncture has developed between volunteer efforts and the more natural forms of caring that once characterized close-knit communities. In one national survey respondents were asked who they could count on if someone in their immediate family became ill and needed help. Factor analysis of the responses yielded two clusters: those who said they could count on their neighbors, friends, relatives, and fellow church or synagogue members, on the one hand; and those who said they could count on volunteers and social welfare agencies, on the other hand.[13]

Churches and schools of course remain common locations for organized voluntary effort, attracting approximately half of all the people who do any kind of volunteer work. Significantly, these organizations retain the community ideal better than most, giving people a chance to do something for themselves or their children while indirectly helping others as well. Change in the wider definition of community, nevertheless, is making a profound impact even among these organizations. Zoning ordinances in large numbers of cities make it impossible for churches to be built in actual residential neighborhoods. Members drive farther to attend mega-churches where they know fewer people but find programs tailored to more specialized tastes. Growing denominational diversity at the local level means that churches often appear to be serving sectarian interests rather than the community as a whole. Schools and youth organizations may enlist parents as sponsors, boosters, fund-raisers, coaches, and leaders. But these activities are likely to be seen more as a contribution to one's family than to the wider community, especially when magnet schools pull children away from local neighborhoods and the majority of the neighborhood itself consists of either young singles without children or empty nesters. With salaried therapists, chaplains, and day-care specialists fulfilling the needs of suburbanites themselves, the most likely outlet for genuine helping behavior, therefore, becomes the formal volunteer organization that specializes in providing services to strangers whose lifestyles and needs are quite different from those of middle America itself.

The most significant consequence of these developments is occurring at the level of moral understanding. Services themselves are being provided through an ever-expanding array of nonprofit organizations, especially as government programs undergo drastic cutbacks. It is, however, the moral meaning of these services that has changed. Consider, for example, how different Norm Lundström's experience with volunteer work has been from Ellen Montgomery's sense that helping her neighbors is simply natural and beautiful.

Having been raised in a small town, Norm Lundström always thought fostering community spirit was a good thing to do. When he first moved to suburban Minneapolis, he joined Kiwanis; he even served a stint as president of the League of Women Voters. But after a few years he dropped out. Nobody in the community knew him personally. They didn't understand why he was so interested in volunteer organizations. Instead of assuming that he was interested in the good of the community, they told each other he must be power hungry, doing these things to make himself feel stronger. Norm eventually decided he didn't need this kind of suspicion. He still believes he is a good, other-regarding person. But he has more questions about his values, his commitments, and how to balance his own interests with those of his community than he did before.

Whether they stay on as faithful volunteers or drop out after a few bouts in the nonprofit ring, a sizable share of the American public registers a mix of conviction and doubt similar to that expressed by Norm Lundström. They worry that self-interest is corrupting the voluntary sector but want it to remain pure, a bastion against the compromises required in government and business.[14] Being a caring person is now a value that symbolizes the antithesis of materialism. In a society where the normal rhythms of community are so obviously lacking, materialism provides a ready explanation of what has gone wrong. Caring becomes the antidote, a way of saving ourselves from utter destruction. In the process, caring becomes all the more important as a value, but more difficult to realize in our daily lives.

Caring as an Antidote to Materialism

The place to begin, if we are to grasp the precarious logic now replacing the earlier communal idea of a moral economy, is a closer look at the meaning of materialism. Surveys remind us that most Americans believe materialism is a serious problem in our society, despite the fact that they themselves are pressing ever onward to make more money and buy more things. In one study, 84 percent of the public agreed that "too much emphasis on money" is a serious problem in our society.[15] In my labor force survey, 89 percent agreed that "our society is much too materialistic." In the same study, 71 percent said our society would be better off if there was less emphasis on money, whereas only 4 percent thought it would be worse off.

We have seen how materialism symbolizes a threat to the family. Middle-class parents say it is corrupting their children. They worry about the growing influence of advertising. Working-class families believe materialism is corroding society from the top down, causing the affluent to be unconcerned about the common good. Both describe it as a force antagonistic to family values. It is but a small step to believe that materialism erodes our capacity to care deeply about people in general.

Wherever one goes, materialism's incompatibility with caring is a common theme. A woman in Los Angeles explains, "When you're consumed with things, you can't be consumed with the needs of people." "When people are materialistic," a Minnesota man echoes, "it's always 'I.' When people care, it's 'we.'" A Chicagoan elaborates, "As long as you're being materialistic, it's difficult to find room in your thoughts and in your heart for people and relationships and love."

If this logic seems entirely sensible, it is nevertheless worth noting that research on the actual relationship between materialism and caring does not suggest any fundamental incompatibility. One study, based on national survey data, showed that virtually the same percentages of volunteers and nonvolunteers said "living a comfortable life" was a personal value they regarded as absolutely essential.[16] Another study, also reporting national data, found no significant differences between volunteers and nonvolunteers on the importance they attached to such materialistic values as providing a good home, furnishings, and clothes, and traveling for pleasure.[17] Other national data, showing a *positive* relationship between the number of hours people work at their jobs each week and the likelihood that they will *also* be involved in community service projects, give indirect evidence of the same pattern.[18]

The trade-off between materialism and caring is nevertheless real in the minds of many Americans. It is a trade-off rooted less in the fact that people literally have to take time off from their work to help others, or in reality have less money to spend on themselves when they give money to charity, than in the fact that each has a moral meaning that contradicts the other.

Materialism is not simply a feature of life that we despise, period. It is a symbol, a token evil that stands for the deeper evils we sense rising up from the lagoons of our half-realized fears. It symbolizes the breakdown of everything positive that community has stood for in the American Dream. Materialism connotes trying to go it alone, rather than recognizing one's interdependence with others. It conjures up notions of power, inequality, and ruthlessness, and its meanings include the loss of community itself.[19] In the same way, caring ceases to be something valued just for its own sake. It is important for reasons other than the fact that people are in need or that it is simply a natural human response to reach out toward others in pain. Caring has become a loaded freight train, symbolizing the way to save ourselves from materialism, the way to demonstrate our virtue in the midst of a materialistic culture, the way to resurrect a dying communal spirit.

Listen to what a New Jersey scientist has to say about materialism: "We lost something. There was a time in this country when people did care about each other. We were more interdependent. Now, the society has started to believe that we're all independent." For him, materialism is clearly something more than going shopping for a new VCR. It conjures up a contrast with the past; it becomes a trend in American life, most clearly associated with a loss of community. Materialism really means each person pursuing his or her self-interest, rather than retaining that traditional sense of interdependence with others.

The same sense of loss, almost a nostalgic longing for the past, is evident in a young Philadelphia woman's remarks. "When you look back, earlier in time, people didn't have as much. They didn't have cars, but they did things more together as a community. They helped more people. And now, people pretty much care about what they have, and nothing else. It's always 'hooray for me, to hell with you. You don't have it, I'm sorry, that's not my problem, I can't help you.'"

For many Americans, complaints about materialism may connote little more than vague misgivings about the price of progress. Underlying this concern, however, may be a conviction that the rules of society have somehow been fundamentally altered, that money is now the name of the game, leaving human relationships a distant second.

For example, Mark Latham still wants to believe that people are more valuable than money, but his years on Wall Street exposed him to an entirely different philosophy. The way the financial world thinks, he explains, is that the person who values friends more than money is a fool. The reason is simple: you can always fall back on money, but your friends may let you down. Although he realizes that this is an extreme view, he also recognizes that society is increasingly structured in a way that allows many people to get along quite well, more on the basis of money than on the basis of other people. "You aren't forced to come together with anyone; you can live all alone and survive." The result, he says, is that feeling a sense of community has become more difficult. "I'm in my house; I get in my car; I drive wherever I want to go, like to the mall. I don't have to see anybody. You are able to have no contact with anyone and survive."

A different conception of the loss of community involves a replacement of horizontal ties by vertical status barriers. Materialism also stands for this sense of loss. It means that people have become obsessed with whether they are better off or worse off than others, rather than focusing on what they have in common. A Chicago woman explains: "I think we'd all be better off if we cared less about what someone's wearing and what kind of a car they're driving or where they're living." Not only does materialism become a measure of status; it creates its own insecurities, a fear of falling, that make people less willing to be generous. Another Chicagoan draws out this connection: "[Materialism] is the 'what I've got' mentality. 'I'll hold on to it no matter what.' But how can you care for somebody else if you're always worried about what you have and who's going to take it from you? If society judges you by what you have, then you've got to keep it so you can be judged right. How can you give it away to somebody?"

Materialism also means something artificial, less than basic to our nature, that is foisted upon us, most often by business. Like a sponge, it absorbs any of the latent discontent people (or their families) may have with their employers. It focuses this discontent, providing an explanation for the way life is when community in the workplace is lacking. If the pace is too hectic to allow for intimacy, it is because one's employer is placing profits ahead of people.

A woman in Washington, D.C., for example, told about a recent event her husband had experienced. To her, it illustrated the point perfectly: "Kevin and I had a death in the family this fall, and it was a real stressful time at work. But it helped Kevin realize what is truly important: just being with his family, being married to someone he loves. He's always running around, trying to make a deal. But what is important is people. His business isn't interested in anything but making a buck. He was shaken out of that. We need relationships. That's what matters."

When materialism means so much about what is wrong with our world, caring then has to mean more as well. Instead of it being a short walk to the door of our needy neighbor, it becomes a feat of supreme effort, like climbing Mount Everest. It carries the weight of civilization on its back. In caring we make a heroic stand on the battlefield for good, we resist the forces of evil advancing against us, driving back the foes that are threatening the very communal foundations of our society, and in the process we get back to basics, rediscovering simpler truths, the older principles on which people lived in bygone days, and by siding with the good, we demonstrate that we ourselves must also be good. This is why capitalism and compassion have always needed each other, why the adulation of Mother Teresa and Donald Trump springs from common cultural impulses: one saves us from the other.

A self-made multimillionaire, a man whose fortune owes much to the much-maligned selling of high-priced "designer sneakers," devotes most of his spare time to charitable and philanthropic activities. He feels compelled to "get back to the fundamental intent of words like honesty, charity, goodness, sensitivity, love." He draws a close connection between the need "to constrain yourself" and "to help the other guy out." These virtues are to him "contrary to just compete, compete, compete, compete, compete, acquire, consume, consume, consume." The latter, he says, "is capitalism, the unbridled capitalism, of which we have in America become so enamored." He's looking for "a balance in there somewhere." Caring for others is fundamental to his search.

But helping others, perhaps paradoxically, becomes a way of redeeming ourselves without actually having to give up anything significant. If caring is indeed an antidote to materialism, then it would seem to work its magic better when it involves genuine sacrifices of money and time. We must remember, however, that materialism stands mainly for something other than money and time. It symbolizes impending corruption in our values, more than it does anything about the economics of our lifestyle. Materialism is a form of mental preoccupation, being too attached to our goods, not with having them in the first place; it concerns *how* we pursue those goods, pushing other people around, thinking of our own self-interest too much, not whether we actually *attain* them. Caring is thus the perfect alchemy. It transforms the meaning of our material pursuits without having to derail us in more than token ways from those pursuits. Even a small act of generosity is enough to demonstrate that a person really has the right set of values.[20]

A Minnesota schoolteacher explains how this is possible: "You're not a bad person just because you own a lot of material things. You're only a bad person if these things mean more to you than everything else. In that case, your priorities are screwed up and you're headed for trouble. Of course somebody can always point the finger at you and say, 'You could have used that money to help somebody else.' But I don't think we need to give up everything to make this a better world. It's just the people who aren't giving at all that are materialistic. We can have nice things and still try to help. If everybody did that, there would be plenty of help to go around."

The heiress of a large family fortune in New York drives the point home with even greater force. "It's not that you're a worse person if you're rich, or a better person if you're not rich. It's a question of your heart. Look at my father. He had all that money. But he'd always say 'reach out to me.' He'd say that to anybody. You know how good a person is when you see how they treat somebody who can't do them any good back. If somebody can't do me any good, and I'm nice to them anyway, then you know I'm a good person."

THE CHANGING MEANINGS OF VOLUNTEER WORK

Curious as it may seem, then, materialism provides the context in which to understand why volunteer work has become so highly valued in our society—and so deeply ambiguous. The more it distances us from the self-interested, go-it-alone world of business and consumption, the more symbolic benefit there is to be gained from it. This is why volunteer efforts that have nothing to do with a person's work so often acquire value above those that are mere extensions of the workplace. It is one of the factors that prompt a majority of Americans (57 percent) to say they can do more to make the world a better place through activities outside their work than they can through their jobs.[21] Physical distance from the workplace helps create the emotional distance we feel we need. As a result, doing volunteer work can make a person feel more different, perhaps more virtuous, than the one who slaves away all day at the office.

A young banking official in Minneapolis came to this realization when he was asked recently to help with a community service project his company was sponsoring in an underdeveloped section of the city. The project involved repair work on low-income housing to give people a sense of pride in their homes and in their community. For this official, the "fun part" turned out to be the work that was least similar to his job. He says he really enjoyed wielding a power saw and interacting with elderly women and teenagers from a different ethnic group. What he intensely disliked were the parts that resembled his regular work. "Half of it was administration and paperwork; that was just awful." Other volunteers speak often of having more freedom than they do at work, doing things that seem more exciting, experiencing closer bonds with fellow volunteers, and gaining enjoyment from meeting different kinds of people.

People who work on assembly lines or in cramped offices might well cherish the variety they can experience at a local shelter for the homeless. These are not the only people, however, who feel volunteer work awakens something inside them that cannot gain expression through their work. A New York theater director, for example, draws a sharp contrast between his life in the city, working with adults, and the volunteer work he does for American Field Service (which he belonged to as a child himself): "It's relaxing to be out of the city. It has this camp atmosphere. It keeps me in touch with the kids, with what's going on in younger people's minds." He says he relishes the time he spends doing this volunteer work, the values it stands for, and what it contributes to his sense of self.

Serving the community through volunteer work takes on added significance in the United States because the world of work itself is generally regarded as a place where caring is absent. There may be isolated pockets of co-workers in which caring takes place, making workers themselves feel more or less wanted and respected.[22] But business as a whole is not regarded as a caring institution. Precisely the opposite. A majority of Americans think business is doing too little to help the needy.[23] Two out of three people say their own preference when conducting business is to keep things strictly on a business level, rather than developing close personal ties with people. And nearly half (47 percent) agree it is necessary to be thick skinned in order to be good in business. None of this is to deny the fact that American business has often played an active role in promoting charitable activities. Indeed, half of all employed Americans say their companies encourage employees to donate money to United Way and other charities, nearly half say their company itself has donated money to a charitable organization, a third say their company directly sponsors community service projects, and a quarter say employees are given released time or other incentives to participate in such projects. The reality of the situation, however, may be less important than public perceptions, not just of business alone, but of the broader materialism and breakdown of community that business represents.

For many people, volunteer work is also a way of keeping something alive that was lost when they chose a career. They had high ideals, but (as we have seen) talk about their careers as being a result of circumstances, something they fell into not for the money so much as for the convenience of it or the fit that seemed to be present with their interests. In the process, however, something got left out, a part of their personality had to be shelved, and the variety they expected turned out not to be so great after all. They feel it is important to do something in addition.

Barbara Jako, a public services administrator in New York, remembers the exact day she became interested in doing volunteer work. "Mother's Day, 1979," she says. "I went to church that morning with my family, and Father O'Hara asked for volunteers who would spend a year working with him at $10 a week plus room and board helping homeless teenagers in Times Square." A senior in high school at the time, Barbara was deeply moved by Father O'Hara's message. She wrote to him asking for more information and seriously contemplated accepting his challenge. But common sense got the best of her. She decided she really needed to go on to college. The hardship of $10 a week appealed less and less to her the more she thought about it. She went on to college, took a job, and now works nine to five doing challenging supervisory and committee work. But one part of her still hears Father O'Hara's call. So to keep this voice alive, she spends every Monday evening at a shelter in the city for homeless teenagers. "It's just my way of giving something back," she explains.

The connections drawn between materialism and the quest for community in our society also shape our understanding of volunteer work by convincing us that it is more blessed to give of one's time than of one's money.[24] This view is of course advanced by volunteer organizations themselves in an effort to get people to give time *and* money, rather than money alone. The problem is that money is devalued in the bargain. People figure it makes little difference whether they give money or not; time is the really important thing. So they give time when they can but otherwise go around feeling guilty. A woman in Chicago who gives money to charities on a regular basis, for example, says she still feels guilty because she has tried to do volunteer work and can never find the time to keep it up. A man in New York donates money sporadically to several charities, but when asked why, he fumbles for words. "I don't know why. It probably doesn't do any good. Who knows? I suppose it doesn't do any harm either. At least it makes me feel good."

Views such as these still generate enough charitable giving that the nonprofit sector has been able to function reasonably well. It is estimated, for example, that three-quarters of all American households give at least some amount to charity each year. Nevertheless, analysts of this behavior believe it is often regarded so casually, and grounded in such sporadic habits, that it may be far lower than it could be. In one recent national study, for example, the average household donation for the year totaled only $734, a mere 2 percent of average household income.[25]

People who do give money also tend to believe it is better to give to an organization to which they also give time. That way they know the "inner workings," as hospital chaplain Amy Oldenburg notes. Many people say they give money to their church for this reason. They attend regularly, they know the people, so they believe the money is likely to be well spent. Besides, they themselves are getting something out of being there. "You'd pay money to go to a movie," observes Jena Forsythe, "so why not pay to go to church?"

People who do volunteer work, though, still generally find themselves bombarded with requests for money from other voluntary agencies. Consequently, the image of the voluntary sector as a whole has begun to suffer. Many people fear these agencies may be purveyors of materialism itself, rather than impregnable bulwarks against it. Organizations that just send solicitations in the mail, people often figure, are trying to rip you off. If it is necessary to give to an organization outside one's community, it is thus preferable to support a smaller charity than a large one. The big ones are too much like bureaucracies and too little like the ideal supportive community. Bureaucracies are burdened with high administrative costs that prevent the money from getting through to those most in need. People feel particularly incensed when they learn that some charity they thought represented the old-fashioned virtues of neighborhood responsibility, like the local volunteer fire company, was really using professional fund-raisers ("from the outside") to help them win support. They prefer to give five bucks to the kid next door who comes around soliciting for a project at school.

Giving money, while not as valued as giving time, nevertheless can function as a way of placating emotions. Having no sense of ongoing obligation to these organizations, people respond when they happen to feel like it. According to surveys, fewer than one person in twelve makes an advance commitment to support charitable organizations (other than a church) with a pledge, and an equally small number tries to give a certain total amount each year; the vast majority make a decision about each separate gift.[26] Qualitative information from donors suggests a similar conclusion. Something catches their attention: perhaps a picture of an orphan in a magazine, a beggar with a dirty glove thrust in one's face, an urgent appeal from a speaker on television. "Sometimes I just get a hair-brained idea, so I give," one woman explains.

People living in close, interdependent communities would not respond to a sick or bereaved neighbor this way. When these communities no longer exist, however, giving to charity comes to depend much more on the mood of the moment. Many people say it depends on whether they have some spare cash. Others admit it makes a difference if they are feeling generous, like at Thanksgiving or Christmas. The gift can no longer be taken for granted as part of what people are expected to do. Each decision to give involves a choice. Indeed, some people find it especially irksome when their company expects them to donate to United Way or when their church suggests they pledge a certain amount of money each year. They consider these unwelcome attempts to influence their decisions. True giving must come from within, reflecting something about a person's values, how he or she derives good feelings, the nature of empathy, the alleviation of guilt.

Most people vehemently deny that guilt has anything to do with their giving and volunteering. The changes that have taken place in the moral logic of American life over the past generation, however, cry out for guilt to be registered and acknowledged. When June Cleaver was free of household and workplace obligations, she gave generously of her time to neighbors and civic organizations alike. The Cleavers' sons and daughters may now be giving as much time to volunteer efforts as anyone (and even more than their father did), but somehow this may not seem to be enough. Their mother's model still guides their thinking. A good neighbor should do more.

A young woman in Washington, D.C., for example, says her mother was a "real activist" who spent most of her time doing volunteer work in the community, helping the poor, organizing benefits, and encouraging her family to be more concerned about social issues. Her mother's example, she feels, had a lot to do with her decision to become a clinical social worker. Still, she feels guilty because she is not doing volunteer work herself. She fantasizes about getting involved with Habitat for Humanity once she is more established in her career. At present, though, all she can do is visit a shelter once a year at Christmas. She says her life is just "too hectic" for anything else right now. But she also worries that she's becoming corrupted by selfishness.

This view adds pressure to the harried lives that people already lead. It also encourages most people who volunteer at all to do so in small, symbolic doses, like taking their families to homeless shelters on Thanksgiving. Volunteer agencies are, in fact, set up to take what they can get, dividing the labor, filling short time slots, and using volunteers for odd jobs that busy professionals cannot complete. Most of us, of course, would not treat needs in our own families this way. When the need is close to us, we give wholeheartedly; when it is distant, we dole out help in small doses. One's own child, seized with appendicitis in the middle of the night, will not wait; a stranger's child on the other side of town will have to make do, whether the volunteer center is staffed that night or not. Overcommitted volunteers may feel guilty about the consequences, but the choice to stay or to quit, they believe, is still theirs.

Jena Forsythe, the Wall Street broker, tries to be a big sister for a teenage girl she met through a volunteer organization, but there is no connection between this activity and her work, so Jena has trouble finding the time for it and often feels guilty. "I didn't call her on Thursday and I felt really guilty," she admits. "I've been thinking to myself, God, if I can't even call one person, I must really be selfish." Sometimes Jena thinks she'd better quit before this girl becomes too attached to her. So she helps a little, but she still feels guilty.

If guilt is not commonly recognized as a motive for wanting to do volunteer work, good feelings nevertheless have become a vital part of the meaning of community service. Were one to pitch in alongside one's neighbors to sandbag the levee and keep the community from flooding, good feelings might result, but they would scarcely be the determining motive. Putting in an extra Saturday at the lab searching for a vaccine against AIDS might be enormously meaningful, but it would also be so similar to the rest of one's work, so much a part of the serious side of life, that a momentary emotional "high" would probably pale as a decisive consideration. When volunteer work has to be generated in contrast to the rest of life, however, extraordinary feelings may become its most prized result. There is often a heightened emphasis on what these activities contribute to the person. Self-fulfillment becomes the key word. This means personal enrichment, a widening of experience, a feeling that one is indeed a good, worthy human being. The logic is not so much to benefit one's community for its own sake, but to do something that rounds out the person's own life, something that is different from one's work.

What keeps Jena Forsythe volunteering is chiefly the good feelings she derives from it. She says it is "fun" to watch this girl grow and discover new ideas. She even admits there is an "ego thing" involved, "instant gratification" from making a difference, like the rush she experiences from making a big junk bond sale. Except there's a qualitative difference. "Maybe it's spiritual gratification," she ventures. "It's just my way of trying to make a difference." And yet she seldom sees tangible results in the community itself. So the feelings she receives become all the more valuable, especially because they must compensate for her guilt.

Searching for good feelings encourages people to seek volunteer experiences likely to generate these feelings. Working with an appreciative recipient for an hour a week becomes a better choice than doing administrative work. This is another reason why giving money is devalued. It is done in hopes of alleviating guilt or generating an emotional high; it may subtract from our resources but add nothing to our lives. People talk about it as being too indirect, as not making a discernible difference, as not giving them a sense of personal satisfaction, like giving of one's time.

"I don't feel anything when I write out a check," is the way Audrey Cole explains the difference. The volunteer work she does for Amnesty International and for various feminist organizations in Minnesota speaks deeply to her sense of who she is. This is "where my values are at," she says. And she gives money, too. But she gains little satisfaction from doing so. She seldom senses that it makes any difference. Intellectually, she thinks it probably does; emotionally, she's not so sure. "Nobody comes up to me and says, 'That's a good idea' or 'thanks for helping out.'" She admits she needs this, just to know she is doing something constructive.

In the end, volunteer work that is separated both from one's immediate community and from one's gainful employment becomes much like another leisure activity. The time it requires competes with the things we would like to do for fun, for ourselves, or for our families. It, too, must be fun to keep us involved. It is part of the discretionary arena of our lives, a matter of choice and personal interest. Thus, many people excuse themselves from doing it at all, saying they do not have the knack for it or lack the time. They mean they do not have the time they need to do their own work and maintain themselves mentally and emotionally. As a working woman in San Diego explains, "I just need that time for myself, I need it to keep myself together mentally." Or, says a working woman in Massachusetts who occasionally does volunteer work for a Head Start program: "Part of me would like to be able to put more time into it, but part of me is saying, no you have to keep that time for yourself. So it's a struggle with balancing my time." And since it is leisure activity, it should also nurture one's family. "I'll do it if it involves Girl Scouts, or something like that where my daughter benefits," says a man in Louisiana. "It's got to be with the family; I wouldn't go out and shoot pool with the guys either."

Helping in the Helping Professions

There is, however, another type of person who integrates volunteer work and paid work more closely. These people are often in the helping professions, doing work that already involves caring. They do not have to seek out special opportunities to pit compassion against the perceived onslaught of materialism in our society. Yet they too become volunteers. A librarian in Portland, for example, spends several evenings a month on a volunteer project concerned with developing information facilities for the disabled. The project grew directly from her work: she saw the need, realized nobody was doing anything about it, and felt responsible to get something started. A New Jersey dietician drives to a pregnancy counseling clinic thirty miles away once a week where she advises mothers-to-be on how to eat right. A Chicago banker who lives in the suburbs spends one night a week at a crisis center in another part of the city giving free financial advice. Why do people like this do volunteer work? And with what cultural consequences?

For many aspiring professionals, doing volunteer work is a way to move up in their careers. Providing counseling or legal services free of charge gives them valuable experience. It looks good on their résumés to have organized a community fund-raising drive. Later, they may take on extra cases to catch their boss's attention. Self-employed professionals sometimes speak of such projects as trial balloons: if they succeed, consider them a good investment; if they fail, call them volunteer work. In such instances, providing voluntary services may not be a very good way of restraining the hours one works at all. Volunteering simply extends work into the other areas of one's life. The responsibility many professionals feel toward their work, whether it is for pay or for free, may in fact *add* to the sense that there is too much to do and too little time in which to do it. For people like this, doing volunteer work probably does not change the pace of their lives as much as reading a good novel or taking a walk in the woods.

How then, if at all, does volunteer work provide a restraint on economic commitments? Probably much the way it did for farmers and craftspeople when they devoted their skills to helping out their neighbors: not so much by changing the pace, but by changing one's orientation. The clinical social worker in Washington, D.C., who does volunteer work with the homeless recognizes that this activity resembles her paid work a great deal. She even worries that she is doing it to gain experience. But she also feels it broadens her, gives her a different perspective, and puts balance in her life. "I think it adds a different aspect to my life. It takes me out of my day-to-day job and gives me a different perspective. I've always liked to have something else to give me balance."

Doing volunteer work provides a contrast for some professionals because it harks back to the basic values that drew them into their profession in the first place. A Chicago man, for example, explains that his wife recently decided to take a promotion to an administrative job at the hospice where she works. Part of the reason was to expand the family budget because their children were nearing college age. Partly, it was to accept a challenge set before her. But moving into administration also meant less direct contact with dying patients. The answer was to work and do volunteer work as well.

Doing good deeds voluntarily can be particularly effective for making a symbolic stand against materialism and everything it represents. Like the heiress who insists that helping others shows she is a good person, professionals sometimes need to do something dramatic, too, to show they have not been personally corrupted by affluence. For the past two years a New Jersey social worker has been donating five hours a week to counsel AIDS patients free of charge. She says her private practice has become "pretty lucrative" and this is a way to give something back. A wealthy publisher takes on projects he knows will lose money just because they uphold values he feels are lacking in the marketplace. A college senior risks damage to her grade-point average in molecular biology to direct a play because she feels somebody needs to "make a statement" about what is wrong in today's world.

There is, however, one important respect in which professionals' volunteer work contrasts radically with neighbors in the same community helping each other. The sense of reciprocity that typically prevails in a community is likely to be limited or lacking entirely. To be sure, professionals may become involved in volunteer work as a favor to another member of their trade, hoping perhaps that this favor will earn them something in return. But in most cases, the volunteer work itself is unlikely to be performed for or with one's immediate neighbors. It is likely to be done for a client who is unable to reciprocate. It may not even be the norm among one's co-workers to engage in such activities. Reasons for going the extra mile, therefore, must to a greater extent come from within the individual.

Under these circumstances, good feelings are likely to play an important role in legitimating caring behavior, just as they do for other kinds of volunteers. "Why spend my evenings and weekends tutoring underprivileged students?" a Chicago physicist muses. "I guess because it gives me a charge." Thinking about the extra time he spends with youth at his church, a Nashville pastor gives a similar response: "It's fun!"

Good feelings, however, generally falter when it comes to more serious sacrifices of one's time. A Los Angeles family planner who gets up at 4 o'clock every morning to wage war against pickets from Operation Rescue does not think of the time she donates as fun. Nor does the woman who counsels AIDS patients. For professionals like these, the extra effort it takes to do volunteer work stems from deep introspection about their values. Neither money nor community norms are enough to drive them the extra mile. They want more out of life than their work alone provides. As they try to think through their values, it helps them to find alternative settings. As they donate time in these settings, their values often become further unsettled. "Why am I doing this?" is a question they struggle to answer.

Symbolic Uses of the Poor

All this suggests that the poor play a strong symbolic function in the lives of middle-class Americans. The poor help us see another side of ourselves, express another set of values. It isn't so much that we fear becoming poor ourselves. It's more that we have become poor in spirit, impoverished in our ability to express deeper human values, living as we do in anonymous middle-class suburban communities. So we reach out, trying to find a more authentic existence by engaging in token service projects for the poor.

What exactly do the poor symbolize? Among the many images that middle- and working-class Americans carry around in their heads, three images of the poor stand out with particular clarity: the poor as carriers of wholesome values, the poor as victims of materialism, and the poor as an opportunity for service. Each of these images conveys some truth about the reality of poverty in the United States, but they are collectively even more revealing of how the majority of Americans are struggling to rediscover their souls.

As carriers of wholesome values, the poor provide a romanticized image of something important that has been lost in America's headlong rush to achieve material success. What we think has been lost is what we see surviving among the poor. It is no longer their closeness to the land, the image of being "dirt poor," that once attracted so many comfortable suburbanites to romanticize the suffering of rural America during the Great Depression. Nor is it the raw, uncivilized manners, the course humor, or the untamed muscularity that once provided a stark counterpoint to the pallid gentility of the bourgeoisie. Middle Americans who romanticize the poor are now taken chiefly with the idea of a lost sense of caring.

"I lived with a family in the slums of Mexico City for two months," recalls a businesswoman in Los Angeles. "They were wonderful. They just loved me and took care of me. I learned so much from them." Another person told of traveling in the third world and being impressed by the way families in rural villages cared for each other despite their poverty. Still another, an Asian woman who has become an advocate for the poor in her city, believes a lot of poor people at least have strong ethnic ties that are lacking among white, middle-class individualists.

The reason the poor seem so caring, we tell ourselves, is that they remain unfettered by the bonds of materialism. Their lives are uncluttered with toys and trinkets; all they have is each other. They have to care. Oh, that we could be like them. It is like journeying back in time to be among them, refreshing in fact to spend a few hours in their midst. This view is particularly prominent when the poor themselves live in some other setting than our own, perhaps one that neither threatens our way of life nor makes claims on our tax dollars.

As victims of materialism, the poor serve up a remarkably dramatic illustration to many privileged but concerned Americans of what is wrong with their economic system. This imagery generally stops short of pronouncing the entire system corrupt and needing to be replaced. It does, however, lead many observers into an analysis of how the work ethic and the American Dream that went with it are finally reaching a breaking point. The continuing presence of grinding, endemic, inescapable poverty for so many in the United States points to the possibility that materialism has become excessive.

Specifically what has gone wrong with the American system is a matter of contention nowadays, just as it always has been. But with homeless people crowding subways and bus stations in ever more visible numbers, armchair diagnosticians seldom falter for words. "It was Reagan," one man begins. "His crowd wanted to make mega-bucks fast, and now look where we're at." Says another man, it was the labor unions that caused the trouble. They hired people who could scarcely read or write, paid them big wages, but then had to lay them off because products could no longer be priced competitively. The unemployed, having no real skills, now find themselves on the street. "Maybe what we need is a little more socialism," ventures a New York woman. "I know they're tearing that down in Eastern Europe, but I look at Donald Trump, and I say, it's just not right for some people to have so much and others to have so little."

Political analysts make much of the differences between those who see problems with the American system and those who don't. There is a common thread that runs through both types of comments, however. Consider how a Minnesota businessman describes the most vivid case of poverty he had dealt with in recent memory. She was one of his office staff, a divorced mother of two, so destitute that she could no longer pay her grocery bills. The problem? Her husband. His problem? He'd become so materialistic that he was driving a fancy car, spending too much money, building up gambling debts. Some people just conceptualize the problem more at the individual level than others. But in either case, the underlying issue is materialism. This is what the needy symbolize.

Even "blaming the victim" is never as far removed from these conceptions of victimization as political analysts would like to think. If the system is at fault, then surely the victims must be blameless. There is, however, plenty of room in middle-class Americans' views of the poor for spreading the blame. Why are the poor that way? Something has gone wrong with our system. We are not quite sure what. Maybe it is that the system generally promotes materialism instead of community and caring. But maybe the trouble is more subtle than that. Materialism need not mean that the whole system is off base, only that some part of its logic has gotten out of kilter. It can mean a malignment of values, perhaps the very decoupling of work and money that so deeply characterizes the middle class itself. Sensing half consciously that we have begun to think this way in our own lives, it is easy to see it in stark relief as the trouble with the poor. They want material things but fail to see the importance of working hard to get them. "No wonder they are in the shape they are in," remarks a businessman. "You give 'em a job and they don't even get to work on time." Or the poor simply become extreme manifestations of the difficulty everyone has knowing how to handle their money wisely. Says another man, "You have to treat them like children; they wouldn't know what to do with money if they had it."

As an opportunity for service, the poor give middle- and working-class Americans a chance to redeem themselves by doing something other than advancing their careers and spending their earnings in the quest for a comfortable life. The same people who may romanticize the poor, and who may argue that materialism *totum bonum* is at fault, will then throw up their hands, pleading too little knowledge of politics or economics to suggest solutions. What they do see in the poor, however, is a way to save themselves. The secret is to help one individual, hopefully a person with whom one can identify, giving that person a "lift," so that he or she can climb out of poverty and become more like us.

"If I could recommend something," says a Philadelphia man, "I'd say get out there and teach somebody, even if it's just one person. If you give him bread, he'll feel like a beggar. But if you teach him to grow wheat, he'll have dignity. I think that's what we all want." A Tennessee man sees special benefits for the caregiver, too. "In the opportunity to help people materially," he explains, "lies the chance to express our compassion." If people are in touch with the God of compassion, he says, then they will need an outlet for their own desire to care.

A woman who pastors a suburban church in Los Angeles gives perhaps the most revealing example of all. Watching people in her congregation working with the homeless for the past few years, she has begun to wonder who is really helping whom. It would be just as effective, she figures, to send money or spend time lobbying city government to do more. The chief value of getting people directly involved with the homeless is that these volunteers have to confront themselves. "They sometimes realize they're all gross and ugly, just like the homeless; they just have better ways of hiding it." Other people have confronted their own alcoholism by working with the homeless. "They see where they could end up." Sometimes the messages are less politically correct, too. Like the people who come away feeling proud of themselves: "I've worked hard for what I have; the homeless haven't." Sometimes, too, people come away feeling superior just because they've helped someone less fortunate than themselves: "It's nice to feel like you have an upper hand on somebody, that there's somebody under you who needs your help, and that makes you feel good."

The Cloak of Ignorance

The problem we have with *really* coming to grips with poverty, hunger, and other desperate needs in our society lies ultimately in the fact that we seldom see these needs at all when we look at them. All we see is a projection of ourselves. The needy appear in our minds as distorted inversions of the materialism that obsesses us. As long as we refuse to understand it, we have no hope of understanding the needy in our midst either.

The most basic feature of our obsession with materialism is that we prefer to regard it as a mysterious force, an evil spirit of some kind that beckons, possesses, but does so in a way that no mortal can understand. It is this same mysterious presence, projected onto the poor, that prevents us from thinking clearly about the issues involved. Asked what should be done to help the poor, otherwise articulate middle-class professionals suddenly grope for words. They profess ignorance. This, they say, enters the realm of politics and economics, neither of which is possible for ordinary people to understand. Probably it will take experts to figure it out. We are not so sure that even the experts know what to do.

Because materialism is seen by the most prescient in our midst as a system, a vast complex of social institutions, the needy are also thought to be part of this system. This too prevents us from probing further. The problem, liberal-minded individuals say, must be capitalism. In what way? Well, somewhere along the line it failed to reward certain kinds of people. And then things got worse, so that these people had difficulty climbing back into the system's incentive structure. After a while, even they began to depend on being where they were. You cannot reform the whole system, though. Maybe some tinkering here and there is what it takes. We are not quite sure.

What we can do is suggest the importance of being compassionate at the individual level. It seems callous, we must recognize, to throw up our hands and say that nothing at all can be done. So the solution is to look after that one needy person we know. Make a small difference. Give one person hope (that person or ourself?). It makes us feel better just knowing we've done something.

"When I think of the whole system, how big it is, and how out of control—it's very overwhelming!" The speaker is a woman who has thought a lot about what's wrong with America. She is no flag-waving patriot. She's been on the streets herself, seen the destitute, tried to help them. She has to do something, but working at the individual level is all she can think of; anything else is, as she says, too overwhelming. "If an individual will just look at one other individual and see the need, then you can do something to help out."

What must not be done, though, is actually to give the poor money. To do so will only corrupt them. Why? They are pure, truly deserving *because* they have no money, because they stand apart from the forces of materialism that threaten the rest of society. To give them money is like putting children with bad teeth in a candy store. They won't be able to resist. Furthermore, the antimaterialist orientation of the middle class leads readily to assertions about the importance of other values, relative to money itself. What's important? Surely not just having money. The basic values in life are self-esteem, knowledge, knowing how to be self-reliant, taking responsibility for the poor. They need to be taught these virtues. This is another reason why volunteering is better than philanthropy. Spend time tutoring the needy. Take canned goods and blankets to shelters for the homeless. Remember the neediest by helping at a volunteer center in one's free time.

Hungry mouths are then fed, at least on Thanksgiving. The news media pick up the story and report it everywhere. Times are hard? Well, thank goodness for the volunteers. With a little sleight of hand, journalists can prove to the public that when needs arise, volunteer activity increases apace. Let's not make our news stories too complex. The public wouldn't understand. After all, they are sort of ignorant. It's best anyway to be upbeat about what we write. Who wants to read about bad news all the time. Stories about volunteering should be the bright side of the news. So not to worry. A little token community service can go a long way toward restraining our materialism—psychologically. An hour here. A dollar there. The giving is relatively painless. It only haunts us in the midnight hours when we ask, "Why am I doing this?" Some of the answers are ones we do not like to consider.

Chapter Eleven

THE QUEST FOR SPIRITUALITY:
AMBIGUOUS VOICES FROM AMERICA'S
RELIGIOUS COMMUNITIES

SINCE EARLIEST TIMES, religious leaders have drawn a sharp contrast between the pursuit of material gain and the life of the spirit. "I undertook great works . . . owned possessions . . . amassed silver and gold . . . found pleasure in all my labor, and . . . this was my reward . . . it was futility, all of it, and a chasing of the wind, of no profit under the sun," proclaimed one of the early Hebrew writers.[1] The patristic John Chrysostom vehemently denounced the love of money. "Like a fire catching a wood, that desolates and destroys all around," he wrote, "this passion has laid waste the world."[2] St. Augustine's denunciation of the lust for material gain was scarcely less mild, likening the person who sought security in riches to a fish caught in a net or an animal flailing in a trap.[3] Centuries later, St. Francis de Sales admonished his followers that their hearts should "be open to heaven alone and impervious to riches and all other transitory things." The heavenly spirit, he cautioned, must never become captive to earthly goods, for these possessions are like poison, debilitating the whole body with an avaricious fever that may not even be recognized or excused with all sorts of high-sounding commitments.[4]

Only in the Protestant teachings that grew out of the Reformation did this extreme separation of the material from the spiritual come to be challenged, and even then the positive connection portrayed between the two was often less straightforward than later interpreters were to assume. "There is almost no one whose resources permit him to be extravagant who does not delight in lavish and ostentatious banquets, bodily apparel, and domestic architecture; who does not wish to outstrip his neighbors in all sorts of elegance; who does not wonderfully flatter himself in his opulence," Calvin wrote in his famous *Institutes*, and he concluded, such people "are certainly defiled by these vices."[5] Indeed, even in theological treatises written long after the Reformation, seeking God is generally presented as a higher calling than the quest for money. Faith requires allegiance to things unseen, not security in one's labor or possessions. The love of money is indeed the root of all evil, for it replaces God with something transient and ephemeral.

How is it, then, that a nation as prosperous, as hardworking, and as governed by the quest for economic profits as the United States can also espouse an overwhelming religious faith, claim near-universal belief in God, and devote itself regularly to the teachings of its numerous churches, synagogues, meeting places, and fellowship halls? Has the ancient tension between the material and the spiritual dissolved in the secular prosperity of American society? Or does spirituality still provide an effective rein on the nation's passion for work and money?

THE RELIGIOUS HERITAGE

To suggest that spirituality might restrain economic behavior is, of course, to fly in the face of what most people understand to have been the case in American history. Religious teachings seldom deterred people from working hard and making money; they *encouraged* it. The Puritans, after all, became known for their divinely sanctioned emphasis on hard work and frugality, traits that despite the Puritans' disdain for worldly possessions often resulted in precisely that sort of accumulation.

These teachings, however, represent only one side of the American religious tradition. The ascetic moralists, as we have seen, drew from biblical texts to argue that work and money were *not* the ultimate values in life. Although the importance of working hard and saving has often been defended on religious grounds, arguments cautioning against these puritan-like virtues can also be found with considerable frequency and consistency. The problem with saving for the future is that it encourages people to trust too much in themselves rather than realizing their dependence on God. Like the rich fool in the New Testament who built large barns to store his crops, the fool of today finds that his life may also be snuffed out in an instant. Instead of saving, one should live generously, trusting in God to provide. Frequently cited is the example of John Wesley, who wrote in 1744, "if I leave behind me ten pounds . . . you and all mankind [may] bear witness against me, that I have lived and died a thief and a robber," and who indeed died with only a few coins in his pocket, having given everything else to the poor.[6]

Working hard has also been criticized because it too can provide a false sense of security. Believers have been admonished to spend their time storing up treasures in heaven by doing deeds of kindness for the needy, engaging in prayer and Bible study, and helping spread the gospel through their churches. Even the Puritans have come to be seen in a more balanced perspective as a people who worked hard, but whose sense of time was much more intimately associated with the rhythms of nature and the inscrutable ways of God than with the contemporary pace of assembly lines, trading floors, intercontinental travel, and electronic communication. Harvard historian David Hall, taking the life of one New England merchant as a detailed case study, has written perceptively: "[His] sense of time was ahistorical. Time was really time*less* in a world where the coincidences mattered, and not the passing moment. Like the artisans who fashioned New England gravestones, he overrode the rhythm of the clock with the time-scheme of the coming kingdom and the resurrection of the saints."[7]

Deeply ingrained in American religion also is an orientation that diminishes the importance of the struggle for material success. Arguing that heavenly rewards tend to differ from earthly rewards, this perspective has given solace to the downtrodden, telling them that true spirituality can only be obtained by the poor, that the wealthy cannot know God as deeply, and that loyalties to church, family, helping others, and seeking deeper knowledge of God should take precedence over secular aspirations. Such teachings have been noted historically in the slave religions of the antebellum South, in populist folk religions, and in the otherworldly orientations of urban pentecostalist sects, and they can still be found in fundamentalist and evangelical writings today. Counseling its readers to shun "the model of self-actualization that is at the root of many contemporary career-development materials," for example, a Christian magazine suggests that the New Testament concept of servanthood should be interpreted as the idea "of taking the lowly place, of doing the menial work, and of receiving no immediate reward for doing so."[8] People should not be unhappy with humble, obscure jobs that fail to meet their career expectations, it cautions, because they can still find ways to tell others in these situations about Jesus.

The religious heritage, then, has at least the potential for curbing material appetites. And yet many people wonder today whether religious institutions any longer have anything to say on these matters—and if they do, whether anybody is listening. Former U.S. Steel executive William Diehl says, for example, that never in thirty years did his church (which he attended faithfully) give him any guidance in how to apply his spirituality to his work. "I received no affirmation, no training, no support, and no prayers," he recalls. "There was absolutely no connection between Sunday and Monday."[9]

CHANGING PATTERNS OF AMERICAN RELIGION

In the 1950s, when Will Herberg was collecting information for his widely read book *Protestant–Catholic–Jew*, American life seemed to be guided overwhelmingly by its religious institutions. So powerful were these institutions that Herberg considered it virtually un-American not to be affiliated with at least one of the major faiths.[10] That sense of religious power is in many ways still evident today. On the surface at least, it is impressive that 85 percent of Americans have received religious training during their childhoods, 84 percent believe God is a heavenly father to whom they can pray, three-quarters think Jesus was the Son of God, 71 percent believe in life after death, two-thirds hold membership in a church or synagogue, 40 percent can be found in the pew on any given weekend, and 38 percent describe themselves as born-again evangelical Christians.[11]

Most observers, viewing these statistics, have concluded that the often predicted demise of religious faith in modern culture has thus far bypassed American soil.[12] A closer look at opinion polls, however, reveals that all is not well in the American Eden. On virtually every standard indicator of religious commitment, significant erosion has been gauged since the immediate post–World War II period. Since 1947 church membership has dropped from 76 percent of the population to 65 percent. Weekly church attendance has declined since 1955 from 49 percent to 40 percent. The number saying religion is very important to them personally has decreased since 1952 from 75 percent to 56 percent.[13] And belief that the Bible is literally the word of God dropped from 65 percent in 1963 to 32 percent in 1992.[14]

More important than the changes polls can pick up, however, are the subtle shifts that people *perceive* to be taking place in their own lives and in the lives of their families. These changes have more to do with qualitative characteristics of faith than they do with numeric shifts, and they generally focus squarely on intergenerational comparisons within families. Herberg, of course, was among the first to recognize the importance of generational dynamics, borrowing from historian Marcus Hanson to suggest that first-generation immigrants tended to be highly religious, their children to be less so as they tried to assimilate, and the third generation to seek spirituality again as a way of rediscovering their roots. Unfortunately, most studies attempting to validate Hanson's theory have found little support for it, and it is in any case limited to the immigrant experience. But there is a kernel of truth that needs to be retained.

That kernel actually finds clearest expression, not in any observer of American religion, but in the writings of psychoanalyst Carl Jung. In *Dreams, Memories, Reflections*, Jung describes a patient who came to him suffering from an undiagnosed neurosis.[15] Upon questioning her, Jung learned that her grandfather had been a deeply spiritual Hassidic Jew, her father an atheist, and she herself was plagued with misgiving about her religious heritage. Jung advised her to become a spiritual seeker but does not indicate what the outcome of her quest may have been.

This case, which in some ways follows the pattern suggested by Hanson (but in a different setting), has deep implications for understanding spirituality in the United States. Americans may not have had Hassidic grandfathers or atheist fathers, but they know what the religious orientations of their forebears was, and many feel that their own faith is somehow less substantial. Some take pride in being less devout than their parents or grandparents. Others express doubt, misgiving, and even a sense of loss in relation to these memories. Still others consider themselves spiritual seekers or claim to have found a deeper faith than their parents, but they often describe this faith in such personalized terms that its connections with long-standing authoritative traditions seem tenuous.[16]

It must be with some caution, then, that the role of organized religion as a source of moral guidance, inspiration, or restraint is considered.

Herberg himself believed religious commitment in America was much wider than it was deep. Despite heroic efforts on the part of many religious organizations in recent years to improve educational programs, spirituality may be even more shallow today. Certainly religious knowledge, even of basic biblical tenets, is so shallow that much of the American public must be considered spiritually illiterate. In one study, for example, fewer than half of the public could name all four gospels, and an even smaller percentage knew who delivered the sermon on the mount.[17] In another national survey, four people in ten thought Jesus was born in Jerusalem, and a quarter said the book of Acts was in the Old Testament—and this was a study of people who were involved in support groups such as Bible studies and Sunday school classes.[18]

The reason that such knowledge is often superficial is not hard to understand. When adults are asked about their religious training as children, the vast majority say they participated in some kind of religious organization; and yet very few received reinforcement at home for what they were taught in these organizations. Only four in ten say their parents ever read the Bible at home, less than a quarter (23 percent) had family devotions, and even fewer (16 percent) knew their parents prayed about financial decisions. Younger people nowadays are even less likely to have had these experiences.[19]

Apart from huge gaps in biblical knowledge, the American public also appears to have been little exposed to specific teachings about the connections between faith and work or between spirituality and money. When asked if they recalled having learned any religious teachings about money as children, virtually everyone said they could not. Those who had ever discussed work or money in the context of some religious organization were rare exceptions. Other than several members of the clergy, nobody could remember ever reading a book that tried to address work or money from a religious standpoint. Even fairly common were those who could think of little in their religious training that had to do with anything specific, whether it was teachings about money or just simple biblical knowledge. One woman whose mother and father had been devout Catholics and had taken her faithfully to catechism classes as a child put it eloquently when she admitted, "I didn't like going, so I think I blocked it all out. All I remember is singing a lot, like 'Michael, Row Your Boat Ashore,' but I don't really remember the teachings." Almost wistfully she added, "I hate to say it, but I really don't know the Bible."

Views such as this are not atypical. When asked in the labor force survey how much they had thought about "what the Bible teaches about money," only 29 percent responded more than a little or none. Asked if they had thought about "what the Bible teaches about work," 32 percent responded similarly. And when asked if they had thought about how to connect their faith to their work, only 33 percent gave these responses.[20]

The Varieties of Religious Presence

Experts on matters of religion insist, of course, that the United States is a rich tapestry of competing beliefs and practices. No generalizations can be made, say some of the experts, because the diversity of traditions is too great. Indeed, sorting out this diversity has been an important preoccupation of scholars and practitioners alike.

There are, to be sure, pockets of believers here and there (Amish farmers, for example) for whom religious teachings serve as a powerful source of values over and against the demands of the marketplace. But seeking to understand the wider role of religion in American culture forces us to recognize such groups as the exceptions rather than the rule. The important question for most scholars of American religion has not been what happens in particular communities, but whether being involved in any religious community is likely to have a discernible impact on the ways in which people do their work, spend their money, and carry out the ordinary details of their lives. One way of approaching this question is particularly worth noting.

In view of the fact that American religion has not remained altogether unaffected by forces of modernity and secularity, it has been common for students of the topic to distinguish between religious institutions that have largely tried to make peace with these changes and those that have attempted to oppose them.[21] Accommodationists, on the one hand, try to see the good in contemporary society and bend their teachings to people who have long since abandoned the pious ways of their forebears. Resisters or antimodernists, on the other hand, try to stand up against change, asserting the value of traditions such as biblical inerrancy, the Latin mass, or keeping kosher. It has made a good deal of sense to many people to see things this way, especially when progressive religious groups and orthodox religious groups seem so often to be locked in cultural combat.[22] And yet this view must be seriously modified in at least two important respects.

First, to divide American religion into two opposing camps this way is to miss a third alternative. This is not simply the excluded middle that public opinion pollsters worry about. It is the group that copes with the inevitable conflict between spirituality and secular culture through *avoidance*.[23] For present purposes, this alternative depends on drawing a firm distinction between spirituality and material life. Many Americans are able to do this, it appears, despite the fact that they believe in some sort of God and lead busy lives in the marketplace. Their conceptual machinery allows them to keep the two realms apart.[24]

Second, the assumption that liberal or progressive religious orientations involve greater adaptation to the forces of modernity than conservative or orthodox orientations must be qualified. On balance, this assumption may be true. More important, however, is the fact that accommodationists and resisters alike have adapted in serious ways to the wider culture. The two represent different initial positions, perhaps traceable in some cases to the fundamentalist-modernist conflict at the end of the nineteenth century, or in other cases to struggles between factions within denominations or confessional traditions. Starting with those orientations, though, both sides have moved in subtle ways so that the relationship between spirituality and material life within each now represents a great deal of cultural adaptation. This is one reason why it is wrong to think of the two sides as being engaged in a "war" involving fundamentally opposing worldviews. The two agree on so many other things, and they have drunk so deeply at the well of American individualism, that they are often indistinguishable.[25] In their views of work and money, the one emphasizes harmonious relations between the material and the spiritual, while the other stresses conflict. And yet neither side poses moral restraint on economic commitments with a very high degree of effectiveness.

What I wish to emphasize, then, is that the influence of religious institutions on economic behavior is unlikely to correspond closely with the ways in which maps of American religion have generally been drawn. The spiritual realm and the material realm can be compartmentalized, viewed as separate worlds, within virtually any of the major faith traditions. The two realms can be synthesized in such a way that little but harmony between them can be imagined. They can also be pitted against one another as combatants fundamentally opposed in how they envision the good life. Which of the three perspectives is taken will be important to an individual's outlook on life. But any of the three will also reveal how difficult it is for religious organizations to make strong claims about work and money.[26]

All three of these orientations also need to be understood as broad categories or styles, each of which encompasses much internal variety. Although the style of avoiding conflict by compartmentalizing the spiritual from the material can often be found among the nominally religious, for example, it includes many devout believers of all faiths as well. Those who imagine harmonious relations between the spiritual and the material tend to be relatively liberal in their religious orientations but include Catholics, Jews, Protestants, and people with their own idiosyncratic beliefs. Similarly, the view that spiritual life and material life are fundamentally in tension with each other characterizes not only the members of conservative Protestant sects, but people of other persuasions as well. It is thus important to consider specific examples of all three if we are to grasp their underlying moral languages.[27]

Separate Worlds: From Dual Kingdom to Multiple Realities

Medieval theology drew a sharp distinction between the spiritual kingdom and the earthly kingdom. One was the heavenly realm that people entered after death; the other, a fallen order to be endured in the present life. Despite his break with the medieval church, Martin Luther retained much of this earlier dualism, drawing the two realms together chiefly by suggesting that believers could serve God in performing their secular work as a divinely appointed duty. In emphasizing that salvation was attained by faith in God's grace alone, he continued to encourage a separation of realms, just as other reformers did in distinguishing the church's authority in ecclesiastical matters from the temporal powers of political rulers. Although countless theological positions have been articulated in the interim, present understandings of the relationship between spirituality and material life are often less distant from these conceptions than we might imagine. Metaphysical distinctions between the natural and the supernatural are still widely believed at the popular level. Reality may now be more complex, more a feature of human imagination, but it is still commonly divided into separate spheres. Work and money make up a significant part of the wide-awake, pragmatic reality in which people live from day to day; ecstasy, transcendence, prayer, and the sacred make up an order of a different kind.

Popular religion in the United States includes at least three perspectives on spirituality, all of which emphasize the separation of the sacred from material life. One, reminiscent of the medieval view, includes a clear conception of God as a supernatural being and yet removes this God from the day-to-day functioning of most things here on earth. In this view, God is described variously as the creator, the maker of nature, Mother Nature, a force that holds the universe together, or simply the sense people have on a starry night that all this "didn't just happen." It is significant that nearly all these images view God in close relation to nature, the raw world that somehow exists independently of human will or action; in contrast, the human realm, including the material world that has been artificially crafted by humans, tends to be separated conceptually from the sacred. A second view is not unlike Luther's orientation, stressing the importance of faith over works, but also making faith so purely a matter of the soul that it seldom has discernible consequences for daily behavior. God is more often conceived in anthropomorphic terms here than in the first view, sometimes as a parent or as an authority figure. The question of how individuals relate to this being is thus more pressing. Having faith is like beaming an invisible laser toward heaven. It can open a channel of communication, but mostly it just establishes contact, reassuring the individual that everything is okay. The third view is a de facto agnosticism that holds forth the possibility of a realm other than the one in which we normally live but conceives of this realm with sufficient doubt and in such vague terms that its impact on ordinary conduct is negligible. What is interesting about the three is that they span all the major faith traditions and include people who are relatively devout as well as those whose faith is quite marginal, yet all three have similar consequences for the way in which spirituality and material life are related.[28]

A mother of two who lives in Texas and takes in typing to help pay the family bills provides a vivid illustration of someone who conceives of spirituality and the material world in dualistic terms. She believes the two are fundamentally separate but is nevertheless able to see some delimited connections between them. Raised by an alcoholic father and a devout fundamentalist mother, she decided as a teenager to quit believing in the wrathful God she had been taught about in the Baptist church. "I already had one angry parent," she explains, "I didn't need another one." As she matured, she therefore retained a more generic sense of the sacred, not so much an anthropomorphic God but simply a vague sense of some other reality, given occasional concreteness with a wide variety of ideas that struck her fancy: Catholic teachings about miracles and the saints that she picked up from her Hispanic neighbors, ideas about reincarnation and karma from the books she read, and simple notions about God and human behavior from thinking about life.

She asserts bluntly that spirituality and the material realm "don't mix." Asked about money and God, she says she prefers not to think of them in the same context. She also denies that religion ever influences her work. In everyday life, she prefers to envision herself acting out an entirely human drama composed only of herself and other individuals. Yet this drama runs parallel to one that she imagines being performed in some metaphysical plane. She says, for example, that she believes there is a fundamental struggle going on in the universe between the forces of good and the forces of evil. She does not describe it quite in the way one talks about a fight on the street corner. She entertains the possibility that things are not like this at all. The metaphysical is, in this sense, closed to her, but imagining its existence helps her try to side with the good and resist evil.[29]

Thus her notion of a two-tiered universe leaves the supernatural realm largely distant and ill-defined, like a New Yorker might view a town in Kansas. The reason the sacred seldom connects to the human world is that God seems to have meant for humans to take care of themselves. They have to live right, think right, and take the consequences. She does not believe, for example, that God cares anything about the specific work she does or the particular things she spends money on. It is important, however, for her to cultivate a positive attitude. She should work hard, but not worry. She should enjoy the material goods she has, but not become too attached to them. Because the human realm is so much a world of its own, it makes sense to work hard. In most instances, hard work will pay off in some way. If it does not, God is not to blame. The natural order simply provides some unanticipated twists and turns (cancer, divorce, automobile accidents). But the individual still is fundamentally in control of these situations because it is not so much what happens, but how one thinks about it, that counts.

Where God connects to the material world is by giving this woman an occasional sign. Because the supernatural exists out there somewhere, she does not find it at all odd to pray. Usually the supernatural is so remote that she has no way of knowing whether her prayers have been heard or answered. But just often enough to keep her convinced of its existence (and not so often to be intrusive), the supernatural does break into her life. Moreover, its interventions always have good outcomes. They do not influence her life materially, but they help her have a better attitude.

She tells the following story as an example of her experience with the supernatural. "This is going to seem silly," she begins, "but it was a real turning point in my life. I had been doing some spiritual reading for a couple of years because I just felt I needed to make a decision once and for all about what I believed and get off the fence. And I read that you can pray about the most minor things, even to help find a lost shoe, and you'll get help. So one morning I was going nuts trying to find my daughter's shoe because we were taking my son to nursery school and, as usual, we were late. I looked everywhere for that shoe. Finally I just sat down in the bathroom and folded my arms and said, 'That's it, I'm not looking for that shoe. If you're there, God, *you* find it.' I was being really defiant. And my head just turned to where I could see into my son's room, where there was a big cardboard box the kids had been playing in, and the words 'The shoe is in that box' just came into my head. And I *know* that thought came from somewhere else, not from me, because it never occurred to me to look in that box. I went and looked and there it was. I was so excited. I never doubted again that God exists."

A different way of compartmentalizing spirituality from one's material life is illustrated by a middle-aged executive who attends a Presbyterian church in New York. As a child, he believed that everything a person did mattered to God. It was important, for example, to put his quarter in the collection plate on Sunday and to obey his mother because doing so would make God happy. He now regards this view as naive. From reading the Bible and from participating in Sunday school classes and Bible studies at his church, he has come to believe that faith is all that matters. "I don't think God will hold up a scale on judgment day and balance out everything you've done," he explains. "If you believe in Jesus Christ, then everything will be all right." In his view, it really doesn't matter whether a person is rich or poor, or how a person uses his or her money, as long as he or she believes in God.

Theologians would argue that this sort of fideism is far from what the architects of Presbyterianism (and most other faith traditions) actually taught. Yet this man's view is probably widespread. Believers who might otherwise be devout enough to let their faith influence their economic behavior separate the two by associating faith entirely with a subjective attitude. By this logic, true believers can even be slightly ruthless or unethical, and thus make a lot of money, as long as they don't actually brutalize their neighbors. A Wall Street broker who attends church faithfully observes, for instance: "[Work] is like an arena, you go out and fight every single day; it's a battle. Yeah, you might have to hit a few people to get ahead or maybe step on a couple of people. But I hope I never have to step on too many people or hurt people who can't help themselves in order to make money and get ahead."

Confronted by Jesus's statements concerning the difficulties of the rich entering the kingdom of God, people in this category generally accept the terms of the statement, viewing the kingdom of God literally as a place people go when they die. But the saying itself annoys them. They cannot imagine why it would make any difference to God whether someone was rich or poor. "What's he got?" asked one man. "An income bracket, and if you're above that, you don't get in?" Because God basically leaves the world alone, their logic goes, we have to accept the world as it is, rather than attempting to judge it by some metaphysical standard. Lots of people (like us) are rich, and it is inconceivable that they have done anything very immoral, so why should they *not* be included in the kingdom of heaven?

Philanthropy is often invoked as proof that rich people are not immoral. There may be some, of course, who are so selfish that they would never give anyone a dime, and thus not merit being included in the kingdom. But most people have enough innate goodness in them that they give when they see a pressing need. Charitable giving thus becomes a kind of token, rather than being directly connected to believing and getting into the kingdom; it is merely a social expectation, something that establishes one's humanity and respectability in the community. Just as going to church does, philanthropy helps people to feel good about themselves.

It does not necessarily follow that churchgoers with this view never do anything to help others. Because of the programs available at their church, or out of respect to common human decency, they may perform deeds of kindness. The view that there is a God out there whom we believe in without being able to fathom very deeply, however, can also lead to this God becoming a *deus ex machina* for coping with the world's needs. A Catholic schoolteacher in St. Paul, for example, says he believes firmly that God is "a higher power who doesn't interfere with life on this earth." This God, he believes, will do nothing directly to help the poor. But there may be some kind of mysterious divine logic by which the poor will eventually be rewarded. He thinks maybe it's like getting a hardship deferment from the draft: the poor will spend less time in purgatory because they have already suffered here.

All of these views, then, draw such a sharp distinction between the sacred and the profane that religious teachings have little impact on economic behavior. Contemporary Americans hold these views, not because heaven and earth are literally separate kingdoms like they were in medieval thought, but because their imaginations distinguish between the "seen" and the "unseen." The economic life is in this sense bounded. It is clearly not everything in life. Yet the sacred holds forth mainly the prospect of being able to think differently. Reality is less "what is" than "what one makes of it." Indeed, there are multiple realities, all dependent on the perspective one takes. Attitudes count more than anything else. Good intentions and positive thinking make for a better life. Lost is a divine being who authoritatively reveals moral standards.

Just how widespread the tendency to compartmentalize the spiritual from the material may be in American society depends, of course, on how that tendency is understood. If it means failing to think very much about biblical teachings concerning money or work, then as many as two-thirds of the population could be so classified. If it means not believing, for example, that "the Bible contains valuable teachings about the use of money," then half the public either disagrees with this statement or doesn't know how to respond. Or if it means taking a more extreme stance, such as that implied in the statement "God doesn't care how I use my money," then fewer than a quarter (22 percent agree) would be included.[30] The important point is that at least a sizable minority of the American public compartmentalizes spirituality from economic life to a significant degree.

HARMONIOUS WORLDS: FROM COLD WAR TO
INNER PEACE

A second strand of thinking brings the spiritual and the material closer together, so close, in fact, that any serious tension between the two becomes virtually inconceivable. It, too, has deep roots in American culture. In some versions of Puritan doctrine, for example, serving God and working hard at one's calling provided a powerful way of integrating spiritual and material life. Throughout the past two centuries, numerous variants on this teaching have been popularized. From Russell Conwell's popular *Acres of Diamonds* to contemporary pray-for-riches schemes advanced by televangelists, religious themes have been harnessed to desires for prosperity.[31] With antimaterialistic leanings still prominent in the wider culture, however, it is difficult to consider such schemes as the primary means by which the spiritual and the material are reconciled. The more subtle ways in which the sacred has been domesticated must be considered if we are to understand why many Americans envisage no conflict between the spiritual and the material. These views are highly idiosyncratic, influenced more by individuals' personal experiences and the multiple religious languages they have been exposed to than by particular creeds or doctrines. Finding harmony between the spiritual and the material is often the result of conscious effort; indeed, this orientation is often expressed by people who have spent considerably more time struggling with their faith than is the more compartmentalized orientation.

The fact that spirituality has become more private and idiosyncratic has, of course, been widely commented upon. Many writers argue that privatization is the principal reason why religious institutions have been losing adherents in recent years.[32] A static assessment of the situation would support this view, revealing, for instance, that many Americans do regard their faith subjectively, holding eclectic views that wed them to no particular tradition or organization. As people themselves tell their stories, however, an entirely different picture emerges. They say they were interested in deepening their faith, wanted to understand more about God and the spiritual life, had questions, asked questions, and tried to fit in. But in many such cases, the churches failed them. Turbulent times in the 1960s, higher levels of education than their parents had ever achieved, dual careers, professional work, travel, mixed-faith marriages, broken marriages, living in new communities away from their relatives—all these experiences left them uncomfortable and unnurtured by the Catholic, Baptist, and Methodist churches in which they had been raised. They needed to mature beyond the faith they had learned in kindergarten, but they increasingly found their parents' churches too dogmatic, inflexible, or theologically simplistic.

The fact that they *had* received religious training as children is, of course, significant; it stems in part from many of these people having been reared in upper-working-class or lower-middle-class homes where religious training was the norm. But these were precisely the social strata from which so many young people in the 1960s went on to exceed their parents. They saw their fathers as weak, distant, and not particularly interested in religion, gained their primary religious sensibilities from their mothers, to whom they were closer, but as they matured came increasingly to see their mothers' religious ideas as childish, naive, and overly traditional. Many had been raised in liberal religious settings, such as Presbyterian or Episcopal churches, and some of the renegade offspring of families in more conservative settings experimented with these liberal offerings too. After a brief attraction to social justice or civil rights that left many more enamored with social change than with religion, they increasingly found too little in liberal settings to sustain their appetite for the sacred.

The spirituality they were left with was thus the result of gleanings in many scattered fields: community churches, college classes, conversations with friends, new religious movements, books, therapy sessions, television, self-help groups, to name a few. It was also a product to a very great extent of their own thinking, a characteristic deeply rooted in the confidence this upwardly mobile generation had in its abilities to make choices for itself. In contrast with those who simply compartmentalize the sacred from material life (often as a result of having taken religion for granted), this group is more likely to have consciously rebelled against something, often meaning that personalism and relativism are themselves vital features of their values, or in other cases, a new commitment to orthodoxy. For those who remained actively involved in religious congregations, spirituality was unlikely to be presented in a way that challenged any of the fundamental assumptions underlying their commitments in the economic sphere. Those who broke entirely with religious organizations became, for many purposes, mirrors of the wider culture, assimilating values from educational institutions, the mass media, and special interest groups that seldom openly defied spirituality but spared nothing in taming the spirit.

To understand the religious views of some, especially the older members of this category, the Cold War provides a convenient metaphor. By the logic that an enemy of my enemy is my friend, the Cold War wedded American religion and American capitalism together in joint opposition to godless communism. It was not so much that the churches and synagogues became active cheerleaders for the material life, just that faith and the American way seemed friendly options in view of the alternative. The ambivalent alliance that was forged in the 1950s fit well with the bland, increasingly secular orientation of the post–World War II era. Faith was easily reconciled with material pursuits because it no longer focused on a fearsome transcendent being. If anything, it connoted a kind of stability, something you could count on as a force for goodness in the world. It undergirded the American Dream, reassuring people of the goodness in themselves and in their fellow citizens. A person of faith could work more confidently, knowing there were mysterious strengths within himself or herself.

A Jewish couple in suburban Chicago provide one illustration of the secular faith that rose to prominence during the 1950s. As young professionals in that period, they distanced themselves dramatically from the old-world origins of their parents. With the Holocaust so recent in their memories, they shed all vestiges of belief that there could be a God of justice who intervened in history on behalf of his people. Still, they attended synagogue faithfully and made sure their boys learned the tradition. God became a hopeful symbol of a different kind: that rational people living under the right sort of political system could lead good, decent, and prosperous lives. "I don't believe in God," says she. "I believe in humanity, in what people can accomplish, and how they should be treated." He elaborates: "God is a representation of man's idealistic ambitions, a source of ethical strength. But a God that intervenes in human affairs, I don't believe in that at all."

Belief that God does not intervene in human affairs, for the compartmentalist, leads as we have seen to a type of material sphere in which the spiritual plays no role at all. In the present case, the logic is different. The noninterventionist God no longer stands outside of human reality; the divine now becomes subsumed within the human realm. Prayer, religious observance, faith, and the language of God itself all remain meaningful, but their meaning is redefined. "You pray," says the same man, "so you can hear yourself pray. It's a commitment to take action, but you are not praying to anybody who listens." Engaging in religious ritual serves a similar function. It is "a way of preparing yourself for conduct" rather than a commitment to a certain set of beliefs. And the idea of God becomes "an abstract notion" that stands for ethical purity, a source of order, "a force in nature that's regular and faithful."

Faith of this kind imposes some ethical structure on the world of work and money. These are neither chaotic nor evil in themselves, but subject to orderly norms of conduct. Indeed, infusing the sacred into everyday life, rather than viewing it as a metaphysical entity, forces greater attention to be paid to the ethical behavior of human beings. A person should work hard. A person should also benefit materially as the reward of hard work. Money is not to be denigrated, but enjoyed. And shared. It should be used for good purposes, such as educating one's family, paying one's bills, and contributing to respectable charities in one's community. As long as people follow the simple ethical norms they assimilated as children, and as long as they recognize the natural orderliness of all things, their spirituality will neither actively redirect nor interfere with the way they live their lives.

This orientation may also assert a rational ordering of means and ends. Quite often this means-ends logic derives from children being taught a kind of "works-righteousness" religion, namely, that doing good will get you to heaven, whereas doing bad would land you in hell. As people with these views grow older, they may abandon the tight connections between earthly behavior and otherworldly rewards, but retain the idea that religion is basically an activity that functions according to naturalistic laws.

A New York man who was raised a Catholic and who dabbled with Eastern religions in college says he still views spirituality in terms of "you get what you give," karma, and the idea that "what goes around comes around." In his view, the ethical system that individuals should follow is a similar formulaic code, whether it be the Golden Rule or the Ten Commandments, to that of the people considered in the previous section. But this code is now understood in a different way. Knowing what is right depends basically on knowing yourself, on paying attention to how you feel and what you want in life. The Golden Rule is no longer an absolute rule that tells you to treat others as yourself; instead it becomes an epistemology, a way of finding truth. You look for guidance within yourself and then let that wisdom govern your behavior toward others as well, because they probably want the same things you do. "I know how I want to be treated," explains another man, "and if I want to be treated a certain way, then I would think another person would want to be treated the same way."

The reason economic life goes on as it does is that the moral restraint provided by religious faith has ceased to be a function of positive instruction or willful obedience to a divine authority. Instead, restraint is simply built into the system of which one is a part. The system is composed of natural laws and institutionalized ethical standards. The natural laws govern behavior by providing circumstances that a person cannot avoid. How a person becomes involved in a particular line of work, for example, is understood largely as a matter of circumstances, ranging from individual talents, to educational experiences, to opportunities at a particular time in the labor market. Some individuals might continue to describe their work as a "calling," but they would mean this conjuncture of natural circumstances.

By the same token, good fortune in finding a job might be described as a "miracle," but the meaning of miracles ceases to imply supernatural intervention. Miracles are fortuitous combinations of circumstances, just as misfortunes and catastrophes are accidents—still to be expected within any conception of an orderly universe. It thus becomes possible to experience special moments of ecstasy and joy, on the one hand, or trauma and sadness, on the other hand, without these events fundamentally defying a person's sense of the natural order. Many people, when asked about miracles, for example, describe the birth of their children in these terms. Childbirth is a moment of rare joy, but understandable within the natural realm. In this view, miracles may also be part of ordinary life itself. One man, for example, says the greatest miracle in his life is simply waking up each morning.

The natural order provides moral restraint, therefore, but as a hidden hand, gloved by the fabric of institutional arrangements. Acquiring huge sums of money, for example, is not problematic because the American legal system provides institutional standards ensuring that material gain must be pursued within constraints of honesty and fairness. The rich man in Jesus's parable has no difficulty entering the kingdom of heaven because the system has required him to behave ethically. His heavenly reward, moreover, is likely to be peace in this life rather than eternal bliss in the hereafter. In this sense, ethical behavior brings its own rewards. Riches gained at the expense of others will eventually cause unhappiness—not guilt, but a lack of peace with oneself, or perhaps isolation from former friends and loved ones. Poverty, though, is not to be understood as the mirror opposite of wealth. Whereas the rich are thought to be ethically responsible problem solvers, the poor are more often understood in terms of some failing in the institutional structure. In both cases, of course, it is the institutional fabric that ultimately makes wealth and poverty understandable, but in the case of the poor, wide cracks in this edifice must be identified. Otherwise, it becomes a small step (as suggested in the last chapter) to blame the victim. If ethical behavior generally results in material success, asked a number of people, then isn't the fact of continuing poverty an indication of some shortcoming in the moral behavior of the poor?

Stewardship also makes sense within this larger worldview, less as a specific religious doctrine than as a term that can be applied to the way in which normal, responsible citizens already live. It means living one's life according to the deep ethical traditions that all responsible citizens uphold. It means, for example, "using your individual talents in a responsible way," as 40 percent of Americans define stewardship, or perhaps "remembering that God made everything" (the definition preferred by 16 percent of the public). More distinctively, however, it means upholding the natural and ethical order itself. Thus environmentalist interpretations of stewardship are not uncommon. Defying natural laws can ultimately lead to chaos for the world.[33] "You're a steward over the earth," says the Chicago woman. "I taught my kids from little on, you should put the litter in your pocket. You don't throw it on the ground. I mean, my kids always tell me their pockets are full of all this stuff they can't throw on the ground."

Stewardship may also mean donating money to good causes in the community because these causes help maintain the moral fiber of society. Political organizations, charitable foundations, and churches and synagogues become virtually interchangeable in this conception because they can all contribute positively to the ethical improvement of society. Churches, in particular, have no special advantage in dispensing goodness. "I'd rather give money to a needy family than to a church" is a statement, for example, that elicits agreement from 58 percent of the labor force. "We've inherited traditions that we're stewards of and should pass on," says the Chicago man. "For instance, I have inherited certain values from my parents and I figure I'm a steward in that sense." One of these traditions, he says, is philanthropy: "giving and endowing hospitals or universities, endowing chairs. Instead of spending it and frittering it away, building edifices that last." Because people have an ethical sense already built into them, because they believe themselves to be basically good, though, they deeply resent being asked to give money. If the situation makes it possible for them to give, and if they happen to feel like giving at that moment, they will do so. But anyone telling them what to do, especially on the basis of some absolute rule or principle, is an annoyance.

Curiously, the sense of harmonizing spiritual order within the American system appears to be as strong today and it was during the 1950s. Younger Americans may be more critical of the system itself, but their religious views often undergird a conviction that life is pretty good the way it is. If anything, the bonds of convention rest more lightly on their shoulders. Rather than religion necessitating positive commitment, it functions mainly to legitimate diversity. A person of faith should still work hard, but enjoying life becomes even more important. Dogmatism should be resisted. Faith should result in joy, inner peace, tolerance, getting along with one another, and indeed just getting along.

A fashion designer in his early thirties who lives in New York brings together the thinking of many people his age. Members of the baby-boom generation, they now have children of their own whom they take to church. They personify confidence and success in their work. They fall squarely into the vast majority who still believe in God and who still pray on a regular basis. But it takes close consideration to understand what they mean by God and prayer. In this young man's case, the Episcopal church provides him with a way to characterize his faith. He and his wife attend with their young son once or twice a month. He mostly likes the Episcopal church because it is not dogmatic.

"I tend to be quietly religious," he explains. "I'm not dogmatic. I'm not literal, as far as the Bible is concerned." To show what he means he draws a contrast between the Catholic church, as he understands it, and his own beliefs. "Roman Catholics do not believe in birth control or female ministers." He finds such narrowness objectionable. He's glad (for more reason than one) that the assistant rector at his church is a woman. "She's absolutely wonderful. A gorgeous, gorgeous woman in every possible way, which is a delight when she's up on the pulpit. At least it's something good to look at." Not wanting to sound too lustful, he also explains how nice it is that his son can see from an early age that God is an equal opportunity employer. He's also glad the Episcopal church believes in birth control. This, he notes, is consistent with his own view that people are basically in control of their own lives.

What he appreciates most about the Episcopal church is its tolerance of diversity. "You're not damned to hell just because you might be unorthodox. There really is room for differences. People can be themselves." He has no patience for the "literalists and fundamentalists." Who made them God, he wonders. It seems absurd to him that "little men in Rome" should tell other people how to behave. That's as ridiculous, he says, as some man in a turban ruling the Middle East or somebody in a kimono overseeing the sun.

Church practice for him is much like his beliefs. Take it or leave it; live and let live. He enjoys the parties and the progressive dinners most. They provide opportunities to meet people, to network. "Sort of keep the old social fabric intact." He's proud of the fact that the church has programs for everyone but doesn't expect anyone to take part in them unless they really want to. "They do have Bible studies and all that stuff. It's optional. If somebody wants it, it's there; if somebody doesn't want it, forget it." He's like 48 percent of the church members in one study who agreed that "it doesn't matter what you believe, as long as you are a good person," and like the 53 percent who said "my spirituality does not depend on being involved in a religious organization."[34]

To the skeptic, it might sound as if this is mere social-club Christianity. Does spirituality really play an important role in his life? "Oh, yes, to a great extent. It's not a dogmatic, pound the Bible sort of thing, but it's just the feeling that God is everywhere. God is watching out. God is accepting. That the right or wrong you do is within you and that's your own personal relationship to God. It's there. But there's no morality carved in marble. It's your morality. What's a sin to one man is not a sin to the next man."

The key, then, is not simply a principled decision to respect others, but a spiritual basis on which to do so. If God is everywhere, if God accepts everyone, and if morality is what each person makes of it, then the human realm is genuinely infused with spirituality. There is no supernatural realm standing over against the material world. Work and money should be closely integrated with spiritual meaning. How?

Working as a fashion designer has spiritual meaning because it involves beauty, and beauty is spiritual, basic, godlike. There need be no conflict between one's faith and this kind of work because anybody can appreciate beauty. Jews, Christians, it makes no difference. Faith is not totally disconnected from money either. The Episcopal church teaches, he says, that it is okay to have money as long as you don't flaunt it. "It's just part of their culture." The important thing is your attitude. For him, being spiritual does not require any special orientation toward his work; it just undergirds his sense of contentment. Like 75 percent of the workforce, he's sure his religious values had nothing to do with choosing his particular line of work. But like two-thirds of the workforce, he believes "God wants me to have the kind of job that will make me happy."[35]

Stewardship itself isn't a concept this man understands very well (he talks vaguely about leadership qualities). He is, in this respect, like approximately half of his generation who say the term has very little meaning at all, and not much different from another third who say it is only fairly meaningful.[36] He does, however, believe firmly in the importance of people with money helping those who don't have enough. The reason is not so much that God expects it, but that life is just this way. "We're all part of a circle." Thus it does not take special teachings or programs to encourage people to give. He recognizes there are some people who have somehow missed out on being raised correctly. They behave without regard for anyone but themselves. Most people, though, just respond to need as part of the moral intuition that lies deep inside them. "If you don't have your gauges, of course, you can't fly your plane. But if you have your gauges, then you have enough. When the occasion arises, you'll know what to do."

A person like this even leads a fairly active devotional life. Work and money are not so separate from spirituality that one never prays about them. But the purpose of prayer is to talk to yourself for a while, to get your gauges in focus, to think straight, and, above all, to calm yourself down. He is among the 51 percent of all working Americans who agree that "praying in the morning helps me have a better day at work." He adds: "I've been known to walk into a church in the middle of the day and make a dip or two. I ask for wisdom. It helps me do the right thing." Basically, then, he takes care of things himself. He doesn't ex-pect God to do anything for him. Nor does he expect anything dramatic to occur. The most vivid results of his prayers, or trying to live right, are "coincidences," moments when something special happens. He likes those moments because they make him feel better. They don't convince him that God exists as some force outside himself, but they do reassure him that things are going well.

"It's not so much an outward sign, nothing blatant, nothing cornball, no stars and stripes going up, just little things." Sometimes a good ser-mon is the bearer of these feelings. "It's just the slightest touch, and then it disappears." Or there have been times when someone showed up and helped him work out a personal problem. The feelings involved are generally quite intangible. He finds it easier to describe them by analogy: "I'm walking through a fog, and all of a sudden there's a ra-vine. And I say, 'Hell's bells, I'm going to fall in.' But a little bridge appears out of the fog. Okay, I walk over that bridge. And no sooner do I walk over it than it disappears. Whoever the person is who helps will no longer be with us. That person will just have done what they're supposed to do. After that, the bridge can evaporate. You don't need it any more. It evaporates like Brigadoon. It's very subtle, very quiet. Nothing loud. Nothing banging."

CONFLICTING WORLDS: FROM VANITY FAIR TO THEME-PARK SAFARI

In John Bunyan's classic allegory *Pilgrim's Progress*, a dramatic image of a third relationship between spirituality and material life is presented. On his way to the Celestial City, Christian endures many hardships, but none is so great as having to pass through Vanity Fair. In Bunyan's thinly disguised version of contemporary London, Christian is be-seiged by hawkers and merchants trying to sell every conceivable kind of merchandise. Refusing to be tempted (saying he wishes only to "buy the truth"), he and his companion Faithful are beaten and put in a cage; Faithful perishes; and after Christian escapes he is subjected to the be-guiling discourse of Money-Love, Save-All, and Hold-the-World.[37] The lesson is clear: believers must pass through the material world, but they will experience deep conflict there; their faith will be tested, and if they persevere, their faith will be strengthened.

A number of believers still regard the material world with the suspicion Bunyan projected from his prison cell in the seventeenth century. They worry about greed and immorality in the workplace, fear that economic business and God's business are fundamentally at odds with each other, and strive to be salt and light to a lost generation. They sense deeply that things are not right in God's New Israel; perhaps they never were, but in comparison with even a few decades ago, the moral fabric has become badly tattered and torn. If they still imagine themselves living in the Cleavers' neighborhood, they nevertheless view it as an island threatened on all sides by the immoral tempests of secularity and materialism. They are among the third of the labor force who say that "people turning away from God" is an extremely serious problem in America.[38] They desperately want to live orderly lives but lack confidence that an ethical order simply exists or that people outside their community are capable of living by it. Like Christian in Vanity Fair, they need the added strength of divine guidance, perhaps even a few special favors from the supernatural.

Compared with the other people we have considered, they have a more personalized conception of God, as one man expressed well when he asserted, "the God of the universe cares very deeply about the lives of individuals." Another distinguishing feature in many cases is that the Bible provides a specific guide for knowing what God wants individuals to do. Moreover, a religious congregation usually functions as a kind of "counterculture" in relation to the wider world of work, advertising, and consumerism. Participating actively in such a counterculture gives people a distinct identity, a core definition of themselves that they can separate from the roles they may be asked to play in the economic arena. "I'm a Christian who also happens to sell Canon copiers" is how one man puts it.

The contrast between spiritual life and the material world is accentuated by the fact that the former tends to be considered primordial, either because it stems from childhood, thus preceding the world of work, or because it was consciously chosen as an adult, often in response to some crisis involving work, career, or personal finances. A man now in his late forties, for example, tells of dropping out of church for sixteen years because of Vietnam, living in California, then one day just falling to his knees feeling that something was missing in his life, praying to God for peace, and the next day quitting his job and moving to Pennsylvania. Now he prays constantly (even at traffic lights and between meetings). He says everything about his life is programmed by God.

Some of the people in this category witness loudly to their co-workers about the need to repent and believe in Jesus. A few (4 percent, judging from the survey) participate in religious groups that meet in the workplace. Others read their Bibles and pray every day for God's protection as they go forward to meet the challenges of the jungle. Their experience is a little like Christian's in Vanity Fair. But it is more like taking a safari through the jungle at Disneyland.

On the surface, the theme park seems dangerous, chaotic. But the believer knows how to avoid the worst dangers. Not rocking the boat is the first rule of caution. It makes sense to stick with one's friends and to stay close to the guided path. In the midst of seeming chaos, one can have a pretty good time, especially if one has a plan. Spirituality ultimately points to something that has been domesticated. Rather than the divine symbolizing some raw, turbulent, wild, mysterious force in life, it is now the safest haven in an otherwise chaotic world. "I'm not big into miracles," says a Presbyterian man who considers his faith central to his life. "I'm really not. But my confidence and my equanimity throughout life has been a basic belief that I'm an individual whom God cares about and therefore I'm immune from the slings and arrows of outrageous misfortune (or fortune) and from the tremendous susceptibility people have to other people's opinions. I think a Christian can be free of that."

The way to have a plan is expressed well in the frequently mentioned phrase "seeking the mind of God." In most cases this is a process involving some understanding of the Bible and faithful attendance at church services featuring sermon expositions of the Bible. It is, in this respect, rooted in fairly widespread assumptions and institutional practices in the United States; for example, 69 percent of the labor force agrees that "the Bible is a detailed book of rules that Christians should try to follow"; a third participate in religious services every week; and of these, 43 percent say they have heard a sermon within the past year about "personal finances."[39]

The "mind of God" is assumed to be rational, a higher wisdom than anything present in the human world. It is composed essentially of principles that can be found by "searching the scriptures." These principles are absolute, universal truths, but how they are applied is generally considered a matter of individual soul-searching. This process mainly involves hunches or intuitions that the individual receives by paying attention to his or her feelings, following the counsel of trusted others, and receiving guidance from external circumstances. That there is a specific "will of God" for an individual in a particular situation is beyond doubt. That this "will" may lead a person to behave differently from co-workers or the proverbial man in the street is also beyond question. But any radical departure from social conventions is minimized because believers generally do not hear the voice of God directly or blindly follow the advice they receive from the Bible. They formulate a plan of action for themselves through a combination of reason, feelings, situational promptings, and social interaction.

A few brief quotes will illustrate how individuals from a wide variety of backgrounds express remarkably similar notions about bringing the sacred into a direct relation with their material lives. A Baptist man says of the Bible, "I seek to find out what principles are there and apply them, not rigidly, but in terms of human situations." A Catholic woman emphasizes that guidance comes to her from God, but she also notes the need to render her own interpretations: "God doesn't just say, 'Oh, lo and behold, here's a new car. It's parked in front of your house.' It doesn't happen like that. I've prayed to God long enough to know that he just guides you. A lot of times there aren't signs, you have to make a decision on your own, but I think he guides you in making a decision." An Episcopalian schoolteacher also seeks divine guidance on a moment-to-moment basis. She says she mostly just "wails at God" and every once in a while a "small miracle" happens to one of the children. A Nashville man provides perhaps the clearest statement of how divine guidance helps to make life orderly, reasonable, a life that can be lived confidently. He says, "I believe that as I pray for wisdom and as I maintain a relationship with God through his Word, He directs my life. Not in any overt, obvious 'voice from Heaven' way, but, yeah, this is the wise thing to do. This makes a lot of sense. This is consistent with what scripture says. If there was a decision I was making where it became obvious that I would have to disobey something in God's Word, well, that would be clear guidance, you know. If I'm consulting God, then I believe He's working in me to do the right thing."

In each of these cases, the spiritual realm is differentiated sufficiently from material life that the two can sometimes come into conflict. The Catholic woman, for example, describes where she works as an alien place where "all they do is conduct business and manufacture things." Her faith does not prevent her from working there; instead, it empowers her to make the best of a bad situation. She does her work responsibly, but instead of becoming wrapped up in it, she redefines the workplace as a mission field, not to proselytize her co-workers, but just to "get into their lives" and show them some kindness. The spiritual and the material are thus differentiated in a way that prevents them simply from being kept apart. Instead, there is a running dialogue between the two, sometimes literally. The Episcopal woman, for instance, admits that anytime she has some money to spend on herself she asks herself, "What would God do in this situation?" Or sometimes she hears something inside her (which she assumes is God) tell her to spend her money or to invest it.

The reason believers like this resemble the tourists at Disneyland more than the pilgrim in Vanity Fair is that the guidance they receive from the spiritual realm consists mainly of easily digestable formulas and results in feelings of reassurance. Instead of being mocked, ridiculed, thrown in jail, and beaten for clinging doggedly to the truth, believers walk through the theme park with their own prerecorded guided tours, having their experience enriched by virtue of knowing what to do and where to go at any given moment.

These are believers who often feel strongly that their religious values have influenced their choice of a career, perhaps they even feel God has called them to their work, but their idea of a calling is rather easy to live with, and it helps them feel better about their work, while conflicting little with the rest of their lives. In the labor force as a whole, 30 percent agree with the statement "I feel God has called me to the particular line of work I am in." But to many of these people, this means simply that "God wants us to do something with our lives that will be useful to the world" (43 percent), and to many of the remainder it means "God wants us to find work that best suits our individual talents" (29 percent).[40] Those who have experienced a calling are more likely than others to value their work, and to express satisfaction with it, but are also *no less likely* to value making a lot of money, living a comfortable life, and spending time on hobbies and leisure activities.[41]

The image of a "guided tour" is not entirely fanciful. Religious periodicals and popular religious books tell readers how to live their lives much in the same way that advice columnists do. "How can I find the right job?" asks the puzzled reader. Apply these three principles: Ask what needs do I see in my world, ask what gifts and abilities do I have to meet these needs, and ask which particular combination of needs and gifts do I feel compelled to pursue. Or for the person having trouble on the job because of disagreeable co-workers, follow such principles as these: remember that kind words will help, pray for that person, guard yourself against becoming bitter, don't be afraid to speak up if you need to, and make sure you don't have the same faults. What sounds like basic common sense is wrapped in religious phraseology that gives it added moral authority. These principles can be seen in the life of Jesus, or come from talking with mature Christians, and each one is backed up with references to specific verses in the Bible.

Like those who scarcely distinguish the spiritual from the material at all, the followers of such advice generally do not believe God will tell them exactly what to do; they mostly derive peace of mind. But this feeling is more acute and situationally specific. Rather than it being a general, background sense of well-being, it provides affirmations for specific decisions. These affirmations are especially important for believers who feel they must make the "right" choice in each situation but lack confidence in their own abilities to do what is right and feel overwhelmed by the uncertainties they experience. Consulting God becomes a way to do what is right by following the right set of procedures. Exactly what choice to make may still be unclear, but a person feels better knowing that prayer and Bible reading have been part of the process. Decisions made simply from intuition can result in guilt, but intuition labeled "God's leading" become acceptable.

"It's real important to me to read the Bible daily," explains a nurse in her mid-twenties. "I feel if I get away from it, there's a sense of guilt that comes up inside me that feels like I'm getting farther and farther from God." Recently, she and her husband bought a new car, and prayer was an important part of the process: "We make decisions so emotionally that we needed something to feel like we weren't just doing it because we liked the car. We were doing it, too, because it was something that was a smart decision and something we needed. And I needed to feel a peace about it, not guilt. I needed to feel that we were making a responsible decision." This was just one example. In general, she feels she needs to rely heavily on the Bible to tell her not only how to behave, but who she is. "I think I have a real loose sense of what my identity is, and when I open up the Bible I can read and get an idea of what kind of person God would want me to be. And I believe that it's in me to be all of what he asks, but you just need to tap into it and realize it." The Bible is especially helpful to her at work because she feels different from her co-workers, most of whom she considers atheists. She prays a lot just to get through the day. "If I didn't have my faith, I don't know how I could work here." Mostly, she prays for patience and understanding. Having these makes hard work easier.

For people like this, the enrichment from spirituality comes from knowing more clearly where one is headed. For many it involves added motivation. Stewardship, for example, is often considered to be a kind of generic responsibility that an individual has to work hard and to be responsible. If a person has nothing but talents that are gifts from God, then proper stewardship requires using these talents wisely. Those who say the idea of stewardship is very meaningful to them, for example, are much more likely than other individuals to agree that "people who work hard are more pleasing to God than people who are lazy." Wanting wealth and expensive material possesions per se runs contrary to this view of spirituality. Valuing the idea of stewardship, for instance, is also positively associated with agreeing that "riches get in the way of our truly knowing God." It is better to live within one's means, being content, for instance, with one's Honda, rather than wanting a Porsche. It may even be better to be a low- or middle-income person rather than a rich person because the latter becomes too self-sufficient and forgets God. Valuing stewardship is also associated, for example, with agreeing that "the poor are closer to God than rich people are."[42]

Believing that spirituality and materialism constitute conflicting worlds may thus be a factor in curbing some of the worst excesses of the quest for money and possessions. To a certain degree, it provides arguments about moral responsibility that help to limit material wants. And yet these arguments alone are often insufficient to make any discernible difference in behavior itself. For example, having experienced a calling and regarding stewardship as a very meaningful idea seem to make no difference to the likelihood of actually working in a high-paying job or admiring people who make a lot of money or having control over one's own expenditures. Despite the antimaterialistic sentiments that prevail among these people, moreover, a quarter say having a beautiful home, a new car, and other nice things is very important to them, a third say this about having a high-paying job, and three-quarters say having money gives them a good feeling about themselves.

If there is an inherent tension between the spiritual and the material, this perspective can also turn the two into partners without extreme difficulty. Rather than having to sell all one's possessions to lead a life of purity, the pilgrim can struggle effectively for career success and even material gain, turning spiritual wisdom into an advantage. Those who take this view generally have religious convictions quite dissimilar from the evangelicals and fundamentalists who take it upon themselves to resist the material forces of evil. Yet there are similarities as well. Both have come to emphasize mind over matter to a high degree. What a person *thinks* is the key to victory, whether that be contentment in poverty or the attainment of prosperity. In both cases, the material world is wild and unruly, the spiritual realm more dependable. By following a plan involving some special knowledge of the sacred, it becomes possible to lead a productive life in the economic sphere as well.

Reared by a devout aunt who took him faithfully to the African Methodist Episcopal church, Jim Washington, a Philadelphia housepainter, still believes firmly in the existence of a Supreme Being even though he's gotten too busy lately to attend church. He's talked to people from all different backgrounds to find out what they believe—Catholics, Buddhists, Muslims, he's talked to them all. His conclusion is that everything is sustained and protected by a divine energy "that's closer to you than your own jugular vein." The problem, though, is that most religions spend all their time on definitions. In his view, "defining your life is not half as important as living it." But living your life takes some know-how, and this is how faith comes to influence your work and money.

"If you want to get to California," Jim explains, "you too must make the trip." He pauses for a moment to savor the metaphor. It's one he's used before. "You see, you can't get there just by lighting a bunch of incense and sitting around. You have to start walking. And if you know how to walk, you'll eventually get there. You can't keep taking two steps forward and two steps backward, though. You've gotta keep going forward." This, he says, is what "livin' your life" is all about.

Having a lot of money is like walking to California. You have to know how to get there. Faith can help. God didn't intend for people to be poor. It's beautiful to be rich. There's a book called *The Magic of Believing*. Jim's been reading it. He says it shows him how to be rich by thinking right and developing pictures in your head. Part of the deal, too, is tithing. He hasn't tried it yet. But he's heard you'll get back ten times the amount you give. He thinks it might be worth trying.

Jim's faith also helps him out at work. "You'll get along better at work if you understand things," he says. "Like these Satanic forces. If you're going around being all negative, they'll attack you. So you'd better be positive about things. If you look for the divine, you'll find it."

Religion and the faith it stands for are too uncontrollable, too powerful to be bracketed off from work and money in the life of a person like Jim Washington. Spirituality can produce unexpected wonders. But they can also be harnessed. This is why living a life of faith is like walking to California. It may be possible to get there simply by the magic of believing; it is more likely if a person follows a plan. Jim admires the Puritans, for example, because they had a plan and stuck with it. "If you're going to grow," he says, "you need a spiritual path to follow. The more clear-cut it is, the better you can see how to achieve."

Unlike so many middle-class Americans, Jim Washington is not talking metaphorically when he says he can achieve. In his work he has tried consistently to follow a spiritual path. He believes his innermost being is spiritual. It is this essence in him that strives for perfection. There is a self inside him wanting to be fulfilled, always striving for a higher worth. It is this attitude that makes him competitive, that gives him endurance, that focuses his attention on his gifts. He says he could out-compete "any Japanese" in what he does. "It's because I have the spirit. I merge into everything I do." This attitude helps him especially when he feels sick some mornings and doesn't want to go to work. "But I feel I have a duty in the world and my spiritual life helps me walk in the world."

Not surprisingly, prayer is an active ingredient of Jim Washington's life. In fact, one reason he enjoys being a painter is that he can pray constantly. He prays for peace of mind. He meditates, sometimes on a verse or a poem. Sometimes he keeps saying something over and over just to plant it more firmly in his mind so he won't forget it. He thanks God for giving him health and strength especially. He knows these are gifts God gives him so he can get his work done. He also knows more directly that God cares for him. Twice in his life he's almost drowned and twice God has rescued him. Twice he's also been able to rescue someone else. There was just a quiet voice prompting him to know that danger was abroad. He's sure there are angels monitoring his life.

The Power of the Sacred

If spirituality has adapted so deeply to American culture that it seldom interferes very dramatically with the work people do and the way they spend their money, it nevertheless does make some difference. It is not simply irrelevant to the harsh realities of economic life, as so many corporate analysts, journalists, and social scientists have come to believe. Nearly half the adult population takes time away from their leisure activities each weekend to attend religious services. At least a quarter spend one of their weekday evenings at a Bible study or prayer fellowship. Charitable giving to religious organizations adds up to billions of dollars each year. Statistical studies show that religious commitment contributes more to most people's sense of well-being than either their work or their personal finances. It is not uncommon, as we have seen, even for people who separate God radically from the rest of their lives to pray or to experience miracles. What, then, does the sacred *do* in relation to the material realm, even in limited ways?

One inescapable conclusion is that the sacred helps people keep order in their lives. It gives them a perspective, an alternative framework from which to derive psychological peace, confidence, and reassurance, or that simply reminds them of the truths they learned in childhood or the security they received from their parents. A Madison Avenue executive, for example, says she attends church every week because it helps her "get back on the path"; it's a form of "attitude adjustment" after she has strayed during the week. A Chicago attorney regards his faith in a similar way, saying it reminds him to be caring and to treat people fairly as he practices law. Fundamentally it helps him through the day: "When I'm walking to work in the morning, occasionally I try to think and keep things in perspective and remind myself that all the chaos that's going to take place that day is secondary to what is important."

Believing the world is orderly has important consequences for the way people lead their lives. If hard work no longer seems to pay off, when money has become private and subjective, and when family and community moorings have been destabilized, there has to be some reason to go through the day thinking that things still matter and that what one does makes a difference. Contemporary piety no longer gives most people meaning by placing them within earshot of a fatherly being who listens to their problems and pats them on the back after a good day's work. God is now more distant for most people—or in other cases remains close but operates mainly at the level of intuition. The divine nevertheless sacralizes daily life by grounding parts of it at such an elemental level that it need not be questioned. For many of the people who separate the spiritual from the material almost totally, there is still a tacit assumption that God supplies them with certain talents at birth. Their own capacity to make choices is thus accorded legitimacy. Many of the people who blend the spiritual and the material tacitly assume that their circumstances embody a divine presence or energy. Paying attention to these circumstances as they make decisions is thus a sensible thing to do. As situations change, the individual must take cues from these changes, functioning always as a problem solver, knowing that good decisions will not always lead to desirable outcomes, but believing that the problem-solving process is itself worthwhile. Those who see conflict between the spiritual and the material generally believe themselves to be the bearers of a higher wisdom, a special plan, greater confidence, or an inner calm that others in the same situations do not possess. They are thus strengthened to carry on with their daily responsibilities.

In interview after interview, this comforting sense of order emerged as people talked about their religious beliefs. What is also dramatically evident, however, is that this sense of order grows as much from early childhood experiences in the family as it does from formal religious instruction. Believing that one's efforts will have predictable consequences (and therefore are worth engaging in) is part of what philosopher Alasdair MacIntyre has called a social practice, not simply an abstract system of ideas.[43] A practice in MacIntyre's terms consists of moral expectations that govern behavior within some concrete social grouping, such as the family. Standards of evaluation are vital elements of any social practice, and these standards are intrinsic to the performances and rewards associated with behavior in those settings. They do not depend on money or on being vested with power and prestige in some larger setting. A child plays soccer on a neighborhood team, for example, not in hopes of becoming rich and famous someday, but for the experience of being part of a team and for the occasional joy of winning; virtues such as self-discipline, dedication, and courage are intrinsic to this practice itself. Similarly, the family encourages virtues such as hard work, honesty, and family loyalty, not so much as a way of making money, but as an orderly way of living in peace and harmony with others.

The reason family experiences come up so often in conjunction with religious teachings is that these teachings tend to be associated with childhood experiences; indeed, are symbolized and concretized by stories people remember from their early years. Generally they do not discuss what they read in the Bible or learned in Sunday school, but some slogan their mother repeated to them over and over again, some vivid encounter with a grandparent, or some behavior they observed in their parents. The religious teaching is important primarily because it summarizes in language, in an easily repeatable formula, what the lesson drawn from those experiences was. The power of the sacred is thus linked closely with the capacity of the family to undergird it. As the rules governing family life and child rearing have increasingly come into question, this capacity of course is seriously weakened. For an increasing number, the power of the sacred has also diminished, and for others it has been rediscovered only with difficulty, often in small support groups such as prayer fellowships or twelve-step groups that serve as surrogate families. It is in these settings that new rules can be learned, creating a new "practice" in which an orderly relation between moral conduct and its consequences seems to prevail.

Uncertainty in Zion

Despite their continuing capacity to impose some moral understandings on the economic life, religious institutions at the end of the twentieth century speak in uncertain voices that, on the whole, do more to raise questions about *how* to relate ultimate values to economic behavior than actually to make these connections. The optimistic religious teachings from earlier in the century that so often linked American capitalism with the coming of God's kingdom itself have long since given way to more sober assessments. After World War II, and increasingly after the 1960s, religious leaders recognized that poverty in our own country and abroad was not being dealt with adequately, that the American Dream had been rife with racism and sexism, and that too often their own organizations had comforted their middle-class members rather than challenging them to think hard about justice and mercy. For a time, Christian-Marxist dialogue was encouraged in hopes of finding common ground with the Soviet bloc and discovering a kind of socialism that Christians could embrace. Having given up on the idea of a literal devil, and having turned evil into a category of neurosis, religious leaders focused increasing attention on institutions as a way of healing the nation's problems. Political solutions came to be favored over personal ones, first in liberal circles, and then increasingly in conservative circles as well. Having devoted large shares of their attention to political struggles for more than a decade, though, many prominent religious leaders are asserting that the quieter, more gradual methods of instructing children and adults in spiritual and moral values may be more effective in the long run.

The difficulty is that few religious leaders seem to have a clear sense anymore of what those values are or how best to communicate them. The leaders who have the clearest vision tend to be Protestant fundamentalists and evangelicals, many of whom have been able to launch large mega-churches, television ministries, or publishing enterprises as a result of their clarity about fundamental values. Whether a value system that excludes all but the born again, that rails against liberal Christians as if they were devil worshipers, that excludes Jews (not to mention Muslims), that has been slow in coming to terms with racial and gender equality, and that attempts to impose its morality on the nation through legislation can be effective in healing the ethical malaise in American society is, however, doubtful at best. Liberal religious leaders seem to be in an even more precarious position as a result of declining memberships, a shrinking financial base from which to launch their programs, and deep uncertainty about what exactly religious belief should be in the contemporary world.

While there is much debate in religious organizations about programs and values, the veritable sea of words that has been produced continues to say little about the economic commitments of individuals. To be sure, "how to" books abound, providing commonsense tips for church members on how to be happy at work, choose a meaningful career, or organize the family budget. Every local congregation exposes its members periodically to stewardship campaigns. Yet few of these efforts take into account the ways in which the American public actually understands its economic commitments, and few make a meaningful attempt to stimulate sustained thinking about the actual connections between spirituality and material life. Many of them focus so narrowly on raising money for the church's programs that members feel their spiritual mentors are becoming obsessed with materialism itself. Others take an overtly antimaterialistic stance and yet practice what one clergyman described as a "demonic worship of orderliness" that tacitly reinforces materialism and may be worse than a doctrine of acquisitiveness itself. It is perhaps a hopeful sign that the problem itself is now being recognized in a variety of quarters and that some significant theological attention is being paid to issues of work and money. Whether these efforts can spread widely into popular thinking, especially in opposition to the massive influences of the workplace and the marketplace, is a more perplexing question.

PART FOUR

THE LANGUAGES OF MORAL DISCOURSE

Chapter Twelve

MATERIALISM AND MORAL RESTRAINT:
THE ROLE OF ASCETIC
AND EXPRESSIVE VALUES

I BEGAN this inquiry by asking whether economic commitments in contemporary society can be effectively curbed by subjecting them to moral restraint. The tendency for these commitments to expand has been widely taken for granted in the theoretical literature. The empirical evidence I presented in chapter 1 demonstrated that most Americans perceive this expansion to be part of their own experience. They feel that they are working harder than they were a few years ago, and by many indications they are in fact working longer hours. Most say they have more money than ever before, but a majority also say they feel financially strapped, they worry about being able to pay their bills, and they wish they had more money than they do. Consumer expenditures do in fact indicate high levels of personal spending, and credit-card debt suggests that an increasing share of these expenditures is in excess of family incomes. Reported levels of job-related stress, burnout, money-related anxiety, and complaints about inadequate time for family and self also point to a widespread impression that economic commitments have expanded to an undersirable point.

Yet it is also true that most Americans regard their work as one of the most meaningful aspects of their lives and, compared with previous generations, have more discretionary income to spend, live more comfortably, do less physically demanding work, and perhaps even enjoy greater amounts of leisure time, especially if retirement years are counted. These observations, taken together, have led me to suggest that the problem facing many Americans today cannot be understood simply in terms of being overworked and underpaid. Instead, we need to consider the possibility that something has been happening to our cultural assumptions to make it more difficult for many of us to piece together our various commitments in a way that seems satisfactory. I invoked the widely referenced metaphor of the American Dream to talk about these cultural assumptions, suggesting that it may have provided more of an ordering mechanism for understanding the complex relationships among work, money, and other personal commitments in the past than it does at present.

By surveying social thought in the early nineteenth century, prior to the advent of large-scale industrial capitalism, and prior to the development of modern economic perspectives, I identified two perspectives—ascetic moralism and expressive moralism—that actually attempted to situate economic commitments in a moral framework and thereby imposed moral restraints on these commitments. I also suggested reasons, however, why these moral frameworks have eroded over the past century and a half. Returning to the present, we were thus confronted with two questions requiring empirical examination: why is it that economic commitments occupy so much of our personal attention, are regarded as deeply meaningful, and yet seem somehow to fall short of our expectations; and how do the institutions that have traditionally served as sources of values external to economic commitments—namely, family, community, and religion—function in that capacity at present, not only as sources of restraint, but also as arenas subject to changes that may be raising more questions about values than they can easily answer?

The question of why work and money are personally engaging yet problematic has led us to consider the ways in which each is culturally understood. I argued that work, while engaged in most of the time as a means of earning money, cannot be understood in these terms as well as it can by recognizing that most people work in order to give a culturally legitimate account of themselves, only one possibility of which is to say they are attempting to earn money. The need to provide legitimate accounts of ourselves immediately places work back in the context in which moral considerations and values apply. It is in fact these moral considerations that render work meaningful for most people and encourage them to remain committed, if not overcommitted, to their work. Yet close consideration of the accounts people give of their work reveals that these accounts are taken-for-granted scripts supplied by the workplace itself (or by schooling experiences), reinforced by certain power arrangements in the workplace, yet at odds with many of the experienced realities of contemporary work, and generally posed within compartmentalized frameworks that do not connect easily with other values, aspirations, or personal commitments. Work is thus meaningful, and for the most part satisfying, but difficult to incorporate into a broader understanding of what life is all about.

Money is problematic for a somewhat different set of reasons. Although it is the subject of much discussion in public life, the more objective monetary realities known at this level are largely separate from the subjective experience of money that characterizes most individuals' private lives. This disjuncture is reinforced by a widely taken-for-granted taboo against discussing the intimate details of one's personal finances with friends, family, neighbors, or co-workers. At the same time, money remains terribly important to most individuals, who also believe it is their responsibility to use it wisely, and indeed to control their thoughts and feelings about it. Money is thus a subject of considerable anxiety, and this anxiety has relatively little to do with how much or how little money an individual actually has.

Consumer expenditures are also problematic. They are so in part because of the uncertainties that surround money itself. In addition, the increasing disjuncture between work and money increasingly severs the latter from one of its traditional underpinnings, allowing it to float more freely, as it were, and to be understood more exclusively in relation to consumption than production. Consumer needs expand for a wide variety of reasons, including age-graded expectations built into the life cycle as well as the appeals of advertising. Like work, these needs are legitimated by personal accounts supplied and manipulated by the marketplace itself (such as ideas about brand loyalty, comparison shopping, and dealer service)—accounts that often exclude paying explicit attention to other personal values. Getting and spending are seldom restrained by rational budgeting procedures but are often subjected to the implicit restraints offered by rituals and symbolic boundaries. Consumer rituals suggest a range of comfort that is appropriate to maintain, and symbolic boundaries raise questions about the spread of consumerism into family relationships and other zones of personal life that have been protected from the market. These rituals and boundaries help to curb the spread of consumer commitments but again set up fences without providing explicit understandings of the nature of these barriers.

Traditional understandings of the American Dream have always tried to integrate issues of work and money with ideas about the role of family and community, and to some extent religion as well. In most instances, work and money have been regarded as means of attaining a better life for one's family, but the pursuit of these activities has also been restrained by understandings about family loyalty, community responsibility, and the priority of the spiritual over the material. I have presented evidence on the ways in which Americans today understand their family, community, and religious obligations in order to see if these understandings still pose moral restrictions on economic life. What I have suggested in simplest terms is that each continues to do so, but that changing social and cultural conditions have also made the relationships between these institutions and economic commitments more problematic.

The relationship between family and economic life has clearly become problematic as a result of dual-career households and, more generally, the transition away from a gendered division of labor between breadwinning and moral pedagogy. Working men and women find it increasingly difficult to reconcile not only the time demands of their work and their families but the priorities and assumptions each entails.

Community involvement at one time was also more readily reconciled with economic commitments because helping one's neighbor, or working to improve one's community, could be connected directly with one's economic self-interest. The breakdown of such communities has made it necessary for concerned individuals to make greater efforts to set aside their own careers and financial concerns and to balance these with voluntaristic efforts. In the process questions have arisen more forcefully about what the appropriate balance is, and indeed about motives and values underpinning community service more generally.

Religious commitments continue to undergird symbolic distinctions between the spiritual and the material. Yet two of the three dominant orientations we have considered—the tendency to compartmentalize and to trivialize the relationship—fail to supply ways of thinking very clearly about how the spiritual may actually restrain material commitments, while the third orientation perceives more conflict between the two but often provides comfort and personal security in the face of economic chaos more than it does a clear sense of moral restraint.

Family, community, and religion, therefore, all continue to serve as sources of human values that are set apart to some extent from economic or market considerations. But in each case we can also see most clearly that social changes have taken place that encourage people to raise questions about their values rather than to supply ready answers about how to integrate the various parts of their lives.

In trying to flesh out the foregoing relationships, I have found it necessary to postpone explicit consideration of moral reasoning itself. Clearly that is the remaining piece of the puzzle that we must now try to understand. I suggested in chapter 3 that nineteenth-century thought had been fundamentally ambivalent about work, money, and other aspects of the material life, often articulating this ambivalence by posing moral arguments about how these commitments should be limited. I traced some of the main arguments of the ascetic moralists and the expressive moralists, largely to demonstrate that there are good reasons to search once again for moral frameworks in which to understand better—and perhaps with which to restrain—our economic commitments.

I also had another reason for introducing the ascetic and expressive moralists' arguments: those are part of our cultural heritage, and, while often neglected in formal discussions of economic life, they probably still have some resonance in popular understandings of work and money. Put differently, we may find residues of these earlier arguments, perhaps modified by late-twentieth-century cultural orientations, that still guide and restrain economic commitments.

At numerous points the foregoing discussions have in fact hinted at some of these connections, although it was not possible at the time to pursue these various clues to their full implications. For example, accounts of work sometimes emphasize personal fulfillment or service to humanity in ways that would perhaps be recognizable to the ascetic moralists, and these accounts also hint at expressive arguments when they emphasize the demons within. Similarly, our considerations of the ways in which men and women try to reconcile their work and family commitments can in some ways be taken as an application of ascetic and expressive logic, the compartmentalization evident in men's lives being more reminiscent of ascetic orientations, and the compositional strategies of working women running somewhat more parallel to expressivist orientations. Rather than reviewing these various hints from the foregoing chapters, however, it will be more useful to turn now to an explicit consideration of moral reasoning.

PAM JONES

It will make the analytic sections of this chapter clearer if we begin with a concrete example. Many of the individuals we have met in previous chapters employ discourse about personal goals and values at various points in discussing their lives. Indeed, virtually everyone feels strongly that values are important, and most people regard themselves as ethical, morally guided individuals. Yet the main point of what we have considered in previous chapters is that these same people have difficulty bringing those values into their discussions of work, money, and material goods. They also recognize that family, community, and spirituality, as alternative sources of values, have given them trouble, causing them to think about priorities but not necessarily providing good ways of resolving these issues. This was as true of thoughtful or articulate people as it was of those who spent less time reflecting on their lives. It will thus be helpful to consider what a person who has been more successful in utilizing moral discourse might sound like. There were in fact a few among those we interviewed. None of them felt that they had been able to put their lives together in a way that satisfied themselves completely, let alone that would serve as a model for others.[1] Nevertheless, an example is useful, and in choosing one, I am drawn again to Pam Jones, the software engineer whom I introduced in chapter 7 as someone with alternative views of consumerism.

Pam Jones has been able to keep her work and money in perspective by relating them to a broader set of moral values and commitments. Reared in Puerto Rico by Anglo parents, she has always prided herself on being bicultural and has wanted to work in a setting where she can put the several languages she speaks (Spanish, English, and French) and her knowledge of several Carribean and Central American countries to use. Her father was a doctor, a deeply religious man, whose desire to help people led him to practice in Puerto Rico. Pam was sufficiently influenced by him to serve as a volunteer in various clinics during her college years. For the past eight years she has been developing applied semiconductor technology for a large communications firm in Illinois. She likes the money she makes and has become absorbed with the technical aspects of her work. It would seem that Pam, like so many other Americans, has been seduced away from her youthful ideals by the comforts of a secure life in the suburbs. Yet if we listen to the story

Pam tells about her life, we soon realize that she is better able than most to frame her economic behavior in a language of moral restraint.

When asked about the fulfillment she receives from her work, Pam mentions the satisfaction associated with the technical aspects of her job but quickly turns to what are often termed transferrable skills. "I'm learning about managing things and negotiating. I'm learning about managing my own time and being productive and making sure that I do what needs to be done rather than just pretending it doesn't have to be done and then have it bite me in the back later. So I think I'm learning some good self-discipline skills." These are skills that attach to her person rather than to her job alone. In her view, they make her a more useful, responsible person. They are traits she can apply in her church work, in her home life, and in other jobs she may take in the future. They are intrinsic to her work, unlike money or prestige. They also connect her to the values her parents taught her. Both parents emphasized taking responsibilities to other people and to the community very seriously. As a young adult, Pam feels she is still learning how to realize those values. "I've grown a lot," she says. "I feel like I could go into some other, totally different environment, like teaching or managing a school system or even working in hospital administration, and apply some of the basic things I've learned. It's not like something you learn in school, it's maturity that comes from being out in the world and experiencing real-life situations."

She is also keenly aware of the ways in which her work does *not* help her to realize some of her deepest values. Although she feels good about the people her work benefits, she worries that these are not the truly needy people she learned to care for as a volunteer in college. "As a company, we are developing features for the rich, for businesses, rather than getting plain old telephone service to more of the world community. I would feel much better ethically about doing that, about working in Bolivia, for example, so some mother could call the hospital when her child has swallowed poison. Three-way calling is nice but it's not necessary. I want to work on the bread for everybody instead of cake for some."

These are values she learned from her parents, who always cultivated a simple lifestyle in order to be of service to those less fortunate than themselves. She still hears these values expressed at her church. She does not hear them very much among her co-workers. Yet she recognizes that her current job can be a stepping stone for something more fulfilling in the future, even within the same company. "My husband and I have talked about going overseas," she remarks. Her company often has new contracts in developing areas, and those opportunities attract her. "I'm interested in becoming involved in on-site work, such as installation." Having language skills, she feels she would be prepared for such a position. She also values these skills enough that she wants to shift into something where she can use them. "I mean, if I don't start using them pretty soon, I feel like I'm going to lose them forever."

So Pam Jones is keeping her horizons open. Remembering some of the other values she holds dear allows her to do so. In the meantime, she still finds meaning on a daily basis at her job. She is not alienated from it, as she might be if she saw no connection between it and the rest of her life. At the same time, she sees it clearly as a means toward realizing other values, rather than as an end in itself. She is especially careful to view the money she makes in this way. "It does bring in good money," she admits. But that is important to her mainly because it allows her husband to work at a job he really enjoys, rather than struggling "to earn top dollar."[2] Between the two of them, they can pay their bills and still have time left over to serve in their church and plan for the future. As we saw in chapter 7, she and her husband restrain their consumer expenditures enough to help refugees, and they protest military expenditures by refusing to pay part of their taxes.

But having a broader language in which to understand work and money does not exempt people like Pam Jones from experiencing pressure on a day-to-day basis. Wanting more out of life than just a good-paying job, Pam often struggles with setting her priorities. "There's not enough time to do everything I want to do," she complains. "I'm really trying hard to learn how to say no to things." And that sometimes means saying no to things she values even more than her work. "Like right now, I feel like I've said yes to too much stuff at the church. I've got too many responsibilities there. I don't have enough time to play, to do things around the house, to be with my husband, read, and work on my own spiritual growth." Rather than simply capitulate to the demands of the moment, though, Pam is able to allocate time and energy to these various interests. She is able to because her understanding of herself keeps all of them in view as explicit values. As she turns her attention to each one, spending time at her church, going for a walk with her husband, and getting together with other women in her community, her values are also reinforced.

As I say, I do not wish to idolize this one example. It nevertheless brings out some themes that are not evident in many people's accounts of their lives. In the following pages I want to look more closely at such themes, not only in the moralist language that this example suggests but in another kind as well. I shall discuss the contemporary manifestations of each, describe how they differ from each other, and suggest how they do in fact pose restraint on economic commitments. To round out the discussion, I shall also try to indicate the limitations and pathologies to which each of these orientations is subject.[3]

Moral Discourse in Two Keys

The two languages of moral discourse on which I wish to focus can be thought of as descendants of the ascetic and expressive moralism of the nineteenth century, and for this reason I shall use these labels in describing them.[4] I shall argue that many of the assumptions of the earlier moralists remain intact and still provide relatively distinct views of how that which is fundamentally good in life is to be known and pursued.[5] At the same time, both must be situated within a late-twentieth-century context in order to grasp their contemporary meanings and implications.

It is difficult to say with certainty how common these two languages are in contemporary society. Were they not only widely shared but also powerful in their effects, I doubt that the accounts of work, money, and material possessions that we have considered in previous chapters would appear quite as they do. Yet these languages would clearly be of less interest if they were common only to a few scattered thinkers, sages, or keepers of tradition. Indeed, by some indications a considerable share of the American public seems to have at least some grasp of the importance of moral absolutes, on the one hand, or of the value of feelings and of inner conviction as moral guides, on the other hand. For example, nine people out of ten agree that "certain values must be regarded as absolutes," and a majority agree *strongly* with this statement. Eight out of ten say they agree with the statement "I believe in following a strict set of moral rules" (with half of these agreeing strongly).

The statement "getting in touch with your inner feelings is more important than doing well in your job" evokes agreement from two people in three. And about four in ten agree that "working on my emotional life takes priority over other things," with an equal number agreeing that "exploring my inner self is one of my main priorities."[6] Yet when consistency across a variety of questions is invoked as a criterion, relatively few Americans hold firmly to such indicators of ascetic or expressive moralism.[7]

What exactly to make of these orientations on a large scale is, of course, difficult to determine. I shall, however, be more interested in considering the nuances of these languages and how they are practiced than in estimating how widely shared they may be. Even to say this much, though, is to get ahead of the story. We must retreat a few steps and, at the risk of repeating some of what was said in chapter 3, discuss the basic assumptions of ascetic moralism and expressive moralism, and then suggest why both remain relevant as alternatives to the logic that normally governs economic affairs.

For its nineteenth-century proponents, ascetic moralism connoted a commitment to absolute values from which a fixed set of morally prescribed rules of behavior could be derived. In popular usage, such rules were probably articulated in simple dictums, such as "waste is wrong," "clean up your plate," "earn the respect of your community," and "be completely honest in all your dealings." These dictums supplied uniform standards for the handling of work and money, as well as other parts of life. Doing one's best, as a general guideline for working, for example, could be translated into specific norms about accuracy and efficiency. For example, an older man recalled that his father, who had earned a living painting signs, always insisted on "painting a line right the first time." Such dictums of course functioned well in jobs that entailed a clear definition of right and wrong. They were also external to the person, serving as standards to be conformed to, not ones to be defined or deliberated.

Contemporary ascetic moralism is less external and less certain about what is absolute, although it is still both of these to a greater extent than expressive moralism.[8] The same man, for example, said his father taught him the value of family, community, and personal integrity. But these values are now tempered by norms of tolerance, relativism, and a belief in thinking for oneself. Thus he feels a sense of continuity with his father's emphasis on unwavering loyalty to traditional values, but he also distances himself by saying he is better able than his father was to understand and appreciate why other people may hold different values. There is also a looser connection between absolute values and the means by which these values are put into practice. Thus, avoiding waste may still be valued, but it is less certain whether cleaning up one's plate is how to do this. Pam Jones, for example, believes in being frugal but says her parents were so rigid about saving money that they sometimes wasted it; she expends more effort trying to decide what being frugal means.

Expressive moralism can also be understood by contrasting it with some of its historic manifestations.[9] If scholars such as Thoreau and Bushnell provided scholarly treatises defending it, a more popular image that connotes some of its meaning was the adventurer. The lonely nonconformist of the past went in search of adventure, hoping to find something to do that was heroic and challenging. The adventurer of today goes out in search of the self, hoping to escape boredom, but also wanting to indulge something inner that is struggling to find an outlet.[10] Wanderlust is the closest idea from the past that conveys the restlessness of today. Some who were smitten with this obsession spent a few years traveling in hopes of finding themselves; others struck out in search of fame and fortune. The historic wanderer was a ne'er-do-well who was looked on with suspicion by respectable folks. The seeker of fame and fortune was viewed more positively as a brave soul who, even in failure, was more easily understood. The expressive moralists of today generally have a more secure threshold under their feet than the wanderers of the past. They need not go out in search of fortune either, because they can always find a secure income if they wish, or even if the worst happens, go live in their parents' suburban palace and cash out some securities from a trust fund. They simply have the luxury to engage in a series of inner explorations. Despite these differences, there is nevertheless continuity. Expressive moralism still draws some of its language from the adverturers of the past, speaking, for example, of spiritual journeys and inward explorations.

Expressive moralism is also rooted in an aesthetic tradition. In the eighteenth and nineteenth centuries a person of sensibility was someone with a natural (or cultivated) ability to feel deeply, to register and express emotion, and especially to enter sympathetically into the suffering of others. Compared with the ascetic moralist, persons of sensibility were sometimes dismissed as being ruled by their emotions. They were sentimentalists whose behavior was guided more by feelings than by reason, or dilettantes swayed by the winds of passion, and therefore undependable, wasteful, and difficult to understand. Sometimes they were thought to be weak and effeminate; often, sensibility was regarded as a female trait, whereas common sense was its male counterpart, but there were exceptions.[11] The ability to feel, especially to sense God's love or to emulate divine compassion, was also taken as a sign of spirituality. The moral component of contemporary expressivism sometimes bears a close affinity with these aesthetic arguments. A person of sensibility does not simply have feelings but has an obligation to express powerful feelings without holding back, especially feelings of tenderness toward others, or feelings of rapture inspired by the beauty of nature or art, and should trust and follow these feelings, letting them influence one's choices and activities.

These at least are among the intellectual underpinnings of expressive moralism. For most people, though, the central tenets of expressive moralism lead to less exotic or aesthetic journeys. Paying close attention to their emotions has been forced upon them by stress, anxiety, dysfunctional family backgrounds, or more acute personal crises, such as divorce, illness, or unemployment. Others have been encouraged to engage in introspection by cultural emphases on the self and personal growth. Religious instruction, encouraging self-exploration as a way of gaining spiritual insight, has provided similar encouragement.[12] Karen Kelsey, the clinical social worker, for example, has been deeply influenced by reading philosophy, Buddhist writings, and therapeutic literature. "There's a person inside each of us," she explains, "who needs to grow and who is trying to express herself."

Both forms of moral discourse are centrally concerned with values, but the two can be readily contrasted in terms of *how* values are conceived.[13] On the one hand, a value can be an object that you attach yourself to, or pursue, or say you are committed to as a desirable goal in life, such as your family or your community or your religion. In each case you can feel committed, loyal, devoted to these objects. You enter into an exchange relation with them. You give time and energy and in return receive pleasure. You may also receive a sense of worth, identity, and security. But to do so, controlling the self, channeling it toward its goals becomes crucial. As Pam Jones observes, "being responsible" is an integrating value. On the other hand, a value can be thought of as a domain of behavior or even as a domain of yourself. Family is not something external to which you are committed; it is an arena in which you live and interact. Community is something you immerse yourself in and it becomes an integral part of you. In this conception the boundary is not drawn between you and it. The boundary here is drawn around the arena, with you inside it. Your identity is expressed and amplified within it.[14]

In the first conception, moral discourse would define proper behavior toward a valued object, such as its rights and your responsibilities. From any stock of personal resources it would be necessary to decide how much to commit to one object or another. A person should also be able to order these objects in terms of a means-ends continuum or according to a hierarchy of priorities. For example, showing up at work on time might be a high value, but transporting a sick child to the doctor would take precedence over that commitment. In the second conception, moral discourse is likely to be more concerned with basic definitions of domains. For example, instead of assuming that there is a self and a family, both being more or less fixed objects, this discourse would say that I am more myself when I am with my family, or that coming to know who I am depends on my family, or that my identity and my family's are relational. The important thing is not so much what you do (how much energy you spend doing it), but what it means to you and how you think and feel about it.

Both, therefore, demand moral responsibility from the individual but cast the individual in different roles. In the first, the actor is a strong ego-type, allocating energy, paying out time, and receiving various rewards; in the second, the actor is part of a system, immersed in a context as part of a cybernetic process, a processor of information that has a feedback mechanism built in; the actor is one who defines domains in which to seek and learn and grow.[15] The first view is exemplified in Pam Jones's desire for self-discipline in the pursuit of higher values. The second view is evident in Karen Kelsey's description of her personal quest to understand moral responsibility: "I started getting the sense that there is no totally objective morality that's been communicated and codified to humans," she recalls. But that raised a question for her: "How do you protect against your own selfish impulses for the greater good?" She began looking inside for answers and pursuing them intentionally. "I was more and more attracted to meditation which says, clear all the stuff out of that space that teaches you how to be a person. You know, clear all those extra thoughts—what am I going to have for dinner, what am I going to do tomorrow, am I going to be important—all the attachments, so to speak. When you clear that space, then you can take in more information from the deeper parts of yourself that can guide you more appropriately toward solid, selfless decisions."[16]

In neither case does moral discourse tell exactly which choices to make, but it lays out considerations to be taken into account and suggests some of the consequences. The language in which moral admonitions are cast differs sharply between the two. In ascetic moralism, behavior to be avoided is likely to be described in terms of laziness, lack of ambition, lack of financial responsibility to one's family and community, a failure to use one's talents wisely, not making good investments, not taking good care of one's body and mind, engaging in foolish activities, making poor consumer choices, displaying intemperate behavior, behaving greedily, or pursuing otherwise good activities to the point that they become destructive to one's physical health or family or social responsibilities. Expressive moralism is more likely to describe undesirable behavior in terms of addictions, being overly committed to anything, not taking time to think things through, letting others make decisions for you, failing to take responsibility for one's decisions, not knowing who one really is, following others rather than defining one's own goals, not paying attention to one's thoughts or feelings, or not attempting to grow as a person.[17]

Bad or improper behavior is thus possible to define within both frameworks. But failure to avoid such behavior is also understood differently in the two. Whereas asceticism implies responsibility and guilt, contemporary expressivism is rooted in therapeutic understandings that mostly deny guilt, arguing instead that a person need not feel guilty about any behavior. In some formulations the idea of "should" drops out of explicit usage. In its place, greater attention may be given to the idea of paying attention to one's limits, recognizing what is beyond one's control, and thus avoiding trying to control things too much. Responsibility to define and take charge of one's circumstances is thereby tempered by a sense of the inevitability of some circumstances and by recognition that one is to a degree a product of these circumstances.

Expressive orientations can, of course, be devoid of moral overtones entirely. Yet their historical manifestations in the work of writers such as Thoreau and Emerson clearly entail the idea that inner feelings are to serve as a standard for ordering one's life and one's values, not simply as a mood or sensation to be followed without thought or self-discipline. Expressivism in contemporary culture has been more problematic, causing some observers to believe it runs contrary to any sense of right and wrong as standards existing independent of inner feelings. But empirical evidence seems to run against these arguments. Among those who say they would give top priority to their feelings when making an ethical decision, for example, nine out of ten also say "trying to do what is morally right" would be a major consideration. Even among the small number of Americans who are willing to define ethics in terms of feeling good (rather than honesty or deciding between right and wrong), more than 90 percent also agree that "certain values must be regarded as absolutes."[18]

Expressive moralism does, however, raise one very important question: does it in fact provide a firm basis for living one's life in an ethically responsible manner, or does it implicitly encourage moral relativism, even ethical license? One way of answering this question is to compare people who elevate their feelings over their jobs to see how they behave when faced with ethical dilemmas at work or in their personal lives. In my labor force survey about one person in six agreed strongly with the statement that "paying attention to my feelings is more important than doing well in my job." Comparing these people with those who gave different responses showed that the former were indeed more likely to say they would follow their feelings when faced with an ethical dilemma at work. But they were *no more likely* than anyone else to have actually bent the rules or the truth at work in the past year, to have arrived late, or to have falsified expense records. They also disagreed that it was all right to do these things, said it was not all right to fudge or look for gray areas on one's income taxes, and were just as likely as other employees to say they would confront someone who was doing something unethical rather than looking the other way. They *were* somewhat more likely to define ethics as doing something that made you feel good, but only about one in ten chose this definition, the remainder opting for responses emphasizing honesty and deciding between right and wrong. Indeed, they were no more likely than other respondents to say ethics depended on circumstances rather than being universal. And they were *more likely* to say they felt personally responsible for the ethical behavior of others.[19]

In short, feelings provide an internal compass that seems to guide these people at least as well as other such compasses. Despite the subjectivity of feelings, those who emphasize them are thus able to govern their behavior and take responsibility for the actions of others. The reason is that people who emphasize feelings check in with themselves but do not make their decisions entirely in a vacuum. In fact, when asked what they would do if confronted with an ethical dilemma, they were more likely than average to say they would discuss the issue with their boss, talk it over with co-workers, read books to see what others had done, and even seek advice from members of the clergy.[20] Furthermore, they often believe that formalized moral codes exist and make sense largely because they are compatible with what truly paying attention to inner feelings would reveal anyway. Karen Kelsey, for example, asserts that morality is not a universal truth, but that there is "a crossover between what an act does to the spirit in everybody, or in most people, and what you can and can't do." She explains, "I think murder hurts the spirit, so most people can't think of doing it, and thus it's not bad to have it in an ethical code because most of us couldn't do it anyway."

ALTERNATIVES TO ECONOMIC REASONING

These two modes of discourse are probably among the most viable alternatives to the various presuppositions of naturalism, utilitarianism, and instrumentalism so widely in evidence in the economic arena. I do not mean to suggest that they are sufficient in themselves to set limits on what many feel is an economic system guided entirely by its own internal mechanisms. But they are surely among the most prominent repertoires that must be considered if moral discourse is to have any role in regulating economic life. Both are, as we have seen, deeply embedded in American history, and it would not be an exaggeration to say they have been prominent in modern culture more generally. Their legacy has been modified by the economic changes that have taken place during the past century and a half and in the philosophical debates that have accompanied these changes. And yet their basic premises remain largely unchallenged, and they have been the subject of continuing interest even at the popular level at least partly because they appear to be firmly embedded in the language and practices of some of our most powerful social institutions.

The opposition between moralism and economic reasoning can be understood partly in historical terms. The intellectual origins of nineteenth-century moralism in the United States can be traced to the eighteenth century when British writers such as Anthony Shaftesbury and Francis Hutcheson began to rethink earlier theistic conceptions of an absolute moral standard both as a reaction to and as an accommodation with the naturalistic orientations gaining prominence in Restoration and Enlightenment thought.[21] Already there was a strong assumption in theism that everything in the world was ordered and regulated for the best, and increasingly this sense of order was associated with nature. The moralists, however, argued that purely naturalistic, instrumental, or utilitarian frameworks failed to appreciate fully the extent to which the cosmos was ordered for human good and, therefore, could not provide an adequate basis for moral conduct. At the same time, they affirmed the reasonableness of acting honestly and respectfully because the cosmic order was indeed a system operating for the highest benefit of all.[22]

The moralist emphasis on order can in turn be traced to Greek conceptions of a golden mean and of beauty in symmetry. These ideas were also very much evident in the moralist literature of the eighteenth century in which, with the growing interest in nature, an aesthetic of spatial proportion and perspective came to be emphasized, and they provided a central principle for someone like Benjamin Franklin. Order implied, as it was often said, a place for everything and everything in its place. Determining appropriate courses of action required individuals to conceive of the whole order of things as a way of gaining the proper perspective in which to see and appreciate their own place. Right understanding depended on taking the larger picture into account so that narrow interests did not lead one astray. Tocqueville's assertion in the early nineteenth century that Americans pursue a form of self-interest that was "rightly understood" was very much a positive application of the moralist perspective.

The moralist perspectives that have gained prominence since the eighteenth century place special emphasis on the capacity of rational beings to love rational order when they see it. An essential feature of human nature is to be morally inclined, much in the same way that goodness was associated in the Enlightenment with nature in its precivilized state, and only subject to being sidetracked by false teachings or the narrowing of perspective that may come with the pursuit of self-interest or vice, among which excessive work or devotion to money might be included. This conception asserts a kind of correspondence between the moral order inscribed externally in the universe and the moral sensibility present internally in the individual soul. The congruence between universe and soul makes it possible for the individual to know what is good and right. It also implies that individuals must examine their own desires, aspirations, and inclinations. Modern moralism, in this sense, maintains an assumption of objective moral order but also heavily subjectivizes morality by placing so much of its ultimate evidence within the consciousness of the individual.

From its inception, the moralist tradition self-consciously opposed the narrow atomistic and utilitarian thinking perceived to govern economic models of human behavior. Hutcheson in particular formulated his ideas explicitly in opposition to Mandeville and later found himself equally opposed to the economic writings of Adam Smith, because both in his view were too quick to blur the distinction between vice and virtue by arguing that self-interested pursuits would necessarily benefit the common good. Moralists denied that benevolence could be reduced simply to egoism, arguing that no matter what the specific consequenced might be, there was still value in loving the good for its own sake and trying to be moral because morality itself is right, not simply because it is in our self-interest.

In historical perspective, it is therefore not entirely accidental that ascetic moralist and expressivist languages remain vital alternatives to the fragmented, valueless discourse so much in evidence within the economic domain. Both emerged in reaction to perceived inadequacies of Enlightenment deism and naturalism, especially their alleged one-dimensionality or flatness that allowed no room for what makes life significant. This was the same unidimensionality that was increasingly embraced by the political economists of the late eighteenth and nineteenth centuries. Ascetic moralists objected strongly to the separation of fact and value that seemed to be an inevitable consequence of regarding the individual as a detached observer of nature, while expressivists sought a closer linkage between the interior realm of subjectivity and nature itself.

In addition to these initial concerns, both orientations have come to deplore the instrumentalism that many social observers perceive to be prevalent in contemporary society. According to this criticism, it is within the economic realm particularly that everything appears to be regarded as a means, rather than being something of intrinsic worth;

thus, work and money both appear as means for the attainment of other ends. But as ends are bracketed from consideration within the economic realm itself, action is increasingly governed by norms of efficiency, effectiveness, and rationality in the arrangement of means.[23] Humans are thus cut off from considering other humans as beings of ultimate worth but regard them as instruments to be manipulated for limited purposes. The same is true of nature, insofar as it becomes merely an object to be mastered or a tool to be used in attaining other ends. This critique of instrumentalism is, at least, the way moral discourse has often been portrayed in the philosophical literature. And yet we will need to modify some of these claims if we are to understand more clearly how moralist language may actually differ from the legitimating claims we have examined thus far in our discussions of work, money, and other spheres of everyday life.

A better characterization would be to say that work and money are no longer understood at the popular level as means alone but have become implicitly associated with certain kinds of ends that give them worth, or intrinsic meaning, of their own. For instance, work is not a means of attaining money which is in turn a means for securing opportunities for one's children; rather, work is inherently meaningful because of the variety and choice embedded within it. Or, put differently, one does not work as a means of obtaining variety and choice; those values are simply present in the structure of work itself. From the moralist perspective, the problem then is not that work comes to be governed strictly by norms of efficiency, effectiveness, and rationality (it is often, in fact, none of these), but that a mythology of variety and choice (or performance) provides it with legitimacy without regard to the goals being pursued.

For the ascetic moralist, the main pitfall of economic reality is thus its tendency to subvert or preclude knowledge of that which is of intrinsic worth. A common complaint voiced by ascetic moralists even today is that people have lost their sense of priorities, and these priorities cannot be rediscovered unless the economic realm is brought into proper perspective by a consideration of broader or transcendent principles. The ascetic emphasis on balance is particularly important for determining what is appropriate behavior in the workplace. Although success may legitimately be sought, excess is to be avoided, meaning that aggressive or overzealous commitment to a career or a job is morally inappropriate, just as is too much interest in making money or securing material goods. Keeping all things in balance requires a commitment to family and neighbors, civic duty, and time for self-examination.

Someone like Pam Jones is thus an example of ascetic moralism because she employs a language of order and priorities to achieve a balance among such commitments. For her, competitiveness and greed constitute violations of the injunction to live temperately and in harmony with one's co-workers and neighbors. Above all, she argues that work must suit the long-range goals she sets for herself, rather than being allowed to subvert these goals. She realizes how easy it is to be caught up in meeting short-term deadlines in the workplace, almost "like a game," she says. When this happens, she finds it helpful to step back and ask herself, "what will have seemed important to me ten years from now?" Talking over these issues with her husband, a close friend, or her Bible study group is essential. Otherwise, she admits, she would begin to behave like a workaholic.

The symptom of imbalance (or disorder) that is of greatest concern to ascetic moralists is selfishness. This, more than greed, ambition, overwork, or material obsessions, is the corrupting force that must be restrained, especially in economic affairs, because these activities encourage self-seeking behavior.[24] Restraining self-interested behavior is of course not always a popular idea, especially when self-gratification has become a cultural expectation. Ascetic moralism may thus sound like a call for puritanism or self-sacrifice. Its moral meaning, however, is better understood as a rejection of self-aggrandizement, which in the economic sphere would imply using material gain solely for one's own comfort, power, or fame. It involves keeping a sense of something other than self clearly in mind, such as a service ethic that champions the interests of other people or what religious writers might refer to as transcendence or submission to the divine. "One clear sign of whether we have godly or selfish ambition is whether we keep our priorities straight," writes California businessman President Robert Heavner. "When our drive to achieve something makes us slight our families, our quiet devotional time with God, our health, or our local churches, we can be sure we have succumbed to selfish ambition."[25]

"Keeping our priorities straight" is thus reminiscent of the moralist arguments of the nineteenth century. Yet this slogan takes on additional meaning in contemporary moral discourse. Choice and human diversity have been emphasized to such an extent that moral standards, while still regarded by many as absolutes, are less likely to be considered universalistically applicable. Knowing how to apply these standards to concrete situations is at least difficult. Consequently, thinking about the relative merit of various priorities becomes good advice, as does finding an appropriate balance among them. Among other things, this means recognizing an inherent tension between self-interested and other-directed behavior, and thus attempting to balance the one with the other. In concrete terms, it may therefore be possible for an individual to be hardworking, ambitious, or rich, and yet be considered morally responsible by virtue of balancing these traits with generosity, kindness, and service. Any specific action may involve complex motives, but a morally acceptable account of these motives will require evidence of having attempted to strike a balance among worthy priorities.[26]

For the expressive moralist, a similar concern for balance is suggested by the charge that economistic thinking separates individuals from nature, thereby cutting them off from their essence or ultimate source of wisdom and inspiration. Sensing that human relationships have been broken by instrumentalist orientations in the material realm, expressivists are also deeply concerned about healing these relationships, overcoming the divisions between people, and creating community. Karen Kelsey, for example, has been involved in volunteer projects ever since she was in high school. She has tutored disadvantaged students, operated a hotline, and organized groups to promote dialogue between Jews and Arabs. At first these efforts seemed instrumental and awkward. They were not part of her ordinary life. But her goal is to integrate them more fully. The idea, she says, is not to look around and ask "what good volunteer thing can I become involved in this year?" That seems too much like "joining" or doing something extra. "I just want to be so much a part of the world, so tuned into things," she explains, "that something will come into my life and I won't be able to stand not getting involved."[27]

As far as broader social divisions are concerned, images of peace, oneness, and the commonness of humanity typically suggest the kind of world desired. Structures that may actually contribute to the alleviation of social problems may be supported intellectually, but not elicit as deep a commitment as those that involve individuals in one-on-one relationships.[28] In more intimate relationships the quest for community is likely to engage the whole person, or at least the person seeking wholeness, and emphasize communication at the level of feelings because these are taken to be the essence of human reality. Community is also likely to be connected closely with concepts of personal growth, such that the nurturing of individual potential comes about through a sharing of feelings (expression) and the originality that results from dynamic interpersonal interaction. Family relationships, involvement in voluntary associations and community organizations, and participation in spiritually oriented groups are all of value because they provide occasions for the sharing of feelings and the mutual nurturing of original and dynamic selves. Some intimate relationships of this kind may also be found, as we have seen, within the workplace or in the market arena, but these are less likely to sustain such relationships because of their competitive, instrumental emphases.

THE ROLE OF FEELINGS

The two moralist languages differ most clearly of course in the role they attribute to feelings or emotions. The ascetic moralist tends to be distrustful of feelings, associating them with nature, from which the reasoning intellect still remains somewhat detached and can be fully objective only so long as it is detached. The impulsiveness of the person guided by feelings is also a matter of some misgiving because the ascetic moralist prefers to work out a rationally ordered system of principles and priorities against which to evaluate the requirements of everyday life. Expressive moralism has, however, become acceptable in contemporary society because of a shift away from some of these conventional views. Emotivism may still be regarded as an inadequate philosophical basis for deriving moral principles. But emotions themselves may well be viewed as advantageous in comparison with detached reason alone. As Robert Nozick suggests, "When we respond emotionally to value, rather than merely judging or evaluating it mentally, we respond more fully because our feelings and our physiology are involved."[29] Moreover, feelings may now be more nearly under our control as individuals. Rather than being nature speaking in an immutable way, they have become the result of circumstances and our own efforts. Thus we have a need not only to escape from work to quiet ourselves in order to listen to our inner nature, but also to escape in order to vary our circumstances, to escape unpleasant pressures, and to expose ourselves to more enriching experiences.

Art Kaufman, 35, a San Francisco psychiatrist, illustrates one way in which an emphasis on feelings and moral responsibility are connected. Ever since he was in high school he has tried to grow by cultivating his creative impulses, by paying attention to his emotions, and by learning to understand these feelings better. The material he works with is of course his life, but he doesn't think of it that way. Instead, he talks about narratives, thus turning feelings into something he can create and control, rather than viewing them simply as natural impulses. In relating to his patients, for instance, he says "you're working with kind of a narrative of a person's life and someone reconstructs who THEY are from the past and memories, feelings, you know, kind of a 'works-in-progress' thing." The narrative, we might say, stands between his feelings (or memories) and the choices he eventually makes. It is important as a kind of template for his behavior. By being conscious about it, he is able to reconstruct it, and thus he is able to integrate his experiences, drawing his thoughts about work and money together with other parts of his life. The result might be described simply as an examined life. But what makes it possible is a two-stage process that involves, first, perceiving his feelings as an important manifestation of himself, and second, constructing an interpretive framework about those feelings and drawing his sense of values and moral obligations into that framework. This framework, moreover, remains fluid, always adapting and incorporating new ideas and feelings. It cannot be described as a structure or a tapestry or a web, all of which convey too static a sense of meaning. Searching for the right metaphor, he likens himself to an improvisational jazz musician. "'Improv-ing' with words," he says, "I guess that's what I do."

The emphasis placed on feelings in expressive moralism may seem to imply that ascetic moralism is, by comparison, entirely cognitive and rationally detached, devoid of feeling. This is by no means the case. But feelings do play a different role in ascetic moralism. Rather than signaling an inner state or natural impulse seeking expression, they are symptomatic of right and wrong conduct, telling individuals whether they have acted morally or not, like the joy or delight that comes from doing what is known to be right. Right conduct can thus be directed and enriched by paying attention to one's feelings. As Pam Jones remarks,

"Some people are so busy doing things, they don't have time just to be. For me, the meditative life is important."

Modern moralists also emphasize the role of individual will to a great extent, so pleasurable feelings of pride and worth may follow from facing good and evil and making the appropriate choice. There is also an expectation that good feelings will result, even when conformity with moral principles is difficult, because of the moralists' conception of a beneficent order in the universe. Individuals may not fully understand why a particular course of action should be taken but can be happy in taking it because they know there is a loving and affirming order in the world that ensures goodness when they live according to its moral principles. This conception of ultimate benevolence can also result in a kind of stoic, stiff-upper-lip contentment with life because joy itself becomes a moral principle, while discouragement and tension indicate a lack of trust that the forces of good will prevail.

In popular discourse, the most common sentiment is probably the simple assertion that individuals have a right to be happy, which translated means a right to feel good. If one does not feel good about one's workday or about a recent purchase, therefore, this feeling may need to be taken seriously as a symptom of misplaced priorities or poor judgment, and effort should be expended to alter one's attitudes or behavior to make good feelings return. The way to restrain one's economic commitments, therefore, is to be guided by a sense of emotional harmony. Concretely, it is not the sheer number of hours one works that has moral significance, but how one feels about those hours. For example, consider how writer Malcolm Muggeridge contrasts workaholism with more laudable service-oriented work, such as that performed by Mother Teresa's Sisters of Charity: "Their life is tough and austere by worldly standards, certainly; yet I never met such delightful, happy women."[30] In other words, happiness is the key. Curiously, then, ascetic moralism may converge sharply with expressive moralism in its elevation of feelings as a standard of moral excellence. The chief difference—clearly an important one—is that good feelings are more likely to be considered an end in themselves in expressive moralism, but only an indicator that means and ends are in proper relation for the ascetic moralist.

In either case, morally oriented individuals have a responsibility to reflect on their feelings, to process them, and to decide which ones to affirm and which ones to discard. The individual's responsibility to take charge of his or her own life is in fact one of the hallmarks of contemporary moralist thinking. It is what makes moralist discourse so highly relevant for a society in which discretion appears to have expanded at so many levels.

Yet the responsibility to engage in morally informed behavior depends not simply on present social conditions but on historic conceptions of freedom that are built into moralist discourse itself. The ascetic moralist assumes that the individual is able to know intuitively at least something of what is right or wrong. The individual is not simply a puppet or an apprentice, as in some Calvinistic understandings, who must learn God's grand design but never know for sure whether or not this knowledge will be adequate. In contrast to the inscrutable God of the Calvinist, the theologies and philosophies that became more popular in the United States have assumed that full knowledge of at least the essential truths of life are subjectively possible, either through the inner promptings of the Holy Spirit or through cognitive reflection on the written Scriptures, or nature, or human experience. Knowing the difference between good and evil, the individual is thus genuinely free to choose between them in a way that someone with imperfect knowledge would not be free. Similarly, the expressive moralist is free because of the essence or power or potential that lies within, in the inner being, and the person's ability to probe the depths of this being, or even to create it imaginatively and experimentally.

In both cases, the enhanced reflexivity of the individual subject has also become central to understanding the freedom and responsibility of the individual to make moral choices. Having the ability to know one's self and to sense one's feelings, and having the conviction that self-knowledge and subjective feelings are a valid form of information, the individual can then use this information cybernetically as a self-correcting feedback mechanism for charting courses of action. Thus, for the ascetic moralist the idea of a moral compass becomes an apt metaphor, giving the individual a reading of ethical location with respect to absolute universal standards, but still assuming that the individual is capable of reading the compass accurately and is free to abide by what it indicates or to violate what it suggests. For the expressive moralist this metaphor is less apt because absolutes are less readily evident. But the idea of moral meanings is better because the individual attributes moral significance to its own action and its surroundings. Language, and especially symbolism, becomes important because it enhances the framework in which individuals interpret the significance of their actions. The language itself becomes part of the action because it defines reality and places individuals in a broader interpretive framework.

It is worth noting, too, that the two also assume other foundational principles on which individual freedoms rest, such as the right to personal safety and certain conceptions of justice and equality. Thus expressivists are bound to restrict the expression of their feelings when it violates others' rights to do the same; each person is also equal in the sense of having potential access to feelings and being able to assume that those feelings are legitimate. The ascetic moralist also has no right to infringe on the personal safety of anyone else and, given the assumption of subjective access to moral wisdom, does not regard anyone as being beyond the pale of moral tutelage and responsibility. Thus moral absolutism is tempered by the assumption that if someone else is strongly convinced of a moral position, then that person needs to be treated with respect. For this reason, sincerity of conviction becomes especially important, whereas not having any convictions becomes seriously questionable.

Chapter Thirteen

THE POSSIBILITIES OF MORAL DISCOURSE:

LIMITATIONS, PATHOLOGIES,

AND CHALLENGES

THE ROLE OF moralist orientations is not to restrict economic life by making it less meaningful, but to set limits around its meanings, showing them in fact to be circumscribed, making differentiation possible, as it were, and then providing bridges between these delimited meanings and other conceptions of value. Moral discourse does not necessarily provide legitimate reasons to work shorter hours, but it helps sort out how to know if those hours are really contributing to the realization of one's goals and one's personal identity.

The observation that many people find their work fulfilling because it provides variety might be taken as an example. Variety can be defined, as we saw, within a narrow range that takes the constraints of the workplace largely for granted, and sometimes even exaggerates the importance of these variations. Moral discourse allows a distinction to be drawn between experiences that are etiolated or deadening and those that appear to provide genuine variety and personal enrichment. The difference is not that any absolute standard of "genuine variety" is specified (although it might be for ascetic moralists), but that variety ceases to be an end in itself and becomes a means that makes sense in relation to some greater end. The ascetic emphasis on balance may be realized more fully when variety is present. Expressivism provides a language for arguing that human life itself is varied, and that this diversity should be valued because the originality of each individual attests to his or her quality and worth as a human being. Experiences that are varied may for this reason seem more real or lifelike. Variety in the workplace is thus important because it seems that this is the way life should be. Insofar as our selves are influenced by the situations we experience, we may also feel that we become more interesting and enriched as individuals.[1]

Survey data are always limited, but they do provide a number of revealing indications of the ways in which ascetic and expressive moralism influence conceptions of work and money. The accounts people give of their work, first of all, are more likely to draw connections with other goals and values, rather than being oriented to isolated characteristics of the workplace itself. For example, ascetic moralists are more likely than average to say they chose their line of work because of the challenges it presented them and the opportunities it provided to make use of their talents, and they are less likely to emphasize money. Expressivists emphasize a relationship between work and their desire for personal growth. Both are more likely than average to say their work is meaningful and to express satisfaction with it, and they are less likely than other workers to experience conflicts with their supervisors. But they are also more likely to say they want more out of life than just a good job, and they want more time to think about their basic values and priorities. Both experience stress as often as other workers, and they are, in fact, more likely to sense that work pressures conflict with their families or their need for personal time. But they are also more likely to alleviate stress by talking with their friends and by praying or meditating. And there is a slight tendency for them to resist working long hours.

Orientations toward money are also influenced by these conceptions. Ascetic moralists are less likely than average to say making a lot of money is important to them, less likely to say they value having a nice home or traveling for pleasure, less likely to associate money with freedom, more likely to keep a family budget, more likely to think about their personal values when deciding on consumer purchases, more likely to value helping the needy, and more likely to give money to charities. Expressive moralists continue to value money but worry less about whether they have it or not, exhibit generosity in helping the needy, balance their interest in money with stronger commitments to their families and their communities, and express greater concern than average about the social effects of materialism and advertising. Both are less likely to cheat on their income taxes or falsify expense accounts at work.[2]

Besides posing restraint and alternative commitments in individual life, moralist reasoning also has broad implications for the articulation of public policies concerned with the collective disposition of resources. Although the alleviation of social ills can be defended strictly in self-interested terms, moralist reasoning has also held that it is simply right to attempt to reduce suffering. Consequently, an ongoing debate in moralist discourse, and one that clearly divides ascetic moralists from expressivists, concerns the definition and manifestations of suffering, and how best to alleviate it. Instrumentalist and atomistic assumptions that may be dominant in economic circles—namely, that ordinary means, such as making businesses more profitable, are sufficient for alleviating suffering, or that individuals are atomized units with little awareness or responsibility for those in need—are rejected by both varieties of moralists. Ascetic moralists naturally conceive of suffering in terms of value priorities, so suffering that results from violations of high values (i.e., evil) is especially important to combat (for example, suffering associated with the Holocaust or attributed to an abridgment of natural rights), and purely instrumental efforts to alleviate suffering are likely to be couched in broader considerations, such as the ideal of making the poor self-sufficient by giving them education, rather than merely feeding and housing them. Expressive moralists, in contrast, are more likely to relativize the concept of suffering by asking what the term means in the first place or by conceiving of it as a constructed reality. In their view mental and emotional suffering would thus be important as well as physical suffering, as would any form of inauthenticity. Any instrumental means of helping the needy would have to be evaluated not only in terms of its effectiveness but also in terms of whether it might degrade them or rob them of their originality. The personal growth of the caregiver might also be especially important. Both variants of moralism, therefore, provide legitimate ways of incorporating some of the broader concerns that arise when caregiving can no longer be regarded simply as a natural part of the communities in which people live.[3]

Paradoxically, moralist language has special potential for revitalizing contemporary culture because it emphasizes the individual even more so than community. Ascetic and expressive moralism resonate deeply with the individualism in our cultural heritage. As Colin Campbell asserts in describing the Puritan and romantic traditions from which the two emanate, "both are individualistic, inner-directed ethics, requiring intense introspection and soul-searching, and whilst what is located in each case as 'the real self' is different, it is this inner reality which is appealed to as the ultimate authority for resisting what are seen as unwarrantable demands from without."[4] It is unnecessary to emphasize the interior quality of each to the extent that Campbell does to see that both place heavy responsibility on the individual to decide what is right, and both aim to do so in a way that is morally persuasive rather than politically coercive or legally binding. This means, in effect, that either language or both can be adopted without having to compromise the authority, freedom, and responsibility we associate so dearly with the individual.

If both have ethical potential because of this compatibility with other values in our culture, they nevertheless carry an inherent weakness for the same reason. Just as Puritanism legitimated not only a moral restraint on the economic life, but also a form of acquisitive capitalism, so contemporary moralism contains ambiguities that do not always stand up well against the pressures of the marketplace. The reason is not that these pressures are so overwhelmingly urgent in themselves, but that contemporary moralist language is itself a product of a highly commercialized cultural environment. As a result, moralist language sometimes affirms the same assumptions that prevail in the economic sphere. Only close consideration of the two reveals the differences. Assumptions about freedom provide a clear example.

UNDERSTANDING FREEDOM

The economic conception of freedom includes the following ideas: that the ability to make decisions at work constitutes freedom, as opposed to someone telling you what to do; that greater wealth means greater freedom, because money is a universal means that can be used to do many different things, even as opposed to other forms of capital, such as land that might limit one's options; and that material possessions enhance freedom because they free one's time from routine tasks, such as washing dishes, or because they give one greater social options, such as wearing the right cosmetics or drinking the right beer providing access to beautiful women and attractive men, or because material possessions actually are the means to self-realization, such as travel that broadens one's horizons, or exercise equipment that makes one feel better and prolongs one's life. Especially important is the idea that freedom means the capacity to choose, so a good economic position to be in is to have a market that supplies abundant goods and career opportunities and chances to make money. Also desirable is being in a personal position with lots of individual capital, whether in the form of training or money or goods, that allows one the freedom to exploit as many of these opportunities as possible.

Moralist notions of freedom are not entirely different. Yet they do add different emphases. Freedom may be enhanced through other things, even things that might limit one's economic opportunities. For example, having a spouse and children, or intimate friends, or people in the community to whom one feels responsible might limit one's career options or freedom to buy things but enhance one's opportunities to grow as a person, to realize one's self in different ways because of the multiple relationships and new roles involved, all of which might be emphasized in an expressive moralist orientation. Or an ascetic moralist might regard freedom more as saying no to demands that violated one's sense of principle, such as leaving a job that demanded ethical compromise; or freedom would be seen as requiring obligations, such that someone who simply "knew no boundaries" economically would actually not be free, but be burdened because of having too much uncertainty, or they would have too much responsibility because infinite choice increases responsibility proportionately; whereas having definite commitments to absolutes, such as the value of one's children or one's god, would mean freedom in the sense of not having to worry, but just knowing that some things were already fixed, and thus having more meaning, or being able to focus more on how to serve those ends; or those absolutes actually giving you the freedom to say no, an excuse not to work weekends, for example. Also, the presence of absolute principles gives one a fulcrum, the ability to detach from everyday reality, to stand above it, and to see it more dispassionately. Thus the moralist is a disengaged actor who can transcend immediate situations, demands for social conformity, even the iron cage of dominant values in the present historical epoch.

Merely the realization that one is a person with legitimate interests, needs, and feelings that cannot be fulfilled entirely by work or money can be a liberating experience, especially for those who have been driven by internal demons that respond obediently to the demands of the marketplace. Karen Kelsey, for example, recalls a period in her life when she was "so driven by the demons of my inner world that there was no me." She says she had "no space," no way to think about her "internal computer," so she just acted out "unconscious things." She was driven to "manage" all sorts of commitments but experienced "no quietness at all." Only by "clearing away things" was it possible for her to gain "enough of a self" that she could truly make decisions about what she wanted in life.

Moralist languages can thus restrain economic behavior by giving terms such as freedom alternative meanings. But moralist languages are also subject to being decomposed. Like genes that can now be sliced and spliced to create artificial life forms, bits and pieces of moral discourse can be separated from their own semantic contexts and joined with other logics to form hybrid arguments.[5] The expressivist emphasis on feelings is especially subject to such adaptations. There is in American moral discourse a strong sense of ethical consequentialism, which under normal circumstances forges a close link between means and ends.[6] One example would be the view, which we saw in nineteenth-century moralist writing, that ethical behavior "pays off," a view that is still widespread in American culture.[7] Another example is the notion that good people who work hard will be rewarded with material prosperity, a view that we have seen to be in considerably greater dispute at present. But if ethical behavior cannot be counted on to produce certain outcomes, especially if these outcomes lie in the economic sphere, then a problem conceivably arises about the relationship between economic behavior and goodness, and indeed about how well rational assumptions about human behavior may apply more generally. The idea of good feelings may come to the rescue in the following way. It is common first of all, as we have seen, for people to deny that wealth and happiness bear any systematic relation to each other. Good feelings can thus be separated conceptionally from monetary calculations. If the reward for good behavior (including hard work) is not money, then it can possibly be good feelings. In fact, people do argue that if someone is a responsible person, works hard, and behaves charitably, then peace of mind, joy, serenity, satisfaction, or other good feelings will be the result.[8] This simple argument can perform two valuable services. One, it restores a sense of rationality to the economic sphere by establishing a different connection between good behavior and desirable ends. And, two, it may in fact give people a reason to limit their work and their interest in money by suggesting to them that a point may be reached where good feelings can be obtained only by relaxing or performing good deeds for one's neighbors. The second can be accomplished, though, only if good feelings remain conceptually linked to the larger logic of expressive moralism. If good feelings are simply transplanted into an economic calculus, then there is no way to decide when enough is enough.

RETREAT FROM SOCIETY?

The limitation that has generally been of greatest concern to critics of moralist language historically is this language's tendency to emphasize individual rather than societal issues. As I have noted, both ascetic and expressive moralist orientations provide perspectives on suffering that may lead to distinct social policy concerns. But these may still fall short of providing a full-fledged image of society. Expressive moralism has in recent years been especially vulnerable to criticisms of this sort. In expressivist terms society is sometimes regarded, as the early romanticists theorized, as a kind of spirit that exists more in the subjective consciousness of the individual than as an organized reality. Expressive moralists may in consequence be inclined to identify with the potential goodness of society, perceiving it as a source of nurture, support, and intimacy, but remaining suspicious of complex organizations and the power structures actually governing modern societies.[9]

In this view, the family may well be emphasized as a haven against the world, a place of warmth and love. But this emphasis also places high expectations on the family, perhaps even causing it to break down under the strain. In practical terms, family loyalty and the intimate warmth of family life may become more important as a way of limiting work, but it may also become necessary to work harder and worry more in order to realize the higher expectations that now become attached to family life. Retreating from other public responsibilities may also be the result of this emphasis on warmth and intimacy. The expressive moralist often desires a richer sense of meaning than can be found in the austere arrangements of large-scale institutions. Fulfillment is thus available only within the family, much as it was for the late-Victorian bourgeoisie, for Irving Babbitt, or for the man in the gray flannel suit after World War II. A sharp split between private and public life may also be the result, accompanied by any of the following: complacency about economic injustice, a limited perspective on work that in the extreme pays little attention to the products being produced, an exaggerated emphasis on the material comforts of life, and a desperate quest for self exploration, personal growth, and clearly defined moral standards.

Similarly, the ascetic moralist may also find solace in the family because the larger society is increasingly felt to be devoid of moral principles. In this scenario, the colder the economic realm becomes, the warmer the private worlds of self and family have to be. The more one is dominated by instrumental reason, the more the other has to give expression to deep-felt emotions. The more one is seen as a sphere of chaos and moral compromise, the more the other has to become a protected sanctuary for rigid moral behavior. Large impersonal institutions dominated by morally shallow careerists and bureaucrats stand against the humanness of small babies, strollers, baby blankets, teddy bears, the high moral values made possible only by home schooling, and a vehement moral commitment to the rights of unborn human life.

THE REINFORCEMENT OF DISCOURSE

Another limitation derives from the fact that both varieties of moralism have been influenced greatly by the relativism of contemporary middle-class culture. The choices depicted in moralist writings are typically no longer between good and evil, but between good and better, or better and best. It is assumed that life is pretty good overall, and that most people are unlikely to fail badly or run into deep trouble of any kind. There is, at one level, opportunity to focus on good feelings because we have the luxury to do so. At another level, it is also assumed in this discourse that there are no absolute, readily discernible rules. The point at which one person will feel uneasy about some action may be quite different from when another person will. What accounts for these differences may well be the subculture of norms and expectations to which a person has been exposed. Yet in failing to recognize the origin of these cues, and by treating them simply as individual differences, it becomes more difficult to pose a systematic challenge to taken-for-granted assumptions. Indeed, it even becomes more difficult for an individual to challenge prevailing norms because doing so can lead to unsettling feelings of anxiety and interpersonal tension.

This limitation brings us, then, squarely to the issue of community. Both ascetic and expressive moralism are widely enough institutionalized in American culture that individuals do not have to be deeply involved in a supportive group to be influenced by them. Indeed, survey results reveal, contrary to some studies that show the necessity of group involvement, that moralist and expressive values are just as likely to influence behavior and attitudes whether people are involved in groups that reinforce these values (churches, fellowships, support groups) or not. Nevertheless, these values are more likely to be held in the first place by people who are members of such groups.[10] Moreover, as sources of cultural influence, these groups help to legitimate the priorities and feelings that may be associated with pursuing certain lifestyles rather than others. An ascetic moralist who decides to shift jobs rather than engage in unethical activities, for example, is likely to receive encouragement for such action by being involved in a Bible study group, whereas no such support might occur within the workplace subculture itself.[11] That support can encourage the individual to feel better about his or her decision. It can also, perhaps more importantly, communicate to others that such behavior is legitimate and indeed desirable.

Expressive moralism may be supported in group settings in similar ways. But there is also a more subtle connection between it and such groups. The danger of feelings as moral guides is that they become entirely relative to personal moods and situations. An individual may also be utterly free to follow the counsel of these feelings or to ignore them. Especially if the individual lives in multiple settings, the feelings may be a variable and unpredictable guide for consistent behavior. Participating in groups, whether informal gatherings of neighbors or formalized therapy groups, becomes a way of objectifying and interpreting these feelings. Reinforcement is likely to be given for the individual taking responsibility for his or her feelings. In the group, the individual is able to objectify both the feelings and the self with which they are associated, looking at them with greater detachment, and therefore being able to decide on a course of action. It is through the support of the group, therefore, that moral discourse is put into practice.

Moralist Pathologies

A balanced assessment of moralist restraint in contemporary society must also pay attention to the disruptive and excessive tendencies in these frameworks. Ascetic and expressive moralism are both subject to pathologies of interpretation that can lead adherents toward adopting personal lifestyles or into joining social movements that defy the usual logic of rationally ordered or democratic social action. In relation to economic calculation, instrumentalism, and the rational pursuit of material progress, such behavior will of course appear pathological simply because it represents alternative values. But even in terms of achieving these alternative values, problems may arise because of extremist orientations or because some of the essential assumptions are lost sight of or misinterpreted.

It is generally from the ascetic moralist framework that extremist scenarios arise in which forces of good are pitted against great evils threatening to engulf human society. Having a clear sense of the importance of rationally ordered systems of priorities gives the ascetic moralist reason to believe that some activities are fundamentally disruptive to the entire ordering of the good life. With evil at the door, the ascetic moralist has all the more reason to live morally. Indeed, what is taken as "reason" becomes more than the cold calculations of the dispassionate rationalist. Now the moralists' commitment stems from virtue, freedom, right, and life itself, rather than the mere expediency of self-interest.

Such excessiveness has been precisely the target of counteraccusations by the champions of economically motivated, rational self-interest since at least the second half of the eighteenth century. But what is excessive for social harmony does not necessarily mean wrong in principle or contrary to standards of human good. To take a contemporary example, arguing that choice on matters of abortion and euthanasia may be the only way to maximize the democratic freedoms on which social order may depend does not itself negate arguments about the sanctity of all human life. Nevertheless, millenarian, apocalyptic, and other extremist movements may be the price a society has to pay for ascetic moralism to remain an active force restraining economic commitment.

If contemporary ascetic moralism is popularly associated with intolerant, rule-bound extremism, it is nevertheless important to observe that a more adequate understanding of this tradition recognizes the importance of self-examination, reflection, and diligent scrutiny of motives, perspectives, and behavior, all of which can serve as significant checks on extremism. Ascetic moralism requires the individual to evaluate personal aspirations and priorities in the light of principles that can be rationally sensed and understood. Compromise on these principles may be out of the question, but the principles themselves demand balance, harmony, equilibrium, an even temperament, and a sense of justice or fairness. These emphases strongly encourage peaceable, cooperative, harmonious relations with others, thus undergirding the civility or polite respect of differences that has often been observed in pluralist encounters, as opposed to an authoritarian or fanatical approach to social relations.

A pathology more likely to accompany the expressivist orientation emanates from the precariousness of its quest for personal fulfillment against the demise of confidence in the existence of a unitary self. Sensing the difficulties inherent in the quest for holistic meaning, even when the search may focus on impulsive intuitions rather than grand philosophical systems, a number of modern writers have asserted the importance of being content with lesser gratifications or have at least, in D. H. Lawrence's pronouncement that "nothing is so meaningless as meanings," expressed doubt about the larger significance of this enterprise.[12] Expressive moralism can thus degenerate into a kind of hedonism that emphasizes instant gratification, coupled with cynicism, restlessness, a focus on moods of the particular moment, a denial of the value of planning, an unwillingness to conceive of any notion of fundamental good, experimentation with novelty and excess for its own sake, and a lack of commitment to the betterment of society. An orientation of this kind can also fold back easily to an emphasis on everyday life, where work retains its momentary pleasures and challenges, making it tolerable at a certain level, but leaving it devoid of larger significance. This view may in fact be implicit in the assertion that work or the acquisition of money is a game, apparently to be played for its own sake, but, like all games, separated from life as an escape or a circumscribed arena in which to seek maximum pleasure.

But carried to extremes, the triumph of ordinary life means then that we not only work, but work at working, just as we work at managing our money, work at being good consumers, and work at balancing all the tasks of everyday life, from personal grooming, to sex, to cooking. Everything becomes a domain subject to the logic of instrumentalism and technical rationality; guidebooks, advice columns, and professional experts exist to direct all these activities. Time once devoted to the toilet training of a toddler now expands because the work of accomplishing the task is supplemented by the work required to consult the appropriate authorities, plan the activity, and evaluate it. In addition, the whole enterprise takes on added importance because the task is now defined in emotional as well as in physiological terms, making it necessary to plan and evaluate at both levels. Furthermore, in the absence of certain values or images of ultimate good, which are now bracketed from consideration as part of everyday life itself, everything takes on equal seriousness. Toilet training, automobile and home maintenance, leisure time, and on-the-job activities must all be performed with a balance of quality and efficiency, emotions and effectiveness in mind. What starts as an expressive concern with balancing the emotional needs of the individual against the demands of the workplace thus becomes an undifferentiated playing field on which all activities become more difficult to accomplish.

CHALLENGES FACING MORAL DISCOURSE

In the final analysis, moralist reasoning remains deeply relevant to the question of how to structure personal and social commitments, especially in a way that creates a more integrated and balanced relationship between economic and noneconomic commitments. Yet the limitations and pathologies to which moralist reasoning is subject also suggest that sustained reflection will be required to keep the essential assumptions of these perspectives intact and to adapt them to changing cultural conditions. Several challenges that arise from cultural conditions already evident at the end of the twentieth century are particularly worthy of further consideration.

One of the most serious challenges currently facing ascetic moralism is the increasingly fearful possibility that no force for good ultimately exists in the universe, a possibility that has been greatly exacerbated by the wars, mass executions, and brutal totalitarianism of the twentieth century. It has thus become common for committed moralists to hold forth heroic images of hope, often symbolized through the courageous and compassionate acts of public figures, such as Mother Teresa of Calcutta or Dr. Martin Luther King Jr. Whether these figures can sustain hope, especially when they have sometimes themselves become victims of the forces of evil, remains an open question. But at least the reason why they, and why other symbolic expressions of the good, have become all the more important in contemporary society can be understood. A second challenge facing ascetic moralists is the growing uncertainty in modern culture about the ability of rational people to sense the good and the moral and to agree on what it is. This is perhaps why moralists increasingly emphasize involvement in communities and organizations in which consensus can take place on a small scale, such as local churches, universities, or neighborhood service organizations. It may also be why some moralists place great faith in scientific and quasi-scientific demonstrations, such as rational arguments about altruism, or scientific interpretations of the origins of the universe. It may also be why many ascetic moralists veer toward expressivism and attach more emphasis on feelings in making moral decisions.

Moralist orientations are also faced with the continuing challenge of attempting to provide a sense of personal integration or, as I have noted, holistic meaning amidst the fragmenting conditions of modern life. Sensing the disparity and incompleteness of the various roles that make up the self, the ascetic moralist struggles for a tight center of control capable of bringing everything into alignment and providing clear direction in making decisions. Ego-strength, assertiveness, willpower, self-control, and moral conviction are all variants on the same pursuit. The expressive moralist in contrast strives for a redefinition of the self that either conceives of it in more holistic terms or locates a center, core, or true self more basic than the various roles arrayed around the periphery of this center. Interiority often serves this purpose well by identifying the true self with something inward that is more stable and inviolate in relation to the situational demands of the external self. Emotion may serve as well to provide moments of ecstasy or mystical union in which the self is integrated or its fragmentation at least temporarily transcended.

But neither of course has been entirely successful in combating the compartmentalization of the self; hence, there is continuing interest in efforts to escape the restrictions of the unitary self entirely, as evident in postmodernist attempts to "decenter" the self by emphasizing its dependence on language, or perhaps in more popular ways through formulaic folk wisdom about the impossibility of finding meaning, the need to be different things to different people, or the zigzag journeys on which most individuals seem to be engaged. The quest for a holistic self may also be characterized by epiphanies of the moment. Temporary experiences of the immediate or punctual present block out the passage of time or the temporality implied in planning and goal-oriented behavior. For example, jogging creates such epiphanies for some people by pushing them into sufficiently strenuous exercise to escape for a brief time from the ordinary rhythms of the day. Television, placing the viewer in a fantasy world suspended from real time, probably serves a similar function. As we have seen, such activities take on great significance for people nowadays who have no other means of determining how economic behavior should be restrained. Thus, one of the challenges is to find ways of understanding the relationships between such temporary escapes and the ordinary rhythms of the workplace.

In a parallel fashion, expressive moralism also appears to be especially concerned with providing alternatives to the world of economic rationality by constructing different conceptions of history through the rediscovery of myth and symbolism. So much of the past has been engulfed in modern images of economic development and material progress that it is often difficult to see beyond the unilinear cultural transformation suggested by these images. Society has improved, according to these indications, by harnessing the forces of nature, applying technological inventions to these tasks, and turning the impoverished parochial settings of the past into the abundant, consumer-rich wonders of the present. Expressivism argues for the need to recover an alternative past in order to achieve a more complete vision of the future.

Rousseau and Whitman found this alternative past in a romanticized conception of nature, and some scientists and environmentalists appear to be fascinated with nature today for the same reasons. The recurrent popularity of tribal myth and ancient folklore, as evidenced in the writings of figures such as Joseph Campbell or Robert Bly, attests to the significance of these alternative conceptions of the past as well. Some of the continuing appeal of such literature surely must be attributed to the fact that it avoids the Western tradition entirely, from Christianity to the present, rooting arguments about human needs instead in primordial stories whose wisdom is magnified by their survival through various periods predating written civilization. At a more personal level, the popularity of individual myths of origin, from efforts to trace family histories to psychological theories of primal pain to therapeutic efforts to rediscover and rehabilitate the inner child, also suggest ways of creating alternative and sometimes highly original conceptions of the past.

We must also consider the challenge that arises in conjunction with current speculation about the future of the human condition itself. Moralist thought has been diminished by some of its detractors for posing an overly pessimistic view of human nature. Others regard it in precisely the opposite terms, arguing that only social institutions, rather than moral restraint of any kind, are capable of sustaining the common good. Both arguments draw implicit comparisons between moralist conceptions of human nature and those alleged to be the underpinning of rational economic relations. It is thus of value to consider these comparisons more explicitly.

In some ways the moralist tradition takes a more optimistic view of human nature than is evident even in classical economics. The latter has often been taken to be the more optimistic because of its assumption that goodness will prevail from the pursuit of self-interest. But moralists assume that people are inspired by a better nature than self-interest, that goodness and generosity are also natural to the human spirit. This optimism in fact is probably one of the reasons why moralism itself has been transformed to some extent in the twentieth century and why economic reasoning seems to have become more persuasive. The hope that human goodness would prevail, still evident in the American progressivism and modernism of the early twentieth century, suffered terrible devastation as a result of the subsequent wars and economic catastrophes that overtook much of the world. The erosion of faith in human goodness that followed also reinforced another, more pessimistic view of human nature, namely, the one that had been present in American culture as a result of its Calvinist and Puritan heritage.

In light of the more cynical interpretation of humanity that developed, an economic system aimed at turning evil to the best possible outcomes that could be anticipated has seemed more realistic to many social analysts. Moreover, this economic system has also found some of its strongest supporters among conservative religionists who espouse this view of human evil most strongly. But one of the factors that has weakened the moralist tradition's capacity to challenge prevailing economic assumptions is that these conservative religionists, who are often the ones who champion a strict conception of objective morality, have nevertheless opted to support rather than criticize the American economic system. In their place the strongest voices of criticism from religious quarters generally come from old-line denominations that were the principal centers of mainstream moralism in the nineteenth century but now find themselves weakened both numerically and because of uncertainties about the natural goodness of humanity and, for that matter, the presence of a rationally knowable moral order.

Whether moralism can be a powerful check on economic life in the future will thus depend greatly on whether compelling arguments can still be made for the existence of an orderly and harmonious or ultimately beneficial moral sense that can be sensed and understood by the individual or collectively. But the impression sometimes voiced by observers of American society that moralism cannot prevail in this context because American culture contains *too much* optimism seems beside the point. If high levels of optimism about human nature are present, as much evidence suggests they are, then moralism makes more sense than an economic system that assumes the worst in human nature. It is only the pessimistic, authoritarian moralism of those who believe human nature is so fundamentally perverse that moral rules must be established by the coercive power of the state to which such an economic system can make sense.

The way to buttress moralism is probably not, therefore, to put on public display the worst cases of political and corporate corruption, as journalists are sometimes prone to do, let alone to parade rapists and murderers through the city streets, as more extreme proponents of law and order occasionally suggest. Moralism is more effectively reinforced by the good, reflection on which empowers us to be good ourselves, to exhibit benevolence toward others, and to trust them to respond in kind (and in kindness). This does not mean taking a Panglossian view of society that diminishes the reality of suffering and evil, but finding reasons for hope in the possibility of goodness. Moralist frameworks originally found such hope in arguments about the universal goodness of God's love and the possibility of experiencing divine grace. Belief in these conceptions is still widely in evidence, despite growing influences of secularism in public discourse. Research demonstrates strong relationships between perceptions of experiencing God's love and a principled willingness to engage in ethical and charitable behavior.[13] In addition, human instances of heroism and benevolence continue to inspire widespread admiration and generate a collective sense of hope about the future and faith in the power to realize that hope.

But one of the features common to contemporary ascetic and expressive moralism is the difficulty they both have in making room for heroism. Exceptional virtue, things worth dying for, and even clarity of fundamental purpose in life are difficult even for the morally principled to articulate and understand. We are still products of the passionlessness of our age and the decline of high aspirations that Kierkegaard and Nietzsche wrote of in their time. And so ascetic moralism makes room for small acts of heroism by emphasizing balance and temperance and by discouraging extremism. Expressive moralism accomplishes the same task by elevating the value of the moment, the temporary or impulsive commitment that may spark moral insight even if it does not generate sustained involvement.[14]

In this respect, then, even small doses of morally principled behavior can count for a great deal. They become emblematic, serving to remind others that there are indeed higher values than they may have considered during a particular day at work or in the marketplace. "In every generation," noted one of the people we interviewed, "there are people who know this knowledge and manage to pass it from one generation to the next. I value the people who know and preserve and contain that knowledge. And when I say knowledge, I'm talking about ideals such as peace and love and community which end up preserving society."

Since Marx, if not before, social observers have been tempted to seek irony and contradiction in explaining economic life. The present analysis could be extended in that direction as well, suggesting, for example, that economic utilitarianism generates its moral opposites, and that these opposites inadvertently reinforce the economic behavior they oppose. But this type of theorizing rests on a faulty view of the very moral languages to which I have drawn attention.

To be sure, my claim is that ascetic and expressive moralism contain arguments that legitimate restricting the pursuit of wealth and material success. But this is not all they contain. Like all ethical discourses, they are less dialectic than dialogic. They establish a polarity, an opposition between related concepts and symbolic categories, drawing boundaries between the two, and adding positive and negative valences. But they also authorize the individual, the actor, to make choices, and they suggest the need for complex strategies of behavior. They do not simply negate the economic realm. They seek to re-*vision* it, placing it in a wider framework, and providing individuals with ways of talking that make sense of the movement back and forth between their economic activities and other realms of their lives. Such re-visioning can play a vital role in rescuing the American Dream.

METHODOLOGY

B
ESIDES published literature, historical texts, and other studies cited in the notes, I have drawn extensively from a survey of the U.S. labor force that I conducted in 1992, the Economic Values Survey. A copy of the questionnaire and a description of the sample are available in the appendix of my book *God and Mammon in America* (Free Press, 1994), which reported results to some of the questions that asked about faith, work, and money. Briefly, the survey was based on a national sample of approximately 2,000 adult men and women who were currently employed full-time or part-time. The decision to exclude persons not in the labor force was based on the fact that a large share of the questions focused on work experiences and attitudes toward one's job, career, and place of employment. The survey also included numerous questions on the uses of money, attitudes toward money and material possessions, personal values, family relationships, community involvement, religion, and moral understandings. Each person interviewed for the survey was interviewed in person by a trained interviewer from the Gallup Organization. These interviews included more than 500 fixed-choice questions and lasted an average of eighty minutes.

The 200 in-depth, qualitative interviews were conducted separately from the survey. These respondents were selected purposively, rather than randomly, and were chosen to provide a wide variety of orientations and experiences, including different occupations, ages, regions, and religious and ethnic backgrounds. We conducted interviews primarily in the following metropolitan areas: New York, Philadelphia, Trenton, Boston, Chicago, Minneapolis, Portland, San Francisco, Los Angeles, Houston, and Atlanta. In each area we selected respondents from central city, suburban, and exurban areas. We interviewed approximately equal numbers of men and women and younger people and older people. We included African Americans, Asian Americans, and Hispanics in numbers approximately equivalent to the proportions in the U.S. population. The first 150 interviews were conducted among working men and women. Some of these interviews were done before the survey and helped in the design of fixed-choice questions.

Twenty-five interviews were conducted with men and women who were currently unemployed. And twenty-five were conducted with men and women, both employed and unemployed, who were recent immigrants to the United States and who added to the ethnic diversity of the study. The interviews lasted approximately two hours, covered a standard array of topics but included different follow-up questions depending on respondents' answers, and yielded approximately 10,000 pages of verbatim transcript.

NOTES

CHAPTER 1

1. Arlene Skolnick, *Embattled Paradise: The American Family in an Age of Uncertainty* (New York: Basic Books, 1991), 220.

2. Graham Hueber, "Baby-boomers Seek More Family Time," *The Gallup Poll* (April 7, 1991), 1.

3. Timothy Belknap, "Reeling in a Fly-Fishing Collectible," *Business Week* (June 17, 1991), 116.

4. T. George Harris and Robert J. Trotter, "Work Smarter, Not Harder," *Psychology Today* (March 1989), 33.

5. Others who predicted a time when work would be minimized, freeing humanity for higher pursuits, include Thomas Jefferson, Karl Marx, John Stuart Mill, and John Maynard Keynes; for an overview, see Benjamin K. Hunnicutt, *Work Without End* (Philadelphia: Temple University Press, 1988).

6. Sam Keen, *Fire in the Belly: On Being a Man* (New York: Bantam Books, 1991), 67.

7. Thomas J. Kniesner, "The Full-Time Workweek in the United States," *Industrial and Labor Relations Review* 30 (1976), 3–15; *Business Statistics, 1961–88* (Washington, D.C.: U.S. Department of Commerce, 1989), 51; "ILO Report Predicts Shorter Workweek, Longer Vacations Before End of Century," *Daily Labor Report* (January 18, 1985), 4–5.

8. Susan E. Shank, "Women and the Labor Market: The Link Grows Stronger," *Monthly Labor Review* 111 (1988), 3–8; G. H. Moore and J. N. Hedges, "Trends in Labor and Leisure," *Monthly Labor Review* 94 (1971), 3–11. Polls that attempt to measure the average workweek by asking individuals themselves how much they work contain certain biases but suggest that Americans on the whole are actually working harder than in the recent past. For example, Harris surveys conducted in 1973 and again in 1990 revealed a rise in the average workweek from 40.6 hours to 48.8 hours. Among professionals, people with incomes over $50,000, and those termed "baby boomers," the average was 52 hours, and among small businesspeople 57 hours. These figures are reported in Benjamin K. Hunnicutt, "No Time for God or Family," *Wall Street Journal* (January 4, 1990): A12. Results of a 1991 Gallup survey, though reported in less detail, also indicate that many Americans work more than the standard forty-hour week. Thirty-nine percent reported they work more than forty-five hours in a typical week; one person in eight works more than sixty hours a week. Larry Hugick and Jennifer Leonard, "Job Dissatisfaction Grows; 'Moonlighting' On the Rise," *The Gallup Poll* (September 2, 1991), 10.

9. *The Gallup Poll* (July 1989).

10. According to Hugick and Leonard, "Job Dissatisfaction Grows," 10, the percentage of Americans who say they are regularly scheduled to work evenings and weekends increased from 24 percent in 1989 to 36 percent in 1991.

11. Shank, "Women and the Labor Market."

12. Juliet B. Schor, *The Overworked American: The Unexpected Decline of Leisure* (New York: Basic Books, 1991).

13. Hugick and Leonard, "Job Dissatisfaction Grows," 5.

14. My survey was conducted in February and March 1992, among 2,013 randomly selected adults who were currently working full-time or part-time. See the appendix on methodology.

15. "Time at a Premium for Many Americans; Younger People Feel the Pressures Most," *The Gallup Poll* (November 4, 1990).

16. Anastasia Toufexis, "Drowsy America," *Time* (December 17, 1990), 78.

17. Economic Values Survey.

18. John P. Robinson, "Time's Up," *American Demographics* 11 (1989), 33–35.

19. Henry D. Thoreau, *Walden* (Princeton: Princeton University Press, 1973 [1854]), 16.

20. These observations are borne out by figures from the annual Consumer Expenditure Survey conducted by the U.S. Bureau of Labor Statistics; see, for example, Margaret Ambry, "The Age of Spending," *American Demographics* (November 1990), 16–23.

21. Economic Values Survey.

22. Unpublished results from a survey designed by the author and conducted by the George H. Gallup International Institute in November 1990 among a national sample of 1,000 U.S. adults. Fourteen percent of the younger group said having nice things had become less important, as did 21 percent of the older group. Among persons over age 50, having nice things was also more—rather than less—important by a margin of 26 percent to 22 percent.

23. Economic Values Survey. The figures are percentages of the sample who said each statement describes them very well or fairly well.

24. U.S. Bureau of the Census, *Statistical Abstract of the U.S., 1990* (Washington, D.C.: Government Printing Office, 1990), 506.

25. "Credit-Card Delinquencies Growing, Bank Group Says," *Wall Street Journal* (March 13, 1991).

26. "Personal Savings," *Wall Street Journal* (May 23, 1991); Clint Willis, "Americans and Their Money," *Money* (April 1991), 74–76.

27. Robert F. Black, Don L. Boroughs, Sara Collins, and Kenneth Sheets, "Heavy Lifting: How America's Debt Burden Threatens the Economic Recovery," *U.S. News and World Report* (May 6, 1991), 53–61.

28. Keen, *Fire in the Belly*, 52–53, quotes this bumper sticker, adding: "Debt, the willingness to live beyond our means, binds us to the economic system that requires both surplus work and surplus consumption."

29. Quoted in William Heyen, "Death of a Salesman and the American Dream," in *Arthur Miller's Death of a Salesman*, ed. Harold Bloom (New York: Chelsea House, 1988), 51.

30. These figures are from a 1989 national survey of 2,100 persons conducted for the author by the Gallup Organization. A description of the survey and details on sampling and questions are available in Robert Wuthnow, *Acts of Compassion: Caring for Others and Helping Ourselves* (Princeton: Princeton Uni-

versity Press, 1991). The present figures are from my own tabulations of the data. I shall refer to this study as the "Values Survey."

31. Quoted in Larry Martz, "True Greed," *Newsweek* (December 1, 1986), 48.

32. Brief summaries of these two studies were reported in Lynn Asinof, "Fraud is Common," *Wall Street Journal* (March 1, 1990), 1.

33. Economic Values Survey.

34. These are 1991 figures are reported in Larry Hugick and Graham Hueber, "Pharmacists and Clergy Rate Highest for Honesty and Ethics; Senators and Police Decline," *The Gallup Poll* (May 22, 1991), 1–3. The authors assert, "When the ratings of all twenty-five professions are considered, they seem to eflect a more pessimistic attitude about the state of honesty and ethics in U.S. society today. In 1991, not one of the 25 professions saw their ratings increase significantly. Overall, fourteen professions saw their ratings decline, five had small increases, and six remained constant" (p. 1).

35. *Ibid.* Between 1981 and 1991 the percentages scoring the ethics and honesty of each profession very high or high declined 9 points for bankers, 7 points for TV reporters, 6 points for journalists, 6 points for newspaper reporters, 3 points for lawyers, and 5 points for stockbrokers.

36. "Opinion Roundup," *Public Opinion* (November/December 1986), 22.

37. "What Bosses Think about Corporate Ethics," *Wall Street Journal* (April 6, 1988), 27.

38. "Values Survey."

39. Arthur Miller, *Death of a Salesman* (New York: Penguin, 1949), 13. Although there are numerous interpretations of *Death of a Salesman*, I follow William Aarnes in suggesting that Willy Loman is a character whose life is "essentially meaningless," which is in turn consistent with at least one rendition suggested by the playwright himself, who once described the play as a "steady year-by-year documentation of the frustration of man." See William Aarnes, "Tragic Form and the Possibility of Meaning in *Death of a Salesman*," in *Arthur Miller's Death of a Salesman*, ed. Harold Bloom, 95. Miller's statement is quoted in Brian Parker, "Point of View in Arthur Miller's *Death of a Salesman*," in *Twentieth Century Interpretations of Death of a Salesman*, ed. Helene Wickham Koon (Englewood Cliffs, N.J.: Prentice-Hall, 1983), 55.

40. Toward the end of the play (p. 132), Biff says to Willy, "You were never anything but a hard-working drummer who landed in the ash can like all the rest of them."

41. *Self-Esteem Survey* (Princeton: The Gallup Organization, 1982).

42. Hugick and Leonard, "Job Dissatisfaction Grows," 4, report that 40 percent of the labor force claims to be completely satisfied with their jobs, while 43 percent say they are somewhat satisfied. They also note a small decrease in the proportions who express satisfaction in recent years, and they suggest that this decrease is probably attributable to economic conditions.

43. Economic Values Survey.

44. Hunnicutt, "No Time for God or Family."

45. Emily T. Smith, "Stress: The Test Americans Are Failing," *Business Week* (April 18, 1988), 74–76.

46. National Center for Health Statistics, *Health Promotion and Disease Prevention: United States, 1985* (Washington, D.C.: U.S. Department of Health and Human Services), series 10, no. 163, p. 30. Among men and women age 30 to 44 who earned more than $50,000 annually, 69 percent complained of stress, compared with fewer than a third of men and women in their sixties in the lowest income categories.

47. Lawrence K. Altman, "Changes in Medicine Bring Pain to Healing Profession," *New York Times* (February 18, 1990), 1; William Celis, "Broad Teacher Dissatisfaction Is Pointed Up in National Poll," *New York Times* (September 2, 1990), 1; "Lawyers Have High Rate of Mental-Health Woes," *Wall Street Journal* (November 30, 1990), 1.

48. Hugick and Leonard, "Job Dissatisfaction Grows," 5–6, 10.

49. Economic Values Survey.

50. James T. Wrich, "Beyond Testing: Coping With Drugs at Work," *Harvard Business Review* (January-February 1988), 120–28.

51. Helen LaVan, Marsha Katz, and Wayne Hochwarter, "Employee Stress Swamps Workers' Comp," *Personnel* (May 1990), 61–64.

52. James P. Markey and William Parks II, "Occupational Change: Pursuing a Different Kind of Work," *Monthly Labor Review* 112 (1989), 3–12.

53. Hueber, "Baby-boomers Seek More Family Time," 4.

54. Economic Values Survey.

55. Center for Education Statistics, "Teacher Job Entry, Separation and Transfer Rates," *Bulletin of the Office of Educational Research and Improvement* (November 1986), 1–3; "Who Is Leaving the Federal Government? An Analysis of Employee Turnover," *Report to the President and the Congress of the United States* (Washington, D.C.: U.S. Merit Systems Protection Board, 1989), 6–48.

56. Markey and Parks, "Occupational Change."

57. Economic Values Survey.

58. For estimates of the emotional impact of various life events, see Barbara Snell Dohrenwend and Bruce P. Dohrenwend, *Stressful Life Events: Their Nature and Effects* (New York: Wiley, 1974), and Peggy A. Thoits, "Dimensions of Life Events as Influences upon the Genesis of Psychological Distress and Associated Conditions: An Evaluation and Synthesis of the Literature," in *Psychosocial Stress: Trends in Theory and Research*, ed. Howard B. Kaplan (New York: Academic Press, 1983), 23–45.

59. *Faith Development in the Adult Life Cycle: Pretest Results* (Princeton: The Gallup Organization, 1982), 55. These results are from a national survey involving 557 respondents. I was the principal author of this report.

60. Robert N. Bellah, Richard Madsen, William M. Sullivan, Ann Swidler, and Steven M. Tipton, *The Good Society* (New York: Knopf, 1991), 85.

61. In a 1991 Gallup survey that asked "how well does the term 'workaholic' describe you," 77 percent of the U.S. labor force said "very well" (24 percent) or "fairly well" (53 percent). The proportions who said "very well" rose steadily from 15 percent among those age 18 to 29, to 47 percent among those age 65 and over; Hugick and Leonard, "Job Dissatisfaction Grows," 10.

62. Economic Values Survey.

CHAPTER 2

1. Hugh A. Mulligan, "Companies Give Workers Piece of the Action," *Trenton Times* (May 19, 1991).
2. LaVan, Katz, and Hochwarter, "Employee Stress," 64.
3. For example, see those quoted in Annetta Miller, "Stress on the Job," *Newsweek* (April 28, 1988), 40–45.
4. *Ibid.*
5. David J. Abramis, "Finding the Fun at Work," *Psychology Today* (March 1989), 36–38.
6. Keen, *Fire in the Belly*, 61.
7. Economic Values Survey.
8. Diane Fassel, *Working Ourselves to Death: The High Cost of Workaholism and the Rewards of Recovery* (San Francisco: Harper San Francisco, 1990), 46.
9. Economic Values Survey.
10. Useful surveys of recent debates concerning the role of the state in regulating economic forces include Alan Wolfe, *Whose Keeper? Social Science and Moral Obligation* (Berkeley: University of California Press, 1989); Robert Dahl, *A Preface to Economic Democracy* (Berkeley: University of California Press, 1985); and Fred Block, *Post-Industrial Possibilities* (Berkeley: University of California Press, 1990).
11. This result and the other figures reported in the text are from the "Values Survey." See chapter 1, note 30.
12. Government intervention in the economy is also favored less than the work of the voluntary sector. For example, in the "Values Survey," 72 percent agreed that "private charities are generally more effective than government programs."
13. The relationship between economic institutions and personal discretion is clearly described in Milton Friedman, *Capitalism and Freedom* (Chicago: University of Chicago Press, 1962); for a more recent statement, see Peter L. Berger, *The Capitalist Revolution: Fifty Propositions about Prosperity, Equality, and Liberty* (New York: Basic Books, 1986), especially chapter 5.
14. Robert Jackall, *Moral Mazes: The World of Corporate Managers* (New York: Oxford University Press, 1988). I have benefited greatly from the insightful analysis presented in this book.
15. Bryan Wilson, *Religion in Sociological Perspective* (Oxford: Oxford University Press, 1982), 161. Wilson also discusses the ways in which moral questions have been moved into the sphere of political reform.
16. As a guide to this literature, I have found especially valuable the work of my colleague Jeffrey Stout, *Ethics after Babel: The Languages of Morals and Their Discontents* (Boston: Beacon, 1988). I have also borrowed quite selectively from Alasdair MacIntyre, *After Virtue: A Study in Moral Theory*, 2d ed. (Notre Dame: University of Notre Dame Press, 1984), and Stanley Hauerwas, *Truthfulness and Tragedy* (Notre Dame: University of Notre Dame Press, 1977).
17. John Dewey, *Theory of the Moral Life* (New York: Holt, Rinehart and Winston, 1960 [1908]).

18. *Ibid.*, 6–7.
19. *Ibid.*, 3.
20. "There is not simply a succession of disconnected acts but each thing done carries forward an underlying tendency and intent, *conducting*, leading up, to further acts and to a final fulfillment or consummation" (*Ibid.*, 11).
21. The thesis of "lifeworld colonization" is developed in Jürgen Habermas, *The Theory of Communicative Action*, 2 vols. (Boston: Beacon, 1984, 1987), especially 2:332–73.
22. Wolfe, *Whose Keeper?*, 7.
23. Karl Polanyi, *The Livelihood of Man* (New York: Academic Press, 1977).
24. On the importance of institutions for moral language, see Bellah et al., *The Good Society*.

CHAPTER 3

1. Max Weber, *The Protestant Ethic and the Spirit of Capitalism* (New York: Charles Scribner's Sons, 1958), 53.
2. Among these studies, see, for example, Irvin G. Wyllie, *The Self-Made Man in America: The Myth of Rags to Riches* (New York: Free Press, 1954), and Peter Baida, *Poor Richard's Legacy* (New York: Morrow, 1990).
3. Maxims such as "those who would eat must work" and "all work and no play makes Jack a dull boy" were widely disseminated to American children during the late eighteenth century and the nineteenth century through such books as *Mother Goose's Melody* (London: Newberry, 1765); reprinted in Jacques Barchilon and Henry Pettit, *The Authentic Mother Goose Fairy Tales and Nursery Rhymes* (Denver: Allan Swallow, 1960). "Busy as a bee, that's the kind of little girl people like to see. . . . Gentle as a dove, that's the kind of little girl every one will love" is from an anonymous nineteenth-century poem entitled "Ambition"; reprinted in *Saint Nicholas Book of Verse*, ed. Mary Skinner (New York: Century, 1923), 47–48.
4. Jonathan Edwards, "Sermon Seven: Charity Contrary to a Selfish Spirit," in *Ethical Writings*, ed. Paul Ramsey (New Haven: Yale University Press, 1989), 271.
5. Nathaniel W. Taylor, *Practical Sermons* (New York: Garland, 1987 [1858]), 139.
6. *Ibid.*, 135.
7. *Ibid.*, 140.
8. Francis Wayland, *The Moral Law of Accumulation: Two Discourses* (Boston: Gould, Kendall & Lincoln, 1837), 10.
9. E. H. Chapin, "Advice to the Young," in *Osgood's Progressive Fifth Reader for the Young*, ed. Lucius Osgood (Pittsburgh: A. H. English, 1858), 254.
10. Jonathan Edwards, "Love the Sum of All Virtue," in *Ethical Writings*, 136.
11. John Todd, *American Educational Reader* (New York: Ivison, Blekeman, and Taylor, 1873), 34–35.
12. Chapin, "Advice to the Young," 252.
13. John Randolph, "Advice to a Young Relative," in *Holmes' Southern Fifth Reader*, ed. George F. Holmes (New York: Richardson, 1867 [1834]), 324.

14. Henry Ward Beecher, *Eyes and Ears* (Boston: Ticknor and Fields, 1862), 235.

15. Wayland, *The Moral Law of Accumulation*, 14.

16. Samuel Hopkins, "Disinterested Benevolence," in *American Christianity: An Historical Interpretation with Representative Documents*, H. Shelton Smith, Robert T. Handy, and Lefferts A. Loetscher ed. (New York: Charles Scribner's Sons, 1960), 543.

17. James Northcote, *One Hundred Fables: Original and Selected* (London: Saville Passage, 1828), 93–94.

18. Alice Mitchell, *Tales of Instruction and Amusement* (London: Harris, 1807), 21.

19. *Ibid.*

20. Isaac Watts, *Divine Songs* (New York: Mahlon Day, 1837 [1715]), 51–52.

21. Edwards, "Sermon Seven," 262.

22. Colin Campbell, *The Romantic Ethic and the Spirit of Modern Consumerism* (London: Basil Blackwell, 1987), traces the affinity between the Puritan and the romantic tradition as background for considering the significance of this variety of moralist thought in English and American culture.

23. Henry W. Bellows, "Influence of the Trading Spirit upon Social and Moral Life in America," *American Review* 1 (1845), 95.

24. Horace Bushnell, *Work and Play* (London: Alexander Strahan, 1864), 7.

25. *Ibid.*, 10.

26. Bellows, "Influence of the Trading Spirit," 98.

27. Thoreau, *Walden*, 14.

28. *Ibid.*, 17.

29. Bushnell, *Work and Play*, 13.

30. Thoreau, *Walden*, 8. It is easy from a twentieth-century vantage point to make Thoreau into a kind of bohemian or hippie who never worked preferring instead to relax and take his leisure. But that image separates him too far from the other moralist writers of his day. He was, as Emerson said of him, "a born protestant," a man who was "never idle or self-indulgent," who simply refused to devote himself to an ordinary craft or profession in order to work hard at the art of living." Emerson, "Thoreau," in *Lectures and Biographical Sketches* (Boston: Houghton Mifflin, 1904), 452; originally published in 1863 (a year after Thoreau's death) in the *Atlantic Monthly*.

31. Ralph Waldo Emerson, "Character," in *Lectures and Biographical Sketches*, 95; originally published in the *North American Review* (April 1866).

32. Quoted in Paul F. Boller, Jr., *American Thought in Transition: The Impact of Evolutionary Naturalism, 1865–1900* (Chicago: Rand McNally, 1969), 72.

33. George Opdyke, *Treatise on Political Economy* (New York: G. P. Putnam, 1851), 16.

34. Francis Bowen, *The Principles of Political Economy* (New York: Garland, 1974 [1856]), 27.

35. John Stuart Mill, *Essays on Economics and Society* (Toronto: University of Toronto Press, 1967), 321; a reprint of "On the Definition of Political Economy," originally published in 1844.

36. Quoted in Boller, *American Thought in Transition*, 72.

37. *Ibid.*, 319.

38. Bowen, *Principles of Political Economy*, 8.

39. *Ibid.*, 19.

40. Thoreau, *Walden*, 14.

41. Horace Greeley, *Essays Designed to Elucidate the Science of Political Economy* (Boston: Fields, Osgood, 1870), 15.

42. For an overview, see Albert O. Hirschman, *The Passions and the Interests: Political Arguments for Capitalism before Its Triumph* (Princeton: Princeton University Press, 1977).

43. Alexis de Tocqueville, *Democracy in America* (New York: Vintage, 1945 [1835]), 2:129.

44. Quoted in Boller, *American Thought in Transition*, 72.

45. Bowen, *Principles of Political Economy*, 20.

46. Warren J. Samuels, *The Classical Theory of Economic Policy* (New York: World, 1966), especially 21–97.

47. Anthony Giddens, *Modernity and Self-Identity: Self and Society in the Late Modern Age* (Stanford: Stanford University Press, 1991), 144–80.

48. *Ibid.*, 167.

49. *Ibid.*

50. Wilson, *Religion in Sociological Perspective*, 161.

51. *Ibid.*

CHAPTER 4

1. Daniel T. Rodgers, *The Work Ethic in Industrial America, 1850–1920* (Chicago: University of Chicago Press, 1974).

2. Clair F. Vough, *Tapping the Human Resource* (New York: Amacom, 1975), 14.

3. E. A. Locke, D. B. Feren, V. M. McCaleb, K. N. Shaw, and A. T. Denny, "The Relative Effectiveness of Four Methods of Motivating Employee Performance," in *Changes in Working Life*, ed. K. D. Duncan, M. M. Grunberg, and D. Wallis (New York: Wiley, 1980), 379.

4. "Labor," *Index to International Public Opinion* (1987–1988), 489.

5. Economic Values Survey. The question read, "Following are some reasons people give for getting into their present line of work. Which ones were most important for you?" And: "Which *one* was the most important reason of all?" Among the responses listed were options such as "the chance to become successful," "the opportunity to use my talents," and "knowing people in this line of work." "The money" was selected by 53 percent as an important reason and by 29 percent as the most important reason of all.

6. *Connecticut Mutual Life Report on American Values in the '80s: The Impact of Belief* (New York: Research & Forecasts, 1981), 182.

7. "Occupations," *Index to International Public Opinion* (1988–1989), 210.

8. "World Surveys," *Index to International Public Opinion* (1988–1989), 601.

9. *Connectual Mutual Life Report*, 167.

10. *Ibid.*, 171; the two extreme income categories in this study were separated

by a 16 percentage point spread on frequency of making decisions at work, but only a 5-point difference on frequency of feeling dedicated.

11. "Why Are Employees Leaving the Federal Government? Results of an Exit Survey," *Special Report* (Washington, D.C.: U.S. Merit Systems Protection Board, 1990), 1–19.

12. My own analysis of data from the "Self-Esteem Survey" conducted in 1982 by the Gallup Organization; beta statistics were .200 for fulfillment and .129 for finances when the two were entered simultaneously as predictors of work satisfaction; when satisfaction with family was included, the coefficients were .178 for fulfillment, .102 for family, and .098 for finances.

13. Hans Zetterberg and Greta Frankel, "Working Less and Enjoying it More in Sweden," *Public Opinion* (August/September 1981), 41–45.

14. "Multinational Surveys," *Index to International Public Opinion* (1988–1989), 604.

15. "Traditional Social Values," *Index to International Public Opinion* (1988–1989), 651.

16. "Multinational Surveys," 618.

17. "Occupations," *Index to International Public Opinion* (1986–1987), 280.

18. "Single Nation Surveys," *Index to International Public Opinion* (1986–1987), 270.

19. For a critical assessment of postscarcity theories and evidence of new scarcities, see Daniel Bell, *The Coming of Post-Industrial Society: A Venture in Social Forecasting* (New York: Basic Books, 1973), 456–75.

20. Daniel Yankelovich, Hans Zetterberg, Burkhard Strumpel, and Michael Shanks, *The World at Work: An International Report on Jobs, Productivity, and Human Values* (New York: Octagon Books, 1985), 41.

21. "Job Satisfaction," *Index to International Public Opinion* (1987–1988), 492.

22. From my own analysis of data from the 1989 Values Survey described in Wuthnow, *Acts of Compassion.*

23. "Business and Industry," *Index to International Public Opinion* (1985–1986), 254.

24. From my own analysis of data from the Values Survey, described in *Acts of Compassion.*

25. Cooperative Institutional Research Program, *The American Freshman: Twenty Year Trends, 1966–1985* (Los Angeles: Higher Education Research Institute, 1987), 97.

26. "Status and Role," *Index to International Public Opinion* (1985–1986), 511.

27. In the Values Survey data, 31 percent of professionals valued "making a lot of money" as either an essential or very important value, compared with 39 percent of managers, 37 percent of skilled workers, 39 percent of semiskilled workers, and 47 percent of service employees.

28. Marvin B. Scott and Stanford M. Lyman, "Accounts," *American Sociological Review* 33 (1968), 46.

29. Accounts are thus a special case of the discursive self-reflexivity that characterizes all human beings. Giddens writes, "All human beings continuously monitor the circumstances of their activities as a feature of doing what

they do, and such monitoring always has discursive features. In other words, agents are normally able, if asked, to provide discursive interpretations of the nature of, and the reasons for, the behaviour in which they engage" (*Modernity and Self-Identity*, 35).

30. Charles Taylor, *Human Agency and Language: Philosophical Papers*, vol. 1 (New York: Cambridge University Press, 1985), 15–16.

31. Harry Frankfurt, "Freedom of the Will and the Concept of a Person," *Journal of Philosophy* 67 (1971), 7.

32. Max Weber, *Economy and Society*, translated by Guenther Roth and Claus Wittich (Berkeley: University of California Press, 1978 [1922]), 4.

33. See especially Peter L. Berger and Thomas Luckmann, *The Social Construction of Reality* (Garden City, N.Y.: Doubleday, 1966).

34. This point is stressed in Robert N. Bellah, *Beyond Belief: Essays on Religion in a Post-Traditional World* (New York: Harper & Row, 1970), especially 3–19.

35. Weber, *Economy and Society*, 8.

36. See, for example, Scott and Lyman, "Accounts," 46–62.

37. Robert B. Horton, "Myths and Truths, but No Challenge: Make Some Piece of the World Care," *Vital Speeches* 54 (1988), 688–90.

38. Ann Swidler, "Culture in Action: Symbols and Strategies," *American Sociological Review* 51 (1986), 273–86.

39. Michael Lewis, *Liar's Poker: Rising Through the Wreckage on Wall Street* (New York: Norton, 1989).

40. *Ibid.*, 247. Elaborating, Lewis writes: "the belief in the meaning of making dollars crumbled; the proposition that the more money you earn, the better the life you are leading was refuted by too much hard evidence to the contrary. And without that belief, I lost the need to make huge sums of money" (p. 248).

41. The work-for-money approach has been subjected to particularly compelling criticism in E. E. Lawler, III, "Motivation: Closing the Gap Between Theory and Practice," in *Changes in Working Life*, ed. K. D. Duncan, M. M. Gruneberg, and D. Wallis (New York: Wiley, 1980), 539–50.

42. Worthwhile contributions and overviews to this literature include F. J. Landy and D. A. Trumbo, *Psychology of Work Behavior*, 2d ed. (Homewood, Ill.: Dorsey Press, 1976); E. E. Lawler, *Motivation in Work Organizations* (Monterey, Calif.: Brooks/Cole, 1973); C. C. Pinder, *Work Motivation: Theory, Issues, and Applications* (Glenview, Ill.: Scott, Foresman, 1984); E. F. Schumacher, *Good Work* (New York: Harper & Row, 1979); and V. H. Vroom, *Work and Motivation* (New York: Wiley, 1964).

43. Monetary rewards have also been deemphasized in theories that adopt Maslow's hierarchy of needs and therefore focus more attention on such "higher" needs as sociality and self-actualization; see, for example, Frederick Herzberg, B. Mausner, and B. B. Snyderman, *The Motivation to Work* (New York: Wiley, 1959). Herzberg's influential theory has of course been the subject of much debate and revision.

44. This view has been seriously challenged, however; see Arlie Kruglanski, "Can Money Enhance Intrinsic Motivation? A Test of the Content-Consequence Hypothesis," *Journal of Personality and Social Psychology* 31 (1975), 744–50.

45. The influential treatise by Martin Morf, *Optimizing Work Performance: A Look Beyond the Bottom Line* (New York: Quorum, 1986), for example, bases its arguments about work motivation explicitly on behaviorist theories of needs and rewards that deny the culturally constructed character of both.

46. The recent emphasis on corporate culture in some literature goes beyond the need-reward literature in recognizing accounts as well; see Theodore Peters and Robert H. Waterman, Jr., *In Search of Excellence* (New York: Harper & Row, 1982).

47. Scott and Lyman, "Accounts," 54.

CHAPTER 5

1. The extent to which accounts of one's work and accounts of one's self begin to overlap in childhood is suggested strongly (for males at least) by Sam Keen, who writes: "Long before a boy child has a concept of the day after tomorrow, he will be asked by well-meaning but unconscious adults, 'What do you want to be when you grow up?' It will not take him long to discover that 'I want to be a horse' is not an answer that satisfies adults. They want to know what men plan to do, what job, profession, occupation we have decided to follow at five years of age! Boys are taught early that they are what they do" (*Fire in the Belly*, 51–52).

2. I am extending an argument here that has been made in the organizational literature to account for similarities in formal structure under uncertain market conditions; see, for example, Paul DiMaggio and Walter W. Powell, "The Iron Cage Revisited: Institutional Isomorphism and Collective Rationality in Organizational Fields," *American Sociological Review* 48 (1983), 147–60. My argument is that organizations also develop isomorphic accounts of themselves that provide employees in these organizations with stories to tell that transcend the specific workplace. On the importance of organizational myths and ceremonies more generally, see John W. Meyer and Brian Rowan, "Institutionalized Organizations: Formal Structure as Myth and Ceremony," *American Journal of Sociology* 83 (1977), 340–63.

3. The accounts reported in this chapter are drawn from interviewees' discussions of their work. A variety of questions were used to elicit these accounts. Most people were asked to give a brief history of their work experience, say why they had chosen their particular line of work, describe a typical day, talk about what they like and dislike about their work, say what motivates them to do well in their work, and discuss the extent to which and in what ways their work gives them personal fulfillment. Most people talked openly, freely, and with animation about their work. The typical interview yielded from ten to fifteen pages of verbatim commentary about work.

4. Earl Shorris, *The Oppressed Middle: Politics of Middle Management, Scenes from Corporate Life* (Garden City, N.Y.: Doubleday, 1981), 30–31. I disagree with many of Shorris's specific arguments, but his general emphasis on the power of the modern corporation to secure loyalty by defining happiness is consistent with the thrust of my own analysis. He writes: "The most insidious of the many

kinds of power is the power to define happiness. It is the dream of merchants, despots, managers, and philosophers, because whoever defines happiness can control the organization and the actions of other men: he not only assigns aspirations and desires, he constructs the system of morals by which the means of achieving happiness is judged" (17–18).

5. I have included a few direct quotes in the text as illustrations; further examples are provided in the notes to this chapter.

6. I apologize to my friend Mark Granovetter for the blatant adaptation here of his well-titled article on social networks.

7. Ann Swidler has provided valuable examples of such accounts in her work on love, one version of which was given in a talk at Princeton University in 1989.

8. My colleagues and I culled through dozens of these brochures. Phrases such as "variety of assignments," "different kinds of tasks," "new challenges," "diversity," and "trying out different roles" were much in evidence.

9. Economic Values Survey. The proportions who scored high (9 or 10) on a self-rated job satisfaction scale were 41 percent among persons who said the statement about variety describes their work very well, 20 percent among those who said it describes their work fairly well, 9 percent among those who said "not very well," and 8 percent among those who said "not at all."

10. An elementary teacher in Los Angeles, for example, talked about how she liked being able to teach many different subjects and introduce new ideas in the classroom. A doctor in New Jersey emphasized how he is always having to learn new techniques to keep up with his profession. A Philadelphia psychiatrist, like Maxine Weingard, emphasized the room for creativity that he enjoys: "There's a tremendous amount of creativity in it for me. I can be working with someone and while one approach isn't working, so, you know, you go around and find another approach. I think there's some therapists who just have one way of doing it and kind of put the patient in their box and that's it. But that's not the way I work."

11. Economic Values Survey. Among those who said variety described their work very well, 39 percent said work was absolutely essential to their basic sense of worth as a person and 26 percent said they work 50 or more hours a week; among those who said variety did not describe their work, only 16 percent gave each of these responses.

12. In some instances middle-class workers specifically single out lower-ranking employees with whom they interact to indicate how much better their own situation is. Melissa Schneider, the CPA, provides an example: "Being a professional gives you so much more flexibility. Like the secretary and the data-entry person—they have a lot less flexibility. I have what's called comp time. I can take off, I can take two-hour lunches, I can come in late and leave late. But they have to be there eight to five. I wasn't even thinking about that when I got an office job, but boy, I'm glad I chose to be a professional."

13. A typical "frame" for these accounts is to indicate some other job the person previously held or considered holding, then depicting their present va-

riety in comparison with it. A 42-year-old Chicagoan, a black woman who had worked for Johnson Products before starting her own graphic design business, for example, used the contrast between the two to indicate how satisfied she is with the variety in her present work. "I like working for myself, because when working at Johnson Products, it was always hair every day, all day. It was hair. And now I might be working on hair at ten in the morning, I might be working with education at two, tomorrow I might be working with soap suds. So I like the diversity of it."

14. A personnel manager for a public administration agency in New York remarked: "When I was growing up the teachers always said this is the way it should be done. You follow steps A, B, C, and D. Which was okay in some instances but I guess I always like to be able to try to set a goal and try to go about attaining that goal maybe in different ways. And I think that's what makes working on different projects with different people so interesting."

15. Harold Bentley's remark, which is quoted in the text, is a typical example.

16. Melissa Schneider, the CPA who is quoted in the text, reveals some awareness of how her work delimits the variety she can experience in her remark that it is, after all, accounting. Some accounts also take what seems like a constraint and turn it into something likeable. A physician who runs an emergency room at a Philadelphia hospital provides an interesting example: "I'm the only physician required by Federal law to see absolutely everyone that comes to me, no matter what. Every other physician can choose not to accept Medicare or Medicaid. They can choose not to accept HMO, and so therefore those patients won't come to them. I'm required by federal law to accept everyone and anyone, no matter who comes, no matter whether they can pay or can't pay. And so I see a lot of the ills of our society, too, which gives an interesting perspective."

17. Observe how this respondent, a dentist, admits to leading a very structured work life and yet tries to emphasize some form of variety *within* this framework: "Unfortunately I work under a very strict or structured day, I'd say. It's schedule-oriented. . . . Every minute of my day is accounted for, from the minute I walk in. Basically I am a type of individual that walks in about five minutes before the patients come, takes off my coat and goes right to work. An average day, let's say with the hygienist, I'll probably have to deal with anywhere from 18 to 22 people. And though I may not be directly treating every one of these patients, I do interact with all of them. It could be quite trying, depending on the individuals we deal with. Some are friendly, some are not friendly, some are anxious, some are new, some are old, so it really is different circumstances. So your personality's changing constantly with each individual, I would say, because you have to approach each person differently."

18. In Minneapolis a 68-year-old independent sales representative often referred to himself as an "entrepreneur," even though in a strict sense he is not an entrepreneur, not someone who develops and brings a product to the market. He basically represents an industrial equipment manufacturer in a company-

determined territory, selling their equipment in his area. Although he likes the autonomy that being an entrepreneur connotes, he actually reports to a large company that determines much of what he does.

19. Economic Values Survey.

20. The Long Island restaurant manager also used a hierarchical image in describing what he likes about being his own boss: "It's not dictated too much by emergencies and other things that might happen, and nobody is looking down on me at all, I'm totally my own boss."

21. Nursing, for example. "I like the autonomy," explains a Los Angeles nurse. "I think nursing has gotten out of the role of being subservient to the physicians. They've given us a lot of power. I like managing my patients, and thinking ahead of potential problems and confronting the doctor about them."

22. These particular phrases are taken from a brochure published by AT&T.

23. The Los Angeles nurse also observes, "I like the autonomy, being able to make suggestions, because years ago nurses couldn't do that."

24. Middle-class people from working-class backgrounds are especially likely to dramatize the choice in their own work by contrasting it with that of their parents. A number of people, though, also talked of middle-class parents whose lives were more highly bureaucratized than their own. A New Jersey dentist, for example, remarked that what he enjoyed most was being his own boss; then to clarify the point he noted: "I grew up in a family where my father worked as an executive and I saw the ups and downs of that. When he was successful, times were good. And when the economy would slip or the company would be in trouble and he'd lose his job, the disappointment and anguish he went through, especially as he got older, was just terrible."

25. An assistant district attorney in Chicago who complained that her ability to make decisions had recently been taken away also had this to say: "I have never been told I can't make a decision on something, but now I am being told, 'Well, try your best not to have to say anything until the people up on top decide on what our policy is going to be.' I am hoping that is going to change since we have a new state's attorney who will take office in about another week or so." Similarly, an inventory planner for an electronics distribution firm in Philadelphia said she hated her work because the company had just been taken over by a large corporation in Harrisburg and she no longer had any control over what she did. She observed, however, that she still knew the difference between right and wrong and tried to do what was right.

26. A young woman who says she works in a high-stress job at a Los Angeles printing firm doing troubleshooting on software problems every day nevertheless emphasizes that she feels she is able to use her brain a lot and make her own decisions. "I'm able to pretty much do what I please. Not that I would abuse it or anything but I have the autonomy to do what I want to do and make the changes that I—if this isn't efficient, let's change it. You know, we can do that. We're not stuck in any sort of system. It really makes your job more satisfying."

27. A woman in Portland who was especially candid about her career trajectory explained how she had started a pie-baking business, only to have it drive her crazy with long hours and not prove financially viable. At wit's end one

night in a fit of tears she decided to go into gerontology work because she knew it was a growth industry. After experiencing all kinds of roadblocks, she eventually earned an MPA and started working with older people. Yet in concluding her account she still felt it necessary to show how much she liked her present work by linking it with her own talents and interests: "I love working with the elderly that have all these stories. I love to listen to their stories and that kind of thing. So I just needed to find something that will match me up with that."

28. A middle-level manager for a large retailer in Los Angeles described how her loyalty to the company was enhanced by its conscious strategy of providing employees opportunities to make decisions, something that she tries to pass on to the employees she hires: "The people that you employ, you let them make decisions and have responsibility and be accountable, and therefore they will thrive. That's the way I felt about it. I was given a lot of responsibility and I had a lot of opportunities to do things that made positive changes in the company and that meant a lot to me. And that still continues today. That's why I'm still with them. I'm very loyal to the company, and I'm very committed because they are still carrying on the same kind of things that were there when I first started."

29. A New York attorney described law school and the larger world of law in much these terms. It was a benign system that presented him with tempting opportunities. All he had to do was follow his instincts and at each step do what he enjoyed. "The momentum just started rolling towards practicing some kind of a business-oriented, big-practice kind of law," he explains. "But I enjoyed those courses very much. I knew very little about the world of business, but I enjoyed it very much and as time proved, my instincts were pretty good in it and that's how I sort of ended up where I am today."

30. Peters and Waterman, *In Search of Excellence*, 282.

31. An account that emphasizes several of the themes mentioned in the text—symbolic victories, companies providing special occasions to reinforce those victories, competitiveness, and bigness—comes from a young computer salesman: "The satisfaction part of the job comes from the fact that I do my job very well. I really do think I know my product, probably better than anybody else in the office and better than probably most of the people in the country. I ranked in the top ten for sales, nationwide. . . . It was like 1.1 million dollars for the copiers. We flew out to California for an awards ceremony. . . . It was a sense of satisfaction that I really do know my product. I take pride in knowing it, knowing everything about it, keeping up to date on the technology."

32. Another woman, a typist, remarked: "It's the way I'm made. I'm a perfectionist. I can't live with myself if I do less than my best."

33. Quoted in Keen, *Fire in the Belly*, 55.

34. In the professions especially, there is a credentialing process, and these credentials become part of one's identity, often with letters attached to one's name, a résumé, and so on. This identity is further reinforced by the fact that one associates with similar people, and they know whether or not you have the credential, and you know theirs, even if it is in a different field.

35. Steed Wellman, 26, a corporate auditor for a Fortune 500 firm, illustrates how organizational pressure is often translated as internalized pressure. In one of his periodic reviews, he was criticized for leaving some unanswered questions in the audit he had done for one of the branch offices of the company for which he works. He said the criticism was unjustified, pointing out that he had done ten weeks of work on the project to the full satisfaction of his boss, only to have the entire review focus on this one issue. Nevertheless, he vowed he would be more punctilious in the future so nobody would ever again call him up about unanswered questions. The account he gave emphasized that this was his own decision and that he made it because he himself was a perfectionist who always liked to get everything right.

36. A Washington-based psychiatric social worker, Kala Osborne, described the difference between internal and external pressure in precisely these terms. The internal pressure was good: "I feel pressure in the session. I feel pressure to give as much of myself as I can, to get knowledge and give it to the client, to interact in the appropriate way, to be fully aware of what is going on. That is where it is draining, exhausting. Probably I put the pressure on myself." But she contrasts this with the external pressure she associates with getting her paperwork in on time, meeting deadlines, and attending staff meetings. She believes nothing serious will happen if she slacks off on these responsibilities. The internal pressure is thus higher, more intrinsic to herself, something that connects her performance to her training and her worth as a person.

37. Kala Osborne, the psychiatric social worker, is an example of someone whose work involves a high level of ambiguity. She is a good therapist but always wants things to be even better. Not knowing exactly how to define "good enough," she attributes the pressure she feels entirely to herself. One of the stories she relates shows the kind of words she uses: "I had a couple that I worked with and the man tended to throw out sarcastic, angry comments at me. This family really was into sarcastic humor as a way of relating to each other, and this particular way of expressing anger was very hard for me to relate to and hard for me to call and say, 'it seems like you're angry at me,' or 'I hear anger in your sarcasm.' So I felt the pressure to call on him when he did that, but it was fairly rare, and when he did it, I felt stunned and unable to confront him. And so I would always be putting pressure on myself to do something about it, but rarely really feeling like I had completely approached the issue. So that's the kind of pressure I would put on myself. Occasionally I would say something about it, but it would be a tense moment; I would be wanting to say something. I wouldn't quite feel like I said the appropriate thing."

38. The classic study of this imagery is Irvin G. Wyllie, *The Self-Made Man in America: The Myth of Rags to Riches* (New York: Free Press, 1954).

39. According to a 1991 Gallup survey of the U.S. workforce, for example, 79 percent said "chances for promotion" were either very important (53 percent) or fairly important (26 percent) as job characteristics; Hugick and Leonard, "Job Dissatisfaction Grows," 6.

40. Economic Values Survey. Among peole who scored high on job satisfac-

tion, 36 percent said "good opportunity to advance" described their job very well, compared with only 8 percent who scored low on job satisfaction. How much people valued their work and how many hours they worked each week were also positively associated with their perception of having opportunities to advance.

41. For a valuable study of the changing rules of success among corporate managers see Robert Jackall, *Moral Mazes*. Jackall's field work, conducted in the early 1980s, convinced him that "managers' rules for survival and success [were] uppermost in their minds [and form] a moral code that guides managers through all the dilemmas and vicissitudes that confront them in the big organization" (3–4). His conclusions appear on the surface to differ sharply from the ones I report in the text. One reason is perhaps the changes in corporate culture that have taken place during the past decade. A more important reason may be that the rules Jackall examined are indeed operative norms for survival in bureaucratic settings, something that many of my respondents spoke about as well, but tell us little about the overarching values and goals that people resort to in legitimating the role of work in their lives. I am in substantial agreement with the main contention of Jackall's study, however, which is that the organizational contexts in which people work have a fundamental influence on their consciousness in general, and that more specifically "bureaucratic work causes people to bracket, while at work, the moralities that they might hold outside the workplace or that they might adhere to privately and to follow instead the prevailing morality of their particular organizational situation" (6).

42. Among numerous discussions of the service ethic, see especially Bell, *The Coming of Post-Industrial Society*, Chap.2.

43. This combination of internal and external standards of success is also well evidenced by an inspector at a Japanese electronics firm in Portland, Oregon, who looks to himself for motivation to do well in his job but also needs to believe that his work will be appreciated and that he would be rewarded by the company. He says, "As far as external motivations coming from the company that make me feel good about doing my work, recognition and the fact that I can see that by doing this that there's a reasonable chance of going up within the company. I still do it anyway because of my own personal beliefs, but it makes me feel even better about it if I do receive some recognition. If I do see there's a reasonable chance of moving up within the company, that makes it even better."

44. Thomas Friedman, *Up the Ladder: Coping With the Corporate Climb* (New York: Warner Books, 1986), 6, estimates that only 5 percent of middle-level managers in American corporations, for example, make it into the ranks of senior management.

45. It is perhaps noteworthy that the one person who spoke positively of his work as a game was a pastor who said he treats writing his sermons as if he were playing a game!

46. Hugick and Leonard, "Job Dissatisfaction Grows," 6; characteristics such as health insurance, interesting work, job security, opportunities to learn new skills, and vacations headed the list.

47. Economic Values Survey.

48. Also like money, though, success is beginning to be regarded by social scientists as something to which fewer people may now be aspiring than in the past. University of North Carolina sociologist Arne Kalleberg, for example, is quoted as saying, "Success won't be measured in monetary terms any more. People will be looking at family and leisure time and personal development as the new markers of success." Quoted in Jim Nesbitt, "American Dream Dims for Young," *Trenton Times* (September 22, 1991), A16.

49. Peters and Waterman, *In Search of Excellence*, 260–62.

50. A number of people interviewed also implied by their remarks that they expected most workplaces to be plagued with impersonality or with competition and conflict; thus, the mere absence of these problems was sometimes enough to convince them that their workplace functioned like a family. A Boston schoolteacher provides an example: "There's very little in-fighting, back-fighting, people who can't stand this one, that one. A faculty of about eighty people all get along really well."

51. Philadelphia attorney Stanton Haynes provides another example of the importance of stories in reinforcing the family image of the workplace. His story was more than a decade old but still stood out in his memory because of the emotional significance of the occasion: "My mother passed away in 1976 and I think my partners and other people in the firm were very considerate in the last couple years of her life because I knew at that time that she was failing—this would be her final disease—it was a terminal disease—and I had a difficult schedule to balance. She was living out of state in Florida and my major case was in the Pacific Northwest, and many people were good about covering things. Also after she did die there was a tremendous attendance at her personal service held for her on successive evenings during the period of mourning and I think, I think there's a lot of caring in the firm—more so than in a lot of other firms that—I would say—there's somewhat of a family type of arrangement there."

52. Brad Diggins, the travel agency owner, says he spends more time with people at work than with his family. Even though he finds it necessary to keep some distance between himself and his employees in order to be an effective manager, he tries to treat them like a family. Why? He believes a family-like environment gets better results from people in the final analysis and is good business. Banker Harold Bentley says he prefers to deal with his clients this way, too, and likes businesses that treat their employees as family. "It's the Mom and Pop operations that keep the world going," he argues.

53. Victor Turner, *The Ritual Process: Structure and Anti-Structure* (Ithaca: Cornell University Press, 1969), especially chap. 4.

54. Another example is provided by an AT&T pamphlet for college seniors entitled "Getting the Right Job." Counseling readers on page 3 to "assess your values," the pamphlet then lists the values that should be considered: achievement, advancement, aesthetics, challenge, creativity, excitement, high income, independence, leadership, power, prestige, recognition, security, social service, variety. This list commits the logical fallacy of assuming that work

values are somehow different from values in general, and then compounds the problem by failing to make this distinction explicit. As a result, many other possibilities are excluded from the list—for example, free time, family loyalty, serenity, personal relationships, intimacy, moral standards, and religious commitment.

55. As one woman, with more than typical self-clarity, admitted, "What I dislike most is constantly feeling I should be doing more." Not wanting to become a workaholic, she nevertheless found herself lying awake at night trying to solve problems associated with her job. It took some stern lectures from her husband, a job change, and lots of internal struggle before she was able to get herself on track.

CHAPTER 6

1. Karl Marx, "The Power of Money," reprinted in *Karl Marx: Early Writings*, trans. T. B. Bottomore (New York: McGraw-Hill, 1963 [1844]), 189–90. Marx's quotation of Shakespeare is from the Schlegel-Tieck translation of *Timon of Athens*, act IV, scene 3.

2. Georg Simmel, *The Philosophy of Money*, 2d ed., trans. Tom Bottomore and David Frisby (London: Routledge, 1990 [1900]), 253.

3. For an overview of recent literature, see Richard Swedberg, "Major Traditions of Economic Sociology," *Annual Review of Sociology* 17 (1991), 251–76; and in anthropology, see especially Beatrice Orlove, "Barter and Cash Sale on Lake Titicaca: A Test of Competing Approaches," *Current Anthropology* 27 (1986), 85–106. Swedberg correctly points out that the current cultural perspective actually has deep roots in other nineteenth-century theoretical traditions, especially the work of Marcel Mauss, Emile Durkheim, and Max Weber. He also notes that cultural approaches as such are still relatively underdeveloped compared with utilitarian, rational-choice, and institutional theories of economic behavior.

4. Viviana A. Zelizer, "The Social Meaning of Money: 'Special Monies,'" *American Journal of Sociology* 95 (1989), 342–77.

5. *Ibid.*, 347.

6. *Ibid.*

7. Sigmund Freud, *Totem and Taboo*, trans. James Strachey (London: Routledge, 1950).

8. Though challenged in some recent perspectives, this so-called functionalist view of taboo was widely emphasized in classical anthropological and sociological studies, including James G. Frazer, *Psyche's Task* (London: Macmillan, 1909), see especially 20; Emile Durkheim, *The Elementary Forms of the Religious Life* (London: Allen & Unwin, 1915), especially 300–10; and A. R. Radcliffe-Brown, *Structure and Function in Primitive Society* (London: Cohen & West, 1952), especially 133–52.

9. See, for example, Max Weber, *Ancient Judaism* (New York: Free Press, 1952 [1921]), especially 149–93. Some suggestive evidence on similar relationships between hierarchical development and taboo in primitive settings is given in

Guy E. Swanson, *Birth of the Gods* (Ann Arbor: University of Michigan Press, 1960).

10. Among numerous studies that have advanced this argument, see especially Philippe Ariès, *The Hour of Our Death* (New York: Knopf, 1981). Similar arguments about insanity, illness, and sexuality have been made by Foucault; see, for example, Michel Foucault, *Madness and Civilization: A History of Insanity in the Age of Reason* (New York: Random House, 1965), and *The Birth of the Clinic: An Archeology of Medical Perception* (New York: Random House, 1975).

11. The following exchange with an inventory planner for a large firm in suburban Philadelphia also reveals how informal norms in the workplace deter financial discussions:

Q: Would you discuss your personal finances with people at work?
A: No.
Q: Why not?
A: Because I know at work everyone gets paid something different. And I don't want them to know what I'm getting paid or what I'm not getting paid. It's just not their business. I don't have that kind of relationship with my friends at work.

12. Lewis, *Liar's Poker*, 21.

13. Conflict between spouses that arose from one of them discussing personal finances with his or her parents came up frequently in our interviews. A young military officer who was in his second marriage admitted, for example, that "me and my parents talk about financial situations, especially when they've helped me out. We've talked a lot. To me it's an embarrassing subject to bring up to my wife. Money just brings you to fights a lot of times." Implicit in some of these accounts is the assumption that people are violating norms of marital intimacy by mentioning finances to anyone else.

14. The subculture of bargain hunting that develops among some groups of friends and co-workers further legitimates discussions in which prices are revealed. Here is an example given by a woman talking about several of her co-workers: "Fran treats herself nicely. She'll go and say it wasn't expensive at all. It was just $125. Marge and I look at each other and say, '$125 is when we think we've treated ourselves.' So it comes up in a very casual kind of way. I mean, I know what Fran spends on her clothes. She'll say, 'Look at these two coats that I got.' I go and show them all the bargains that I bought, too. It's like look at this great buy that I bought."

15. We discovered in conducting our interviews that these were exceptional "ice-breaking" settings for many people that gave them the freedom to talk in depth about personal finances with someone outside their family for the first time. Most people still found it difficult to be specific about their incomes or investments, but some appeared to find it cathartic to be able to reveal these matters to someone. In a few notable instances, people acknowledged their unease about discussing finances and then launched voluntarily into lengthy monologues about monetary matters.

16. The most commonly mentioned device for opening up detailed discussions of personal finances with a family member was asking some relative who

has special expertise to help prepare one's tax forms. This created a quasi-professional, confidential relationship in which people felt comfortable raising questions that went well beyond the tax forms themselves.

17. The taboo on talking about money has, however, been promoted in many tight-knit ethnic groups as well. Some of our respondents indicated that silence about money was part of the immigrant culture their parents or grandparents had learned; for example, this woman of Italian stock observes that she never talks about money with anyone in depth and then explains: "I really think that may be 'Old World,' tied up with a man's image and what's going on. That's not really anybody else's business."

18. The story reported by the man who had worked in China is also revealing because of how he explains the American taboo against talking about money: "When I was in China, they had some young fellows working in the, what they call their foreign affairs office. These guys were 22, 25 years old. Spoke English, and so after lunch we had about an hour or so before the next activity. And I used to like to go for a walk or go out in a park that was behind the hotel where we were staying. Well, anyhow this one fellow wanted to know more—he wanted to practice his English. So we went out to the park and he asked me all about my—what I did and family and what I earned while I was working and what my sources of income would be when I retired, and so I told him. And then after we were through I said, you know, in the United States nobody would tell you these things because they're very personal and if you're gonna ask any of the other people the same questions, be sure to tell them that this is confidential and you're not gonna reveal it to anybody and don't you reveal anything I told you either."

19. A number of the people we talked to recognized explicitly that their parents had taught them to keep quiet about money. Here is one example: "I think I got that secrecy thing from my family, you know, that you don't talk about it. It's private."

20. On the development of private life in the eighteenth century, see Richard Sennett, *The Fall of Public Man* (New York: Random House, 1978). Although many of Sennett's specific claims about narcisissm have been widely criticized, his discussion of the separation of public and private life remains a valuable introduction.

21. Jürgen Habermas, *The Structural Transformation of the Public Sphere: An Inquiry into a Category of Bourgeois Society* (Cambridge: MIT Press, 1989 [1962]), discusses the social processes giving rise to a more fully developed, autonomous public arena in the eighteenth century.

22. I have examined the conditions in a number of European countries in the eighteenth century that contributed differentially to the development of the public sphere and discussed the impact of this development on literary and philosophical conceptions of private selves and public roles in my book *Communities of Discourse: Ideology and Social Structure in the Reformation, the Enlightenment, and European Socialism* (Cambridge: Harvard University Press, 1989).

23. A brief overview of the concept of privatization is presented in Peter L. Berger, *Facing Up to Modernity: Excursions in Society, Politics, and Religion* (New

York: Basic Books, 1977), 130–41. Privatization in the sense used here is not to be confused with discussions focusing on the transfer of social functions from government to the "private" (for-profit) sector; see *Between States and Markets*, ed. Robert Wuthnow (Princeton: Princeton University Press, 1991), especially chap. 1.

24. A comparison with religion is helpful for understanding more clearly the nature of privatization with respect to money. Religious privatization is generally assumed to have been furthered by the gradual exclusion of religion from the dominant secular institutions of modern societies. Because of separation between church and state, the exclusion of religious teachings from public schools, and the diminishing role of religion as an economic institution, believers have presumably come to define religion more in terms of their own personal needs for meaning, comfort, security, and sociability. Religious institutions, on the whole, become significantly weaker in public life, while retaining their importance in the private realm. If this argument is correct, however, we would not be accurate in seeing the privatization of money as a parallel case. Surely the role of money in public life has, if anything, become stronger, rather than weaker. Solving this problem requires us to rethink the sources of privatization. A closer look at religious developments shows that greater emphasis on the private aspects of religion has not come at the expense of its public functions. Instead, the strength of one appears to vary in direct proportion to the other, as the resurgence of religious activity in political life throughout many parts of the world suggests. In the case of money and religion alike, the significant development has been an increasing bifurcation between the public and the private. Among numerous discussions of privatization in the religious area, see especially James Davison Hunter, *American Evangelicalism: Conservative Religion and the Quandary of Modernity* (New Brunswick, N.J.: Rutgers University Press, 1983), 13–14.

25. My use of the term "objective" derives primarily from the discussions of this concept in cultural sociology in Berger and Luckmann, *Social Construction of Reality*, especially part II, and in Peter L. Berger, *The Sacred Canopy: Elements of a Sociological Theory of Religion* (New York: Doubleday, 1967), especially chaps. 1 and 2. Berger and Luckmann emphasize as features of objectivity institutionalization, standing outside of or being perceived as external to the individual, sharing that results in cultural objects gaining collective recognition, and a sense of legitimacy or facticity that gives objective culture power over the individual.

26. Both functional and procedural rationality as modes of objectification are suggested by Berger and Luckmann, *Social Construction of Reality*, 54–64, whose discussion draws heavily on the theoretical formulations of Max Weber.

27. What Daniel Bell, *The Cultural Contradictions of Capitalism* (New York: Basic Books, 1976), chap. 1, has described as a "disjunction of realms" (i.e., between institutionalized social structure and cultural expression) may thus be applied to the topic of money as well.

28. The discussion of subjectivization, which again follows loosely the previously cited work of Berger and Luckmann, must not be taken to refer simply to a distinction between internalized and externalized culture, but to the special

features of internalized culture that obtain under the conditions of "disjunc-tion" between public and private in modern society.

29. Of religion, Berger, *Sacred Canopy*, writes: "privatized religion is a matter of the 'choice' or 'preference' of the individual or the nuclear family, *ipso facto* lacking in common, binding quality. Such private religiosity, however 'real' it may be to the individuals who adopt it, cannot any longer fulfill the classical task of religion, that of constructing a common world within which all of social life receives ultimate meaning binding on everybody. . . . [V]alues pertaining to private religiosity are, typically, irrelevant to institutional contexts other than the private sphere" (pp. 133–34).

30. On norms of civility, see especially John Cuddihy, *No Offense: Civil Religion and Protestant Taste* (New York: Seabury, 1978).

31. Bellah et al., *Habits of the Heart*, especially 55–84.

32. Despite the emphasis placed in American culture on "leaving home," it is important to recognize the relationship between this emphasis and the sense of arbitrariness that was discussed earlier in the text. Berger and Luckmann, *Social Construction of Reality*, write: "The original reality of childhood is 'home.' It posits itself as such, inevitably and, as it were, 'naturally.' By comparison with it, all later realities are 'artificial'" (143).

33. The "anchoring" effects of linking money with work have been suggested in a variety of discussions, including ones emphasizing the relationships between affluence and anomie, between anomie and sudden or unexpected windfalls such as lottery winnings, and between work and locus of control; see William Simon and John H. Gagnon, "The Anomie of Affluence: A Post-Mertonian Conception," *American Journal of Sociology* 82 (1976), 356–78; Mark Abrahamson, "Sudden Wealth, Gratification and Attainment: Durkheim's Anomie of Affluence Reconsidered," *American Sociological Review* 45 (1980), 49–57; R. Vecchio, "Workers' Beliefs in Internal Versus External Determinants of Success," *Journal of Social Psychology* 114 (1981), 199–207; and J. Younger, A. Arrowood, and G. Hemsley, "And the Lucky Shall Inherit the Earth: Perceiving the Causes of Financial Success and Failure," *European Journal of Social Psychology* 7 (1977), 509–15.

34. Adrian Furnham, "The Protestant Work Ethic, Human Values and Attitudes towards Taxation," *Journal of Economic Psychology* 8 (1983), 112–28.

35. Research conducted among 5- and 6-year-olds also suggests a reason why the taboo on money itself may be a factor in its being dissociated from work: children generally realized there was some connection between working and getting money, but they were also likely to be quite confused about the relationship because (a) they realized governments, banks, mints, and even God were also sources of money, (b) they recognized that many people, including themselves and often their mothers, worked but did not receive pay, and (c) they saw no intrinsic connection between how hard people worked and how much money they received. The implication is that explicit discourse about money and work is needed to clarify these connections. See Hans G. Furth, *The World of Grown-Ups: Children's Conceptions of Society* (New York: Elsevier, 1980), especially chap. 5.

36. These studies are reported in Daniel Yankelovich et al., *The World at Work: An International Report on Jobs, Productivity, and Human Values* (New York: Octagon Books, 1985), 139, 155, 284.

37. Lewis, *Liar's Poker*, 32.

CHAPTER 7

1. See, for example, Roland Marchand, *Advertising the American Dream* (Berkeley: University of California Press, 1985).

2. The example reported in the text of Pam Jones illustrates that the question of values comes up both in deciding to enter the market in the first place and then in making more finely graded choices once one is in the market. A Los Angeles attorney talking about his decision to purchase a $500 suit, rather than one half this price, reveals that the question "Do I need this?" is probably the biggest hurdle that defining oneself "in the market" brackets from consideration. "Do I really need it? We've got more than we possibly could use in this country. And, if we're honest, most of us have more clothes then we will ever use. We buy nicer cars than we need. All we need is transportation. I'm sometimes self-conscious that I bought too much or too good when I don't really need that." When asked to explain, then, why he bought the suit, he paused, asked how honest he should be, and then explained, "At a surface level there was the motivation that I needed a new suit. At another level I bought a better-quality suit that I would need to have just to wear every day at the office, because there's a motivation for me to look sharp or I place personal value in good quality clothes or appearances. Appearances are important to me." In short, having to think through the question of "need" in response to the interviewer's question forced him to admit that looking nice at the office was one of his values.

3. As one example, consider the following remarks by a young woman in Washington, D.C., who had struggled recently with the question of whether to purchase a new camera for her part-time photography business: "I just felt very materialistic—like, I'm draining all our resources, you know, and I don't have to have a new camera, that I'm just kind of being petty. I would jump back and forth between, 'No, I really need it. This is for my business. It's important.' And then, 'How good a camera should I get? Should I get top of the line? Should I not?' I just started getting really obsessed about this materialism thing and it was disgusting."

4. This is a recognized sales tactic to reduce "buyer's remorse," something that many of our interviewees admitted having. For example, one man mused at length about the anxiety he had experienced in deciding on a new car: "How do you justify spending that extra $3,000? If you amortize it out over a six-year period, it's really nothing, but at the time it's a whole bunch, and you get into little nitpick situations like that. I had an old car that I could fix up. That was a great car. Is it worth me putting out all this huge amount of cash versus fixing it up and driving this other one? And it was a real battle. It was a real battle. I had buyer's remorse for a long time."

5. Teri Silver, the systems analyst, was an exception. She felt she should follow a budget but had not been disciplined enough to do it: "I never followed a budget and I know I should. . . . I want to, but I never have done it."

6. A man in his late sixties who considered himself financially prudent illustrated the logic of fixed and discretionary expenditures when he remarked, "We know what money's available, we know what our responsibilities are, and so that's what you follow. You know what's left as to how much spending you should do. And so if you want to call that a budget, why it's an invisible budget."

7. Stuart Cummings, the Chicago lawyer, says he and his wife have found a way to avoid these disagreements: "Once a month I sit at my desk and I write all the checks out, and I become tenser and tenser as the process goes on. And my wife is suspiciously quiet and stays on the other side of the house when that process goes on."

8. Robert Wuthnow, *Meaning and Moral Order: Explorations in Cultural Analysis* (Berkeley: University of California, 1987), 109.

9. Mary Douglas, *Purity and Danger: An Analysis of Concepts of Pollution and Taboo* (Baltimore: Penguin, 1966), 137, writes that the cultural boundaries of any society "contain power to reward conformity and repulse attack. There is energy in its margins and unstructured areas."

10. Token behavior of this kind, we might say, has "symbolic utility" because it stands for something else, often a larger category of behavior; for example, for the dieter eating dessert one time symbolizes personal dissipation and weakness in the face of temptation. I am grateful for this example to Robert Nozick, who discussed it in his 1991 Tanner Lectures at Princeton University, entitled "Principles of Decision, Decisions of Principle."

11. Italian and Japanese wedding customs often involve the use of a ceremonially decorated envelope in which guests place cash or checks; the Japanese custom generally does not require anonymity as is the case in some Italian traditions.

12. Another example that partially illustrates this point is the finding that parents who give or loan money to adult children seldom negotiate with siblings to determine who will pay the best rates of interest, or make decisions based on calculations of differential need (which would require estimates of earning power, net worth, debts, and other financial obligations); instead, they usually impose extrinsic standards of equity and give all siblings exactly the same amount; see Marcia Millman, "They Do Come Home Again . . . for Money," *Lear's* (November 1991), 94–97, 138.

13. Although studies of marital financial arrangements are rare, those that exist suggest that global agreements are quite common and are often orchestrated in such a way as to minimize actual monetary negotiations. For example, allowances given by wage-earning husbands to unemployed wives in early twentieth-century London appear typically to have been long-term agreements based on a *percentage* of the husband's total wages; see M. Pember Reeves, *Round about a Pound a Week* (London: G. Bell and Sons, 1914).

14. Allocations of family finances between husbands and wives are often

based on this principle; one spouse (usually the husband) taking responsibility for certain routine payments (such as rent or mortgage) and large unusual expenditures (purchasing a new automobile), while the other spouse is put completely in charge of other items, such as food and children's clothing. British examples are presented in Jan Pahl, "Patterns of Money Management within Marriage," *Journal of Social Policy* 9 (1980), 313–35. What some have called "gendered money," such as allowances and pin money, can from this perspective be understood as one specific example of a more general class of symbolic mechanisms used to minimize the likelihood of money discussions becoming a contaminant of intimate human relationships. Cultural boundaries are simply applied, rather than market-type negotiations having to take place. As one student of the subject observes, "The allocative system is a normative rather than a bargaining process" (quoted in Pahl, 321).

15. The frequency with which people fight about money has been suggested in a number of studies. For example, in one study of urban families money ranked at the top of the list both as the "chief disagreement" mentioned and among the "total disagreements" mentioned. See Robert Blood and Donald M. Wolfe, *Husbands and Wives: The Dynamics of Married Living* (New York: Free Press, 1960), table 118. In this study, money was implicated in 42 percent of all family disagreements.

16. See, for example, Marcia Millman, *Warm Hearts and Cold Cash: The Intimate Dynamics of Families and Money* (New York: Free Press, 1991).

17. I am grateful to Richard Epstein of the University of Chicago for this insight.

18. One recent example is Joel Martin, *Sacred Revolt* (Boston: Beacon, 1991). Personal conversations with Professor Martin also suggest the interesting hypothesis that the ambivalence expressed toward traders by Native Americans and others in premoney societies can be understood as a functional equivalent to the ambivalence many people today express toward money.

19. Research summarized in Barry Schwartz, "Altruism: Why It is Impossible . . . and Ubiquitous," paper presented at the conference on "Altruism: Exploring the Intellectual Concept," University of Chicago, 1991.

20. Quoted in Leo Rosten, *Infinite Riches* (New York: McGraw-Hill, 1979), 361.

21. One man summed up the consequences this way: "Most of the loans I know between individuals have turned out just to separate them."

22. Nonmarket monetary transactions are also considered dehumanizing in American culture because people are supposed to be economically self-sufficient. As one man explained: "I hate ever having to ask anybody for anything, in a sense, because you feel obligated to them, or you feel the way our country works, that you're sort of stupid. And like no one in this country—everybody can make it on their own. If you have to ask, you're a failure. And I know I don't like to feel that way, and I wouldn't want to make somebody else feel that way."

23. The woman quoted in the previous paragraph in the text went on to say that she would feel comfortable borrowing from or loaning money to her par-

ents, but not her siblings: "I feel very comfortable with my parents and we trust each other and that's all really good and well. One time I talked to my sister about borrowing money from her and she was like right away to say, well, we want to have it written down and thoroughly understood how much it would be and how much the interest would be and when it was going to be paid back. And I just felt like, you know, if you're that uptight about it, I don't want to do it. I mean, I know that's wise, but just to have that attitude. . . ."

24. The reasons for negative attitudes toward money as a gift have been explored empirically in P. Webley, S. Lea, and R. Portalska, "The Unacceptability of Money as a Gift," *Journal of Economic Psychology* 4 (1983), 223–38.

25. Women were more likely to give handmade items than men. One woman's comment provides an especially good illustration of the symbolism of making something yourself: "My values about [gifts] have changed over time. I prefer, much prefer, to make something for somebody. Do needlework. Mostly it's arts and crafts kinds of things. And to put my precious time into doing a piece of personal work like that that not only doesn't cost as much, but I think has a value that is much more me." She added that she also likes to give gifts she finds in unusual places, like when she is on vacation, rather than at the places where everybody else shops.

26. A respondent who worked at a department store bought most of her gifts there because of the discount but often had them monogrammed in order to "add a personal touch."

27. As one example, consider the following remarks from a middle-aged man who said he had changed his views about gifts over the years: "A lot of the things I did for certain people, which I thought they would really appreciate, it turns out that they really didn't, and that kind of turned me off to it in a lot of ways. So I am much more careful nowadays as far as who I do for and what I do for them. You tend to be suspicious of everyone's motives. Why are they looking for this? Why are they looking for that? What are they trying to gain? And that's a bad way to be, and I try to keep that to a minimum, but I don't do as much for people as I used to as far as, you know, buying them things, other than the people who are very close to me. I tend to take care of the people who are very close to me and more or less let other people fend for themselves."

28. Arthur Kleinman, *Patients and Healers in the Context of Culture: An Exploration of the Borderland between Anthropology, Medicine, and Psychiatry* (Berkeley: University of California Press, 1980), 209–23.

29. Virginia A. Hodgkinson and Murray S. Weitzman, *Giving and Volunteering in the United States: Findings from a National Survey* (Washington, D.C.: Independent Sector, Inc., 1990), 9–10.

30. In a national survey I conducted in 1989, 70 percent of the American public agreed that "a lot of the money given to charity is really given for tax reasons," 75 percent agreed that "many charities fatten the pockets of their administrators instead of really helping the needy," and 62 percent agreed that "giving to charities is a way of making yourself feel good without really getting involved." The details of this survey are described in my book *Acts of Compassion*.

CHAPTER 8

1. Quoted in David Kusnet, *Speaking American* (New York: Thunder's Mouth Press, 1992), 133; Kusnet, offering advice to political office-seekers, adds: "Remember—America is a middle-class country. Most people identify themselves and others as middle class, and consider the middle class to be society's economic, social, and moral norm" (152).

2. Figures reported in this chapter from the Economic Values Survey are drawn from comparisons of full-time workers who are employed as laborers or in skilled, semiskilled, service, or clerical occupations and whose family incomes in 1992 were $30,000 or lower with full-time workers who are employed in professional or managerial occupations and whose family incomes were $50,000 or more. For most purposes, "working class" and "professional-managerial class" refer to these operational definitions.

3. See, for example, William Simon and John H. Gagnon, "The Anomie of Affluence: A Post-Mertonian Conception," *American Journal of Sociology* 82 (1976), 356–78.

4. Ely Chinoy, *Automobile Workers and the American Dream* (Boston: Beacon, 1955).

5. David Halle and Frank Romo, "The Blue-Collar Working Class: Continuity and Change," in *America at Century's End*, ed. Alan Wolfe (Berkeley: University of California Press, 1991), 152–84.

6. Mark Granovetter and Charles Tilly, "Inequality and Labor Processes," in *Handbook of Sociology*, ed. Neil J. Smelser (Beverly Hills: Sage, 1988), 175–221.

7. Bell, *The Coming of Post-Industrial Society*, 137–42.

8. "The Union Label," *Forbes* (September 14, 1992), 302; Italy, Japan, Sweden, the United Kingdom, and Germany all had higher proportions of union membership in 1990 than the United States.

9. National statistics released in 1992, for example, showed an average hourly salary decline of 7.6 percent since 1987 for blue-collar workers, compared with a 3.5 percent decline over the same period for white-collar workers; reported in Sharon Cohen, "Blue Collar: A Vanishing Dream," *The Intelligencer* (September 6, 1992), A8.

10. Among other examples, see Nelson Foote, "The Professionalization of Labor in Detroit," *American Journal of Sociology* 58 (1953), 371–80; Arthur L. Stinchcombe, "Bureaucratic and Craft Administration of Production: A Comparative Study," *Administrative Science Quarterly* 4 (1959), 168–87; and Theodore Caplow, *The Sociology of Work* (Minneapolis: University of Minnesota Press, 1954), 48, 139.

11. Harold L. Wilensky, "The Professionalization of Everyone?" *American Journal of Sociology* 70 (1964), 137–58.

12. Nina Munk, "A Convenience-of-Living Index," *Forbes* (September 14, 1992), 218.

13. Forty-three percent of working-class respondents in the Economic Values Survey gave high job satisfaction scores (8, 9, or 10), compared with 66 percent of professionals and managers. Some of this difference is, however,

attributable to the fact that younger working-class respondents (who perhaps see their present job as a way-station to something better) are considerably less likely to express high job satisfaction (31 percent) than are older working-class respondents (58 percent).

14. Working-class respondents are only marginally less likely to agree with that statement "I feel good about the work I do" (89 percent compared with 98 percent among professionals and managers).

15. The proportions among working-class respondents and among professionals and managers, respectively, who said each of the following describes their present job fairly well were: provides a lot of variety, 65, 90; suits my personality, 77, 94; people at work care about me personally, 76, 89; pays very well, 61, 79; is mentally stimulating, 59, 93; I have a lot of freedom, 57, 80.

16. The percentages, respectively, for working-class men and women in manual occupations and in service occupations were: control over daily schedule, 43, 57; control over goals, 40, 50. By a considerable margin (59 percent to 30 percent), more of the former said their work left them physically exhausted.

17. For instance, 67 and 62 percent of manual and service workers, respectively, said "provides a lot of variety" characterizes their work very or fairly well; 39 and 43 percent, respectively, said they experience at least a fair amount of variation in their daily tasks.

18. Whereas 53 percent of professionals and managers said they worked for organizations employing more than 100 people, only 35 percent of working-class respondents did; respectively, the percentages who said they had to work closely with more than 10 people were 44 and 30; and the percentages who described themselves as working in a huge bureaucracy were 47 and 32.

19. Joan Larsen makes a similar point about caring. She says it makes all the difference in the world that a couple of the lawyers in her office are very warm, personable human beings. "That's life," she asserts, "it's probably true whether you dig ditches or work in a law firm." Murial Johnson also emphasized the caring or family aspect of her work: "I'm the type of person I like to feel needed and I like to feel that what I'm doing is appreciated or liked. So therefore, since in my situation I am liked by all of them, those that are higher ranked than me and lower ranked than me, they consider me a person. You know, a lot of times, okay, like in the beginning they tried to class me once I made supervisor. 'Well, I shouldn't say this because you're one of management,' you know, they tried to like throw me off into another class, but because of my personality it was hard and they couldn't do it, and they still relate to me as one of them as well as their boss." In the survey, women and employees in service occupations were more likely than men and manual laborers to say their co-workers cared about them.

20. Ed Butler's story was typical of many others. Jack Paretti, for example, told about a recent job that gave him a great deal of satisfaction: "It was a complete mess. Nothing was typeset. We quoted it at being half the size it was, with half the pictures and everything. He brought in something twice as big, twice as many half-tones, and they had to have it for Friday. It was a mess because they had five people on their committee and five people apparently

thought they were in charge of the committee. I was getting calls from all these people all week about the job. And actually when we finished it yesterday, it looked pretty good. They were real happy with it, and they called up. Actually, the guy called me at home yesterday morning and told me they were real happy with it. You feel good about that. I mean, everybody in the shop worked real hard to get it out. It's kind of like a teamwork thing."

21. In a statement that reveals much about the symbolic value of expertise, Mike Kominski says, "I'm not afraid to say that I'm very good at what I do, at driving concrete. I've been doing it for fourteen years. I've been with three different companies. I've been all over, in different situations, all different kinds of pours, all different kinds of trucks, all different kinds of situations, and after you put in so many hours for so many years, you hopefully get a certain amount of experience and a little bit of knowledge out of that as far as what you can and what you can't do with the truck. And my boss realizes this, so what happens sometimes is if there is a real bad job, something that's very muddy or very difficult to do, a lot of times I will be the one that goes to do it. If the truck gets stuck, if the truck's in a bad situation where it might roll over, a lot of times I'm the one he sends out to try to pull the truck out and save it. And I like that and, you know, that makes the boring, boring hours that you put in, the repetition of doing the same thing over and over, when something like that happens it makes it worthwhile."

22. Sixty-six percent agreed that their work is making the world a better place, compared with 81 percent of professionals and managers.

23. Discriminant models were examined in which age and gender were controlled and predictions of high job satisfaction were estimated separately for working-class respondents and for professionals and managers. Coefficients among working-class respondents were as follows: work is boring (–.33), emotionally draining (–.26), too much pressure (–.18), co-workers care about me personally (.24), mentally stimulating (.27), suits my personality (.35), pays very well (.27). Coefficients among professionals and managers were of similar magnitude; exceptions were that the coefficient for boring work was not significant, while there was a positive effect for work providing a lot of variety.

24. A more pointed example comes from a man who says, "I met a couple people who are wonderful in offices and such, but, in general, I wouldn't do that type of work because, unfortunately, the pressure is there to perform too greatly, and—it's almost like a Shakespearean play—who is king and who is on the way up to get there—the line of succession. And how do you do it? Well, you slice everyone's throat getting up there." Another man explains, "I work by myself, so it's not like I have that phony image in the office. I can be myself wherever I go. I don't hide anything."

25. A working-class man who is earning a modest living as a free-lance photographer says, for example, "I'm a terrible critic with my own pictures. I'm always saying I could have done something better, dah duh dah duh. When I was up in Alaska, I got some beautiful shots of whales, which I've always wanted to do in my life is just to see whales. I have a great love for whales. And as nice as these pictures are, I'm still frustrated."

26. Asked what the most important reason was for choosing their present line of work, 38 percent of working-class respondents said "the money," compared with only 16 percent of professionals and managers.

27. Another example, less typical, is worth considering because it makes the same point about circumstances, choice, and reasons for liking a job in even more pointed terms. Larry Leonard, 30, spends his days delivering bottled water to restaurants, clubs, and private homes—even to "go-go bars" (always fearing he'll be seen and mistaken for a customer). He was a good student in high school, but his main love was soccer. During his first semester in junior college he realized he didn't have the "umph" to make it any longer in the classroom. He'd worked at fast food places, had a girlfriend, needed money. So he quit school and got a job with a burglar alarm company. That lasted a couple of years. Then he spent a year working nightshift as a janitor at an oil company. He spent another year as a carpenter's apprentice making cabinets. For the past six years he has been hauling water. Asked how he got into his job, he emphasizes circumstances: "It wasn't my choice. It was a job. I just got laid off, and I needed work. I had a wife and a child, and I could not afford to sit around, and this happened to be a friend who said, 'I can hire you. Do you want the job?' I was like, 'Fine,' and I took it." But he hastens to add: "I've never found myself to be an inside person anyway. I always much prefer to work outside. So in a way, I didn't mind taking the job. It happened to be pretty good in that sense. And I like the job. There's a lot to it that I do like." Asked what, he stressed the job's variety. "Every day is different, something always happens."

28. Among working-class respondents, the percentages who said they never or hardly ever discussed each of the following with anyone outside their immediate family were: income, 79; family budget, 88; purchases, 78; financial worries, 70; the routine cost of goods, 75; and charitable gifts, 93. Only financial worries was significantly lower than the proportion among professionals and managers. The percentages of working-class respondents who said they never or hardly ever discussed personal finances with the following were: co-workers, 86; clergy, 97; therapists, 99; financial experts, 97; fellow church members, 98; and close friends, 75. Only close friends was significantly lower than among professionals and managers. A significantly higher proportion of working-class respondents than professionals and managers agreed that parents should not talk about money in front of children.

29. In the Economic Values Survey there were no statistically significant differences in the responses of working-class men and women to questions about discussing money.

30. In the Economic Values Survey, the proportions who said "very clear" were 12 percent and 35 percent, respectively, among respondents age 18 to 29; among respondents age 50 or older, there were no differences, suggesting that children of all social strata were perhaps more likely to be exposed to family financial decisions a generation ago.

31. They are also grandchildren of the Great Depression, often feeling that their parents made it or almost did, but weren't wise, and followed whims. Sometimes they look back to their grandparents, finding a common bond there

because they are working and scrimping like their grandparents. Here is one example: "I've been there [at my job], God, I said twelve years, it's probably been like fourteen or fifteen. My grandparents respect it because I've been there for a long time, because my grandfather worked at B & B in production for twenty-some years or whatever. So to them if you're in a job, and you work your way up and you stay there, that's the good thing. I think my dad's happy that I've held a job and financially held my own. My mom's kind of like, 'you've been there too long. Go get something else,' because my mom's jumped from job to job since she's been out, and she really hasn't moved ahead at all. She gets somewhere, jumps somewhere else, and she starts lower and moves up, and she's not getting anywhere."

32. Eighty-two percent of working-class respondents said they had worried about paying their bills recently, compared with 58 percent of professionals and managers; 42 percent (versus 12 percent) had worried a lot. Among working-class respondents, 76 percent had experienced anxiety recently about money decisions, and 58 percent had felt guilty about their purchases.

33. Seventy-one percent of working-class respondents said they had a lot of control over their attitudes toward money, and 56 percent said this about how much they thought about finances, compared with 31 percent who said they had this much control over their earnings and 34 percent who said the same about family spending. None of these figures was statistically different for professionals and managers.

34. Compared with professionals and managers, working-class respondents were more likely to say making a lot of money was very important to their sense of worth as a person; they were also more likely to say they had been worried recently because they were feeling bad about themselves.

35. Jack Paretti, for example, doesn't just worry about paying the bills. He also feels guilty. He feels he didn't learn how to handle money properly because his mother always abused their credit cards. Until he was married he paid the rent and then just blew everything else. He says he wishes now he would have saved so they could buy a house.

36. Although it might be assumed that perceiving a lack of relationship between hard work and making more money is merely sour grapes among poorly paid members of the labor force, these responses were not statistically different from the percentages giving the same responses among highly paid professionals and managers.

37. Working-class commitment to hard work as an ideal is evident in the fact that 47 percent expressed high admiration for someone who was rich but still worked hard, compared with only 5 percent who said the same about a rich person who didn't work. Evidence of work that results in wealth being more valued than work that does not comes from the 69 percent who expressed admiration for someone who works hard and earns a lot of money, compared with 51 percent who said the same about someone who works hard but earns little.

38. The percentages of working-class respondents who said they would be very willing to do each of the following to make more money were: work

longer hours each week, 33; take a high-pressure job, 13; take a job that is less interesting but pays better, 23; and move to a different part of the country, 16. These percentages should not, however, be interpreted as evidence of laziness or lack of ambition among the working class. Among professionals and managers, the proportions were even lower (21, 9, 7, and 10, respectively).

39. On simple survey items asking how much of a consideration mileage, the best deal, and preference for a particular model would be in purchasing a new car, working-class respondents and professionals and managers did not differ, with one exception: the former were actually more likely than the latter to say they would pay a lot of attention to how this purchase fit into their broader values.

40. One man explained why he is planning to buy a conversion van in these terms: "Right now, the conversion van is sort of looking more interesting. For one thing is, I kind of, right now, say, I kind of deserve a little toy. A little plushness in my life, you know."

41. The symbolic, as opposed to purely economic, value of ritualized cutbacks is also clearly in evidence, however, as illustrated by this statement: "When the paycheck goes down, everything gets tight, and all the bills, and then you start saying, well, don't leave the water running, or make sure you shut the light off, and you've got to think about that. I don't want to have to think about leaving a light on. I mean, that shouldn't have to happen."

42. Jack Paretti gives an example of splurging that shows clearly how such an episode gets defined, why it is remembered, and how it relates to rules about ordinary expenditures. He says he and his wife have an agreement that neither will spend more than $25 without consulting the other. "I won't spend more than $25, unless it's grocery shopping, on anything that could be considered a luxury or whatever unless I bring it up with her and vice versa, because we both violated that agreement once, her on my birthday one year and me on hers. [What happened?] She spent about $50. I kept telling her the whole time, 'Look, don't. I don't want anything. Don't spend.' 'Well, I'm going to spend some money. I'm going to get you something.' She spent $50. I got kind of annoyed. I mean, I appreciated the gift obviously, and then I did the same thing. But it wasn't like a major argument or anything. It's just like, better not do it again, so we haven't had any problems with it."

43. One man provided this illustration: "We try to figure out, like we need a TV, so we figure out exactly what we want, and how much you want to spend on it. It goes back to the old don't buy junk. I didn't want to get a piece of garbage for $100, and yet I wasn't going to pay $600 or $800. The salesman was trying to sell me this one with the picture in picture, and stereo sound. I'm looking at this one TV, which was on sale, and he goes, 'Well, it doesn't have stereo sound.' I said, 'Well, turn it on,' and he did. I said, 'I can hear it. What's the problem?' That's the kind of thing. I didn't want to waste money on the TV for stuff we really didn't need. I only watch one channel at a time. Why do I need a TV screen with four channels on it for?"

44. Jack Paretti talks about his brother who has been in jail for theft as someone who is "materialistic," so in this case materialism doesn't mean paying

attention to making ends meet, but being so obsessed with money that one breaks the law, or in some other way ruins one's life.

45. A third of working-class respondents said wealthy people are generally less happy than other people, compared with only 16 percent of professionals and managers; only 10 percent of each group thought the wealthy are happier.

46. The following quote also provides a good illustration of borrowing and lending being disliked because they alter the balance of power in family relationships: "There was one time where her father loaned us money, and then it was kind of like the thing we purchased was his. He helped us also move into the first apartment, and now all of a sudden it's like, 'Well, you should arrange it this way, and you should—' and he tried to just kind of take over. And we're like, 'Well, it's my place. Don't do that. Just because you gave us the money doesn't mean it's your place.' But we worked through that and kind of straight away said, 'Let's get this up front. This is my house, and thank you, here's your money back, and we'll do it this way.'"

47. The connection between materialism and negative attitudes toward the rich is also particularly evident in this remark from Mike Kominski: "One of the things that gets under my skin the most in this world is materialism. I despise people, even though I hate to say despise, but I really have problems with people who are yuppies, who it seems like they judge the sum of their lives by their possessions, by their BMWs, their Porsches. I can't stand it when I see people who live their lives just to obtain possessions, because something I've learned from standing out here on the street corner collecting for the Fire Department is that over the course of a couple days you'll notice that the poor people will always stop and give you something, even if it's just a couple quarters or whatever it is they have, an old dollar bill or something like that. A lot of times your more well-to-do people, they won't."

48. Figures cited in the text are from Urban Institute, Census Bureau, and Immigration & Naturalization Service statistics reported in Michael J. Mandel and Christopher Farrell, "The Immigrants: How They're Helping to Revitalize the U.S. Economy," *Business Week* (July 13, 1992), 114–22.

49. *Ibid.*, 122.

50. Christopher Power, "America's Welcome Mat Is Wearing Thin," *Business Week* (July 13, 1992), 119.

CHAPTER 9

1. This quote is from an actual story carried by the Associated Press about a national survey conducted by Mellman & Lazarus, Inc., for the Massachusetts Mutual Life Insurance Company; see "Poll: Importance of Family Rises," *Trenton Times* (November 18, 1991), D3.

2. My question is quite different from the considerable literature that examined the circumstances of work-family conflicts, rather than the moral understandings of these relationships; some of that literature is summarized in Francine D. Blau and Marianne A. Ferber, *The Economics of Women, Men, and Work*

(Englewood Cliffs, N.J.: Prentice-Hall, 1986), and F. J. Crosby, ed., *Spouse, Worker, Parent: On Gender and Multiple Roles* (New Haven: Yale University Press, 1987).

3. According to George P. Murdock, *Social Structure* (New York: Macmillan, 1949), the nuclear family was the dominant custom prior to this time in approximately one-third of all societies.

4. In this I follow Skolnick, *Embattled Paradise*, 51, who defends the 1950's family as a baseline from which to assess recent changes in family life.

5. Arlene Skolnick, *The Intimate Environment* (Boston: Little, Brown, 1973), 97.

6. On the distinction between "postmodern" and "modern" families, see Judith Stacey, *Brave New Families* (New York: Basic Books, 1990).

7. Although many observers distinguish extended from nuclear families on the basis of physical residence in the same household, the present discussion takes a somewhat broader view, focusing on the geographic proximity and social, economic, and emotional interdependence of family members.

8. On romantic love, see especially Ann Swidler, "Love and Adulthood in American Culture," in *Themes of Work and Love in Adulthood*, ed. Neil J. Smelser and Erik H. Erikson (Cambridge: Harvard University Press, 1980), 120–47.

9. The close connection between the American Dream and the nuclear family is also symbolized by the importance that was attached to homeownership.

10. Christopher Lasch, *Haven in a Heartless World* (New York: Basic Books, 1977), xxiii, writes: "Most of the writing on the modern family . . . assumes [it is] impervious to outside influences. In reality, the modern world intrudes at every point and obliterates its privacy. The sanctity of the home is a sham in a world dominated by giant corporations and by the apparatus of mass promotion."

11. The resulting resentment of parents toward their children is one of the "injuries" described in Richard Sennett and Jonathan Cobb, *The Hidden Injuries of Class* (New York: Vintage, 1972). The corresponding feeling of abandonment on the part of children can also be acute. A Hispanic man in Chicago who was the first member of his family to attend college told us: "My family takes no interest in my work. They don't know what I do, or why I do it. It really doesn't matter to them."

12. Skolnick, *Embattled Paradise*, of course suggests this imagery in the title of her book.

13. Economic Values Survey; specifically, 44 percent agreed strongly, 45 percent agreed somewhat, 7 percent disagreed somewhat, 2 percent disagreed strongly, and 2 percent were unsure.

14. Her view is typical. In the Economic Values Survey, 75 percent agreed (35 percent strongly) that "advertising is corrupting our basic values."

15. In the Economic Values Survey this statement elicited stronger agreement that any other statement about materialism: 53 percent agreed strongly, 37 percent agreed somewhat, 6 percent disagreed somewhat, 1 percent disagreed strongly, and 2 percent were unsure.

16. Sylvia Ann Hewlett, *When the Bough Breaks: The Cost of Neglecting Our Children* (New York: Basic Books, 1991), 102.

17. Writer Austin Winters, a Philadelphian, drew another direct connection between the power and innocence of children. The problem with materialism, he explained, is that children gain a sense of power from the television programs they watch and the video games they play, but they do not yet have the ability to discriminate between good and bad uses of this power.

18. The questions and responses in the Economic Values Survey were, "How sure are you about what to teach your children?" Very sure (54 percent), somewhat sure (38 percent), somewhat unsure (3 percent), very unsure (1 percent), and don't know (4 percent). "How do you feel, in general, about the way children are being raised in our society? Do you feel our nation is doing an excellent job (1 percent), a good job (9 percent), a fair job (41 percent), a poor job (33 percent), or a very poor job (15 percent)?"

19. The chief reason, of course, is that married women are increasingly in the labor force themselves. Between 1960 and 1988 the proportion of married women with children under the age of 6 who were in the labor force increased from 19 percent to 57 percent. Panel on Employer Policies and Working Families, *Work and Family: Policies for a Changing Work Force*, ed. Marianne A. Ferber and Brigid O'Farrell (Washington, D.C.: National Academy of Sciences, 1991), 102. The fact that fewer men are married, and that fewer married men have children, is also a reason for the changing relationships between work and family.

20. In the Economic Values Survey, 38 percent of married men with full-time jobs and with employed spouses said they often relieved stress by watching television (another 35 percent did so sometimes), whereas only 29 percent of women in comparable situations said this.

21. Specifically, 12 percent of men in the Economic Values Survey with full-time jobs said they experienced serious or very serious conflict between their work and their families; among married men with children, this figure rose only to 15 percent. In the latter group, 33 percent said they experienced some conflict, 42 percent experienced hardly any, and 10 percent experienced no conflict. By a margin of 31 percent to 41 percent, married men with employed spouses are also less likely than married women with employed spouses to say they experience stress as a result of having too little time for their families.

22. One indication of this tendency may be the fact that 34 percent of working men in the Economic Values Survey said they often deal with job-related stress by keeping it to themselves, compared with 23 percent of working women.

23. As discussed elsewhere in the chapter, married working women are more likely than married working men to complain that their families do not appreciate their work.

24. Among respondents in the Economic Values Survey who were working full-time, married, and had employed spouses, 69 percent of the women said

they did most of the housework, compared with 8 percent of the men. Three percent of the women said their spouse did most of it, compared with 57 percent of the men. Twenty-eight percent of the women said they shared it about equally, as did 35 percent of the men. See also Diane S. Burden and Bradley Googins, *Balancing Job and Homelife Study: Managing Work and Family Stress* (Boston: Boston University School of Social Work, 1987).

25. Panel on Employer Policies and Working Families, *Work and Family*, 102, "Approximately 10 percent of full-time employees are actual or potential caregivers for elderly relatives. This group is expected to increase substantially over the next several years."

26. For example, 37 percent of women in the Economic Values Survey said they had worked part-time instead of full-time because of obligations to their families, compared with 16 percent of men; 17 (vs. 12) percent had refused to work overtime; and 24 (vs. 16) percent had refused to travel or be away from home.

27. Gender differences in providing emotional support to children are striking. Among women in the Economic Values Survey who were working full-time and had children, 60 percent said their children came mainly to them for emotional support, whereas only 11 percent of the men said this. Among married respondents with children and an employed spouse, 52 percent of the women said their children came mainly to them, compared with only 6 percent of the men.

28. Nineteen percent of working women in the Economic Values Survey said that "arranging child care" had been a big or very big issue for them (compared with only 10 percent of working men); 33 percent said the same about "getting household chores done" (compared with 19 percent of working men).

29. This difference was more pronounced in open-ended interviews but was also somewhat evident in the survey. Thirty-eight percent of women with full-time jobs said "it drains me emotionally" described their work very well or fairly well, compared with 33 percent of men with full-time jobs. An indirect indication of the same pattern may be that equal numbers of men and women said their work was physically exhausting, yet only 22 percent of married women with full-time jobs said they have a lot of energy left after work, compared with 27 percent of married men with full-time jobs.

30. The need to do personal repair work, coupled with added household tasks, is one of the reasons why working women are more likely than working men to say they have too little time for themselves. Among married women with full-time jobs and employed spouses, 55 percent said getting time for themselves had been a big or very big issue (compared with 28 percent of men in comparable situations). It is worth noting that the absolute figure and the relative difference between women and men are greater on this item than on household and child-care items, suggesting that repair work is indeed part of the issue. On another question, 68 percent of these women said that "I seldom get enough time for myself" described them very well or fairly well, compared with 39 percent of the men.

414   NOTES TO CHAPTER TEN

31. Among married women with full-time jobs and employed spouses, 30 percent said they often relieve stress by taking about it with friends (another 45 percent said they sometimes did this), whereas only 22 percent of men in comparable situations said this. Thirteen percent of the women said feeling their work was unappreciated had been a big issue in their family, compared with only 6 percent of the men.

32. Twenty-five percent of working women in the Economic Values Survey said they were involved in a support group that meetings regularly, compared with 15 percent of working men.

33. Mary Catherine Bateson, *Composing a Life* (New York: Atlantic Monthly Press, 1989), 166.

34. Fifty-one percent of married women with full-time jobs, children, and an employed spouse said that "I need more time to think about the really basic issues in life" described them very well or fairly well, whereas 38 percent of men in comparable situations gave this response.

35. Fifty percent of married men with children said they had taken on extra work because of family obligations; 38 percent of married women with children had done so.

CHAPTER 10

1. An earlier draft of part of this chapter was originally published under the same title in the series *Essays on Philanthropy* (Indianapolis: Indiana University Center on Philanthropy, 1992), no. 7.

2. Tocqueville, *Democracy in America*.

3. Robert H. Bremner, *American Philanthropy*, 2d ed. (Chicago: University of Chicago Press, 1988). Precise levels of volunteer activity have not been measured, but rates of church membership and the foundings of fraternal and civic associations point clearly toward overall growth during the nineteenth and early twentieth centuries.

4. I have examined the language of motives for caring and discussed the need for a clearer sense of reciprocity in my book *Acts of Compassion*, esp. chaps. 3 and 10. Difficulties of reconciling altruistic and self-interested motives in popular discourse find parallels in the academic literature. See, for example, C. Daniel Batson, "Prosocial Motivation: Is It Ever Truly Altruistic?" *Advances in Experimental Social Psychology* 20 (1987), 65–122; Barry Schwartz, "Why Altruism Is Impossible—and Ubiquitous," paper presented at the Conference on "Altruism: Exploring the Intellectual Concept, University of Chicago, 1991; and Jan Osterberg, *Self and Others: A Study of Ethical Egoism* (Dordrecht: Kluwer, 1988).

5. Discussed in chapter 3.

6. Prominent examples are, of course, E. P. Thompson, *The Making of the English Working Class* (New York: Vintage, 1963), and James C. Scott, *The Moral Economy of the Peasant: Rebellion and Subsistence in Southeast Asia* (New Haven: Yale University Press, 1976).

NOTES TO CHAPTER TEN

7. Kristen R. Monroe, Michael C. Barton, and Ute Klingemann, "Altruism and the Theory of Rational Action: Rescuers of Jews in Nazi Europe," *Ethics* 101 (1990), 103–22, provide another example of altruistic behavior being motivated by a sense of community that renders it "natural."

8. My argument is not that people have no friends in their communities. A substantial literature suggests otherwise. In a national survey I conducted in 1991 (for a project on small-group involvement), for example, four people in ten said they had five or more close friends in their present community. However, an increasing share of physical and emotional needs are being met, neither by families nor by these friendship networks, but by specialized organizations, ranging from support groups (such as Alcoholics Anonymous) to soup kitchens and shelters for the homeless.

9. William H. Whyte, Jr., *The Organization Man* (Garden City, N.Y.: Doubleday, 1956), 391. It is perhaps telling that Whyte stresses the neighborliness of Park Forest in the 1950s, whereas Paul Leinberger and Bruce Tucker, *The New Individualists: The Generation after the Organization Man* (New York: Harper, 1991), found little of this ethic when they returned in the 1980s.

10. Virginia A. Hodgkinson and Murray S. Weitzman, *Giving and Volunteering in the United States: Findings from a National Survey, 1990 Edition* (Washington, D.C.: Independent Sector, 1990), 2. A comparable survey conducted in 1992 showed that the percentage of households contributing volunteer work was down slightly (from 54 to 51 percent), but the average number of hours donated per week was up slightly (Virginia A. Hodgkinson and Murray S. Weitzman, *Giving and Volunteering in the United States, 1992 Edition* [Washington, D.C.: Independent Sector, 1992], 4).

11. The labor force survey found that 26 percent claimed to be "involved in any charity or social service activities, such as helping the poor, the sick, or the elderly." In comparison, my 1989 survey of the general population estimated this figure at 29 percent. Full-time workers are significantly less likely to be involved in such charitable activities than part-time workers (24 vs. 33 percent). But this difference is largely because more part-time workers are women. Among both full- and part-time workers, women are substantially more likely to be involved than men.

12. Hodgkinson and Weitzman, *Giving and Volunteering, 1990*, 31.

13. These are my own analyses of data I collected in 1989 for my book *Acts of Compassion*. A description of the study is found in that volume. Coefficients for factor 1 were as follows: neighbors (.570), church members (.507), relatives (.611), friends (.681), and for factor 2: volunteers (.736), social welfare agencies (.846). Further analysis, using discriminant models, revealed that the likelihood of receiving help from relatives outside one's immediate family (an indicator of naturally occurring networks) is positively associated with the likelihood of receiving help from friends, co-workers, and church members, but unrelated to receiving help from volunteers. In other words, volunteer effort appears to be of a different order.

14. *Ibid.*, chaps. 7–9.

15. *Ibid.*, 264.

16. *Ibid.*, 23.

17. Virginia A. Hodgkinson and Murray S. Weitzman, *Giving and Volunteering in the United States: Findings from a National Survey, 1988 Edition* (Washington, D.C.: Independent Sector, 1988), 37.

18. From my own analysis of surveys collected between 1983 and 1987 as part of the General Social Survey conducted by the National Opinion Research Center at the University of Chicago.

19. An empirical assessment of the meaning of materialism is made possible by examining correlates in the labor force survey of saying that materialism (or an emphasis on money) is an extremely serious problem. Using as predictor variables a list of nine social problems identified in the survey, discriminant analysis shows that all the other problems are positively associated in zero-order models, but only some are significantly associated in multivariate models. Although there is some response bias due to the adjacent ordering of items in the interview, this bias is minimized by the fact that the entire list was rotated at random and by virtue of having two different dependent variables. In the nine-variable models, individualism, selfishness, and the breakdown of community were significantly associated with both dependent variables. Except for the association of the two dependent variables with each other, none of the other items was significantly associated with both of the dependent variables.

20. In the labor force survey, 10 to 15 percent more of those who were involved in charitable activities than of those who were not involved registered concern about materialism and emphasis on money in American society; yet virtually the same proportions of each valued having a nice home, new car, comfortable lifestyle, vacations, security in retirement, and nice clothing, and said they had serious financial obligations.

21. This figure is from my 1989 survey for *Acts of Compassion*. Discriminant analysis of factors differentiating volunteers from nonvolunteers in these data also suggest that volunteer activity is rooted in a different orientation or constellation of values than work; specifically, volunteerism was strongly associated with valuing helping others, valuing one's religious commitments, valuing one's leisure time, and valuing one's family but was virtually unrelated to valuing one's work. These findings, it might be noted, are consistent with sociological arguments that place volunteer activity, religion, family, and leisure in the "private" sphere of personal life, contrasting it with work as an activity that is increasingly removed from the home.

22. These perceptions were discussed in chapter 5.

23. The figures quoted in this paragraph are from the national survey I conducted in 1989 for *Acts of Compassion*. That Americans feel business is not doing enough for the needy is indicated by the fact that 63 percent say "corporations doing more to help the needy" would help a lot to make America a better place.

24. That it may *in fact* be more blessed to give time than money is suggested by further analysis of my 1989 data: values most closely associated with giving time included wanting to make the world a better place, while those closely

associated with giving money were the expectation that others would be kind in return and that generosity would help the giver get what he or she wanted.

25. Hodgkinson and Weitzman, *Giving and Volunteering, 1990*, 1.

26. *Ibid.*, 184–86.

CHAPTER 11

1. Ecclesiastes, 2:4–11 (revised English version).

2. John Chrysostom, *Six Books on the Priesthood* (Crestwood, N.Y.: St. Vladimir's Press, 1977), 8:469.

3. St. Augustine, "On the Trinity," in *A Select Library of the Nicene and Post-Nicene Fathers of the Christian Church*, ed. H. Wace and P. Schaff (Grand Rapids, Mich.: Eerdmans, 1966), vol. 1, sec. 3.7.

4. Quoted in St. Francis de Sales, "Riches, Poverty, and the Spiritual Life," *Discipleship Journal* (January 1, 1985), 32.

5. John Calvin, *Institutes of the Christian Religion*, ed. John T. McNeill (Philadelphia: Westminster, 1977), III.xix.9, 1:841.

6. Quoted in Charles Edward White, "What Wesley Practiced and Preached About Money," *Leadership* (Winter 1987), 28.

7. David D. Hall, *Worlds of Wonder, Days of Judgment: Popular Religious Belief in Early New England* (Cambridge: Harvard University Press, 1990), 238.

8. Marlow C. Embree, "Help Wanted: Finding the Best Place to Use Your Gifts," *Discipleship Journal* (May 1, 1988), 27.

9. William E. Diehl, *The Monday Connection: A Spirituality of Competence, Affirmation, and Support in the Workplace* (San Francisco: Harper, 1991), 12.

10. Will Herberg, *Protestant–Catholic–Jew: An Essay in American Religious Sociology* (New York: Doubleday, 1955).

11. These figures are from 1990 Gallup surveys as reported in *Emerging Trends* 12 (September 1990), 1–6.

12. Examples of such arguments would include Andrew M. Greeley, *Religious Change in America* (Cambridge: Harvard University Press, 1989), and Theodore Caplow, Howard M. Bahr, and Bruce A. Chadwick, *All Faithful People: Change and Continuity in Middletown's Religion* (Minneapolis: University of Minnesota Press, 1983). There are of course many social scientists who believe secularization is happening in more subtle ways. The essays in *The Sacred in a Secular Age*, ed. Phillip E. Hammond (Berkeley: University of California Press, 1985), provide helpful insights into these debates.

13. The current figures reported are for 1990 and are based on comparisons with earlier Gallup surveys reported in "Religion in America, 1935–1985," *The Gallup Report*, no. 236 (May 1985), 1–57.

14. "Literal Belief in the Bible Declining in U.S.," *Emerging Trends* 14 (January 1992), 1.

15. C. G. Jung, *Memories, Dreams, Reflections* (New York: Random House, 1963), chap. 4.

16. Wade Clark Roof, *Generation of Seekers* (San Francisco: Harper, 1993) offers many intriguing examples.

17. "Religion in America, 1935–1985," 57.

18. "Small Groups Survey," conducted in 1991 by the Gallup Organization for the Project on Small Groups and Spirituality under a grant from the Lilly Endowment.

19. These figures are from the Economic Values Survey and thus pertain only to the U.S. labor force. Among respondents ages 18–34, 21 percent had had family devotions as children, compared with 30 percent of those age 50 or over.

20. Economic Values Survey.

21. One thinks especially of Peter Berger, Brigitte Berger, and Hansfried Kellner, *The Homeless Mind: Modernization and Consciousness* (New York: Random House, 1973), as a contribution to this perspective.

22. The image of warfare (which, in my view, has greatly overstated and miscast the important arguments) has become common in recent years; one example is James Davison Hunter, *Culture Wars: The Struggle to Define America* (New York: Basic Books, 1991). My own position on the sources and nature of recent conflicts in American religion (from which Hunter has adapted some of his arguments) was presented in *The Restructuring of American Religion: Society and Faith since World War II* (Princeton: Princeton University Press, 1988), and *The Struggle for America's Soul: Evangelicals, Liberals, and Secularism* (Grand Rapids, Mich.: Eerdmans, 1989).

23. Warfare imagery of course neglects this point by focusing on the polemics of public interest groups. Faced with the shrill appeals of extremists at both ends of the spectrum, many people probably say "a plague on both your houses."

24. Much the same mechanisms might well be present in the relationships between spiritual commitments and views on political issues, but that is not the focus of our attention here. It is a simple matter to suggest that compartmentalization is one of the ways of coping with being pious in a secular world. But just how this is done reveals much about how religion is understood in our society.

25. On the ways in which individualism underlies religious liberalism and religious conservatism alike, see my *Acts of Compassion*, chap. 5.

26. Of necessity, the discussion of religion in this chapter is oriented toward its contemporary implications for the moral restraint of economic life; considerably more detail about the relationships between religious beliefs and economic values has been presented elsewhere; see Wuthnow, *God and Mammon in America.*

27. Although it is especially difficult to separate religious orientations from questions of moral discourse, readers should be alert to the fact that the latter questions are addressed more specifically in chapters 12 and 13.

28. What is also important to recognize is that a dualist view of spirituality and materialism is scarcely incompatible with thinking seriously about the relationship between the two. In the labor force survey, for example, the 10 percent who had thought most about biblical teachings on money and work were overwhelmingly (89 percent) likely to say they had also thought a lot about the *differences* between spiritual growth and material possessions.

29. She also believes life is like climbing a mountain. Everyone is headed for

the same pinnacle. She hints that this pinnacle may be God or heaven. But again the story really only involves human characters. Some people struggle up the mountain with heavier burdens than others. And if some don't make it, nobody does. So it is up to everyone to help everyone else.

30. Economic Values Survey.

31. Conwell's widely read book was first published in 1915; for a discussion of it and other gospel-of-riches literature, see especially Irvin G. Wyllie, *The Self-Made Man in America: The Myth of Rags to Riches* (New York: Free Press, 1954), chap. 4.

32. For example, Wade Clark Roof and William McKinney, *Mainline American Religion* (New Brunswick: Rutgers University Press, 1987), especially their discussion of the "new voluntarism."

33. Economic Values Survey. In addition to the responses reported in the text, 10 percent defined stewardship as "giving a certain percentage of your money to the church"; 12 percent, as "taking good care of our planet"; and 20 percent said they didn't know.

34. Small Group Survey. This was a national survey of 1,000 randomly selected persons who were currently involved in some kind of small group that met regularly and provided caring and support for its members. Because of the high concentration of people in Sunday school classes and Bible studies, this sample was actually more religiously involved than the nation at large.

35. In the Economic Values Survey, when asked, "In deciding what kind of work to go into, did your religious values influence your decision?" 10 percent said "Yes, definitely," 12 percent said "Yes, maybe," 75 percent said "No," and 2 percent were unsure.

36. Economic Values Survey. In the total labor force sample, 22 percent said the idea of stewardship was very meaningful, 40 percent said it was fairly meaningful, 20 percent said it was not very or not at all meaningful, and 18 percent said they didn't know. Among younger respondents the latter percentages were higher.

37. John Bunyan, *The Pilgrim's Progress* (New York: Washington Square Press, 1957 [1678]), 85–103.

38. Economic Values Survey.

39. Economic Values Survey.

40. Economic Values Survey. Other responses given by respondents who felt they had experienced a calling included "God wants us to work at whatever makes us happiest" (18 percent), "God doesn't really care what kind of work we do" (4 percent), and "other" or "don't know" (6 percent).

41. In the Economic Values Survey, 35 percent of those who agreed that God had called them to their particular line of work said their work was absolutely essential to their basic sense of worth as a person, compared with 26 percent of those who disagreed with this statement; the percentages rating their job satisfaction at the high end of the scale were 32 and 21, respectively. The respective proportions saying each of the following were also absolutely essential were: living a comfortable life (21 and 21), making a lot of money (13 and 14), and hobbies or leisure activities (14 and 12).

42. Proportions among those who said the idea of stewardship was very meaningful to them and among those who said it was not very meaningful, respectively, who agreed with each statement were: "people who work hard are more pleasing to God than people who are lazy" (70 vs. 40), "riches get in the way of our truly knowing God" (42 vs. 19), and "the poor are closer to God than rich people are" (27 vs. 13).

43. MacIntyre, *After Virtue* 187; and for an elaboration, see Stout, *Ethics after Babel*, chap. 12.

CHAPTER 12

1. Nor do I wish to set them on a pedestal. We shall in fact turn eventually to a number of the limitations evident in contemporary moral discourse.

2. I noted in chapter 7 that Pam Jones and her "husband" are not legally married.

3. As in previous chapters, I have been able to substantiate these arguments by drawing on evidence from personal interviews and the survey, but will restrict most of this supporting evidence to notes.

4. Discussed in chapter 3.

5. In positing these two as moral languages capable of placing restrictions on economic pursuits, I am of course suggesting certain similarities between them. But I am not the first to have done so. For example, despite the fact that Puritanism and romanticism have often been portrayed as opposing tendencies, the former contained a strong pietistic strain that was conducive to the expressivism found in the latter, and the latter contained a moralistic element that was reminiscent of the former. More importantly, the two spoke with one voice in condemning the cold, calculating reasonableness of economic utilitarianism and called for something higher, or deeper, in the human spirit to be given its due. Some of these common roots are discussed in Colin Campbell, *The Romantic Ethic and the Spirit of Modern Consumerism* (Oxford: Blackwell, 1987).

6. In the Economic Values Survey, the exact percentages of the labor force who agreed (and who agreed strongly) were: "certain values must be regarded as absolutes," 90 (53); "I believe in following a strict set of moral rules," 85 (41); "getting in touch with your inner feelings is more important than doing well in your job," 58 (14); "working on my emotional life takes priority over other things," 42 (9); and "exploring my inner self is one of my main priorities," 45 (11). Other evidence is provided by the fact that 56 percent said "your moral standards" are absolutely essential to their sense of worth as a person, and 25 percent said this about "paying attention to your feelings."

7. As rough indicators of the two kinds of moral language discussed in this chapter, "moralism" and "expressivism" scales were constructed from the Economic Values Survey data as follows. For the former, respondents were given scores ranging from 0 to 3 for their answers to the questions asking how important moral standards were to their sense of worth as a person, their agreement that certain values should be regarded as absolutes, and their agreement with

following a strict set of moral rules. For the latter, scores were assigned similarly for answers to the questions about the importance of paying attention to
one's feelings, agreement about working on emotional life taking priority over
other things, and agreement that exploring my inner self is one of my main
priorities. Each scale was collapsed into four categories and its validity was
examined in relation to other items in the survey that measured similar beliefs.
Twenty-seven percent of the respondents scored in the highest category on the
moralism scale, and 20 percent scored in this category on the expressivism
scale. Statistical relationships reported in notes to this chapter are based on
these two scales.

8. A possible indication of change in views toward moral absolutes is the fact
that 60 percent of those age 50 or older in the Economic Values Survey agreed
strongly that "certain values must be regarded as absolutes," whereas only 46
percent of those age 18 to 34 did so.

9. My use of the term expressive moralism basically follows that of Robert N.
Bellah and his associates who coin the term "expressive utilitarianism" in reference to the view "that each person has a unique core of feeling and intuition that
should unfold or be expressed if individuality is to be realized." While noting
that this view is related to certain strains in nineteenth-century thought, particularly romanticism, they too suggest its distinctiveness in contemporary thought
by remarking on its affinities with therapeutic language. I have dropped their
identification of this outlook with utilitarianism because nothing in their basic
definition necessarily associates it with utilitarian thinking. I agree with their
suggestion that this outlook, while focusing on individuality, "is not necessarily alien to other persons or to nature." See *Habits of the Heart*, 334.

10. "Today's wild man owes more to Rob't Bly than Dan'l Boone. Today's
wilderness is only a site for weekend seminars; rassling grizzlies is discouraged" (Ian Shoales, "Mo' Hicans? No, Thanks," *New York Times*, September 27,
1992, 17).

11. Jane Austen, *Sense and Sensibility* (London: Avalon, 1949), provides one
example of these contrasts. For an example of an exception to the usual gender
imagery, Henry Mackenzie's *The Man of Feeling* (Oxford: Oxford University
Press, 1967) extolled emotionality as a virtue in men. In the Economic Values
Survey, expressivism and moralism were both statistically associated with
being female, although only moderately so.

12. Both the expressivism and moralism scales in the Economic Values Survey data were positively associated with valuing one's relationship with God
and saying that "I'd like to spend more time exploring spiritual issues" described themselves very well. Higher scores on both scales were associated
with a greater likelihood of saying that one was very happy with life overall,
but expressivism was also associated with describing one's work as emotionally draining, with having experienced burnout, and with feeling that one's
work was compromising one's values.

13. In the Economic Values Survey there was a strong relationship between
higher scores on the moralism and expressivism scales and saying that "I think

a lot about my values and priorities in life" described themselves very well. When age, sex, and education were controlled, this emphasis on values and priorities was more strongly associated with moralism than with expressivism.

14. These observations are drawn from a close analysis of the ways in which people talked about their values in the qualitative interviews; the survey did not provide sufficiently nuanced responses to sort out these differences quantitatively.

15. Some evidence supporting the view that ascetic moralism encourages a stronger or more controlling ego orientation comes from the survey data, in which there were positive associations between moralism and sensing that one was in control of one's daily schedule, long-range objectives, short-term decisions, and ability to allocate tasks to others; no such relationships existed between these items and the expressivism scale.

16. She adds that once she learned about "nonattachment," she realized even more clearly the need for "some kind of moral code to live by." She says she realizes that "the individual really needs to listen to the inner voice until that inner voice guides them in what kind of person to be."

17. Data from the Economic Values Survey also suggest some of the similarities and differences among persons oriented toward ascetic or expressive moralism. Among those who score high on each scale, the demographic profile is remarkably similar in terms of gender, age, education, income, and occupation. In both cases, high scores are positively associated with being female but unrelated with education; moralism is associated with being older; expressivism is unrelated to age. Neither is associated with workplace characteristics such as size of firm or sector. Ascetic moralism appears to be rooted more in religious participation, especially attendance at religious services. Expressivism is associated with religious interests, such as valuing one's relationship with God, and with some forms of religious involvement, such as having attended religious retreats, but is unrelated to attendance at religious services. Expressivism is associated with attending support groups and having been in therapy; ascetic moralism is not.

18. Besides the fact that expressivism is empirically associated with moralism, there are also normative reasons for stressing this fact. It is this association that tempers the tendency for expressivism to encourage purely self-interested behavior. Empirically, this is evident in comparisons made possible by the Economic Values Survey. Among expressivists who assert the importance of doing what is morally right, there is only a weak relationship with saying they would also pursue their self-interest. But among expressivists who deny the importance of trying to do what is morally right, there is a strong tendency to pursue their self-interest. Relationships examined were between items asking how much of a consideration feeling good would be and how much of a consideration doing what would benefit yourself would be if faced with an ethical dilemma at work. How important doing what is morally right would be was introduced as a control. When morally right was a major consideration, the relationship between the other two items was weak (gamma = .25) and probably attributable mainly to response set bias due to proximity of the items;

when morally right was only a minor consideration the relationship was stronger (gamma = .45), and when morally right was not a consideration it was even stronger (gamma = .63).

19. Fifteen percent of the respondents agreed strongly that "getting in touch with your inner feelings is more important than doing well in your job" (we use this statement here, rather than the scale, because it pits the issue of job-related behavior vs. personal feelings directly). Comparing answers to other questions given by this 15 percent with all respondents yields the following percentages, respectively: bent rules (within last month), 32, 29; bent truth, 26, 26; would tell someone if they were doing something wrong, 56, 53; say ethics means feeling good, 9, 6; say ethics means always being honest, 35, 31; say ethics means deciding between right and wrong, 30, 32; say ethics is circumstantial, 50, 49; agree it is okay to bend the rules, 50, 49; agree they follow their feelings, 78, 73; agree they are responsible for others' behavior, 58, 53; say one should follow the rules in figuring income tax, 84, 85.

20. Percentages among those who strongly agreed that feelings should be placed above jobs, and among all respondents, respectively, who said they would be very likely to do each were: talk with boss, 62, 54; talk with co-workers, 48, 39; read, 32, 19; seek clergy advice, 22, 10.

21. Charles Taylor, *Sources of the Self: The Making of the Modern Identity* (Cambridge: Harvard University Press, 1989), chap. 15, provides an overview of this history.

22. See especially Anthony Shaftesbury, *Characteristics of Men, Manners, Opinions, and Times* (New York: Bobbs-Merrill, 1964 [1711]); Francis Hutcheson, *An Inquiry into the Original of Our Ideas of Beauty and Virtue* (Hildesheim: Georg Olms, 1971 [1725]), Francis Hutcheson, *An Essay on the Nature and Conduct of the Passions and Affections, with Illustrations upon the Moral Sense* (Gainesville: Scholars Facsimile Reprints, 1969 [1742]); Francis Hutcheson, *A System of Moral Philosophy* (Hildesheim: Georg Olms, 1969 [1755]); and, for overviews and brief selections, *British Moralists, 1650–1800*, ed. D. D. Raphael (Oxford: Oxford University Press, 1969).

23. This contrast was drawn sharply by Karen Kelsey, the clinical social worker, in describing the difference she perceives between the ethos of business and government, and the expressive values she tries to realize in her own life: "I'm nonutilitarian and nondeadline oriented, and I'm not goal-oriented for the sake of some external pressure."

24. Discriminant analysis of the differences between respondents in the Economic Values Survey who said materialism was a serious social problem and those who said it was not a serious problem indicate that "selfishness" and "individualism" are the two specific concerns that explain the most variation.

25. Robert Heavner, "Great Aspirations," *Discipleship Journal* (July/August, 1988), 9.

26. On multiple motives and their depiction in narratives, see my *Acts of Compassion*, chap. 3.

27. She adds that what's important to her is not simply helping another person: "But are they tapping into themselves and being part of the world that has

a lot of suffering? And having their whole self being dedicated to their own growth and health in the world and eliminating that suffering? To me, I really don't think there's such a thing as volunteer work. I don't think that if you're really in touch with yourself at the point where you are doing those things, you're volunteering. I think you're just doing what you have to do in order to be you."

28. For example, Karen Kelsey describes herself as "structure phobic," saying she recognized that people who run agencies want to make the world better, but she herself doesn't like the compromises required of such agencies, and she prefers to change society by working with one individual at a time.

29. Robert Nozick, *The Examined Life: Philosophical Meditations* (New York: Simon & Schuster, 1989), 92. Nozick comes close to offering an emotivist argument when he suggests, "Emotions provide a kind of picture of value, I think. They are our internal psychophysiological response to the external value, a response that is specially close by being not only due to that value but an analog representation of it" (93).

30. Quoted in Frank Barker and Maureen Rank, "The Martha Syndrome," *Discipleship Journal* (March 1, 1988), 13. Another writer, attempting to locate work in a strong moral context based on biblical tradition, asserts that feelings are the best guide for distinguishing between both overwork and laziness. The former, she says, is marked by a lack of joy, laughing, and peace; the latter, by "deep uneasiness." Ruthann Ridley, "Juggling Work and Rest," *Discipleship Journal* (September 1, 1984), 45.

CHAPTER 13

1. Although Pam Jones draws on ascetic language more often than expressive language, the latter surfaces prominently as she talks about variety at work. Rather than variation in the tasks themselves, she focuses on the diversity of people she works with—playboys, overachievers, introverts, homemakers, and so on. Emphasizing this variety helps her feel that the workplace is more similar to life itself.

2. The relationships reported in the text concerning work and money are drawn from the Economic Values Survey data and utilize the moralism and expressivism scales that are discussed in the notes to the previous chapter. All relationships were statistically significant at or beyond the .05 level of probability. Significant relationships were also examined using discriminant analysis in which age, sex, and level of education were controlled.

3. These issues were discussed in chapter 10.

4. Campbell, *The Romantic Ethic and the Spirit of Modern Consumerism*, 220.

5. I have outlined some of the ways in which the elements of moral codes may be deconstructed and recombined in *Meaning and Moral Order*, chap. 3.

6. Consequentialist moral logic is discussed with empirical examples in Steven M. Tipton, *Getting Saved from the Sixties: Moral Meaning in Conversion and Cultural Change* (Berkeley: University of California Press, 1982).

7. In the Economic Values Survey, 58 percent of the labor force agreed that "being ethical will pay off economically," while 35 percent disagreed.

8. A Minneapolis salesman provided one example of how good feelings can substitute for an economic consequentialist argument. Noting that he was taught that those who do good shall also receive, he quickly added: "not necessarily in the same manner, but something different, like feeling blessed." A Philadelphian made a similar point, arguing that "the more good that goes out from you, the more good comes back to you," but "in other ways," like something that might "pick you up" emotionally.

9. Expressivists themselves sometimes raise these questions. The clinical social worker, Karen Kelsey, for example, muses about whether she has retreated from the real world into a kind of therapeutic counterculture. She doesn't feel she has withdrawn from social responsibilities, but she does realize she cannot fully express herself within mainstream institutions. "I don't like the mainstream. I still don't agree with the compromises, I'm still offended by the values. So I find that a very difficult issue to resolve. Did I flee to a counter culture? I don't know. Could I be happy another way? No."

10. The assertion in the text that beliefs are more likely to be put into practice if supported by a social group of some kind is illustrated by a finding in previous research that religious commitment is positively associated with volunteering to help the needy among those who are actively involved in religious organizations, but not among those who are unaffiliated (*Acts of Compassion*, chap. 5). In the Economic Values Study, relationships between the moralism and expressivism scales and attitudes toward work and money were no different for people who were or who were not involved in religious organizations, fellowship groups, or support groups. There were, however, positive relationships between moralist orientations and being involved in one or another of these institutional settings. For example, 57 percent of those who scored high on the moralism scale attended church or synagogue every week, compared with only 12 percent of those who scored low on the scale. Among those who scored high on the expressivism scale, 19 percent said they relieve stress by attending a support group, compared with only 6 percent of those who scored low.

11. In a separate study of small groups and spirituality conducted between 1989 and 1993, I found quantitative evidence that small group members typically discuss issues of work and money as well as other personal problems, and many anecdotes of such discussions appeared in the ethnographic component of the research.

12. Quoted in Ricardo Quiñones, *Mapping Literary Modernism* (Princeton: Princeton University Press, 1985), 144.

13. Wuthnow, *Acts of Compassion*, chap. 5.

14. Karen Kelsey, the clinical social worker, provided an example of being inspired to make a more enduring life change as a result of seeing small acts of heroism. Working with AIDS patients as a volunteer, she saw a marked contrast between the values she aspired to and those she saw enacted among her

co-workers in government. She soon came to detest the "pragmatism" that ruled her work and began defining her co-workers' interests in terms of illness and pathology rather than high values. "I really couldn't stand that they were pretending to be concerned about national interest when they were forwarding their own personal pathological agendas in the political market place. And within the office I worked there were some very sick people who were part of the reason, for example, that we weren't doing something about AIDS because they wanted the senator to pay attention to them, so they cut off time from his schedule to work on legislative issues. And it was really a battle of illnesses and personalities and egos and not of national priorities and compassion and all of that."

INDEX

accounts, definition of, 93; and motivation, 94; ragbag theory of, 95–96; and work, 105–106
advertising, 167, 248–49
alcoholism, 33, 41–43, 301
Allen, Meg, 260–61
American dream, 4–5, 331; in Detroit, 207; immigrants and, 85, 234–36; materialistic aspects of, 18, 237, 242; and success, 124
anxiety, 152–53, 157, 281; gender differences in, 254–55, 262–63; about money, 166–67, 248–49, 333
Aristotle, 19
Arkwright, Ben and Sarah, 252–53
Arno, Tony, 162, 256
ascetic moralism. *See* moralism, ascetic

Bakhtin, M. M., 171
Bateson, Mary Catherine, 262
Beecher, Henry Ward, 66
Bellah, Robert N., 36, 153
Bellows, Henry W., 70, 72
Bentley, Harold, 111, 254
Bible, 63, 66, 294, 298
Boesky, Ivan F., 26
Bowen, Francis, 75, 77, 78
budgets, 181–83
Bunyan, John, 315–16
burnout, 32, 33, 41
Bushnell, Horace, 71
Butler, Ed, 209–10, 217, 218, 219, 221, 222–23, 226, 228, 231

Calvin, John, 292–93, 355
Campbell, Colin, 359–60
Candela, Lou, 31, 158
careers, changes in, 34–35, 88, 102
charity, 67, 202–04, 279, 304, 324
children, 65, 216, 248–50, 253; and discussions of money, 145–47, 191–92; and memories of, 173–74
Chinoy, Eli, 207
choice, in working conditions, 112–15. *See also* freedom
Chrysostom, John, 292

churches, 269, 295. *See also* God, views of; religion, privatization of
Cole, Audrey, 176–77, 282
community, involvement in, 265–66, 270, 334; materialism contrasted with, 267, 271–76
consumer rituals, 172–73, 183, 184–88, 333
consumerism, 6, 9, 174–76, 178, 229
Conwell, Russell, 306
corporate cultures, 6, 117–18, 130–31
Cummings, Stuart, 23, 26, 30, 116, 119, 124, 131, 142, 249, 256

debt, 25
Depression, children raised during, 163–66; and frugality, 163–64; and subjectivity, 164–65; and working class, 214–15, 286
Dewey, John, 52–54
Diggins, Brad, 40–41, 42, 43
discretion, 44, 46–47
disease model, 41–43
divorce, 155, 302
Duryea, Dan, 123

economic growth, 45, 196
economists, 74–79
Edwards, Jonathan, 62, 64, 67, 69
Emerson, Ralph Waldo, 73, 153
emotions, 260, 282, 344–46, 352–55
ethics, 26–29, 56
exercise, physical, 39, 255
expressive moralism. *See* moralism, expressive

family, 231–32; connections and getting jobs, 109; corporations as, 130–31; loans within, 199–200; nuclear, 243–45, 334
feelings. *See* emotions
Fiedler, Leslie, 26
Forsythe, Jena, 23, 158, 281–82
Frankfurt, Harry, 94
Franklin, Benjamin, 3–4, 59–60, 182, 347
freedom, personal, 45, 48–49, 360–63. *See also* choice, in working conditions
Friedman, Marcus, 112

Robert Wuthnow is the Gerhard R. Andlinger Professor of Sociology and Director of the Center for the Study of American Religion at Princeton University. He is the author of numerous articles and books on American religion and culture, including *Acts of Compassion* (Princeton) and *Learning to Care: Elementary Kindness in an Age of Indifference.*